FEMALE PSYCHOLOGY

Contemporary Psychoanalytic Views

FEMALE PSYCHOLOGY

Contemporary Psychoanalytic Views

EDITED BY

HAROLD P. BLUM, M.D.

INTERNATIONAL UNIVERSITIES PRESS, INC.

New York

Library of Congress Cataloging in Publication Data

Main entry under title:

Female psychology.

    Bibliography: p.
    Includes index.
    1. Women—Psychology—Addresses, essays, lectures.
2. Child psychology—Addresses, essays, lectures.
3. Psychoanalysis—Addresses, essays, lectures.
I. Blum, Harold P.
HQ1206.F423   155.6'33   76-53908
ISBN 0-8236-1890-0

Manufactured in the United States of America

CONTENTS

EDITOR'S INTRODUCTION

The fundamental contributions of psychoanalysis have provided the wellspring for the contemporary understanding of female psychology and have influenced a broad spectrum of research on this subject. Psychoanalysis has, in turn, been stimulated and enriched by contributions from other disciplines. Recent years have seen extensive psychoanalytic exploration of feminine traits and tendencies—their definition, origins, and developmental transformations. Advances and innovations within psychoanalysis as well as scholarly critiques from both within and outside of psychoanalysis have highlighted unresolved theoretical questions and have inspired challenge, controversy, and re-evaluation.

Expanding knowledge has spurred our efforts to clarify theoretical assumptions and formulations; to detect and correct our inconsistencies, oversights, and errors; and to propose extensions and modifications of our initial developmental models. Ongoing clinical experience has confirmed many basic psychoanalytic discoveries, while, as Freud anticipated, amplifying and amending earlier hypotheses and propositions. In any science, there is an unavoidable lag in testing and integrating new ideas and a still further lag in recognizing the possible implications of these ideas. As we carefully reconsider our views on femininity, we must clearly differentiate revisions from earlier propositions, and critically compare the two. The expansion of analytic theory is part of a circular process—assimilating and stimulating further investigation.

This anthology covers a variety of topics, introducing new formulations and, inevitably, fresh controversy. The articles included here represent only a sample of continuing psychoanalytic inquiry into an inexhaustible and timeless subject. This book is a survey of female psychology in the broadest sense of that term. Female values and aspirations, maternal attitudes and creative interests are dealt with, in addition to female sexuality and sexual identity.

The book opens with a critical review of Freud's ideas on early female sexuality, followed by articles arranged so that the reader will trace female development from birth through maturity. Direct observational studies are included, as well as considerable clinical documentation. The concluding part of the book deals with special issues crucial to female psychology. Most of the articles stem from a recent supplementary issue of the *Journal of the American Psychoanalytic Association*; a few have been carefully culled from earlier issues.

Despite the descriptive title of this volume, psychoanalysts recognize the psychological bisexuality of both sexes. Female psychology cannot be considered exceptional or separate, as if isolated from other personality factors. There are differences between the sexes as well as similarities and interrelationships in lines of development and personality organization.

I am grateful to the members of the editorial board of the *Journal of the American Psychoanalytic Association* and to various consultants for their counsel. I am particularly indebted to Drs. Selma Kramer, Burness Moore, and Roy Schafer for their editorial assistance in this project.

Harold P. Blum, M.D., Editor

FREUD'S VIEWS ON EARLY FEMALE SEXUALITY IN THE LIGHT OF DIRECT CHILD OBSERVATION

JAMES A. KLEEMAN, M.D.

WHAT IS REMARKABLE ABOUT FREUD'S IDEAS on early sexuality, derived as these were largely from the analyses of adults, is that so many of them have withstood the test of time. It is less remarkable that some of his ideas require correction and modification because of new information from a variety of sources, including the direct observation of children. Direct observation can demonstrate manifestations of early female sexuality that can only be conjectured from reconstructions in adult analysis.

In reviewing his writings on early female sexuality, I shall therefore concentrate on three issues having to do with phenomena that have already been subjected to direct observational study (Stoller, 1972; Galenson and Roiphe, 1971; Kleeman, 1975), and contrast Freud's views with the conclusions arising from these studies.

Before proceeding to examine what Freud actually said about early female sexuality, a word concerning the desirability of restating the details of Freud's writings on this subject 70 years after they were first written: As several recent reviews have pointed out (Sherfey, 1966; Chasseguet-Smirgel, 1970; Fliegel, 1973), Freud's conception of women met an immediate flurry

3

of challenges (Müller, 1932; Horney, 1926, 1933 [see also 1967]; Jones, 1927, 1933, 1935; Klein, 1932), followed by a period of almost 30 years when the little written about the subject was largely in support of Freud's views (Lampl-de Groot, 1928, 1933; Brunswick, 1940; Deutsch, 1944; Bonaparte, 1953). Erikson (1950) and Greenacre (1945, 1948, 1950, 1952, 1953, 1958) made significant contributions to the understanding of infantile sexuality and femininity. Their corrections and additions were made within the framework of Freud's work and without stressing their differences with Freud. Erikson made crucial additions relating to the impact of society on sexual development as well as introducing the concepts of *modes* and *modalities*. Greenacre, especially in her 1950 paper, took up Freud's admonition (1933) to turn to one's own experience, the poets, or science to know more about femininity. On the basis of her experience with adult patients, she made a case for early vaginal sensation, for vaginal awareness in females well before puberty, and for varying relationships between the clitoris and vagina. The recent resurgence of interest in female sexuality (Kestenberg, 1956, 1968; Erikson, 1964; Barnett, 1966; Sherfey, 1966; Horney, 1967; Lidz, 1968; Moore, 1968; Stoller, 1968a, 1968b, 1972; Chasseguet-Smirgel, 1970; Kleeman, 1971a, 1975; Fliegel, 1973), warrants a restatement of Freud's ideas in order to chart further amendment. Although his concept of women has taken a considerable buffeting in recent writings (Chodoff, 1966; Lidz, 1967; Marmor, 1973; Millett, 1969; Money and Ehrhardt, 1972; Cherry and Cherry, 1973; Miller, 1973; Stoller, 1973; Schafer, 1974), Freud's ideas about early female sexuality have been the best theoretical framework available and have had a profound impact in many areas of thought. It therefore seems preferable to continue to re-examine and revise them rather than discard them and start anew.

Many of Freud's essential assumptions are confirmed by the direct observation of young children: the universality of genital self-stimulation or masturbation; the presence of infantile sexuality in many forms, including the castration and Oedipus complexes; the significance of preoedipal attachment to the mother; the role of the inner world in sexual development; the biological basis of sexuality (here, chemical and hormonal data combine with observation); the ubiquitous presence of bisexuality in each individual; the importance of the child's discovery of anatomical difference; and the role of activity as well as passivity in the behavior of little girls. On the other hand, a correction or modification of Freud's assumptions would seem to be dictated in the following areas: the onset, nature of, and reasons for alteration of female genital self-stimulation; the presence of femininity in the first year of life, which is related to the emergence of early gender identity; the importance of the father to the little girl's development; and the relative thrust of learning, cognitive functions, and language, compared with penis envy, in the emergence of femininity.

Freud on Early Female Sexuality

Although Freud's conclusions were based predominantly on memories and reconstructions from the analyses of adults, he had some data from the direct observation of children: "It seems, however, that the sexual life of children usually emerges in a form accessible to observation round about the third or fourth year of life" (1905, pp. 176-177). In a footnote added 1910, commenting on the results of some child analyses, he states: "It is gratifying to be able to report that direct observation has fully confirmed the conclusions arrived at by psycho-analysis" (1905, pp. 193-194). Material for his 1908 paper on the sexual theories of children was partly derived "from the direct observation of what children say and do" (p. 209). His writings, however, include no reference to systematic direct observation of children. He seems aware of this when, after his 1912 discussion on masturbation, he says: "There is no doubt that we have left very many points over to be established and clarified by some future band of observers and enquirers" (p. 246).

Freud repeatedly remarks that we know more about the sexuality of boys than we do about girls (1905, 1908b, 1912, 1923, 1924, 1925, 1926, 1933). Typical of these statements are: "It has been a matter for regret, too, that we have not been able to pay as much attention to female as to male masturbation; female masturbation, I believe, is deserving of a special study..." (1912, p. 247), and "We know less about the sexual life of little girls than of boys. But we need not feel ashamed of this distinction; after all, the sexual life of adult women is a 'dark continent' for psychology" (1926, p. 212; see also 1925, pp. 243-244).

One of Freud's seminal discoveries was the importance of infantile masturbation. He later stressed that the associated fantasy was the crucial psychic aspect (1908a), in addition to the response of the environment and the child's feeling about it, especially the anxiety of castration (1908b). His general conclusions about infantile masturbation have withstood the passage of time more durably than his specific statements about females. He talks about early masturbation in a number of papers (1905, 1908a, 1912, 1917, 1919, 1925, 1926, 1931, 1933, 1940), but his important elaborations are disclosed in three (1905, 1912, and 1925).

He described three periods of masturbation (1912, p. 246): (1) "masturbation in infants, which includes all auto-erotic activities serving the purpose of sexual satisfaction," (2) "masturbation in children, which arises directly out of the preceding kind and has already become fixed to certain erotogenic zones, and 3) masturbation at puberty...."

In a section of the "Three Essays" added in 1915, Freud ascribed a brief efflorescence of sexual activity to "about the fourth year." In other papers he links this second period of infantile masturbation to the Oedipus complex (1925, p. 250), which he variably dates at three to five years or two to five years, (cf. 1940, p. 189). Otherwise he is not very specific about the time of onset of genital self-stimulation or "infantile" masturbation.

One of Freud's fuzziest concepts, especially confusing because it has proven erroneous, concerns the nature of early female masturbation. He concluded that early childhood female masturbation involved only the clitoris and that the clitoris was a little penis; the vagina is still unknown, and therefore essentially all sexuality in boys and girls through the phallic phase (hence the name) is masculine. In 1905 he said: "So far as the auto-erotic and masturbatory manifestations of sexuality are concerned, we might lay it down that the sexuality of little girls is of a wholly masculine character" (p. 219). "The leading erotogenic zone in female children is located at the clitoris, and is thus homologous to the masculine genital zone of the glans penis. All my experience concerning masturbation in little girls has related to the clitoris..." (p. 220).

"If we are to understand how a little girl turns into a woman, we must follow the further vicissitudes of this excitability of the clitoris" (1905, p. 220). Freud goes on to stress that the shift of the leading erotogenic zone from the clitoris to the vagina, amounting to the putting aside of childish masculinity, is intimately related to the essence of femininity. He maintained this position throughout his writings: "With their entry into the phallic phase the differences between the sexes are completely eclipsed by their agreements. We are now obliged to recognize that the little girl is a little man".... "It seems that with them [little girls] all their masturbatory acts are carried out on this penis-equivalent, and that the truly feminine vagina is still undiscovered by both sexes" (1933, p. 118). In another paper (1923, p. 142) he states that the essential condition of the phallic phase is that there is only one genital, the male one, for both sexes; at this time there is only maleness, not femaleness, and it is not until puberty that the sexual polarity coincides with *male* and *female* (p. 145).

Freud's other conclusions on female masturbation should also be mentioned: the awakening of potential masturbatory pleasurable sensation occurs with the mother's cleansing of that area (1933, p. 120); the possibility is that little girls masturbate less frequently and less energetically than little boys (1931, p. 232); bringing the thighs together as a method of masturbation is more common in girls (1905, p. 188); masturbation is further removed from the nature of women than of men (1925, p. 255); probably masturbation starts spontaneously as an activity of a bodily organ and only later acquires relation with the Oedipus complex or other fantasies (1919, p. 187; 1925, p. 250); early sexual activity is of great significance for later sexual maturity and personality development (1905; 1933, p. 127).

Freud tenaciously adhered to the following formula for the little girl's waning interest in childhood masturbation: observation of anatomical difference → castration complex → penis envy → renunciation (in the phallic phase) of pleasure in clitoridal stimulation (masculine sexuality), feelings of inferiority = essential step in attainment of definitive femininity (1925, pp. 255-256; 1931, pp. 232-233; 1933, p. 126; 1940, p. 193): "Thus the little girl's recognition of the anatomical distinction between the sexes forces her away from masculinity and masculine masturbation on to new lines which lead to the development of femininity" (1925, p. 256). "The discovery that she is castrated is a turning-point in a girl's growth . . . the little girl has hitherto lived in a masculine way, has been able to get pleasure by the excitation of her clitoris . . . now, owing to the influence of her penis-envy, she loses her enjoyment in her phallic sexuality" (1933, p. 126).

Freud in all his writings claimed femaleness didn't come into being until puberty and in his early writings stressed the parallel sexual development of boys and girls. In later writings, however (1924, 1925, 1931, 1933, 1937, 1940), he traced a *different* course for males and females in other important respects: One of the two important new points in

Freud's 1931 paper "Female Sexuality" was his discovery of the strength and duration of the little girl's pre-Oedipus attachment to her mother (see 1925, p. 245). "We see, then, that the phase of exclusive attachment to the mother, which may be called the *pre-Oedipus* phase, possesses a far greater importance in women than it can have in men" (1931, p. 230). The differences in male and female development after the phallic phase include an opposite chronology of the castration complex and Oedipus complex and dissimilar superego formation—"Thus the little girl's recognition of the anatomical distinction between the sexes" sets in motion her castration complex, her sense of inferiority, and penis envy. "In girls the Oedipus complex is a secondary formation. The operations of the castration complex precede it and prepare for it. As regards the relation between the Oedipus and castration complexes there is a fundamental contrast between the two sexes. *Whereas in boys the Oedipus complex is destroyed by the castration complex, in girls it is made possible and led up to by the castration complex*" (1925, p. 256) (cf. 1931, pp. 229-230; 1933, p. 126; 1940, pp. 193-194). Freud stressed that the girl's Oedipus complex is much simpler than that of a boy: "it seldom goes beyond the taking of her mother's place and the adopting of a feminine attitude towards her father" (1924, p. 178). This is one of Freud's few attributions of femininity to the young prepubertal female. His general stance is that the path to the development of femininity does not lie open to the girl until she has passed through the phallic phase, the observation of anatomical difference, the castration complex, a sense of inferiority, penis envy, and has entered the Oedipus period by turning from the mother and toward the father (1931, p. 239; 1937, p. 251). Calogeras and Schupper (1972) have documented the progression of his statements about the Oedipus complex, which I shall not consider further.

Freud's steadfast characterization of early female sexuality as masculine was based in part on his assumption that there are no early vaginal sensations and that the young girl is ignorant of her vagina until puberty. He declared this in the "Three Essays" (1905, p, 197) and retained these ideas throughout his writings (1908b, 1923, 1924, 1926, 1931, 1933, 1940). In several passages (1931, 1933, 1940) he acknowledged that others had reported early vaginal sensations, but he dismissed these as indistinguishable from anal or vestibular sensations or as being of no consequence: "The occurrence of early vaginal excitations is often asserted. But it is most probable that what is in question are excitations in the clitoris — that is, in an organ analogous to the penis" (1940, p. 154n).

Freud found the terms masculine and feminine more confusing than clarifying. The difficulty of finding a psychological meaning for "masculine" and "feminine" was discussed in several passages (1905, pp. 219-220n; 1930, pp. 105-106n; 1933, p. 114). He demonstrated the three uses of the terms: in the sense of activity and passivity (the use he felt was essential for psychoanalysis), in a biological sense, and in a sociological sense. He held that *bisexuality* was a characteristic of all humans (1905, pp. 141-144; 1925, p. 255; 1933, p. 144) (cf. Stoller, 1972). He sums up these deliberations: "Psycho-analysis has a common basis with biology, in that it presupposes an original bisexuality in human beings (as in animals). But psycho-analysis cannot elucidate the intrinsic nature of what in conventional or in biological phraseology is termed 'masculine' and 'feminine': it simply takes over the two concepts and makes them the foundation of its work. When we attempt to reduce them further, we find masculinity vanishing into activity and femininity into passivity, and that does not tell us enough" (1920, p. 171). He maintains that masochism is truly feminine (1933, p. 116) and develops the idea of the *active* element in the little girl's attitude toward her mother and in femininity generally (1931). In developing the concept of the little girl's activity, he uses the example of doll play. In one passage he acknowledges this play as a "sign of early awakened femininity" (1931, p. 237), but later (1933, p. 128) denies that the play is an expression of femininity.

Freud was not unaware of the impact of society on development. 'He dealt with the influence as taken for granted. In his wish to emphasize universals like libido, preoedipal attachment, observation of sexual difference, castration complex, Oedipus complex, penis envy, etc., he addressed himself to few societal specifics. What few statements he made applied to mature rather than early female sexuality. Speaking of passive aims, he wrote: "But we must beware in this of underestimating the influence of social customs, which similarly force women into passive situations.... The suppression of women's aggressiveness which is prescribed for them constitutionally and imposed on them socially favours the development of powerful masochistic impulses" (1933, p. 116).

A constant in Freud's writings is the theme that sexual development has its basis in biology. This was proclaimed in 1905: "The unsatisfactory conclusion, however, that emerges from these investigations of the disturbances of sexual life is that we know far too little of the biological processes constituting the essence of sexuality to be able to construct from our fragmentary information a theory adequate to the understanding alike of normal and of pathological conditions" (p. 243). It was restated in subsequent works (1920, p. 171; 1926, p. 210; 1931, p. 242; 1933, p. 116; 1940, pp. 186-188); Freud anticipated the work of Kinsey (1953), Masters and Johnson (1966), and Money and Ehrhardt (1972) when he lamented that the relation of normal sexual development to the emergence of the sexual perversions required anatomical and physiological knowledge that was not available in medical school teaching (1926, p. 210). He returned to this conclusion late in his writing: "We often have the impression that with the wish for a penis and the masculine protest we have penetrated through all the psychological strata and have reached bedrock.... This is probably true, since, for the psychical field, the biological field does in fact play the part of the underlying bedrock. The repudiation of femininity can be nothing else than a biological fact, a part of the great riddle of sex" (1937, p. 252) (cf. Stoller, 1972).

Yet with all of Freud's perseverance in promulgating his particular assumptions, he often displayed a striking flexibility, as when he wrote: "...we are not as yet able to distinguish in this field between what is rigidly fixed by biological laws and what is open to movement and change under the influence of accidental experience" (1931, p. 242; cf. 1905, pp. 327, 329).

The Missing Link: Gender Identity

The study of gender identity has effected a major correction of Freud's theory about early female sexuality (Money et al., 1955; Hampson and Hampson, 1961; Stoller, 1964, 1968b; Greenson, 1966; Lidz, 1967; Kleeman, 1971a; Money and Ehrhardt, 1972). First came a gradual shift by a few analysts away from Freud's point of view that there is no femininity until the phallic phase or later (Horney, 1933; Jones, 1933; Payne, 1936; Zilboorg, 1944; Greenacre, 1945, 1952). Freud's assertion that there is no femaleness until puberty was based on his assumptions about early female masturbation (i.e., it is essentially all clitoral; the clitoris is a little penis; before puberty there are no significant vaginal sensations, and the vagina is unknown until then). Though a number of authors have contradicted Freud by ascribing vaginal sensations to the very young female (Klein, 1928; Brierley, 1936; Payne, 1936; Rivière, 1936; Brunswick, 1940; Greenacre, 1948, 1950; Bonaparte, 1953; Kestenberg, 1956; Barnett, 1966, 1968; Horney, 1967; cf. Sherfey, 1966), the answer to the question of when femininity begins would seem to lie in a study of the origins of the little girl's gender identity. Studying how a girl acquires her sense of being female (the early phase of which we call *core gender identity*) by a variety of methods, including direct observation of children, reveals that the assignment of gender at birth is a crucial moment. One cannot understand gender identity or gender role[1] without giving proper credit to the moment of assignment, which in turn sets in motion a whole process of acculturation which teaches the little girl that she is female and what and how a female is supposed to think, to feel, and to act in the family and in the segment of society that family represents.

Observation of children leaves no doubt that as soon as the infant is given a female name she is bombarded with verbal and nonverbal messages which convey a sense of femaleness, as female is defined in that family. Though the core gender identity will not be firmly secure until age four or five years, evidence of its emergence can be observed clearly by the time the child is walking and may be irreversible by age eighteen months (Kleeman, 1971a; Money and Ehrhardt, 1972). Relative to core gender-identity formation, direct observation of children reveals (Kleeman, 1971a) that there are observable differences between male and female children in infancy and early childhood. These have been detailed in a number of areas, including motility, play and toy preference, fantasy, autonomy and dependence, what constitutes a fear situation, exploratory behavior, response to frustration, and aggression.

Innate differences exist between male and female infants and children, but even more crucial for gender-identity formation are the *learning* experiences of the young child. Parents relate differently to girls and boys from birth. The expectations and selective reinforcements conveyed to a girl are different from those conveyed to a boy, though the process

---

[1] My use of these terms follows Stoller (1968b):

Gender identity originates with the knowledge and awareness, conscious and unconscious, that one belongs to one sex and not the other. In its later forms it becomes more complex, e.g., the person is not just a woman, but a dainty one, an active one a masculine one, and so forth. *Gender role* is the overt behavior displayed in society, the role played with other people which establishes a position with them with regard to their evaluation of gender.

is usually subtle. The known socialization inputs to the two genders are sufficiently dissimilar to produce known gender differences in dependency and aggression, as well as other traits (Mischel, 1966). The learning experiences are powerful enough to make them the predominant factor in determining core gender identity (Money, et al, 1955; Stoller, 1968a, 1968b). Taken together, these facts confirm the existence of a primary femininity in infancy.

A variety of sources converge to establish the little girl's sense of femaleness, in addition to the genetic, hormonal, central nervous system patterning, and anatomical-physiological factors elaborated by other investigators (Money and Ehrhardt, 1972): the emergence of the ego capacity to differentiate—one aspect of the over-all reality-testing function; verbal and nonverbal communication with significant adults and other children; the development of language, including the ability to *categorize;* body-image representation, including genital sensation, exploration, and self-stimulation; sense of self-development; and imitation and identification processes. Observation suggests that learning conveyed through parents and identification mechanisms contribute to the beginnings of gender identity before the phallic phase and before castration anxiety, penis envy, and the Oedipus complex exert their greatest influence (cf. Stoller, 1964). Penis envy need not be the initiator of the feminine gender identity, as Freud claimed, and, indeed, usually is not. Parental attitudes, originating partly in the culture and expressed in the family setting, reflect normative and pathological gender-identity issues in those significant adults.

Cognitive functions play a much more prominent role in the evolution of core gender identity than most major analytic contributors to sexual identity have stressed. Freud (1925), Greenacre (1948, 1958), Kestenberg (1956), and Erikson (1964) have emphasized the impact of anatomical difference on the maturation of certain ego functions and sexual identity. Cognitive aspects of gender learning have been relatively neglected. Direct observation supports the findings of Kohlberg (1966) who, utilizing a cognitive-developmental approach, points to *the maturation of cognitive capacities* as the key to early gender identity. The child's conscious and not-so-conscious labeling herself a girl, which progresses as cognitive apparatus mature, serves as the primary and basic organizer for subsequent gender experience. According to this view, even identification processes, which psychoanalysis has emphasized in gender-identity formation, would be secondary to this labeling. The labeling would come first, and would guide the little girl's identification with a variety of maternal qualities and with only certain paternal traits. The labeling would also organize complementing behavior toward the parent of the opposite gender. Galenson (1973) and Roiphe (1968), through direct observations, arrive at a somewhat different point of view and stress that the emergence of genital awareness (especially arousal), along with anal and urinary body schematization during the second half of the second year of life, has a far-reaching organizing influence on other areas of development, including object relations, the separation-individuation process, and nascent ego functions.

A second way in which cognitive functions operate to establish early gender identity in the girl during her first fifteen months is within the person of *the parent*. The cognition in the parent — *my baby is a girl* — organizes a whole set of cues, selective rewards and sanctions, and directives to the child, and, *after* fifteen months, are increasingly present in the child as the expressable identity of being a girl.

Psychoanalytic theory of *primary identification* leaves unanswered why a normal three-year-old boy is clearly a boy even though his contact has been largely with a female adult The Kohlberg point of view better answers the question. Primarily the child is labeled a boy; this, together with subsequent selective reinforcement from the key adults, overrides the fact of his predominant contact with a female model. What the child learns through vision, kinesthetic sense, and touch similarly would be organized by the mental representation of being male.

Cognitive functions (the maturation of cognitive apparatus in the child and cognition in the parent) play a more primary role in core gender-identity formation before age three years than identification processes, castration anxiety, envy of male genitals, or genital sensation. Stoller (1968a, 1968b) has shown that girls born without a vagina can have an unequivocal sense of being a female and that the sense of being a female and the more complicated *feeling feminine* can be strong, independent of the female genitalia.

The little girl from one year to three can under normal conditions demonstrate a feeling of pride in her being, in her being a girl, in her body, and, specifically, in her genitals, if these attitudes have been conveyed to her. Her femininity is not dependent on believing she is inferior and anatomically deprived. This is not to say that observation of anatomical difference, castration anxiety, and penis envy are unimportant in the second year and thereafter — but it is to say that these latter are not prerequisite, as Freud claimed, for the emergence of femininity.

Language is crucially important in the development of gender identity after the first year: *modes of communication* and linguistic meanings of the family are vital in the transmission of gender identity; words in our language have different meanings for males and females; males and females gradually develop different ways of thinking; gender-identity formation results from *positive* direction within the family, not just from a normal unfolding of predetermined lines of development (Lidz, 1967). Language also contributes to fantasy formation, part of the inner world which Freud so importantly emphasized as contributor to and influencer of sexual development.

Freud has repeatedly stated that the girl gives up penis envy and replaces it by the desire for a child, and, to this end, she turns to her father. Recent observations (Abelin, 1971;

Kleeman, 1971b) indicate (a) many infants have a specific relationship with the father before their first birthday; (b) the most conspicuous "turning toward the father" often occurs around ten to twelve months when he becomes the "other" parent, different from mother; (c) at any rate, somewhere between eight and eighteen months the child is ready for a father relationship; (d) having the father available during that time is vital to the child and to the mother in order for the child to achieve optimum individuation; (e) the triangulation occurring around eighteen months is a developmental landmark but is to be distinguished qualitatively from the oedipal triangle, which usually attains prominence a year or more later; (f) girls show a tendency to demonstrate the father attachment earlier than boys and to be more discriminating with regard to unfamiliar persons generally; (g) beginnings of the differentiation of mother as the expressive-affectional parent and father as the instrumental, centrifugally-directed parent are observable in this ten to eighteen-month period.

Later, in addition to the impact of the inner working of the castration complex and the Oedipus complex, selective reinforcement of the child's behavior by the important adults externally fosters the transfer of the little girl's affection to the father.

Doll play expresses many different issues for the young child. Observation does not support Freud's denial (1933) of doll play as an expression of femininity in the little girl. Perhaps, as Kestenberg (1956, p. 462) claims, the little girl's mothering of her doll is, in part, a projection of her vaginal sensations onto the doll baby. What is unquestionable is that the little girl's "maternal" behavior is an identification with her mother, who selectively reinforces the behavior as appropriate to the female gender. The play is encouraged, rewarded, and confirmed (Kleeman, 1971a) both in its current form and as preparation for a future gender role. The child's core gender identity—"I am a girl"—helps to organize and specify the doll play.

Social factors—the family psychodynamics that so powerfully mold early gender identity—outweigh the influence of biology stressed by Freud in the initial development of femininity (Stoller, 1972). Observation suggests that object-relations theory is more primary than instinct theory in this regard.

Observable Manifestations of Early Female Sexuality

It is a curious fact that very little accurate data have been collected on the directly observable genital behavior of girls in the first three years. Several modest beginnings to fill this gap are now available (Kleeman, 1975; Roiphe and Galenson, 1972; Galenson, 1973), and much additional observational work needs to be done. Herewith are my tentative interpretations of these studies to date:

Pleasurable genital self-stimulation should not be labeled masturbation before the middle of the third year. Psychoanalytic theory has stated that the fantasy associated with the stimulation is essential to the concept of masturbation. Direct observation of children records the external behavior; it gains significant fantasy content only in a limited way before two and a half years.

In normal children the genital self-stimulation behavior is a small fraction of the child's total behavior. Singling out the genital behavior for observation should not in itself establish a hierarchy of importance of this behavior relative to object relations, self-development, cognitive function, or other categories of behavior. Genital sensations and genital self-stimulation contribute to core gender identity and core gender identity is a very significant aspect of the young child's personality development, but I do not believe that this genital sensation and awareness normally acts as a major *organizer* of behavior (cf. Galenson, 1973; Roiphe, 1968; Sperling, 1970; Galenson and Roiphe, 1971). Clearly, the genital events and awareness can alter and influence other behavior in vital ways, but for most normal individuals the genital self-stimulation of the first two years is one of many aspects of experience contributing to healthy personality growth and sexual development. A developmental line emerges from the first chance fingering of the genitals, usually in the first twelve months, to masturbatory stimulation, usually toward the end of the third year and thereafter. The developmental line has discontinuities in frequency and regularity of stimulation and in motivation behind the stimulation. At the outset it tends toward exploration and boundary-setting and later becomes more predominantly pleasure-seeking.

Normal children have a wide range of preferred self-stimulation activities and styles. There is no well-defined or universal sequence of genital self-stimulation leading to masturbation.

Starting in the neonatal period, female infants seem to have a spontaneous rhythm of vaginal lubrication comparable in frequency to the spontaneous erections observed in males (P. Sarrel, personal communication). Generally, infants in the first year are not yet capable of the directed, volitional behavior necessary for the masturbatory act. Spitz (1962) correctly prefers the term "genital play" for the behavior. The shift from genital play to masturbation is a gradual and discontinous process with a poorly defined point in time, varying for different children.

Both innate and environmental factors can lead to heightened genital sensitivity in the first year of life and symptomatic genital self-stimulation.

In normal children approximately between fifteen and 24 months there is an increase in genital sensation and awareness (cf. Greenacre, 1968), as well as a heightened genital sensitivity to external stimulation and an increase of pleasure potential. Observation does not establish without doubt that this is an *endogenous* genital arousal (Sperling, 1970). The combination of improved sensorimotor skills, maturation of apparatus (nervous system serving genital, urinary, and anal structures, both sensory and motor), and the decrease in diffusion of drive tensions results in an increase of genital self-stimulation normally in the second year, which surpasses anything usually observed in the first year. The common innervation of the areas unquestionably results in initial commingling of anal, urinary, and genital sensations. The heightened anal and urethral sensations as well as the increased pleasure potential of the genitals draw the child's attention to the area. Bowel and bladder training results in further focus on the genitals of self and others.

Genital self-stimulation is thus a behavioral manifestation of the multiple factors of maturational processes, progressive awareness of one's own body, the *quality* of maternal care, and the *interaction* of the child and the mothering person. Many other issues, in addition to the parental attitudes and the development of the child's inner world, can influence the nature of the genital self-stimulation, such as experiences with siblings and others or the birth of a new baby in the family. Under particular circumstances, seeing the genitals of the opposite gender can have significant impact.

A climax type of excitement that one could characterize an orgasm does not normally occur in the first two years, and, generally, the genital self-stimulation of this period is without great emotional excitement.

The emergence of body and genital pride and initial forms of exhibitionism and castration anxiety are commonly observable in the course of the second year.

The categorization of gender (who is a girl; who is a boy), largely a cognitive function, starts around fifteen months and reaches a crescendo in the final third of the third year.

The experiencing of sensations in the genitalia contributes to the primitive body ego, the sense of self, and the awareness of gender.

There is a tendency for research observers, as well as parents, to confuse semantically vulva and vagina. Contrary to Freud, observation establishes that little girls in the first three years stimulate the labia and introitus (vulva) in addition to the clitoris and occasionally explore and stimulate the lower part of the vaginal canal (cf. Fraiberg, 1952, p. 187). Most authors who in the past have made a case for the fact of *vaginal* masturbation in this age group have not specified the site of stimulation.

In a small group of girls observed longitudinally (Kleeman, 1973), two patterns of onset of genital self-stimulation could be discerned. In the first pattern, genital touching begins around eight months, gradually increases with discontinuity, until genital self-stimulation reaches an efflorescence around the middle of the second year. In the second, there is a burst of genital self-stimulation in the middle of the second year, preceded by the child's showing almost no interest in exploring or stimulating the genitals. This second pattern negates one aspect of Spitz's work. He made the presence of genital play in the first year and good object relations covariants. Whereas it is true generally that genital play is decreased or absent when the mothering is inadequate, there can be a paucity of genital play in the first year in some little girls growing up in a setting with adequate or excellent mothering.

In some reports, reddening of the genitals is cited as evidence that the child has stimulated herself or masturbated. While this may sometimes be true, under circumstances where an almost complete record was available of the child's self-stimulation, I have found that genital redness encouraged scratching, other stimulation, and attention directed at the genitalia. The skin rash was primary; the self-stimulation followed.

Aside from the initial date of genital touching, which seems in part accidental, usually the genital self-stimulation of girls is later in onset, less vigorous, less focused, less frequent, and shows less intentional self-arousal and self-absorption than that of boys in the first year and early part of the second year.

Girls are capable of intense and vigorous genital self-stimulation during the second half of the second year, and observation does not confirm that genital stimulation is contrary to feminine nature unless society, speaking through the parents, conveys such a message. However, at the end of the second year, usually the boy is more knowledgeable about his penis, scrotum, testicles, and meatus urinarius than the girl is about her clitoris, labia, introitus, ovaries, vagina, and urinary meatus. The vagueness of the girl's explorations and the lack of the visual modality in comprehending her organs result in less well-established mental representations of her genitalia at an age comparable to the boy. The girl also has an unclear mental picture in the first two years of exactly where her urine emerges.

In addition to the visual factor, other reasons for this boy-girl difference include the greater accessibility of the male organs to manual manipulation and exploration, the dual function of the penis—urinary and genital—the existence from birth of visible penile erections, testicular sensation from greater exposure and testicular movement, and the greater stimulation of the protruding male genitals by the child's rhythmic motility. Last and, probably most important, parents react differently to boys and girls. A dramatic example is that mothers generally have much more difficulty naming the girl's genital organs and do it less precisely and at a later date than for their sons. The anatomy of the boy directs his sexuality outward and is more clearly visible, compared with the girl, so that *even the observer* of the girl's genital self-stimulation sees less.

Freud repeatedly made the point that the little girl gives up (masculine) masturbation (of the clitoris) and finally makes a move toward femininity under the impact of castration anxiety and the consequent sense of inferiority. Much additional observational data is needed to determine the motivational conditions operating when a little girl stops genital self-stimulation in a setting of penis envy and a sense of inferiority; when she continues genital self-stimulation despite opportunity to know about anatomical differences; and when she stops genital self-stimulation for reasons other than penis envy. All three eventualities can and do occur, and observation denies the single routine pattern Freud claimed to be universal and which he felt answered so many issues.

Summary

Freud's writings on early female sexuality are reviewed in order to demonstrate which of his central assumptions are supported and which have been corrected by the direct observation of young children. The study of the emergence of core gender identity in little girls is a key to the modification of Freud's statements on the onset of and crucial factors in the development of femininity. Cognitive functions, learning experiences, and language are believed to be more important than Freud stressed, and penis envy and feelings of inferiority are relegated to a less universal and less *necessary* place in the onset of femininity. The role of the father is given different emphasis. Direct observation clarifies many aspects of masturbation or early genital self-stimulation in the young female: its onset; its feminine rather than masculine character; its early vicissitudes; its importance relative to other behavior; the impact of the discovery of anatomical difference; one special way it is affected by parental attitude; and how it contrasts with comparable behavior in the young male. Observation refutes Freud's often quoted statement that masturbation is further removed from the nature of women than of men.

REFERENCES*

Abelin, E. (1971), The role of the father in the separation-individuation process. In: *Separation-Individuation,* ed. J. B. McDevitt & C. F. Settlage. New York: International Universities Press, pp. 229-252.

* All references to *This Journal* are to the *Journal of the American Psychoanalytic Association.*

Barnett, M. (1966), Vaginal awareness in the infancy and childhood of girls. *This Journal*, 14:129-141.

—— (1968), "I can't" versus "He won't." Further considerations of the psychical consequences of the anatomic and physiological difference between the sexes. *This Journal*, 16:588-600.

Bonaparte, M. (1953), *Female Sexuality*. New York: International Universities Press.

Brierley, M. (1936), Specific determinants in feminine development. *Internat. J. Psycho-Anal.*, 17:163-180.

Brunswick, R. M. (1940), The preoedipal phase of the libido development. *Psychoanal. Quart.*, 9:293-319.

Calogeras, R. C. & Schupper, F. X. (1972), Origins and early formulations of the Oedipus complex. *This Journal*, 20:751-755.

Chasseguet-Smirgel, J. (1970), *Female Sexuality*. Ann Arbor: University of Michigan Press.

Cherry, R. & Cherry, L. (1973), The Horney heresy. *The New York Times Magazine*. August 26.

Chodoff, P. (1966), A critique of Freud's theory of infantile sexuality. *Amer. J. Psychiat.*, 123:507-518.

Deutsch, H. (1944), *The Psychology of Women*. New York: Grune & Stratton.

Erikson, E. (1950), *Childhood and Society*. New York: Norton.

—— (1964), Womanhood and the inner space. In: *Identity, Youth and Crisis*. New York: Norton, 1968, pp. 261-294.

Fliegel, Z. (1973), Feminine psychosexual development in Freudian theory: A historical reconstruction. *Psychoanal. Quart.*, 42:385-408.

Fraiberg, S. (1952), A critical neurosis in a two-and-a-half-year-old girl. *The Psychoanalytic Study of the Child*, 7:173-215. New York: International Universities Press.

Freud, S. (1905), Three essays on the theory of sexuality. *Standard Edition*, 7:125-243. London: Hogarth Press, 1953.

—— (1908a), Hysterical phantasies and their relation to bisexuality. *Standard Edition*, 9:155-166. London. Hogarth Press, 1959.

—— (1908b), On the sexual theories of children. *Standard Edition*, 9:205-226. London: Hogarth Press, 1959.

—— (1912), Contributions to a discussion on masturbation. *Standard Edition*, 12:239-254. London: Hogarth Press, 1958.

—— (1917), Introductory lectures on psycho-analysis. *Standard Edition*, 16:241-496. London: Hogarth Press, 1963.

—— (1919), 'A child is being beaten': A contribution to the study of the origin of sexual perversions. *Standard Edition*, 17:175-204. London: Hogarth Press, 1955.

—— (1920), The psychogenesis of a case of homosexuality in a woman. *Standard Edition*, 18:145-172. London: Hogarth Press, 1955.

—— (1923), The infantile genital organization (an interpolation into the theory of sexuality). *Standard Edition*, 19:139-145. London: Hogarth Press, 1961.

—— (1924), The dissolution of the Oedipus complex. *Standard Edition*, 19:171-179. London: Hogarth Press, 1961.

—— (1925), Some psychical consequences of the anatomical distinction between the sexes. *Standard Edition*, 19:241-258. London: Hogarth Press, 1961.

—— (1926), The question of lay analysis. *Standard Edition*, 20:177-258. London: Hogarth Press, 1959.

_____ (1930), Civilization and its discontents. *Standard Edition,* 21:57-145. London: Hogarth Press, 1961.

_____ (1931), Female sexuality. *Standard Edition,* 21:221-243. London: Hogarth Press, 1961.

_____ (1933), Femininity. *Standard Edition,* 22:112-135. London: Hogarth Press, 1964.

_____ (1937), Analysis terminable and interminable. *Standard Edition,* 23:209-253. London: Hogarth Press, 1964.

_____ (1940), An outline of psycho-analysis. *Standard Edition,* 23:139-207. London: Hogarth Press, 1964.

Galenson, E. (1973), A research investigation of sexual behavior and symbolic functioning in the second year of life. Presented at the 6th Symposium— Sexuality and Psychoanalysis Revisited, Society of Medical Psychoanalysis. New York: March, 1973.

_____ & Roiphe, H. (1971), The impact of early sexual discovery on mood, defensive organization, and symbolization. *The Psychoanalytic Study of the Child,* 26:195-216. New York: Quadrangle Books.

Greenacre, P. (1945), Urination and weeping. In: *Trauma, Growth, and Personality.* New York: International Universities Press, 1969, pp. 106-119.

_____ (1948), Anatomical structure and superego development. In: *Trauma, Growth, and Personality.* New York: International Universities Press, 1969, pp. 149-164.

_____ (1950), Special problems of early female sexual development. In: *Trauma, Growth, and Personality.* New York: International Universities Press, 1969, pp. 237-258.

_____ (1952), Some factors producing different types of genital and pregenital organization. In: *Trauma, Growth, and Personality.* New York: International Universities Press, 1969, pp. 293-302.

_____ (1953), Certain relationships between fetishism and faulty development of the body image. In: *Emotional Growth.* New York: International Universities Press, 1971, pp. 9-30.

_____ (1958), Early physical determinants in the development of the sense of identity. In: *Emotional Growth.* New York: International Universities Press, 1971, pp. 113-127.

_____ (1968), Perversions: general considerations regarding their genetic and dynamic background. In: *Emotional Growth.* New York: International Universities Press, 1971, pp. 300-314.

Greenson, R. (1966), The enigma of modern woman. *Bull. Philadelphia Assn. Psychoanal.* 16:173-185.

Hampson, J. L. & Hampson, J. G. (1961), The ontogenesis of sexual behavior in man. In: *Sex and Internal Secretions,* ed. W. Young. Baltimore: Williams & Wilkins.

Horney, K. (1926), The flight from womanhood. In: *Feminine Psychology,* ed. H. Kelman. New York: Norton, 1967, pp. 54-70.

_____ (1933), The denial of the vagina. In: *Feminine Psychology,* ed. H. Kelman. New York: Norton, 1967, pp. 147-161.

_____ (1967), *Feminine Psychology,* ed. H. Kelman. New York: Norton.

Jones, E. (1927), The early development of female sexuality. *Internat. J. Psycho-Anal.,* 8:459-472.

_____ (1933), The phallic phase. *Internat. J. Psycho-Anal.,* 14:1-33.

_____ (1935), Early female sexuality. *Internat. J. Psycho-Anal.,* 16:263-273.

Kestenberg, J. (1956), Vicissitudes of female sexuality. *This Journal*, 4:453-476.
——— (1968), Outside and inside, male and female. *This Journal*, 16:457-520.
Kinsey, A., Pomeroy, W., Martin, C., & Gebhard, P. (1953), *Sexual Behavior in the Human Female*. Philadelphia and London: Saunders.
Kleeman, J. (1971a), The establishment of core gender identity in normal girls. (a) Introduction; (b) Development of the ego capacity to differentiate. *Arch. Sexual Behavior,* 1:103-129.
——— (1971b), Who needs a father? Unpublished.
——— (1975), Genital self-stimulation in infant and toddler girls. In: *Masturbation: From Infancy to Senescence*, ed. I. Marcus & J. Francis. New York: International Universities Press, pp. 77-106.
Klein, M. (1928), Early stages of the Oedipal conflict. In: *The Psychoanalysis of Children*. New York: Grove, 1960, pp. 179-209.
——— (1932), *The Psychoanalysis of Children*. London: Hogarth Press.
Kohlberg, L. (1966), A cognitive-developmental analysis of children's sex role concepts and attitudes. In: *The Development of Sex Differences*, ed. E. Maccoby. Stanford: Stanford University Press, pp. 82-173.
Lampl-de Groot, J. (1928), The evolution of the Oedipus complex in women. *Internat. J. Psycho-Anal.,* 9:332-45.
——— (1933), Problems of femininity. *Psychoanal. Quart.,* 2:489-518.
Lidz, T. (1967), Psychoanalytic theories of development and maldevelopment: some reconceptualizations. *Amer. J. Psychoanal.,* 27:115-126.
——— (1968), *The Person*. New York: Basic Books.
Marmor, J. (1973), Freud's sexual theories 70 years later. *Medical World News: Psychiatry,* 173:86-88.
Masters, W. & Johnson, V. (1966), *Human Sexual Response*. Boston: Little, Brown.
Miller, J., Ed. (1973), *Psychoanalysis and Women. Contributions to New Theory and Therapy*. New York: Brunner/Mazel.
Millett, K. (1969), *Sexual Politics*. New York: Doubleday.
Mischel, W. (1966), A social-learning view of sex differences in behavior. In: *The Development of Sex Differences*, ed. E. Maccoby. Stanford: Stanford University Press, pp. 57-81.
Money, J. & Ehrhardt, A. (1972), *Man and Woman, Boy and Girl*. Baltimore/London: The Johns Hopkins University Press.
———, Hampson, J. G., & Hampson, J. L. (1955), An examination of some basic sexual concepts: The evidence of human hermaphroditism. *Bull. Johns Hopkins Hosp.,* 97:301-399.
Moore, B. (1968), Physiological studies of female orgasm. *This Journal,* 16:569-587.
Müller, J. (1932), A contribution to the problem of libidinal development of the genital phase of girls. *Internat. J. Psycho-Anal.,* 13:361-368.
Payne, S. (1936), A conception of femininity. *Brit. J. Med. Psychol.,* 15:18-33.
Rivière, J. (1936), On the genesis of psychical conflict in earliest infancy. *Internat. J. Psycho-Anal.,* 17:395-422.
Roiphe, H. (1968), On an early genital phase. With an addendum on genesis. *The Psychoanalytic Study of the Child,* 23:348-365. New York: International Universities Press.
——— & Galenson, E. (1972), Early genital activity and the castration complex. *Psychoanal. Quart.,* 41:334-347.

Schafer, R. (1974), Problems in Freud's psychology of women. *This Journal,* 22: 459-487.

Sherfey, M. J. (1966), The evolution and nature of female sexuality in relation to psychoanalytic theory. *This Journal,* 14:28-128.

Sperling, E. (1970), Research in early genital arousal, an overview of theory and method. Presented at a meeting of the American Psychoanalytic Association, Dec. 18, 1970.

Spitz, R. (1962), Autoerotism re-examined. *The Psychoanalytic Study of the Child,* 17:283-315. New York: International Universities Press.

Stoller, R. (1964), A contribution to the study of gender identity. *Internat. J. Psycho-Anal.,* 45:220-226.

————— (1968a), The sense of femaleness. *Psychoanal. Quart.,* 37:42-55.

————— (1968b), *Sex and Gender.* New York: Science House.

————— (1972), The "bedrock" of masculinity and femininity: bisexuality. *Arch. Gen. Psychiat.* 26:207-212.

————— (1973), Overview: the impact of new advances in sex research on psychoanalytic theory. *Amer. J. Psychiat.,* 130:241-251.

Zilboorg, G. (1944), Masculine and feminine. *Psychiat.,* 7:257-296.

80 Bethmour Road
Bethany, Connecticut 06525

SOME SUGGESTED REVISIONS CONCERNING EARLY FEMALE DEVELOPMENT

Eleanor Galenson, m.d.

and Herman Roiphe, m.d.

A RE-EVALUATION OF FREUD'S IDEAS concerning early sexuality must take into account new findings from a variety of sources, such as studies of normal children, genetically and hormonally deviant ones, and those who are emotionally disturbed, as well as the changes in psychoanalytic thinking that have taken place under the impact of ego psychology over the past twenty years. We agree with Lichtenstein (1961) that sexuality has been relegated to the position of only one among several variables from the special and exemplary role in development that Freud (1905, 1940) had originally assigned to the sexual drive organization. Lichtenstein, in arguing against this general trend, maintains that sexuality is the most archaic mode, closely related to the primary process and therefore uniquely capable of conveying the emotional truth of personal existence, while only later on do other modes establish, in thought, the conception that one does in fact exist. In this respect, he follows Freud's views concerning the centrality of sexuality among the other variables of

The research upon which this paper is based was carried out in the Research Nursery in the Division of Child Psychiatry at the Albert Einstein College of Medicine. We wish to acknowledge the important contributions of the many staff members to this work, particularly Dr. Jan Drucker, who assisted in data analysis, and Ms. Catherine Shapiro, head teacher, who has been responsible for the functioning of the Nursery for the past five years.

development, and holds that sexuality both molds and is molded by developing object relations, a position with which we are in agreement. This mutual influence of sexuality and object relations was alluded to in a preliminary and sketchy way in Freud's 1933 paper, where he acknowledged that the early experiences of boys and girls differed, and that the preoedipal relation of the girl with her mother was of a special nature. He described the changing character of the girl's libidinal relations to her mother as "of many different kinds. Since they persist through all three phases of infantile sexuality, they also take on the characteristic of the different phases and express themselves by oral, sadistic-anal and phallic wishes. These wishes represent active as well as passive impulses..." (pp. 119-120).

With the advent of Mahler's infant observational research (Mahler and Gosliner, 1955; Mahler, 1963, 1966, 1968), attention to the area of developing object relations increased enormously, while drive development receded somewhat from both research and clinical interest. In the course of our own research carried out at the Albert Einstein College of Medicine since 1966, we have attempted to encompass both the sector of developing object relations and that of drive organization, focusing upon their interdependence and their reciprocal influence in relation to ego functions. We have been particularly interested in the emergence of the sense of sexual identity during the second year of life.

Review of Pertinent Studies

Before presenting our own data concerning the emergence of genital awareness at sixteen to nineteen months, we shall review two other studies of early sexual development, since these point to a critical period in development coinciding with the one we have described. The work of Money and Ehrhardt (1972) is concerned with genetically and hormonally deviant individuals: these authors suggest that it is the sex in which the infant is reared during the first two years of life that plays the major role in the establishment of the sense of feminine gender identity. They have studied several different groups of children. There are genetically male individuals in whom there has been complete absence of all gonadal hormones during the prenatal period, and are therefore born with female-appearing external genitalia. These children develop along female lines if they have been reared as females during the first eighteen months of life. In contrast to this first group is a group of genetically female children who have been hormonally androgenized during their prenatal period (without having received additional androgenization post-natally). These prenatally androgenized but genetically female girls were also reared as girls. When studied during their latency years in follow-up, although they show certain traits called "tomboyishness," which included preference for rough and tumble play and for boys' toys instead of dolls, as well as a disinclination to have children, their object choice is distinctly heterosexual and they regard themselves as female.

Money and Ehrhardt conclude from the study of these two groups of children that feminine gender identity is primarily dependent upon neither prenatal gonadal hormones nor genetic endowment, but upon the sex of rearing. The presence of tomboyish traits, however, suggests to them that the presence of prenatal androgens plays a minor part.

Another group studied by Money and Ehrhardt consists of genetically male individuals in whom there had been an absence of hormonal androgenization prenatally. Some of these infants were born with normal or near-normal-appearing female external genitalia and were reared as females. These chidren showed feminine preferences for doll play and for having children of their own later on: 90 per cent of them said they were content with their female role, and 80 per cent had already established heterosexual relationships when followed up at the time of early adolescence.

However, those genetically male infants in whom some

but not the normal amount of prenatal androgen hormones had been produced were born with external genitalia that were anomalous in appearance, neither definitely male nor female. In several of these infants reared as boys, sex reassignment was attempted after they had reached the end of the second year of life because of the surgical impossibility of providing a semblance of adequate male genitalia. These children showed profound psychological disturbance. Money and Ehrhardt concluded from the study of this group as well that it is primarily postnatal factors in the human that, in contrast with lower species, account for much if not most gender identity. They nevertheless believe that it is cognitive development, particularly language, that is responsible for the age-specific critical level of eighteen months or so beyond which successful sex reassignment is impossible. Our own findings are in agreement with the critical age for sex reassignment, although we do not consider cognitive factors to be the essential determinants.

The other major research connected with very early sexuality, carried out by Stoller (1968) and his group, emphasizes the decisive influence of early parental rearing during the first few years for the determination of "core gender identity." Stoller has described the importance of the prephallic feminine identification in a small group of transsexual males whose mothers shared a particular type of psychosexual constellation. These transsexual males had apparently reached a critical developmental divide in terms of their sexual identity toward the end of their second year, the same critical period noted by Money and Ehrhardt and in our own research population. However, Stoller does not entirely eliminate the contributions of genital anatomy and physiology, or of endocrine and neurological factors, to the sense of sexual identity, in addition to the effect of the maternal influence.

In regard to female development, Stoller believes there is an early phase of female gender development, followed by a secondary phase, which he feels is the result of the girl's defense against her growing awareness of the genital difference, although no clinical material has as yet been offered in support of this position. A similar point of view was expressed by Horney (1924, 1926), Jones (1927, 1933), Zilboorg (1944), and, more recently, Fliegel (1973), all of whom have disagreed with Freud's emphasis on the phallic phase as the beginning of the gender development of the girl.

In summary, the two most extensive ongoing studies of early sexual development, those of Money and Ehrhardt, and of Stoller, have identified a critical period for the establishment of gender identity which occurs by the second half of the second year of life, a critical period that correlates chronologically with our own findings. There is disagreement among us, however, as to the factors responsible for the occurrence of this critical phase of sexual development.

Research Hypotheses and Research Design

Rolphe (1968) has proposed an early genital phase, which occurs normally and regularly sometime between sixteen and 24 months of age and is characterized by the presence of behavior indicating genital arousal. This would include frequent and intensive manipulation of the genitals and increased curiosity regarding the genitals of others. This early genital phase would be free of any oedipal resonance but would be closely connected with ongoing consolidation of self and object representations, particularly of the genital area. Roiphe further postulated that although reactions would usually be low-keyed, there would be moderate to severe castration reactions at this time in those children who were exposed to the genital anatomical difference between the sexes, and who had sustained, during their first year of life, either some important trauma to the developing body image, such as serious illness and surgical procedures, or had suffered a serious disturbance in the mother-child relationship, due to such factors as prolonged separations or depression in the mother.

Roiphe proposed that these preoedipal castration reactions would consist of a complex of symptoms including negativism, increased dependence on the mother, disturbances in sleep and bowel and bladder functioning, nightmares, fears of being bitten by animals, the fear in boys that the penis would fall off, and, in girls, the question of why they do not have a penis. This early castration anxiety would be indissolubly connected with fears of object loss and self-annihilation unlike the castration reactions of the later oedipal phase.

Finally, the original hypothesis (Galenson, 1971) was broadened to predict that all areas of functioning, including the emergent symbolism of play and speech, would be influenced and organized by the genital awareness and the reaction to the genital difference; in other words, this era would constitute a true early genital phase, preceding by a year or more the later well-known phallic-oedipal phase.

During the nine years of our research, we have studied a population of 70 children who are evenly divided between the sexes, mostly coming from a middle-class group; they have been studied from their tenth or twelfth month of life through the end of their second year in a naturalistic, informal nursery setting. Ten mother-and-child pairs attend four two-hour sessions each week. Two observers gather developmental information from the mother and observe the child's behavior, recording the data immediately after the observation session. Although individual case studies have already been published, this is our first cross-sectional analysis of our population, a group that is now the subject of a systematic follow-up by colleagues who will be comparing their findings with our own earlier ones.

Every mother lends shape to an "identity theme" in her young infant, as Lichtenstein (1961) has felicitously described it, and it is partly through the feeding relationship that this molding occurs, an experience that appears to be a different one for boys than for girls. Murphy (1962) and Korner (1973) have described differences in maternal handling according to whether the infant is a male or a female.

Furthermore, reports in the psychoanalytic literature have pointed to the difference between the early oral experiences of male and female patients. Greenacre (1950), Kestenberg (1956, 1968), and, more recently, Fraiberg (1972) have described the close relation between oral and vaginal themes in the analytic material from both adult and child female patients. Confirmatory evidence of such combined early oral and genital experience comes from the fact that penile erections occur in boys during nursing (as well as at other times, of course).

Although feeding is certainly a highly significant experience of the first year, it is by no means the only one. As Freud (1933) pointed out (p. 120), "the mother . . . by her activities over the child's bodily hygiene inevitably stimulated, and perhaps even roused for the first time, pleasurable sensations in her genitals." Kris (1951) elaborated on this point: "The transfer from general affection to the genital zone itself . . . may also arise as a consequence of the general bodily closeness to which, we assume, the child tends to react with sensation in the genital region" (p. 96). We would add to this that it is likely that the mother's activities are experienced differently by boys than by girls, not only because the genital anatomical structure of each sex provides distinctive sensations, but more particularly because the specific sex of the child provokes special and unique unconscious fantasies in the mother as she handles her infant's genitals. One has only to witness the repetitive and intense genital cleansing practiced by some mothers, in contrast to the almost complete avoidance of the area by others, to be convinced of the impact on the infant of sexual fantasies aroused in the mother.

The mutual influence of drive organization and object relationship just described characterizes all early mother-child interactions. Lichtenstein (1961) describes this as: "An interaction between two partners where each partner experiences himself as uniquely and specifically capable of serving as the instrument of the other's sensory gratification — such a partnership can be called a partnership of sensual involvement" (p. 207). And later on: (p. 250) ". . . there is an innate body responsiveness, a capacity . . . . to respond to contact with another person with a specific kind of somatic excitation which is not a drive, because it has no direction, but which is the innate prerequisite for the later development of a drive. . . . This responsiveness we may call sexual because it forms the matrix of later sexual development."

Patterns of sensuous interaction of mother and child — the expression of early drive organization — seem, then, to involve the genital zone from the very beginning of life, not only in the course of the mother's fondling and bodily ministrations and during feeding, but also probably in connection with transmitted pressure and excitation from the adjacent anal and urinary areas, the totality of these sensuous interactions contributing to a substantially different early body image for each sex.

Correlation Between Drive Development and Object Relations from Six to Eighteen Months of Age

The particular importance of the genitals as well as the face, from about six months of age, for the establishment of the sense of identity has been described by Greenacre (1958) as

> The body areas which are then most significant in comparing and contrasting and establishing individual recognition of the body self, and that of others, are the *face* and the *genitals*. . . . after six months of age and extending into the second half of the second year. During the latter part of this time, however, and especially during the third year, the gradual increase in genital feelings — clitoral and phallic — gives endogenous sensations and pressures from within a kind of sensory peg which combines locally with the body imagery produced by visual and tactile

appreciation of the own genitals and those of the other [pp. 116-118].

It is specifically this new level of bodily awareness, involving first the anal and urinary zones and then the genitals, which emerges during the practicing subphase of Mahler's separation-individuation process, that is, at about one year of age. Behavioral evidence of these psychological developments has been accumulated during the course of our own research. Whereas the infant of six months played with his toes, fingers, and body in a general exploratory fashion, the twelve-month-old examines his body parts in a new way. He compares his own facial features with his mother's by pointing at and touching them, and soon his comparison includes the rest of his body as he proceeds in a regular sequence from facial features to the anal, urinary, and finally the genital area (Galenson and Roiphe, 1974). The emergence of anal awareness is indicated by behaviors such as shifts in the frequency and timing of defecation, attentiveness to the act itself, tugging at the soiled diaper, hiding during defecation, interest in toilets and garbage cans, and the use of anal verbal references. There is also an increased incidence of diaper rashes and diarrhea and/or constipation. With these anal-zone indications come many sequences of play behavior which we have understood as "anal derivative" in nature. These consist of "in and out," filling and emptying, and scattering and smearing behavior, all having structural properties similar to those characteristic of anal-zone functioning (Galenson, 1971).

With the anal awareness, or soon thereafter, the emergence of urinary awareness is signaled by such zonal behavior as attentiveness to the urinary act and such derivative play as interest in faucets and hoses and in pouring liquids. This anal and urinary interest is directed not only at the toddler's own body, but at these specific areas and functions in parents, peers, animals, and dolls as well.

In the midst of the progressive anal and urinary awareness, genital behavior of a different quality from the early genital exploratory play emerges for the first time. All 70 children in our research sample (Galenson and Roiphe, 1974) have demonstrated this heightened and qualitatively distinctive genital awareness along with genital derivative behavior, to be described below, beginning sometime between fifteen and nineteen months of age, confirming Roiphe's original hypothesis (1968). Moreover, in each instance the genital awareness has emerged in regular and predictable sequence, only after the development of both anal and urinary awareness. This finding agrees with Kleeman's (1976) report of the five infant girls he studied.

Clinical Illustration

The following excerpts from direct observational data of an infant boy illustrate the type of behavior that indicates the underlying psychological anal, urinary, and then genital differentiation, as well as progressive differentiation in the object sphere.

John, at twelve months of age, explored his mother's eyes, ears, and mouth simultaneously with those areas on his own body and had become interested in his mirror image. As self-object differentiation proceeded, peek-a-boo games with his whole body were his favorites; he pointed and waved bye-bye, and he took his first unaided steps. As evidence of his increasing individuation and body-image emergence, John's interest began to be concentrated more and more in the perineal area; he began to defecate only at night, and was now very interested in the toilet and toidy seat — both of which he used for splashing and playing — and garbage pails intrigued him for the first time. His genital play, which had begun at about seven and a half months continued to be casual and exploratory in nature.

At thirteen months, John become interested in his

mother's navel and in his own, began to remove his own diapers, was following his mother into the bathroom consistently, and had begun to throw and bang toys and aggressively take them away from other children. At fourteen months, an important shift in the object sphere was signaled as John became definitely less clinging to his mother, but now sought out his father, anticipating his departure in the morning and his return at night. He succeeded in witnessing his father's urination for the first time, as far as was reported to us. Along with this beginning shift in object ties, there was a definite acceleration of his anal and urinary and genital interests. His stools were softer in consistency, they awakened him in the morning and he was irritable until he was changed. He pulled at his soiled diaper and at his outer pants in preparation for the change, and had also developed a diaper rash. Much anal-derivative play made its appearance soon after; he shredded his pampers, banged and threw toys, the "shape box" became his favorite toy, he messed and smeared his food, searched out garbage pails constantly, discovered and operated light switches devotedly (the element of control was important here), loved push-toys (again the anal expulsive characteristic), and was often found filling the toilet with paper. His object ties assumed anal-phase attributes as he became much more demanding and had angry outbursts, during which he screamed and kicked his mother.

Urinary and genital awareness in the body-image area showed similar intensification. John now began to urinate selectively during diapering and could stop and start his stream while standing in the bathtub. At the same time, he pointed to his own penis and smiled as he manipulated it.

At fifteen months, his increasing general autonomy became evident in his "no" behavior and verbalization of that word, but he also began to imitate his father more and more. He now defecated in solitude only, sat on the toidy seat quite voluntarily (but without results), teased, stored and stacked his toys, and still remained very interested in the bathroom.

His urination became even more infrequent as he withheld his urine for longer periods, and he labeled his mother's urination "pee-pee"; futhermore, he pointed to his penis and looked down at it as he pulled in his rather protruberant abdomen. It was evident that the anal, urinary, and genital areas were achieving much greater psychic representation, as was the emerging concept of his own identity as a totality. For example, he called himself by his proper name, he had added the word "yes" to his vocabulary, and he was attached to a new transitional object, a Teddy Bear (his bottle had been his first one).

In the object sphere during the next three months, as an even stronger shift to the father took place, John was increasingly interested in his father, carrying about his shoes and other belongings while he bit and was angry at his mother. As for body-image progression, his own penis became even more interesting to him: he pointed at it through his diaper, pulled at it vigorously, often while it was erect, and in parallel fashion tried to touch his father's urinary stream and penis on many occasions.

This summary description depicts the usual urinary and genital developmental sequence with the concomitant separation-individuation progression, including the beginning shift toward the father which has been observed in most of our normal children.

In contrast to the normal developmental sequence of anal, urinary, and then genital emergence at sixteen to eighteen months just described, 29 disturbed children in our Therapeutic Nursery have shown serious delays, not only in their separation-individuation process, but also in the emergence of their anal, urinary, and genital awareness (Galenson et al., 1975). It seems, then, that the achievement of both the practicing and rapprochement subphases of object relations is correlated with and, in fact, is essential for ongoing drive development, as is illustrated by the delay in progression of anal, urinary, and early genital cathexis and organization, which is evident in these children with serious object-relationship impairment. Drive development is profoundly influenced by the quality of the object relation.

The Line of Development of Genital Drive Organization

It is now generally agreed (Spitz, 1962; Kleeman, 1971, 1975; Galenson and Roiphe, 1974) that the genital play of the first sixteen months of life is, under normal circumstances, in the nature of general body exploration and can not yet be considered true masturbation. The pattern of emergence of this early genital play, as described by Kleeman (1971, 1975) in the five children he reported on, agrees in most respects with our own findings (Galenson and Roiphe, 1974) in the 70 boys and girls we have studied. This early genital play may be summarized as follows: boys and girls show a difference in time of onset and quality of early genital play. Boys begin genital exploration somewhere between seven to ten months, whereas girls begin some months later. In girls, the genital play is less focused, less frequent, and shows less intentionality than in boys, partially, we believe, in consequence of the more indirect mechanical stimulation by diapers and cleansing experienced by the girl.

Genital behavior in both boys and girls then begins to take on a new quality beginning somewhere between fifteen and seventeen months. In the five girls reported by Kleeman and in the 35 girls in our own sample, genital manipulation is now more focused, the infant is absorbed in the activity, she derives intense pleasure from it, and there are signs of concomitant autonomic excitation, such as skin flushing, perspiration and rapid respiration. Masturbation is carried out manually as before, but the action is now rapid and repetitive, with vigorous rubbing, pinching, and squeezing, the fingers being positioned near the mons pubis, or on or between the labia. Because the genital area is so small, it is usually impossible to decide whether the vaginal opening is being stimulated at the same time. However, several of our research group mothers have reported that the little girl's finger has actually been introduced into the opening of the vagina itself. In two deviant female infants we have studied (Galenson et al., 1975), insertion of their pacifiers deeply into the vagina regularly and repetitively was observed in our own nursery.

The usual normal manual masturbation occurs during bathing and diapering, while indirect nonmanual masturbation is achieved mainly through straddling rocking horses, toys, furniture, parents' legs, etc. It is particularly significant that affectionate and erotic gestures toward other people now accompany the genital manipulation for the first time; that is, it appears to be object directed. In the beginning of this period of new genital awareness, the little girl often looks at or touches her mother with an expression of pleasure and delight as she is touching her own genitals. Gradually this object-directed affect is replaced by the inner-directed gaze that soon accompanies all her genital self-stimulation.

We consider this new type of genital activity true masturbation, in spite of the absence of a concomitant verbalized fantasy, for various forms of nonverbal yet clearly symbolic behavior accompany the new genital activity, indicating the presence of some accompanying—albeit rudimentary—fantasy state. For example, among the many objects used in direct genital masturbatory contact by many little girls in our study have been nursing bottles, transitional-object blankets, stuffed animals, and dolls. We think it likely that this early fantasy formation includes a partial memory of the earlier maternal contact, since the genital manipulation so often involves these typical "mother-me" objects. Concrete objects are then gradually discarded, and masturbation approaches the adult model, although some people never relinquish them entirely, as has been reported by Greenacre (1969) and by ourselves (Roiphe and Galenson, 1973a; Galenson and Roiphe 1971, 1974).

Genital Drive Organization and the Sense of Femininity

Our view of early female sexual development, as derived from our research findings, includes the following three propositions: (1) As already stated, we believe that sexual drive organization plays a central and exemplary role for the early sense of sexual identity and profoundly influences object relations and ego development; (2) Although Freud in his later papers (1931, 1933), assumed that the preoedipal development in the girl is crucial for certain aspects of her later development, particularly for the shift of love object from mother to father, he vastly underestimated the role of preoedipal psychosexuality; (3) The early castration complex (not as yet connected with the oedipal constellation), with its component penis envy, is a pivotal factor for the girl's developing femininity, particularly for the crucial and decisive erotic shift to the father as love object. Evidence supporting this view of early female development will be presented under the following headings: (1) the role of early drive development; (2) the discovery of the sexual anatomical difference and its impact on psychosexual development, and (3) ego functioning and the sense of sexual identity.

The Role of Early Drive Development

As already described, the early oral activities with their probable concomitant vaginal stimulation have combined with the stimulation of the mother's affectionate handling and other ministrations to provide the girl with an early sense of the genitals, always in connection with the infant's developing bond to the mother. The early genital exploratory play adds to this vague beginning sense of the genital area. Then, at about sixteen months, a qualitatively new type of genital play develops, which we consider to be true masturbation for the first time. The infant seems now to be newly aware of both the genital area and genital sensations in that she looks at her genitals and alertly attends to her genital manipulations. Furthermore, this zonal behavior is soon followed by a flurry of genital derivative behavior. There are accompanying affective behavioral changes, and ego development now comes under the influence of the genital cathexis. A definite quality of phallic organization appears to both mingle with and finally dominate over the prior anal-urinary organization.

The little girl now not only focuses her attention upon her own ano-urinary-genital area, but from about sixteen or seventeen months on, she becomes curious about this area and its functions in others as well. As evidence for the widespread influence of the new genital awareness, all the little girls in our study succeeded in being admitted to the bathroom with their fathers at this time, even in the most modest of families, and those who had been present during parental toileting during their earlier months began to be interested in the father's urination for the first time at about sixteen to seventeen months. This initial curiosity concerning her father is soon followed by similar attempts to investigate the same area in her mother, her peers, and dolls and animals, if available. Then the curiosity spreads to other aspects of body differences, such as hair and clothing. Furthermore, in those girls where boy/girl differential verbal labeling had already emerged prior to seventeen months of age, distortions in the use of such differential verbal labeling have been noted frequently during the period of their reaction to the genital difference, while use of the word "boy" has often dropped out altogether. A few excerpts from our observational data will give a flavor of the behavioral manifestations of this emerging genital schematization in girls.

Lilly, at fourteen months, had been interested in the toilet and its accessories for some time, although toilet training had not yet been attempted. Now she began to pull at her genitals during diapering and bathing. At seventeen and a half months, she wanted to examine her mother's pubic area and asked to see her mother's "penis"; she also inserted her fingers deeply between her own labia and looked up between her wide spread legs. She undressed dolls continually and watched other children being diapered.

Peggy had touched her genitals in her bath since twelve and half months. At fourteen months she fell asleep with her genitals resting upon her Teddy Bear, and she fingered between her labia frequently during diapering and bathing, then examining her hand visually. At fifteen and a half months, she rubbed her labia with toilet paper, looking pleased and flushed as she did so. She, too, examined dolls, and became very interested in other children's diapering. A little later she became self-absorbed and withdrawn during her genital manipulation.

Winnie had been touching her genitals during diapering for some months, but at nineteen months she began to smile when she did so, and looked up at her mother. She also masturbated while looking at a book.

Jenny was one of our early "rocking horse" children, but this rocking became an intensely erotic activity with flushing and rapid respiration from fourteen and a half months onward. At seventeen months, she began to briefly reach for her genital area manually, although rocking still remained her main form of genital activity. She took possession of her father's pen, hiding it for several days. (This possessiveness and interest in phallic shaped objects, extremely common in girls during this period, seems to be linked with the emergence of symbols [Galenson and Roiphe, 1971].) At nineteen and a half months, while she was still rocking intensely, she insisted that a little male friend with whom she bathed was a girl, and made many male-female errors in verbalization. At twenty and three-fourth months, she demanded full possession of all her father's pens.

Mary began to pull at her genitals whenever she was fatigued, beginning at eight months of age. At fourteen months, tentative but now regular genital touching emerged and soon accompanied every diapering. She also began to consistently straddle trains and place dolls between her legs. During a trip with her parents, her masturbation increased, it was now accompanied by a self-absorbed and dreamy look, and she insisted that she, her mother, and her favorite doll all had penises.

Sara began to finger her genitals at twelve months; this gradually became more intense and erotic in character, until at fifteen and a half months she was giggling and becoming quite self-absorbed during each episode of genital manipulation.

Discovery of the Sexual Anatomical Difference and Its Impact on Psychosexual Development: Boy-Girl Differences after 18 Months

Boys and girls differ in their later genital development in several respects, although they are initially alike. All 35 boys in our normal sample developed an awareness of the genital difference and began masturbation proper by about fifteen months or so, as did the girls, and their sexual curiosity was similar to that of the girls during the early weeks following the initial discovery of the genital difference.

From this point onward, however, there was a clear divergence in development between boys and girls. The boys reflected the effect of the genital emergence in their choice of those toys and play activities which are usually considered typically masculine, such as cars and ball playing, and in the onset of a mild degree of hyperactivity. Furthermore, their masturbation was continuous and fairly vigorous from then on. Only two of the 35 boys showed serious disturbances following the emergence of genital awareness, disturbances that seriously distorted their subsequent development. Both boys had suffered marked interference in their maternal relationship during their first year of life, the details of which have been reported elsewhere (Galenson et al., 1975; Roiphe and Galenson, 1973a).

In contrast to the low incidence of overt reaction in the boys, all 35 girls in our research sample showed a definite and important reaction to the discovery of the genital difference and eight of the 35 developed extensive castration reactions. (It should be mentioned here that our sample is not a random one, since we have selected for inclusion in our research group each year at least two children who, because of certain experiences during their first year of life, would be expected to react with disturbance to the emergence of genital awareness in accordance with Roiphe's (1968) original hypothesis. Thus although the castration reactions are definitely more frequent in the girls, this boy-girl ratio is only an approximate one.

The castration reactions in the girls ranged from mildly transient ones, which seemed to have milder prognostic importance, to some profound disruptions involving almost every aspect of behavior. Our data lend support to Freud's (1933) statement that the girl's discovery that she is castrated is a turning-point in her growth. However, this discovery of the genital difference, with the fantasy that she is castrated, takes place at an earlier age than Freud indicated, and the advent of the crucial discovery seems to wait upon the emergence of a specific cathexis of the genital area, which in turn follows closely upon the emergence of anal and urinary awareness. The subsequent sense of loss may be profound to only moderate, depending upon many factors, such as the quality of the tie to the mother, earlier bodily experiences, the availability of the father at this time, or the mother's conscious and unconscious attitudes.

We believe that these castration responses to the sexual difference are important organizing influences from this time onward (Roiphe, 1968; Galenson and Roiphe, 1971, 1974; Roiphe and Galenson, 1973b) and that they determine not only the direction of much of the girl's subsequent psychosexual development, but other aspects of her personality as well, both in enhancing and inhibiting directions. For in the wake of the castration reactions, we have seen marked oral-regressive behavior; anal-zone exploration and anal masturbation become markedly intensified, and there is re-emergence of the fear of object loss and of anal loss, and a subsequent change in the pattern of genital masturbation in many girls. Manual masturbation is often replaced by indirect masturbation by such means as the rocking horse or thigh pressure, or it is displaced to the anal area or to the umbilicus, while some girls abandon masturbation altogether. Still others continue to masturbate, but no longer seem to derive pleasure from it (Roiphe and Galenson, 1974).

In a previous publication (Galenson and Roiphe, 1971) we described the establishment of a basic depressive mood in connection with a profound preoedipal castration in an infant girl. Many of the girls with less profound forms of preoedipal castration reaction have shown temporary affective changes, such as quietness and loss of zestfulness and enthusiasm, along with facial expressions of sadness. Since these mood changes have been correlated chronologically with the castration reactions, we have hypothesized that there is a causal connection between these two experiences. Mahler (1966) described similar mood changes in many of the little girls she observed during the same chronological period, although she has emphasized a causal relation between mood changes and the rapprochement phase of object relations.

In contrast to the disturbances already described, many advances in ego development have been noted. It is in connection with these preoedipal castration reactions, for example, that many girls develop a special type of attachment to dolls or other inanimate objects, different from the earlier type of doll play, which appears to serve as "infantile fetishes" in support of the wavering genital schematization (see Roiphe and Galenson, 1973a; Galenson and Roiphe, 1971, 1974). These inanimate objects are involved in the remarkable burgeoning of inner fantasy life which has emerged in most of the girls in our sample under the impact of the reaction to their recognition of the sexual difference. Furthermore, they begin to use crayons, pens, and pencils at this time, earlier than most of the boys in our group, in an early but definite attempt at graphic representation. Many defenses, such as displacement, introjection, and projection, are elaborated as the little girls cope with the fantasy of castration and their renewed fears of object loss and self-annihilation.

The general developmental picture of the 35 boys differed in that all the boys continued to masturbate manually; furthermore, all of them showed some increase in the level of their general motor activity, ranging from a very mild to a quite intense degree. Finally, the boys were not as involved in either fantasy play or graphic representation as were the girls in this same age group. (The pattern of development in the boy will be presented in another publication.)

In summary, most girls in our research sample showed an increased investment in inner fantasy life, expressed both in play and graphic representation, an elaboration of many defenses, and a change in basic mood and in masturbatory patterns, whereas the boys showed a definite tendency toward increased motor activity. The latter might be viewed as defensive in nature, in the service of a denial of the genital difference.

Excerpts from our data will illustrate the many different patterns and types of reaction in the girls of our sample, following their discovery of the genital difference.

Lilly, who had been investigating her genital area both visually and manually, began at eighteen and three fourth months to inhibit both these activities. At the same time, she became irritable and clinging, her play less zestful and inventive, and her doll play consisted of labeling all dolls as boys. She called for her father consistently and became distinctly antagonistic toward her mother.

In Peggy at fifteen and three fourths months, all exploration and manipulation of her genitals ceased. She became her mother's well-dressed, neat, subdued, and obedient little girl. Her dolls still remained her prized possessions at four years of age, when she was last seen in follow-up.

Winnie had fluctuated in her level of manual masturbatory activity from her nineteenth month on. At 22 months, while bathing with two little boys, she examined her own genitalia and asked where her penis was. After her baby sister was born, when Winnie was almost 23 months old, her doll play flourished remarkably, whereas her genital play subsided. At 24 months she persistently tried to open her father's underwear and to grab for his genitals. At 25 months she started to masturbate again, and at 26 months tried to urinate while standing up in imitation of a boy. She had remained an extremely avid doll player when last seen in follow-up, at almost four years of age, and her fantasy life was rich and varied.

Jenny, our early passionate horsewoman, was still masturbating this way when last seen in her third year, although there was occasional manual touching as well. She had established ownership of several of her father's pens at the time of the birth of her sister when she was seventeen months old, during a period when her anger at her mother had mounted, and she had made many errors in boy-girl labeling of people as well as pictures. By 21 months, she constantly preferred her father in the flesh, or his pens if he were not available. She had also attempted to take possession of her baby sister, with whom she was a very strict and unpleasant disciplinarian.

Finally, Shirley, whose genital manipulation had become intense and was accompanied by definite arousal at sixteen and three fourths months, showed extensive preoccupation both with long rods, which she stood upright, and with her Bathinette hose, at the same time as she stared at her baby brother's genitals over and over again. Her formerly very close relation with her mother began to be superseded by a definite wooing of her father, crying and calling for him when he was away, excited about him when he returned, whereas she refused to allow her mother to read to her or dress her, and she was often sulky. She, too, developed an abiding preference for two of her dolls at this time and was busily engaged in much make-believe play.

The effect of the castration reaction upon developing object ties has been most striking. Both boys and girls in our sample had developed a special relation with her father toward the end of the first year, as part of their increasing separation from the mother. But it was in the midst of their castration reactions that most of the little girls in our group turned to the father in a newly erotic way, seeking the mother's attention only during periods of distress. These little girls seemed to have had a relatively successful experience during their first year. However, in those girls whose earlier relation with the mother had been of poor quality, or had suffered important bodily traumata during their first year, or if they had experienced the birth of a sibling during the second half of the second year, hostile dependence upon the mother was enormously aggravated in the wake of the discovery of the sexual anatomical difference. There is no doubt that these early events in the psychosexual sphere exerted a decisive influence upon the developing libidinal attachment to the father in these little girls, determining whether a definitive erotic shift towards the father took place toward the end of the second year, or whether there was a persistence of an intensified and even more ambivalent tie to the mother. The character of the subsequent oedipal constellation of the girl will, of course, be influenced in due course. The milder castration reaction would appear to facilitate the girl's turn to the father as her new love object, with a continuing, albeit less intense, attachment to her mother, while the more profound castration reaction would be expected to lead to a predominantly negative oedipal constellation, with the choice of the mother as the primary but ambivalently loved object. (We hope to describe the parallel period of development in the boy when our data analysis for the boys has been completed.)

Our data do not thus far elucidate the question of the site of actual sexual arousal. Intense or exclusive vaginal masturbation has not been reported in any of the girls we have studied, although many have apparently discovered and stimulated their vagina in the course of masturbation involving the labial and clitoral areas. In the two deviant infant girls mentioned previously, extensive and persistent vaginal masturbation using their pacifier was reported by the parents and also observed directly in our own Nursery. This vaginal masturbation began at about twelve months of age and continued during the year or so of our contact with these families.

Ego Development and the Sense of Sexual Identity

Effect Upon Symbolic Functioning:

We must keep in mind that those male/female verbal labels which appear at sixteen or seventeen months of age do not represent true concepts, but are still bound to concrete attributes; "boy" means "the boy next door" or "the boy in the book named Jim," but not all boys everywhere. It should not be surprising, therefore, to find that these boy/girl labels are quite unstable, and that they are either lost altogether for a time, or their meaning is confused under the impact of castration reactions (Roiphe and Galenson, 1973a; Galenson and Roiphe, 1971, 1974). This distortion in symbolic functioning has persisted over many months in several of the girls we have studied, frequently encompassing the use of masculine pronouns as well.

Not only is verbal symbolism affected, but many aspects of the emerging semisymbolic play which is characteristic of the second half of the second year, are profoundly influenced by the developments in the psychosexual area. There is usually a remarkable burgeoning of fantasy life and of graphic representation in the form of early attempts at drawing and writing. The little girl begins to use many new defensive measures, such as displacement and introjection and projection, as she very actively copes with the newly aroused anxieties. If the castration reaction is not overwhelming, it is as if a new level of intellectual functioning is achieved. We will mention only a few examples; the avoidance of broken toys, doll play dealing with the genital anatomical differences, the use of phallic shaped inanimate objects as phallic substitutes, and the attachment to dolls and other inanimate objects as infantile fetishes. These findings have been described elsewhere in detail (Roiphe 1968; Roiphe and Galenson 1973b; Galenson and Roiphe 1971, 1974).

In contrast to the usual reaction, those girls with the more intense castration reactions to the genital emergence suffered a considerable constriction in their fantasy life in that imaginative play of all types became sparse and stereotyped. There was also an interference in their general intellectual curiosity; they explored their world in a much more limited fashion. Their extensive use of such defenses as denial, splitting, displacement to other body areas, total body erotization, and the use of infantile fetishes led to further disturbances in their development. These children have been described elsewhere (Roiphe and Galenson, 1973a; Galenson and Roiphe 1971), as have the two boys whose castration reactions came in the wake of unusually severe traumata during their first year of life.

Summary

In our view, Freud's original position that sexual drive organization exerts a special and exemplary role during the various psychosexual stages remains a valid one, although drive organization is in turn consistently and extensively influenced by events in the sphere of object relations. Very early genital-zone experiences during the first sixteen months of life contribute to a vague sense of sexual identity, and undoubtedly exert an influence over many ego functions. Some genital sensations probably occur consistently in conjunction with feeding, as well as during many other interactions of the mother and her young infant.

With ongoing separation and individuation, the genital zone emerges as a distinct and differentiated source of endogenous pleasure somewhere between sixteen and nineteen months of age, exerting a new and crucial influence upon the sense of sexual identity, object relations, basic mood, and many aspects of ego functioning, such as the elaboration of fantasy and graphic representation in girls and the increased use of the motor apparatus in boys—the latter probably in the service of denial. This era constitutes an early genital phase, preceding that of the oedipal period, and the later oedipal constellation will inevitably be shaped by the preoedipal developments we have described.

The discovery of the sexual difference and the new genital sensations of this early genital phase should not be considered merely as several of many variables that influence the growing sense of identity; they are unique, exemplary, and of equal importance to the oral and anal aspects of psychosexual development which have preceded them. Furthermore, the preoedipal castration reaction rapidly reactivates and becomes fused with earlier fears of both object and anal loss, and is therefore particularly threatening to the child's still unstable sense of self and object.

In other publications, we have presented data from direct observational research indicating that the little girl's early relation with her mother, as well as her early bodily experiences, are important in determining the effect upon her when she discovers the sexual anatomical difference at about sixteen to eighteen months of age. At this juncture, depending upon the nature of her earlier experiences, as well as the availability of the father, she may either turn more definitively to the father, or she may remain even more ambivalentlỹ attached to the mother, a choice having fateful consequences for the oedipal constellation shortly to emerge.

We have described the little girl's reactions to the discovery of the sexual difference: they include complex preoedipal castration reactions and penis envy, basic mood changes, and the development of many defensive measures. There may, in addition, be a partial or complete renunciation of direct masturbation. We believe that Freud's original position was partially correct in that penis envy and the feminine castration complex do exert crucial influences upon feminine development. However, these occur earlier than he had anticipated, they are closely intertwined with fears of object and anal loss, and they shape an already developing, although vague sense of femininity, stemming from early bodily and affective experiences with both parents. Furthermore, the castration reactions vary in intensity from child to child to a marked degree and they profoundly influence ego development, in both enhancing and inhibiting directions, depending upon specific individual factors. From this period on, there are marked differences between boys and girls in many sectors of their psychological development.

REFERENCES*

Fliegel, Z. O. (1973), Feminine psychosexual development in Freudian theory. *Psychoanal. Quart.*, 42.305 100.

Fraiberg, S. (1972), Some characteristics of genital arousal and discharge in latency girls. *The Psychoanalytic Study of the Child*, 27:439 475. New York: Quadrangle Books.

Freud, S. (1905), Three essays on the theory of sexuality. *Standard Edition*, 7:125-243. London: Hogarth Press, 1955.

_____ (1931), Female sexuality. *Standard Edition*, 21:225-243. London: Hogarth Press, 1961.

_____ (1933), Femininity. *Standard Edition*, 22:112-135. London: Hogarth Press, 1964.

_____ (1940), An outline of psychoanalysis. *Standard Edition*, 23:141-207. London: Hogarth Press.

* All references to *This Journal* are to the *Journal of the American Psychoanalytic Association*.

Galenson, E. (1971), A consideration of the nature of thought in childhood play. In: *Separation-Individuation: Essays in Honor of Margaret S. Mahler,* ed. J. B. McDevitt & C. F. Settlage. New York: International Universities Press, pp. 41-49.
_____ (1973), Psychopathology of the very young child (unpublished).
_____ Blau, S. & Vogel, S. (1975), Disturbance in sexual identity beginning at 18 months of age. *Internat. Rev. Psycho-Anal.,* 2:389-397.
_____ Drucker, J., Miller, R., & Shapiro, C. (1975), Detection and treatment of early childhood psychosis (unpublished).
_____ & Miller, R. (1976), The choice of symbols. *J. Amer. Acad. Child Psychiat.,* 5(1).
_____ & Roiphe, H. (1971), The impact of early sexual discovery on mood defensive organization and symbolization. *The Psychoanalytic Study of the Child,* 26: 195-216. New York: Quadrangle Books.
_____ _____ (1974), The emergence of genital awareness during the second year of life. In: *Sex Differences in Behavior,* ed. R. C. Friedman, R. M. Richart & R. L. Van de Wiele. New York: Wiley, pp. 223-231.
Greenacre, P. (1950), Special problems of early female sexual development. In: *Trauma, Growth and Personality.* New York: International Universities Press, 1969, pp. 237-258.
_____ (1958), Early physical determinants in the development of the sense of identity. In: *Emotional Growth.* New York: International Universities Press, 1971, pp. 113-127.
_____ (1969), The fetish and the transitional object. In: *Emotional Growth.* New York: International Universities Press, 1971, pp. 315-334.
Horney, K. (1924), On the genesis of the castration complex in women. In: *Feminine Psychology,* ed. H. Kelman. New York: Norton, 1967, pp. 37-53.
_____ (1926), The flight from womanhood. In: *Feminine Psychology,* ed. H. Kelman. New York: Norton, 1967, pp. 54-70.
_____ (1933), The phallic phase. *Internat. J. Psycho-Anal.,* 14:1-33.
Jones, E. (1927), The early development of female sexuality. *Internat. J. Psycho-Anal.,* 8:459-472.
_____ (1933), The phallic phase. *Internat. J. Psycho-Anal.,* 14:1-33.
Kestenberg, J. (1956), Vicissitudes of female sexuality. *This Journal,* 4:453-476.
_____ (1968), Outside and inside, male and female. *This Journal,* 16:456-520.
Kleeman, J. (1971), The establishment of core gender identity in normal girls. *Arch. Sexual Behavior,* 1:117-129.
_____ (1975), Genital self-stimulation in infant and toddler girls. In: *Masturbation: From Infancy to Senescence,* ed. I. Marcus & J. Francis. New York: International Universities Press, pp. 77-106.
_____ (1976), Freud's views on early female sexuality in the light of direct child observation. *This Journal,* 24(5):3-27.
Korner, A. F. (1973), Sex differences in new borns with special reference to differences in the organization of oral behavior. *J. Child Psychol. & Psychiat.,* 14:19-29.
Kris, E. (1951), Some comments and observations on early autoerotic activities. In: *Selected Papers.* New Haven: Yale University Press, 1975, pp. 89-113.
Lichtenstein, H. (1961), Identity and sexuality: A study of their interrelationship in man. *This Journal,* 9:197-260.

Mahler, M. S. (1963), Thoughts about development and individuation. *The Psychoanalytic Study of the Child,* 18:307-324. New York: International Universities Press.

———— (1966), Notes on the development of basic moods: The depressive affect. In: *Psychoanalysis—A General Psychology,* ed. R. M. Loewenstein, L. Newman, M. Schur, & A. J. Solnit. New York: International Universities Press, pp. 156-168.

———— (1968), *On Human Symbiosis and the Vicissitudes of Individuation.* New York: International Universities Press.

———— & Gosliner, B. T. (1955), On symbiotic child psychosis: genetic, dynamic, and restitutive aspect. *The Psychoanalytic Study of the Child,* 10:195-212. New York: International Universities Press.

Money, J. & Ehrhardt, A. A. (1972), *Man and Woman, Boy and Girl.* Baltimore & London: Johns Hopkins University Press.

Murphy, L. (1962), *The Widening World of Childhood.* New York: Basic Books.

Roiphe, H. (1968), On an early genital phase; with an addendum on genesis. *The Psychoanalytic Study of the Child,* 23:348-365. New York: International Universities Press.

———— (1974), A narcissistic disorder in the process of development (unpublished).

———— & Galenson, E. (1973a), The infantile fetish. *The Psychoanalytic Study of the Child,* 28:147-166. New Haven & London: Yale University Press.

———— ———— (1973b), Object loss and early sexual development. *Psychoanal. Quart.,* 42:73-90.

Spitz, R. A. (1962), Autoerotism re-examined. *The Psychoanalytic Study of the Child,* 17:283-315, New York; International Universities Press.

Stoller, R. J. (1968), *Sex and Gender.* Science House: New York.

Zilboorg, G. (1944), Masculine and feminine. *Psychiat.,* 7:257-296.

Albert Einstein College of Medicine
9 East 96th Street
New York, New York 10028

PRIMARY FEMININITY : ROBERT J. STOLLER, M.D.

IN THE PSYCHOANALYTIC THEORY OF THE ORIGINS of femininity[1] in females as first laid out by Freud, there is a stage unaccounted for in the chronology of the little girl's development: the first many months of life are not considered. We become aware of this, not by its being clearly stated, but rather more indirectly in writing style—e.g., "*At some time or other* the little girl makes the discovery of her organic inferiority" (1931, p. 232, italics added). Skipping over this gap grants the present-day analytic understanding of the psychology of women a substantial logic. But for it we pay too great a price; if we must ignore data in order to retain logic, then our explanation is flawed and should be modifed.

For Freud, the psychology of women opens with a sense of castration, as if what went on before, in the first year or so of life, did not contribute to the development of masculinity and femininity. Femininity, in this theory, is just a defense and shows its makeshift origins in its nature: passivity, masochism, penis envy, renunciation, a weak superego, commitment to

---

Professor of Psychiatry, UCLA School of Medicine.

[1] How shall I use the terms "femininity" and "masculinity" herein? They will have no biological connotations, but will refer only to the sense of one's self (identity) and how that sense permeates role. Thus, for me, femininity is what a person and that person's parents, peers, and society agree is femininity; the criteria change from place to place and time to time. Such usage frees us from the impasses produced by biologizing, e.g., that masculinity equals activity (an allegedly biologically-induced pressure) and femininity passivity.

biological imperatives like reproduction more than social options like friendship, and restitutive operations that result in such secondary narcissistic manifestations as exhibitionism (of nongenital parts of the body).

Starting under such handicaps, a girl is unlikely to escape without serious damage. At least, she has more barriers to overcome than does the boy. Although he can be knocked off the track or forced onto detours, his superior genital and his start in heterosexuality give him the potential for a straight run—biologically and psychosocially—on his journey to masculinity and adult heterosexuality. Not so for the girl. Her start with that inferior organ and homosexual object choice means she must either put out a major effort in childhood to switch onto a new track or she is doomed to irreparable unfortunate consequences.

We know by now that castration anxiety, penis envy, and the traumas and frustrations of oedipal conflict are easy to demonstrate; so if one is not aware of an earlier, nontraumatic and nonconflictual stage, the theory fits together (though for those familiar with women less wretched than the ones Freud said typified the species, his system seems somewhat wobbly). But if the first stage in women is different from Freud's description—if a woman can have a fundamental, fixed sense of being rightfully a female—then our psychology of women needs repair. We should look for that earliest stage and try to fill in the empty space in observations and theory.

Core Gender Identity

My work in recent years, following others (e.g., Horney, 1924; Jones, 1927; Zilboorg, 1944), has tried to announce that gap, point to observations anyone can make of that early time of development, derive propositions from the data, and find a theory that explains and predicts. This paper summarizes that work. The term I made up for this task—core gender identity (1965)—derives from a mixture of experimental data and data observable in infant females, girls, and women (and, of course, males). Let me review the concept. Core gender identity is the sense we have of our sex—of maleness in males and of femaleness in females (and, in the rare case, of being a hermaphrodite in hermaphrodites and, in transsexuals, of being—sort of—a member of the opposite sex). It is a part of, but not identical with, what I have called gender identity—a broader concept, standing for the mix of masculinity and femininity found in every person. ("Male" and "female" refer to sex, or biological state; "masculinity" and "femininity" to gender identity, a conviction about one's self and one's role.)

Core gender identity develops first and is the central nexus around which masculinity and femininity gradually accrete. Core gender identity has no implication of role or object relations; it is, I suppose, a part of what is loosely called "narcissism." I postulate it to be the result of the following:

1. A biological "force": this is an effect, originating in fetal life, usually genetic in source (though occasionally nongenetic),[2] springing—so far as we know at present—from neurophysiological (CNS-systemic-hormonal) organizing of the fetal brain.

2. The sex assignment at birth: the message that the appearance of the infant's external genitals brings to those who can assign sex—the attending physician and the parents—and its subsequent unequivocal effect in convincing them of their child's sex.

3. The unending impingement of parents', especially mothers', attitudes about *that* infant's sex and the infant's constructing these perceptions, via its developing capacity to fantasy, into events, i.e., meaningful, motivated experiences.

4. "Biopsychic" phenomena: early postnatal effects caused by certain habitual patterns of handling the infant—conditioning, imprinting, or other forms of learning

[2] E.g., otherwise biologically normal females somewhat masculinized prenatally in external genitals and brain organization by progesterone given to their mothers to prevent abortion (Ehrhardt and Money, 1967).

that permanently modify the infant's brain and resultant behavior without the infant's mental processes protecting it[3] from such sensory input. The evidence that these "bio-psychic" phenomena exist in humans is, so far, weak. This category is related to the previous one and is listed separately for emphasis, as well as to distinguish it from mental processes (also the result of parents' impingements) with which we are more familiar—castration anxiety, for instance—which probably begin appearing later in infancy and which depend on the infant's having acquired the capacity to fantasy, that is, to change reality by its own mental efforts.

5. The developing body ego: the myriad qualities and quantities of sensations, especially from the genitals, that define the physical and help to define the psychic dimensions of one's sex to oneself, thus confirming for the baby its parents' convictions about their infant's sex.

In the usual case—by far the most common—each of these factors (presumably, i.e., no one has yet been able to make precise measurements) contributes to the resultant core gender identity. Only, however, when one finds a pathological aberrance do we see any of these factors clearly. In other words, they have been discovered more in the pathological than in the normative. Here are examples.

1. *The biological "force."* This exciting new information need only be briefly reviewed since it is becoming familiar to analysts. Without the addition of fetal androgens—in all mammals, including humans—anatomical maleness cannot occur. This is true whether the chromosomes are male (XY) or female (XX). But if these fetal androgens are present at the right time, in the right amount, and of the right chemical structure, both anatomical maleness and postnatal masculinity will be possible, regardless of chromosomal maleness or femaleness. This rule operates in all species tested. Since direct experimental manipulation is impossible in humans,

---

[3] By fantasy, a process that empowers the infant to *explain* perceptions, thereby reducing their potential to traumatize.

"natural experiments" have been used, all of which have confirmed the general mammalian law. Thus, for instance, all people studied with the complete form of androgen insensitivity syndrome have been feminine girls and women despite their having male (XY) chromosomes and their producing normal amounts of testosterone (from cryptorchid testes). Because these people have a somatic inability to respond to testosterone, their anatomical appearance is female and their gender identity feminine. Comparably, all people with Turner's syndrome (XO) are feminine, there being no fetal androgens present (Money and Ehrhardt, 1972).

2. *Sex assignment.* When the appearance of the external genitals is unequivocal, the infant is assigned to the appropriate sex; whether the parents are pleased or not, they do not question the assignment, and while their pleasure or displeasure may contribute to the intricacies of the child's developing masculinity or femininity, the child does not question if its body is that of the assigned sex. The exceptional case makes the point: it sometimes happens that an otherwise biologically normal female with adrenogenital syndrome will have external genitals so masculinized that they look rather (and in rare cases exactly) like normal male. Such infants are, naturally, assigned to the male sex and develop a male core gender identity. Should, however, the proper diagnosis of sex be made at birth and the child recognized to be a female, then a female core gender identity results. In those cases where the sex assignment is equivocal because the genitals are hermaphroditic, the core gender identity is neither female nor male but hermaphroditic (Money et al., 1955, Stoller, 1968; Lev-Ran, 1974).

3. *Parental attitudes.* Let us use the adrenogenital syndrome as our example here also. An otherwise normal female is born with genitals that appear equivocal, neither male nor female but rather, bisexual. On delivery, the doctor tells the mother that she has just had a hermaphrodite, that this is not a boy or a girl; his attention caught, however, by a

female-appearing part of the genital anatomy, he adds, "You might as well raise it as if it were a girl." She does so and in the process communicates her belief to this child, who is given no reason to doubt in early childhood that it is a person who is neither a male nor a female but a member of another sex, of which, the poor creature usually feels, it is the only example in existence. As an adult, the patient believes herself to be neither male nor female, but an "it" who imitates women. (The evidence for these effects and their results are presented in detail elsewhere [Money et al., 1955; Stoller, 1968; Lev-Ran, 1974]).

4. *Biopsychic phenomena.* In the rare case, despite biologically normal sex and proper sex assignment, core gender identity can still be shifted from that expected by nonmental effects—that is, not perceived and worked over by a psyche—transmitted subliminally (unconsciously? preconsciously?) from mother to infant. I believe this occurs in the excessively intimate and blissful symbiosis found in the most feminine of boys (transsexuals), those who believe they are in some way females (while still not denying their anatomy or sex assignment). Although suffering no demonstrable congenital defect, with external genitals normal, and sex assignment correct and accepted by their parents, within the first year or two of life these boys are showing the effects of their mothers' too gratifying ministrations. There is no evidence these infants were traumatized in the symbiosis or subjected to frustrations that could cause intrapsychic conflict as is seen in effeminate homosexuals.

5. *Body Ego.* There is a large literature on this subject (Greenacre, 1958; Mahler [Panel, 1958]), to which I have no new data to add, except a footnote: even when anatomy is defective, so that the appearance of the genitals and their sensations are different from those of intact males or females, an unequivocal sense of maleness or femaleness develops if the assignment and rearing are unequivocal (Money et al., 1955; Stoller, 1968).

Filling the Gap

Let us approach the issue of a stage in girls, primary femininity, from two angles, the first logic and the second observation. The logic is simple. The evidence, first announced by Freud, is that in our society little girls—according to Roiphe and Galenson (1972), very little girls as young as one and a half years—suffer penis envy. But why—except to preserve a fragile theory—need we say, as Freud did, that a girl has penis envy before she knows of the existence of penises? How could she be upset if the discovery were not unexpected? Does not her surprise, dismay, envy, or denial indicate her previous belief she was intact? Is there any reason she would not have taken her anatomy for granted prior to the momentous discovery? Did she suffer pain, restricted mobility, deprivation of the chance for early motor, sensory, or intellectual development in the first year or so of life because of a missing penis, as she would have, say, with a missing leg? Why postulate an inheritance of the memory of penises placed genetically in the fetal female brain? Is it not simpler to argue that the little girl, having been informed from birth on by innumerable exchanges with her genitals and with the outside world, has no reason—no way—to doubt herself as a female until she receives new information? And even then, her surprise, disappointment, and envy in themselves indicate that her belief she is a female is in its depths not changed: she reacts the way she does because she cannot give up her sense of being a female.

The second reason for doubting Freud's assertions about femininity in females is simple observation. Freud himself (1931) seems to have recognized the primary femininity and then to have struggled against accepting his own knowledge. This is suggested by such comments as, "*At some time or other the little girl makes the discovery of her organic inferiority.*" "*When* the little girl discovers her own deficiency, from seeing a male genital, it is only with hesitation and reluctance that she accepts the unwelcome knowledge." "*When* she comes to understand the general nature of this characteristic, it follows that femaleness—and with it, of course, her mother—suffers a great depreciation in her eyes" (pp. 232-233; italics added throughout).

Unfortunately, I know of no systematic—only anecdotal—reports showing that little girls are feminine long before the oedipal phase, and I believe these reports do not exist merely because no one has bothered to measure the obvious. And it is obvious. Anyone who has observed little girls has seen that they can be feminine, as soon as any behavior appears that can be judged gender-related. Only if we were to say that the observed behavior and its underlying fantasy life are not genuine or are defensive constructions used for disguise, or that the little girls are really masculine but we just cannot see it, could we argue that there is "complete identity of the preoedipal phase in boys and girls." If we insist that little girls believe they are little boys who have been castrated, then we must discount evidence to the contrary. If we insist that femininity is defined by passivity, masochism, and a penis envy that will only be assuaged by the substitute of growing a baby, then we may ignore other evidence. But why create such a strange definition of femininity? Why not count the ways little girls move, hold themselves (posture), daydream, play games, choose clothes, use vocabulary? Little girls of two already show differences from little boys in style, inflections, carriage, and fantasy life. Are not attitudes and behavior as much a part of femininity as such theoretical constructs as "passivity"?

Of course it will be best if systematized direct observations become available; then we shall know better how early in children's lives consistent differential behavior between boys and girls can be seen. We may also discover, when large enough populations are studied, to what extent the observed differences are culture-bound and to what extent universal. (My guess would be that very few universals will be found, and most of them will be variants on aggressive behavior, such as play in which pushing and penetrating or being pushed and being penetrated are dominant themes.)

Some such work, still fragmentary, is now being reported. Certainly in animals, these differences appear early in life; observation of monkeys and higher apes, which have gender behavior that is not exclusively linked to reproductive behavior, shows sex differences. Mothers and their infant females are closer for longer, while, for the young males, separation from their mothers is enforced by mothers' breaking the symbiosis (Green, 1976). Play that will in time develop into sexual behavior also differentiates the sexes, with, for example, the males doing more mounting and the females more presenting. (All these behaviors can be reversed experimentally with brain manipulation by opposite-sex hormones at critical periods [Young et al., 1964]).

While the study of neonatal sex differences in human behavior by detailed observation is still rudimentary, there are data available (reviewed in Green, 1976).

Studies of the human neonate hold promise of isolating the early roots of "innate" male-female dimorphism. Several sex differences have been reported, some replicated, others not, and most are difficult to interpret. They group into displays of greater muscle strength, sensory differences, and the degree of affiliative behavior to adults.

Newborn males are more able to lift their head from a prone position (Bell and Darling). Mothers have been observed to stretch the limbs of their three-week-old boys more readily than those of their same-aged girls, but more often to imitate sounds made by the girls (Moss). Mothers have been observed to hold their five-month-old daughters more than sons, and, at thirteen months, these same daughters are more reluctant to move away from their mothers. The same thirteen-month-old children also show a different play style with toys and react differently to a barrier placed between themselves and the toys: boys tend to hurl toys about, girls tend to gather them together. They also react differently to a barrier placed between themselves and the boys: boys more often crawl to the barrier's end (in an attempt to get around it) girls more often sit where placed and cry (Goldberg and Lewis).

In an elegant research design, differential mother-attachment behavior by *opposite-sexed co-twins* was demonstrated. Female co-twins looked at, vocalized to, and maintained proximity to their mothers more than did their brothers (Brooks and Lewis).

Other differences during the newborn period have been reported, sometimes of an obscure nature. Neonatal females increase their formula intake when a sweetener is added; boys do not (Nisbett and Gurwitz). At three months, females can be conditioned to an auditory reward while boys respond to a visual one (Watson). At six months, girls show cardiac deceleration (a measure of attention) while listening to modern jazz, whereas boys decelerate to an interrupted tone (Kagan and Lewis)" (pp. 666-667).

In Kleeman's reports (1971), we also find descriptions of what seems to be primary femininity and, on reading these reports, are reminded that the feminine behavior of these girls is part of what all of us have observed. Were it not for Freud's theorizing, would anyone have doubted the existence of primary femininity?[4]

"Experiments" That Test the Hypothesis

MARKED FEMININITY IN MALES

If we wish an "experiment" that makes the first stage of femininity manifest, and does so regardless of anatomy, we

---

[4] This is not to say that anything that seems obvious is to be accepted. Freud made us aware of the dangers of accepting the manifest as being a complete statement of reality. But we would be equally remiss if we took the position that the manifest is never an accurate view.

can look at the male transsexual. The type of person to be described (the one for whom I restrict the term "transsexual") begins to show femininity sometimes as early as the age of one year. Feminine behavior is found exclusively; there is no masculine development at any time in childhood or later. In childhood, the boys are taken for girls by strangers, even when dressed in boys' clothes; as adults, their femininity is accentuated, as is seen in women with hysterical personality.[5] It is not, however, contaminated with caricature as is found in effeminate homosexuals (the caricature being a marker for a hidden masculine urge that shows itself in its mockery of femininity). My data suggest that this femininity is not the result of preoedipal or oedipal conflict, but is rather the product of the failure of the infant to sense himself as separate from his mother's female body; the process is nonconflictual — is, in fact, an extremely gratifying experience in an excessively prolonged mother-infant symbiosis (Stoller, 1968).

Throughout life, then, the male transsexual retains "her" feminine appearance, behavior, and position vis-a-vis other people. "Her" fantasy life and its manifestations in everyday living are feminine in style and heterosexual in object choice. But, as I have described elsewhere (1975), the rest of femininity — the second meaning, the second phase that is the result of the oedipal complex — is not found. These people have no impulse for pregnancy or mothering, although they may go through the motions in order to simulate the patient's image of a normal woman. I have experienced this absence especially in the transference — a great silence in the patient's capacity to relate to me, unlike transferences with any other kinds of people, with the possible exception of very exhibition-istic women, such as models and starlets. For years I believed there was no transference, until I realized that this absence *is* the transference. It is the recapitulation of an infancy and childhood in which father was absent and mother treated her

[5] And psychological tests of the transsexuals seen by our research team are scored as (and do not distinguish the patients from) females with hysterical personality (see also Finney et al., 1975).

beautiful son as if he were a *thing,* an ideal feminized phallus that she had grown from her own body and then kept all-too-attached in the unending symbiosis. The trouble is that this boy—this creature of his mother's need—has never experienced oedipal conflict. I have never seen a true transsexual (by my restricted definition, not by the one generally used—that the person requests "sex change") without this "empty" transference; and some of these patients have been seeing me (treatment?)[6] for from ten to fifteen years.

It seems to me, then, that a first stage in femininity can occur in early childhood in both males or females and results in a femininity that is genuine (a natural, unstudied, nonmimicking appearance). This primary femininity is however, missing other qualities of what is also designated as feminine, such as impulses to be a mother (the urge to be pregnant, to give birth to an infant, to nurse, to cuddle a baby, to raise and educate a child, or to take on the role of wife). These latter, when not merely transitory imitations, are the products, in the form our society takes in this era, of later experiences, that is, oedipal-conflict resolution; they are not just a matter of appearance, but demand commitments to oneself and others beyond the reach of primary femininity. (One can see, then, that primary and later femininity, arising from different processes, may be rather independent of each other, e.g., a woman not very feminine in demeanor may be a wonderful mother.)

Marked Masculinity in Females

A further test of a theory of the origins of femininity in females can be made by the study of the most masculine girls and

---

[6] In keeping with the odd attachment to mother that I experience in the transference, none of these patients has ever accepted my offer to treat him psychodynamically. They only use me as an effective caretaker who knows how to ease reality for them, or who is to listen attentively and benignly.

women, female transsexuals. In the absence of demonstrable biological (including anatomical) defect, these patients develop from childhood in a most masculine manner. Sooner or later, usually while still children, they ask that their bodies be "transformed" to male.[7] If the thesis is that male transsexuals' femininity results from a too-intimate, gratifying, unending symbiosis with their mothers, encouragement of their feminine behavior by their mothers once it appears, and their fathers' failure to interfere, then opposite parental influences should produce masculinity. Were these opposite influences at work in the infancy and childhood of the female transsexuals? The answer seems to be yes. Not enough cases have been reported for confirmation, but, so far, our research team has found the most masculine female children and adults (numbering fourteen)—and only the most masculine— have fit the thesis.

In brief, the findings (Stoller, 1972) show that sometime during the first year or so of life, the mother-infant symbiosis is severely disrupted. These mothers, usually because of severe depression but at times for other reasons, are unable to mother the infant girl. No other woman is substituted as a mother (as might happen if this mother died), so the little girl is not given adequate mothering, only subsistence. Yet mother is somewhere in the household, out of reach but a tantalizing presence (leading to a lifelong yearning to save and protect feminine-appearing, mothering women).

Father does not assuage his wife's suffering. Instead, the little girl is made to sense that she should function as her mother's cure; father, not serving as a supporting husband for his wife's torment, appoints this daughter as the succorer. Unhappily, such cures do not work; mother does not get well and enfold this daughter. The little girl, however, establishes a good relationship with her father, to whom she turns for

---

[7] They do not merely daydream of being men or at times represent themselves in dreams at night as having male qualities, but consciously, insistently, vociferously demand that their bodies be changed.

comfort and closeness. They become comrades, and, in the process, this father encourages behavior like his own: masculine. So, by three or four years of age, the girl is already acting very much like a boy, unwilling and unable to submit to demands that she be feminine. By this time, she is dressing only in boys' clothes, playing as if a boy, exclusively with boys in wholly boys' games, and imagines herself as having a penis or praying each night that God will affix one. (Disrupted mother-daughter symbiosis, unreachable mother, and encouragement by father to identify with him are found, though in different proportions, in two other categories of women with powerful masculine components: mothers of male transsexuals and women who believe—hallucinate—they have grown a penis [Stoller, 1973].)

There is reason to believe, therefore, that just as excessively close and gratifying mother-son intimacy can produce femininity even in a biologically intact male, so can massive disruption of symbiosis cause masculinity in a female child; just as a psychologically absent father can contribute to femininity in a boy, so can a close relationship based on identification with father (rather than on father as a heterosexual object) contribute to masculinity in a girl; and, just as a mother who encourages graceful and nonmasculine behavior in a boy can contribute to his femininity, so can reinforcing nonfeminine, masculine behavior by a father encourage masculinity in a girl.

Discussion

By now we should know that major aspects of character structure develop from two different ways of learning. The one that has been especially the domain of psychoanalytic study is learning that is the result of frustration, conflict, trauma, and resolution of conflict via defense mechanisms. Freud's theory of the development of masculinity and femininity is almost exclusively of this sort (except for his firmly held though vaguely documented belief in biological contributions).

The other, conflict-free learning, was introduced into our theory to restore balance, but it is still not well secured. Hartmann, especially, laid the groundwork. Theorizing on concepts like "self" and "identity" are other preliminary attempts to absorb these intuitions into analytic theory. We are open to using these ideas, perhaps, when we agree that a major piece of character structure cannot be understood without our investigating the contributions of both ways of learning.

And so it is with the development of femininity in women. I would suggest that this development can be conceptualized as being of two different orders.[8] In the first, which can occur in either males or females, learning takes place that is conflict-free and mostly ego-syntonic, consisting of behaviors with which the little girl identifies and/or is taught and encouraged, especially by her mother. Mechanisms like imprinting(?), conditioning, identification, and imitation contribute heavily to such learning and result in the automatized behaviors and convictions, attitudes, and fantasies that I call core gender identity. The manifestations of this stage—such as what clothes the little girl prefers, what dolls she plays with, how she carries herself—these external appearances are culture-bound, fashions, changing as parents' desires for the appearance of their daughter's femininity changes. (This does not in the least imply that an infant's development is conflict-free, only that *certain* behaviors are learned and maintained by conflict-free processes: unpleasure, of course, increasingly plays its necessary role in creating and maintaining gender identity.)

The second but by no means lesser, order of femininity, one on which psychoanalysis has concentrated, results from

---

[8] I am indebted to Dr. Lawrence E. Newman for discussions in which these ideas were clarified.

conflict and envy in the oedipal situation. It brings a new desire and danger to affection, erotism, awareness of anatomical differences between the sexes, and to wishes for children. And it gives depth and richness, via the fantasy systems the girl creates to manage these problems, to those behaviors we label feminine. This form of femininity is made from conflict and its resolution, and simply cannot appear without such creative tension. For instance, a switch in yearning from her mother to her father will be negotiated in a girl's mind by conscious and unconscious fantasies on such themes as how to be rid of mother and how to get father's attention and then desire; she creates these fantasies in a way that corrects the traumas and frustrations of reality. The little girl's play will be shaped to promote satisfaction of these fantasies. And then she will fill out the play world with something more substantial, more fully experienced in bone and muscle, belly and chest: imitation and automatization of behavior observed in the real world that clearly do or possibly might appeal to father. If the subject preoccupying her is what does father like about and want from females, she will gather in clues from her environment, and, to the extent that she comprehends and refashions these in line with the progress of her ego development, she will convert the observations into behaviors. Those that feel right are likely to be repeated, rounded off for good fit until they are automatic; they become chronic—what we conceptualize as "a piece of character structure" or "identity theme" or "identity." And when these fantasy systems-become-behavior focus on certain topics, we call what we see "femininity."

This is not to deny that girls pick up defensively masculine qualities early in life. But I believe this occurs only after the desires and behaviors have been laid down that mark the presence of primary femininity. Certainly, as Freud discovered, penis envy and blaming mother for the lack of a penis turn a girl to masculine behaviors; and these can be used in the service of a homosexuality that tries to win possession of mother. But that struggle does not kill the earlier femininity. Both — primary femininity and defensive masculinity — persist on into the next phase, wherein successful (i.e., gratifying and without flooding hostility as the blighted harvest) resolution of oedipal conflict brings a more complex femininity, modifications more likely to allow a girl to convert the tasks ahead to congenial, productive womanhood.

For from such chronic and successful resolution of conflicts come attitudes and behavior attached to tasks assigned to females by biology and/or culture, such as means of expressing sexual excitement (e.g., differences between men and women in response to pornography; from which parts of the genitals will one draw erotic sensations), desire for or pleasure from the fruitfulness of pregnancy, capacity to mother infants and rear children, etc., etc.

There are implications for treatment in these ideas (Fleigel, 1973). While the "ideal" of the nonjudgmental analyst may be neither attainable nor desirable, most of us feel that the less we introduce our biases and idiosyncrasies, the more likely that transference manifestations will remain free to be analyzed. Regarding the question whether primary femininity exists or not, we find that a theoretical issue is likely to become a living pressure insinuated into the analyses of women. For instance, an analyst may consider his work finished only when a woman accepts[9] that she believed herself a castrated male in childhood, renounces her wish for a penis, and expresses true femininity by graceful admission that maleness is better. Such an analysis will look different from that of an analyst who believes this woman had an early uncomplicated phase of primary femininity before the disappointments due to the discovery of penises. In the latter situation, the analyst may at times judge as genuine — the true self, in Winnicott's term — certain expressions of joy in her anatomy and its functions, while another analyst — attached to a different

---

[9] Translate: acknowledges masochistically and passively.

theory—will hear the same joy as being defensive, manic, evidence of reaction formation, denial, or splitting.

If primary femininity exists and the analyst does not believe it, what happens to the patient's trust in her analyst? On the other hand, there is the risk I run: If primary femininity does not exist and I act as if it does, what trust will a woman have in an analyst who, even silently, gives her false support?

Conclusion

Although it is old-fashioned to say they exist, it is no secret that there are women with a richly textured and complex femininity who meet anyone's criteria for psychic health. This femininity is the product of a solid core gender identity, permanent and nonconflict-laden identifications with feminine women, and successful grappling with and mastery of oedipal conflicts in which these women participated with their mother and father. We need not doubt it; they unthinkingly, comfortably accept having a female body that is a source of their physical pleasure. Should they marry and have children, they draw from their femininity a capacity for mothering in which there is so little hostility that, with the help of their masculine husbands, their sons are masculine and their daughters feminine.

Summary

In Freud's theory of the origins of femininity in females, there is a stage unaccounted for in the chronology of the little girl's development: the first many months of life are not considered. We know by now that castration anxiety, penis envy, and the traumas and frustrations of oedipal conflict are easy to demonstrate; but if the first stage in female development is different from Freud's description—if a fundamental, fixed sense of being rightfully a female is established in earliest childhood—then our psychology of women needs repair.

The factors that make up this stage, with examples, are reviewed: (1) a biological "force": the effect of circulating fetal sex hormones on the brain of the fetus; (2) sex assignment: the announcement at the time of birth to the parents that they have had a boy or a girl (or a hermaphrodite); (3) parental attitudes: the effects of the sex assignment on parents, then reflected back onto the infant; (4) "biopsychic" phenomena: early postnatal effects caused by certain habitual patterns of handling the infant—conditioning, imprinting(?), or other forms of nonconflictual learning; (5) developing body ego: sensations, especially from the genitals, that define the child's dimensions.

I suggest that one can divide the development of femininity in females into two phases, both of which lead to adult femininity, but each of which contributes in a different manner. The first, nonconflictual in origin, contributes a sense of femaleness and some of what allows for one's looking feminine; the second, the result of conflict, especially oedipal, produces a richer and more complicated femininity, not merely one of appearances, but one enriched by desires to perform with the substance, rather than just the façade, of femininity.

REFERENCES*

Ehrhardt, A. A. & Money, J. (1967), Progestin induced hermaphroditism: IQ and psycho-sexual identity in a study of ten girls. *J. Sex Res.,* 3:83-100.
Finney, J. C., Brandsma, J. M., Tondow, M. & LeMaistre, G. (1975), A study of transsexuals seeking gender reassignment. *Amer. J. Psychiat.,* 132:962-964.
Fleigel, Z. O. (1973), Feminine psychosexual development in Freudian theory: A historical reconstruction. *Psychoanal. Quart.,* 42:385-408.
Freud, S. (1931), Female sexuality. *Standard Edition,* 21:225-243, London: Hogarth Press, 1961.
Green, R. (1976), Human sexuality: Research and treatment frontiers. In: *American Handbook of Psychiatry,* ed. S. Arieti, Second Edition. New York: Basic Books, pp. 665-691.

* All references to *This Journal* are to the *Journal of the American Psychoanalytic Association.*

Greenacre, P. (1958), Early physical determinants in the development of the sense of identity. In: *Emotional Growth*. New York: International Universities Press, 1971, pp. 113-127.

Horney, K. (1924), On the genesis of the castration complex in women. In: *Feminine Psychology*, ed. H. Kelman. New York: Norton, 1967, pp. 37-53.

Jones, E. (1927), The early development of female sexuality. *Internat. J. Psycho-Anal.*, 8:459-472.

Kleeman, J. A. (1971), The establishment of core gender identity in normal girls. I. (a) introduction; (b) development of the ego capacity to differentiate. II. How meanings are conveyed between parent and child in the first 3 years. *Arch. Sex. Behav.*, 1:103-129.

Lev-Ran, A. (1974), Gender role differentiation in hermaphrodites. *Arch. Sex. Behav.*, 3:391-424.

Money, J. & Ehrhardt, A. A. (1972), *Man and Woman, Boy and Girl*. Baltimore: The Johns Hopkins University Press.

———, Hampson, J. G., & Hampson, J. L. (1955), An examination of some basic sexual concepts: the evidence of human hermaphroditism. *Bull. Johns Hopkins Hosp.*, 97:301-319.

Panel (1958), Problems of Identity, D. L. Rubinfine, Reporter. *This Journal*, 6:136-138.

Roiphe, H. & Galenson, E. (1972), Early genital activity and the castration complex. *Psychoanal. Quart.*, 42:334-347.

Stoller, R. J. (1965), The sense of maleness, *Psychoanal. Quart.*, 34:207-218.

——— (1968), *Sex and Gender, Vol. I*. New York: Science House.

——— (1972), Etiological factors in female transsexualism: a first approximation. *Arch. Sex. Behav.*, 2:47-64.

——— (1973), *Splitting*. New York: Quadrangle.

——— (1975), *Sex and Gender, Volume II*. London: International Psychoanalytical Library and Hogarth Press.

Young, W., Goy, R. & Phoenix, C., (1964), Hormones and sexual behavior. *Science*, 143:212-218.

Zilboorg, G. (1944), Masculine and feminine. *Psychiat.*, 7:257-296.

Department of Psychiatry
UCLA Medical School
Los Angeles, California 90024

ON THE GIRL'S ENTRY INTO THE OEDIPUS COMPLEX

Henri Parens, m.d.
Leafy Pollock, m.s.w.,
Joan Stern, m.d., and
Selma Kramer, m.d.

OUR CHILD DEVELOPMENT RESEARCHES have centered on attempts to correlate aspects of the mother-child relationship with the development of psychic structure in the child (Parens, 1971a; Parens et al., 1970). In the course of these psychoanalytic direct observational researches, several findings imposed themselves on us in such a manner that each became an object of formal study.

Mary, two years, three months, and fourteen days of age, shows most unexpectedly a powerful push from within, a most remarkable peremptoriness, to get her hands on Mrs. J.'s one-month-old baby. Seemingly unaware of the obstacle, she climbs over four-year-old Minnie to get to the baby Mrs. J. is holding. The pressure of her wish to hold that baby becomes uncomfortable for Mrs. J., and Mary's mother is called in to help Mary contain her pressured push to hold the baby. Vocalizing sharp unpleasurable feelings, Mary struggles against her mother's intervention. A moment later she chants, beaming, "My baby, my baby." From all indications, in the more than 24 months that follow, Mary is driven to own a

From the Early Child Development Program and Project, Henri Parens, M.D., Director and Principal Investigator; Leafy Pollock, M.S.W., Associate Investigator; Joan Stern, M.D., Associate Investigator; and Selma Kramer, M.D., Consultant-Investigator. Eastern Pennsylvania Psychiatric Institute, Children's Unit, and the Medical College of Pennsylvania, Child Psychiatry Section. Project #3: Studies in Early Gender Formation.

baby, her baby. From all available evidence, this behavior came out of turn, insofar as our expectations dictated. Her castration complex and her Oedipus complex *followed* by several months the observation just detailed.

This was not the course followed by Candy whose marked response to babies followed in anticipated sequence, in accordance with Freud's 1925 (also 1931, 1933) postulate on the girl's entry into the Oedipus complex. We had already found, in Jane, a still further permutation of a normal girl's entry into her Oedipus complex, but it was the particularly startling finding in Mary that spurred us on to a formalized study of these three normal girls, focusing on the course of their respective *entry into the Oedipus complex*. All three children are quite normal, are developing well, and, at the most, can be prognosticated to develop no greater a degree of disturbance than a clinical neurosis and or a neurotic character disorder.

Criteria for the Oedipus Complex

To determine when a child would be entering, or had entered, her Oedipus complex it became necessary to establish criteria by which to identify the phenomenon. For the sake of a graspable and communicable comparative approach, we elected to denote three elements which, it seems to us, in psychoanalysis have formed the major components of a girl's Oedipus complex, although of course we recognize that such an approach reflects a condensation and a simplification of what we know to be an overdetermined and complex network of structural and object-related dynamics. These were sorted out as: (1) evidence of a castration complex; (2) further differentiation of object-relatedness, i.e., development of triadic object relations manifested by increasingly ambivalent and rivalrous feelings and behavior toward mother associated with a heterosexual attitude toward father; and (3) the manifest wish to own, to have her own baby (Freud, 1925).

Evidence of a castration complex: We have found it particularly important to distinguish certain attitudes on the part of the little girl toward her own genitals and those of males. We found it useful to sort out reactions of (a) interest, curiosity, pleasure in, and exploration of the genital—usually visual, but in some instances tactile; (b) moderate *negative* affects, low-keyedness, sadness, disquietude, worry, despondence, associated with readily discernible comparisons of external genital anatomy; (c) overt manifestations of anxiety, wary preoccupation, rage, sadism, derivative symptom formation, including phobias. We also found it useful to take into consideration how much these reactions *dominate* psychic activity, using Erikson's (1959) concept that instinctual impulse *dominance* determines at which phase of psychosexual development the psyche currently functions, i.e., whether oral, anal or (phallic-) genital. Consequently, we do not consider the first type of reaction, when it does not appear to currently dominate the psyche, to represent a genital phase in the child. Since occasional manipulation of the genitalia is common from the first year of life on, and neither this nor a benign interest in the genitals warrant consideration of a castration complex or a genital phase, we felt justified in accepting only the last two types of reactions as suggestive or indicative of a castration complex, or possibly of a genital phase.

Further differentiation of object-relatedness: The child typically manifests a marked change in attitude toward the mother during the rapprochement and early object constancy subphases. The mother who, during a favorable rapprochement subphase—even with the ambivalence of the rapprochement crisis (Mahler, 1972, 1975)—was highly regarded by the child, now begins to be the object of a rather specific type of protracted negative feeling, action, and verbalization; there is much evidence of rivalry for father's exclusive attention, with directly expressed ambivalence or its derivatives. Juxtaposed to these feelings toward mother is open affection for father and men, with clearly erotic attitudes, coyness, and even flirtatiousness. The clinician who has not had the opportunity to observe longitudinally the manifestations in behavior of sexual cathexes in children of this age will be surprised by the intensity and preponderance of *hetero*sexual attitudes they manifest at this point in development. We found that while rivalry with the mother is more or less explicit, as it was in these three girls, it is interspersed with expressions of erotic (negative Oedipus) trends and affection for her, wishes to please her, turning to her preferentially in time of need, and preference for her over all other humans remains very high. This is in contrast to situations that evoke regression, when a recurrence of rapprochement behavior was noted.

The manifest wish to have her own baby: We have found that interest in live babies and dolls begins to emerge in both girls and boys, from twelve to fourteen months of age on. This interest is more or less occasional only, and is characterized by behavior toward the baby or doll that mirrors the mother's holding behavior, and, in well-cared-for children, an affect of affection and tenderness may readily be evident. One-year-olds, however, also will pull the baby or doll's hair, poke at its eyes, and soon cause alarm to the mothers and observers. This early interest in babies and dolls in children of both sexes results from what we have come to view as an identification with the mother, which comes out of the symbiotic (in Mahler's sense) relation to her especially during the differentiation and rapprochement subphases, as that symbiosis is in process of evolving into self/object differentiation.

But with the advent of the girl's *first genital phase*, the wish to have a baby of one's own takes on a significantly different character in the girls we have observed. Not so in our several boys. Briefly, the girl's wish to have a baby now seems not just to be the result of an identification, but, in addition, it seems to have the quality of a drive, of an inborn gender characteristic; this we have not found in our boys.

We want to note here parenthetically—because a more extensive discussion with data presentation regarding this issue is required—that in this paper we will not refer to the girl's "phallic" phase, but rather, as a working hypothesis, to her *first genital phase* or her *protogenital phase*, a term we feel equally applicable to the boy's phallic phase. By the *first genital phase* or the *protogenital phase* we mean that period in psychic development in both boys and girls classically referred to as the *phallic* or *phallic-oedipal* phase. As have most psychoanalysts, we have found it to emerge from the early part of the third year of life. The rationale for this term is that our observations have strongly impressed us with the two- to five-year-old girl's sensuality in her approach to objects, her manner, poise, and communications, her pelvic-perineal (including clitoral) masturbatory activity, all of which seem to us visibly of a *dominantly feminine* disposition; so much so, that speaking only of her phallic preoccupations—which vary widely from child to child—associated with her castration complex does not take into account what we have found to be the *dominant* feature of the girl's awakening genital sensuality. It is, after all, the awakening protogenital sensuality that gives to the Oedipus complex its powerful impetus. We believe that this amply visible sensual activity in the little girl is an expression of her *primary, constitutional feminine disposition*. Direct observation leads us to question the view that the *feminine* activity—behavioral and, by inference, intrapsychic—of the two to five-year-old girl is defensive or reactive. While we speak of this as a *genital* phase, it is to be distinguished from the *adult genital phase* which emerges from puberty on. Hence, we mean that the first genital phase is an *infantile form* of genitality, which, of course, differs significantly from its *adult form*.

Freud's Hypothesis on the Girl's Entry into the Oedipus Complex

Up to 1924 Freud seems to have assumed that boys and girls enter their Oedipus complex in a similar manner—that, by virtue of a biological "programmed" predisposition, a boy is drawn to his mother and a girl to her father. In 1919, Freud for the first time records his dissatisfaction with the view that a precise analogy exists between the sexes regarding their Oedipus complex: "the expectation of there being a complete parallel was mistaken" (1919, p. 196). In "The Dissolution of the Oedipus Complex" (1924) Freud now discards the view that the girl's and the boy's Oedipus complexes are analogous. And in 1925, he arrives at a new statement of his views on the different paths by which the girl and boy *enter* their respective Oedipus complexes.

In 1925 (as well as today) it is understood that the boy's Oedipus complex is innately "programmed" to emerge during the phallic phase of psychosexual development, a development Freud believes to be "preordained," phasic, and following from the child's constitutional and biological time-tables. Freud viewed his biologically determined development to be effected and expressed through the libido. Impetus to the *resolution* of the Oedipus complex in the boy is given most especially by the fear of castration. The girl, however, Freud postulated, has a prehistory that is different. By virtue of the biologically determined dominance of genital impulses — which creates the first genital phase of psychosexual development — the girl's attention turns to her clitoris (phallus equivalent and masculine organ). Feeling herself at a disadvantage when she sees the boy's penis, she is overtaken with jealousy, experiences penis envy, and blames her mother for this "shortcoming." Penis envy then leads to "a loosening of the girl's relation with her mother as a love-object" (p. 254). Disappointed in and by her mother, the girl turns to her father, at which point she enters her Oedipus complex proper. "Now the girl's libido slips into a new position. . . . She gives up her wish for a penis and puts in place of it a wish for a child: and *with that purpose in view* she takes her father as a love-object. Her mother becomes the object of her jealousy" (p. 256).

Freud then postulates an important distinction between

the girl's and boy's Oedipus complex: "As regards the relation between the Oedipus and castration complexes there is a fundamental contrast between the two sexes. *Whereas in boys the Oedipus complex is destroyed by the castration complex, in girls it is made possible and led up to by the castration complex*" (p. 256). The girl's entry into the Oedipus complex is *preceded* by her castration complex. Thus, "In girls the Oedipus complex is *a secondary formation*" (p. 256; our italics).

Therefore, in terms of the three criteria used in our research, the order in which we expected to find them in their emergence, at their origin, to support Freud's hypothesis regarding the girl's entry into the Oedipus complex would be: first, evidence of her castration complex; second, her wish to have a baby; and, third, an ambivalent and rivalrous relation to her mother and a preferential, seemingly heterosexual attitude toward her father. It is not essential that the second and third criteria emerge in the order stated; one may precede the other with little consequence to the question investigated here, or they may emerge at the same time. In any case, the castration complex would precede them.

In line with this postulate, Freud concluded that "The difference between the sexual development of males and females at the stage we have been considering is an intelligible consequence of the anatomical distinction between their genitals and of the psychical situation involved in it" (pp. 256-257). In closing, Freud remarked that he "set some value" on these considerations. He concluded: "I am aware, however, that this opinion can only be maintained if my findings, which are based on a handful of cases, turn out to have general validity and to be typical. If not, they would remain no more than a contribution to our knowledge of *the different paths* along which sexual life develops" (p. 258; italics added).

It is clear that Freud hoped for more research on this issue. It is in the spirit especially of Hartmann that we report the findings that follow: to attempt to effect a "meaningful interpenetration" (Hartmann, 1950) of the findings of psychoanalytic reconstruction with those of psychoanalytic direct child observation.

Methodology

The data to be reported were collected under conditions of direct child observation in accordance with the position and principles stated by E. Kris (1950), Hartmann (1950, 1958), Anna Freud (1958, 1965), Mahler (1975), and Lustman (1963). The three children on whom we report have been known to us as research subjects since their birth. They have been seen with their mothers and other preschool siblings twice weekly for two-hour sessions. Our relation to these subjects is that of participant observers. Data are collected pertinent to several areas under investigation. Written records are kept on each child, as well as film and video data. The material reported here comes from these sources.

Those of us who do psychoanalytic direct observational research side by side with clinical psychoanalyses of adults and children realize that this research method, which brings an encouraging yield, has significant limitations (see all the authors just mentioned, particularly A. Freud, Hartmann, and Lustman). We are therefore especially concerned about the probability that, even though we have observed these children since birth and have seen them four hours every week, not all aspects of psychic activity may have surfaced and come directly to our attention. We do hold, however, that psychic activity *which has dominance in the psyche will manifest itself*—in fact, in children the age of our subjects, cannot remain hidden from such constant observations as we have programmed.

In this study, the method and its yield have compelled us to re-examine an existing psychoanalytic hypothesis which derives from psychoanalytic reconstruction. Our findings dictate a different set of hypotheses.

Data Presentation

An attempt is made here to follow the emergence of the three indices of the girl's Oedipus complex in each child. Of the three indices, an interest in genitalia, along with pregenital masturbation, and an interest in a baby are readily observable in the normal child prior to the emergence of the Oedipus complex. The decision must be made by the psychoanalytic investigators whether the data observed represent a precursor or whether they are evidence of the *protogenital phase* when the Oedipus complex emerges. Pregenital masturbation, for instance, which is commonly encountered in the first eighteen or so months of life, occurs in most instances at a time when orality dominates the psyche; hence, in these instances, it does not represent a genital (or phallic) phase.

We want to pick up the various manifestations of these indices at their origins; therefore, we begin where we first saw them, indeed well before these could be inferred to represent a protogenital phase of psychosexual development.

Candy

Before Candy was born, her mother was somewhat distressed at being pregnant again, but gradually accepted her state. Mrs. H. already has several daughters, and hoped this child would be a boy. After an initial reaction of disappointment that it was "another girl," Mrs. H. came to appreciate Candy, the relation between child and mother stabilized into a largely positive, affectionate and mutually gratifying one. When we first saw Candy she was a well-formed neonate who, from the outset; tended to be calm, easy to feed and comfort; she cuddled well and responded to mother's efforts favorably. Her emotional and physical development proceeded well.

Prior to her entry into the rapprochement subphase, which was recorded to manifest itself from age 1-4-24,[1] Candy

---

[1] Age stated in year-month-day.

showed the pregenital masturbatory activity, and pleasure at mother's cleaning her genitalia and anus that one normally encounters during diapering. We also recorded in Candy an affectionate interest in dolls and babies from age 1-2-9 on. At age 1-2-16, we found that, gradually over several weeks, since neonate Mary entered our project, Candy became interested in dolls, in a notably caretaking, tender, and fascinated manner. This behavior clustered over a period of two months, then waned, to appear occasionally over the next year, when it reappeared in a strikingly different form (see below). It may be pertinent that within one month of this cluster of baby-interest activity Candy entered her rapprochement subphase.

Over the next twelve months a number of significant events occurred. Several months after an extensively manifest and well-delineated rapprochement crisis (Mahler, 1975), we recorded mild interest on Candy's part (then age 2-0-22) in the diapering of a girl peer. From 26 months of age on Candy was toilet-training quite easily.

When Candy was 2-5-22, she demonstrated a marked concern which suggested to the observers that there was something worrisome and puzzling about her genito-urinary-cloacal anatomy. On this morning, sitting at her mother's feet, Candy was upset at having holes in the toe of her sock. While she had had holes in her socks before, today it bothered her suprisingly. For 45 or so minutes, she seemed to try to make the holes go away. She looked troubled and, at moments, depressed. The mounting distress was low-keyed, and many minutes passed before Mrs. H. registered her daughter's reaction and sewed the holes up then and there. When it was done, Candy put her sock on and left, seemingly relieved, to play with the others.

At the next session, Mrs. H. reported that since the holes-in-the-sock episode, Candy had been wetting herself, and on 2-5-23 was so embarrassed over it that she hid in a closet. She wet herself twice on the subsequent day.

At 2-5-29, loss of sphincter-control anxiety showed itself again, with urgency, tearfulness, and near-panic. We also saw Candy seek out and hold onto the large doll she preferred over others. This time she struggled briefly with Jane to retain possession of it. She was especially attentive to its small anatomical features, its fingers and ears.

Candy next showed concern about things being broken and became very upset that her cracker was broken. She was disconsolate until she received another which was in one piece. Similarly, she tried with some preoccupation to put together a lollipop she had broken into two pieces. Now she clearly sought the help of her mother and staff to effect a return of her toileting controls.

Evidence was now (2-6-12) ample that she was in the "phallic" phase. Mrs. H. now recalled that since *just before* the holes-in-the-sock episode, Candy had been wetting her bed at night. This did not distress mother, but distressed Candy, who stayed in bed ashamed and troubled until morning. A period of compulsive handwashing appeared now, which lasted for several weeks. This, associated with her sphincter-control anxiety, was viewed as symptomatic because of its associated anxiety and shame, the source of which we felt to come from within the child. We therefore believed that genito-anatomical concern, i.e., her castration complex, was the source of this regression in toilet control as well as the source of toileting anxiety.

Soon we saw ample genital masturbation, direct and indirect, some of which was of notable intensity and led to much excitation and discomfort for Candy. From 2-6-12 on we saw evidence of an erotic attitude and overtures on the part of Candy toward her mother, with Candy rubbing her perineum on her mother's thigh, or leaning against and touching her breasts. We postulated in this the emergence of Candy's negative Oedipus complex.

At 2-6-26 Candy tried to urinate like a boy. From 2-7-3 she showed a notable interest in a four-month-old female infant with a new depth of warmth and tenderness. Her interest in the genital anatomy of boys continued as she watched boys being diapered. When, in the process of being diapered, a boy urinated, Candy was startled and sober-faced, low-keyed, worried, and sad. For two days she was depressed.

At 2-7-3, Mrs. H. reported that for the last two weeks Candy had become angry with her father when he left the house and when he paid attention to her sisters. She seemed to want his exclusive attention, a tendency she had not shown before, although her relation with father had all along been an affectionate one. Although she had not shown a preferred attachment to any particular male (peer or staff) in the project, she was warmly and coyly responsive to males, and several months later was among the girls who, giggling and squealing, would entice a boy to chase them.

From this time, Candy showed ample evidence of being pleased to be a girl, of wanting to be a mother and have a baby. She told her sister, who teased her about it, that she (Candy) does not have a penis! that she is a girl! She seemed well on the way to pleasurably consolidating her feminine core-identity (Stoller, 1968); she showed a clear maternal attitude toward infants, as well as in her play with peers. The evidence of her negative Oedipus complex seemed more prominent than in Mary, Jane, and our other girls. There was also prominent evidence of her positive Oedipus complex, with a clear heterosexual interest in her father and other males.

In Candy, we saw the entry into the Oedipus complex to follow very closely the line formulated by Freud in 1925. First to appear as a source of intrapsychic tension and conflict was her castration complex. This seemed then to carry with it, simultaneously but less emphatically in the psyche, a "protogenital phase interest in babies" (see Discussion below). These were soon followed by an erotic attitude toward her mother (the emerging negative Oedipus complex) as well as toward her father (the emerging positive Oedipus complex).

She had moved well into her first genital phase and her Oedipus complex, and proceeded to consolidate nicely her feminine core-gender identity.

Mary

Mary is the only girl and youngest of several children of professional parents. Her home environment is relatively stable and secure except for a chronic illness of the father, which is a constant but usually quiet source of stress for the family. Mary's birth was a delight to Mrs. W. who very much wanted a girl. Mr. W. quickly became deeply invested in the child.

We pick up Mary's behavior when she was in her practicing subphase, which was typical, clear, and vigorous. The practicing-subphase conflict (Parens, 1976) imposed by the mother's prohibitions was mounting and creating problems in her relation with mother. At age 1-2-26 we noted Mary's first interest in babies. She tried to cuddle one of the babies sleeping on the spread on the floor. She tried to "hold" Harold (age one year, eight months) too, who was larger than she. One week later she called her mother's attention to a baby playing on the spread on the floor. She was delighted and rattled a toy for him when her mother picked him up, but soon moved on to other things.

Mary's brother Donnie, age 3-7-13, expressed an interest in Mary's (age 1-3-16) genitalia, asking many questions. At this time Mary began to note the genitalia when a male baby was being diapered. She pointed at his penis, smiled, seemed curious and pleased. Mary at 1-4-23 had occasionally alerted her mother to her wish to use the potty. Two months later, at 1-7-9, she resisted having her diapers changed and being put on the potty.

From age 2-3-8 Mary's interest in babies became marked. She held Mrs. J.'s one-month-old baby and referred to her as "my baby." At 2-3-15 Mary was showing an intense push to hold Doris. The inner-driven quality of this push was striking. When Mrs. W. intervened because Mary was climbing all over Mrs. J. and a peer seated next to her to get to Doris, Mary became angry, and when mother pulled her away she melted into tears. Her reaction was intense when her mother told her gently enough that the baby was not Mary's. At 2-3-26 Mary told her mother while she held Doris that only she (Mary) "would hold Doris next time, nobody else."

When Mary was 2-3-26, Mrs. W. reported that Mary had gone through a period of interest in her genitals when she was in diapers, during which time she derived a great deal of pleasure from being washed and powdered. This interest seemed to have declined since the time Mary began wearing pants.

Mary was especially affectionate with her mother at this time. For the next several weeks she spent a lot of time playing with dolls. This was followed by a month's period of intense interest in Doris, referring to Doris as "my baby," approaching her with warmth and tenderness. At times Mary was exhilarated upon approaching the baby, and clearly showed that she shared her pleasure with her own mother as well as Doris' mother. The possession of the baby seemed to fluctuate in Mary's behavior, sometimes it belonged to Mary and sometimes to the baby's natural mother.

In our sessions, most of Mary's activities and affects seemed determined by her interest in Doris; she was depressed when Doris was not in the sessions and exhilarated when the baby was there. At 2-6-16, while at home, Mary was upset. In an effort to comfort her, her father asked Mary several times to come sit on his lap. She finally did and told him, "I want a baby." Father was surprised and asked again what she said, only to get the same reply. He told Mary she could have a baby when she grew up.

At 2-6-16 Mary focused on breast feeding for the first time. After she watched Mrs. J. breast feeding Doris, Mary tried to get her own mother to breast feed her. Later in the session, Mary took a doll, pulled up her shirt and pretended to breast feed, glancing now and then toward Mrs. J.

We found that Mary continued to be excited when touching her mother and to wriggle when she straddled her mother's knee. In addition, for about a week, Mary had been squirming when she sat on her father's knee. There was much evidence to suggest that while still erotic with her mother, Mary was becoming erotic, according to Mrs. W., with her father, and we saw ample, indeed dramatic, evidence that she began to turn for erotic gratification to Donnie (see below).

As on other occasions, now, at 2-7-14, Mary's first greeting in our sessions was for Doris, but she spent less time with Doris than she had before. She was cheerful, played well with other children, and continued to interact preferentially with her mother and Donnie. At this session, Mrs. W. reported that five days before, Mary had said to her father, "I'm gonna have a penis when I get big." Her father gently told her that she would not, that she is a girl. She also asked Donnie if she could have a penis. She said to her mother, "I'm gonna have a penis." Her mother, disconcerted at her daughter's wish, said carefully, "You can't have a penis, but when you get big you can gave a baby." Mary reacted with a beaming smile, but she continued to express her wishful expectations to have a penis. At home Mary once sat facing the back lid of the toilet, as if fusing what a boy and a girl do in urinating.

At age 2-8-15 Mrs. W. told us that Mary had said to her, "Do you have a penis, Ma?" Mrs. W. answered, "No, Mary; how about you?" Mary replied casually, "No." This was the first sign that Mary was beginning to resolve the issue of not possessing a penis. At age 2-9-13, Mary asked Mrs. J. for the first time, "Can I hold your baby?", thereby suggesting she was accepting the fact that Doris was not her baby. From 2-8-33 to 3-0-0, masturbation became more overt. At 2-11-7, Mary straddled a large banana-shaped inflatable plastic toy, and she turned to Doris and tried to kiss her on the mouth.

At 3-0-4, after perfuming herself, Mary dumped her mother's perfume, cosmetic powder, and shampoo into the sink. While mother was at work, Mary (3-1-24) asked father to "go dancing and to the movie." Mr. W. told us that Mary had been "exercising her womanly charms" on him, being seductive and fluttering her eyelashes. He was surprised at the genuinely sexual quality of his daughter's seductiveness.

From the data of our observations and that supplied by Mrs. W. we concluded that Mary had entered her Oedipus complex. Mary expressed the expectation and desire to have a penis and a baby. Her masturbation revealed increased genital sensations. The libidinal cathexis of the mother became erotic in character. A redirection of the libido moved from a dominant cathexis of the mother to include a strong attachment to the father and a specific brother. Rivalry then developed with the mother for the father. However, the *sequence* in which these events made their appearance differed from that of Candy and Jane. The first (from age 2-3-15), longest-lasting, and acutely intense component of the Oedipus complex for Mary was her interest in and desire to have a *baby*, a wish that caused her much excitement, then distress and conflict. Over many months then, we saw a series of defenses emerge, erected to deal with this wish to have a baby. The next to emerge was an erotic relation with the mother (2-4-29) and an interest in her own and her mother's sexual anatomy (2-5-2). From age 2-7-0 we found protogenital-phase masturbation when she was with her mother as well as with her father. Almost simultaneous with this was the beginning of an increased and qualitatively new interest in her father and brother. Then too she first expressed a wish to have a penis.

Jane

When we first saw Jane at birth she had just become the youngest of the K. parents' many children. The family is emotionally warm, strongly bonded together. Father works in a tool factory and mother cares for the large family. Financially, life is not easy for the family, but an over-all down-to-earth sense of well-being is characteristic of its members, except for father who suffers occasional depressions and gastrointestinal symptoms. Jane was a well-developing, active child. Prior to eighteen months of age, Jane's masturbation activity was not remarkable.

Jane's sister was born when Jane was 1-5-26. When mother was still in the hospital we found Jane to be clearly low-keyed. It soon became important that Anni required a great deal of care and attention (including hospitalizations) from mother for months to come, indeed years to come, due to a significant congenital problem. By virtue of admirable efforts on the part of the mother, and a richly supportive familial environment, the relation of Jane with her mother and others around her remained at a notably good emotional level. For quite some time during her rapprochement subphase, one of the major tasks at hand was working through the anger at her beloved mother for the numerous separations created by Anni's needs, separations which lasted several hours. Sibling rivalry made its appearance quite early, but Anni's particular vulnerability made her a very poor target, and Jane, sensing this, it seemed, soon used displacement, making a game of undesirable impulses, as well as neutralization and sublimation. She participated in the care of Anni, identifying with mother; she also identified with Anni, behavior with which the mother dealt well.

While the rapprochement subphase was long, it was benign in quality and allowed much age-adequate work to be done. Several peaks of rapprochement crisis appeared and were worked through with significant observable growth. It was in the midst of such a rapprochement-crisis peak that now, for the first time in our project, Jane, age 2-1-14, made evident her awareness that there are boys' things and girls' things. She picked up a toy and said, "Boy's boat." Mrs. K. said, "It's a girl's boat too." Jane agreed.

At age 2-4-14 we saw the first clear evidence of her emerging Oedipus complex. In the Toddler Area, that morning, there was much talk of getting married; this was started by a five-year-old girl. Jane said she was going to marry daddy. She added that she would have two babies, and, when asked, said she would call them "mommy." (Thus she could have the best of both worlds.)

At age 2-7-1 we saw clear evidence of genital masturbation while she sat on a sheep toy pressing against its erect tail which is ¾ inch in diameter and two inches high. (This toy, for the same reason, it seemed, became a favorite of several of our then two-and-a-half to three-year-old girls.) A further note from our record for this day indicates that two male observers found Jane to be "lovely, coy, charming"; one female observer who was teased by Jane the same morning found her to be "bitchy." The impressions reported on Jane by the observers were, for the first time, divided according to their gender.

We felt the Oedipus complex fully engaged when, at age 2-7-18, Jane devised a game in which she shot various members of her family. Of all of them, only mother had been shot hard and was supposed to be dead. In this session Mrs. K. surprised us when, irritated by Jane's provoking her this morning, she said playfully but pressured from within, that she would gladly give Jane to someone "for one year." Mrs. K. felt that Jane had been gradually becoming difficult with her *for the past four months.* Jane has from time to time now indicated a marked wish to be with her father and for mother to leave. Despite this occasionally clearly expressed wish to be rid of mother, the strongly loving relation between mother and daughter prevails.

From here the full evolving of the Oedipus complex was readily discernible. Genital masturbation, manual and indirect, was often evident. The ego's efforts to cope with dramatically mounting sexuality were most impressive. Jane's seductiveness, charm, sexual discharges and interests were explicitly directed toward males. Heterosexual interest dominated the psyche and was easily discerned. Rivalry and anger toward mother alternated with periods of apparent sexual quiescence and affectionate behavior with mother. Further evidence of her interest in genital anatomical differences culminated in her quiet statement at age 3-1-6, that someday she will urinate like her brothers. And in Jane, the wish to have a baby, to have "a real baby," emerged strongly for the first time at age 3-2-14.

Hence, in this child, first signs of an apparently mild preoccupation with genito-anatomical differences and her first protogenital phase were observed first. Within one month, well before evidence of working through her castration complex, evidence of her Oedipus complex emerged. Whereas there had been no strong evidence of *conflict* over genital anatomy, there was indeed strong evidence of an *oedipal conflict*.

It seemed to us that the intertwining of genital concern and the Oedipus complex in Jane was coincident rather than sequential; her moderate preoccupation with genito-anatomical differences was not yet resolved, and we doubted whether it could satisfactorily be considered to have either led to or given way to her heterosexual attitude to males and to rivalry with mother, or to the protogenital-phase wish to have a baby.

Discussion and Formulation

It is our impression, insofar as the three stated criteria for the girl's Oedipus complex are concerned, that Candy, Mary, and Jane entered their respective Oedipus complexes by somewhat different pathways. Candy showed convincing evidence that first to appear was her castration complex; her "protogenital-phase wish to have a baby" (see below) and her heterosexual attitude toward males and rivalry with mother, as well as her negative Oedipus complex, followed her manifest castration complex. Mary epigenetically first showed a strong "protogenital-phase wish to have a baby." Two months or so later, an erotic attitude to mother was manifesting itself. Three to four months after the wish to have a baby emerged, Mary's castration complex made its appearance. Then a heterosexual attitude toward her father and rivalry with mother emerged. In Jane, the picture was less distinct. The clearest statement we can make is that her genito-anatomical concern, which seemed to be rather mild, and her heterosexual attitude toward father and other males, as well as her strong rivalry with mother, made their appearance in behavior coincidentally rather than sequentially. We could not say that one gave way or made way for the second. Nor did we find satisfactory evidence that Jane's castration complex was replaced by the "protogenital-phase wish to have a baby." In consequence, we felt that Freud's 1925 postulate on the girl's *entry* into her Oedipus complex could not apply to two of these three normal girls.

The Manifest Wish to Have a Baby

Because the first-genital-phase wish to have a baby is pertinent to this presentation, a brief comment will be made here on the contrast between pregenital and first-genital-phase interests in babies. It is by relying on the character of the data of observation and clinical assessment of these data that the following position is proposed: the child in the pregenital phases shows an interest in babies and dolls that derives from an *identification* with the symbiotic partner; in the first genital phase, the girl, in addition and pre-eminently, shows evidence of a *drive-derived* wish to have a baby. We do not believe that the difference in behavior comes solely from or is primarily motivated by a greater development within the ego or in object relatedness.

Evidence of a pregenital identification. From the age of twelve to fourteen months or so, our girls and boys, although our nine normal girls did so more than our four boys, showed an interest in babies and dolls.

Behavior and affect: Each showed a warmth, indeed a new tenderness, holding the doll in arms, rocking motions with it, smiling, looking at mother and others while doing so. Or they patted a baby on the head, softly. Sometimes they used a soft or rubber animal toy in this manner. While exploration seems to be a part of this behavior, it is quite distinguishable from the handling of blocks, cars, or other toys. Surprisingly, a moment of tenderness may be followed by an exploratory pulling of the infant or doll's hair, or poking at the eyes, which, when it is a baby, invariably alarms the mothers.[2] Often the child seems surprised at what she has evoked from the mothers.

Motivational pressure: The pressure to touch or hold the baby is mild; there is no strong, compelling push to do so. Deflection of the interest is easily enough achieved. While there may be a struggle, it is not specifically associated to the doll or baby; the child in the practicing subphase resists all kinds of frustration of autonomous strivings.

Frequency, dominance of activity in behavior: The fourteen-month-olds we have seen show such interest in a baby or a doll-like toy only occasionally. For example, in a two-hour session, this activity may not occur at all, it may occur once for several minutes' duration, then the child's attention cathexis moves on, directed here and there by the push of autonomous strivings which govern the ego at this age (practicing subphase). Sometimes the child may return again for several minutes to a doll or baby, not always the same one, in this two-hour period. Then we may not see this behavior for one or several weeks. Clearly, this behavior does not dominate the psyche at this time.

---

[2] In each of these instances, except in Jane, the exploring one-year-old did not have a younger sibling, i.e., it was doubtful that sibling rivalry motivated aggression toward the infant or doll.

Ego's reaction to this activity: There is no evidence of ego defense against this activity, except against the tendency to poke at the eyes or pull the hair of a live baby, a defense instigated by the mother's sharp disapproval of such activity.

Impression: On the basis of these criteria, we believe this activity to be the direct expression, not of a drive, but of an identification with the mother. Hence it is the direct expression of a reaction in the ego. The drive element in this behavior pertains to the libidinization of the mother—the symbiotic partner—and the *self.* We suggest that it pertains to the work of resolving, of differentiating out of, the symbiosis (see Parens, 1971b).

Evidence of a protogenital phase drive-based disposition. By contrast, from two and a quarter to two and a half years of age on, during the beginning of the protogenital phase, the activity becomes very different.

Behavior and affect: At this age the tenderness and affection become more pronounced, the care-taking more complex: holding, talking to, diapering, bathing, etc. Of course the ego's degree of development, especially fantasy function, is much more elaborate. We no longer see innocent hair pulling or eye poking. There is a notable degree of excitement or despondency associated with the presence or absence of the actual baby which is cathected under the influence of the wish to have a baby. A real baby is treated very differently now from a doll; a much more powerful cathexis toward the real baby is readily discernible (by inference). It is verbalized.

Motivational pressure: It is especially in the *pressure* and *dominance* in the psyche of this activity at this time as compared to the pregenital period that the difference lies. As the data shows for the three girls here presented, the pressure to touch, hold, care for the baby is peremptory. That is the most dramatic aspect of this behavior; it acquires thereby a *new quality.*

Frequency, dominance of activity in the psyche: Also new and dramatic is the notable preoccupation in these girls with a baby, the real baby having a special impact on the child in this phase. In our girls at this time, not one session went by wherein there were not several long periods (anywhere from five to 60 or more minutes) of preoccupation with a baby. The child constantly returns to it. It is often the first thing the child looks for on entering the project area. There also often is a specific baby or doll that is preferred over others. One can even see a set of behavioral and affective reactions to the actual mother of the preferred baby.

Ego's reactions to this activity: Important to this thesis, too, is the fact that now the ego sets up a number of defenses to contain and cope with the peremptory interest in owning a baby. Defenses are erected against the reaction to the actual mother, but most importantly, against the wish itself. This may explain why many girls discard dolls harshly, "never want to play with them," which we frequently hear clinically. It seems that oedipal fantasies underlie the defenses against the wish to have the baby. But also, as Mary and Jane especially showed, ego defenses are employed against the enormous frustration of the wish to have a baby, to allay the pain of drive frustration. It will be noted that Mary's manifest struggle with the wish to have a baby lasted for over one year—indeed over two years.

Impression: We propose that, on the basis of its pressure, inner-driveness, peremptoriness (i.e., primary-process quality), constant activation, and dominance in the psyche, as well as the ego's defenses erected against it, the wish to have a baby in the first genital phase is based on an instinctual impulse that has biological roots and is expressed by the libido, i.e., it is the direct expression of a drive-based disposition. It may, of course, also have inherited ego proclivities (see below). This we found in the girls. From the limited observations we have made so far, it seems that at this developmental phase the wish to have a baby in the boy does not have the same features or inherited ego dispositions as that of the girl.

It can be argued that the girl's wish to have a baby can have the configuration just described and still be reactive to the wish to have a penis, in accordance with Freud's 1925 postulate. But, we found that in Mary this wish to have a baby *preceded* the emergence of the castration complex. Why would clear manifestations of her castration complex first appear *after* the expressed wish to have a baby has emerged? Nor was the evidence that Jane's castration complex was replaced by the wish to have a baby convincing.

It is from two features especially that our discomfort with the 1925 postulate grew: (1) that we found the wish to have a baby in the protogenital phase sometimes *preceded* the emergence of the castration complex in the girl; and , (2) that in some instances this first-genital-phase wish to have a baby has a distinctly fresh drive character which seems to mitigate against the postulate that it is a substitutive or defensive operation.

Suggested Working Hypotheses: A Reformulation of the Girl's Entry into the Oedipus Complex

Because we address ourselves to "subsurface phenomenology" (A. Freud, 1965)—to manifestations of drives and ego functioning—we wish to emphasize that the hypotheses suggested here derive from *inferences* compelled by the behavior of only a handful of normal girls. Such hypotheses, at this stage of psychoanalytic theory assessment—made possible by the investigative method employed in this study—must be regarded with caution. Consequent to the findings reported here, we suggest the following series of hypotheses:

1. The wish to have a baby during the first genital phase does not necessarily follow upon or depend on the wish to have a penis. In psychoanalytic direct child observation we found that the girl's "first genital-phase wish to have a baby" in

certain instances is the first criterion of the girl's Oedipus complex to become manifest.

2. Similarly, as we found in Jane and Mary, increasingly ambivalent and rivalrous feelings and behavior toward mother associated with a heterosexual attitude toward father may arise in parallel with, rather than follow upon the emergence of the castration complex.

3. The evidence suggests that not in every case does the girl enter her Oedipus complex by way of the castration complex. If this is so, the castration complex, which appeared more or less intensely in these three normal girls—and in our experience (research and clinical) appears more or less intensely in all normal girls—is not obligatory for, nor does it necessarily lead the way into the girl's Oedipus complex.

4. While in many of its aspects Freud's hypotheses regarding the castration complex in both boys and girls is supported by our direct observational findings, the 1925 hypothesis is not satisfactorily confirmed, indeed, in some instances seems rejected by our direct observational findings.

5. Hence, we propose that some force other than the castration complex thrusts the girl into her Oedipus complex. This force would have to be capable of forging the variable paths by which the girl can enter her Oedipus complex with regard to the three criteria used in this presentation. We hypothesize this force to be the child's (girl and boy) biological, constitutional disposition to heterosexuality, which expresses itself in the *somatopsychic continuum* (Spitz, 1965) at this time. Central, it seems to us, among these constitutional dispositions, is a differentiation in what Freud called "the sensual current" of the libido.[3] This differentiation, in accordance with Freud's views, is biologically "programmed" to occur at this time: the biological modification in the libido *from undifferentiated (i.e., gender-nonspecific and pregenital) libido into heterosexual (protogenital) libido*. Such a differentiation in the libido

---

[3] Throughout his writings, Freud referred repeatedly to two currents in the libido, the *affectional* and the *sensual* (see Parens and Saul, 1971, Chapter I for a discussion of Freud's writings on this point).

would seem secured by evolution to biologically protect the preservation of the species. It is here proposed that such a drive differentiation is preprogrammed to occur at this time and leads to the emergence of the child's first genital or protogenital phase. This differentiation is probably mediated by neurological and hormonal changes. In conjunction with this drive differentiation may also be constitutionally preprogrammed differentiations in primary ego apparatuses pertaining to perception, synthesis, cognition, motility, and other inherited ego dispositions. Needless to say, as current work suggests (Money and Ehrhardt, 1972; Stoller, 1968) postnatal experience plays a most significant part in facilitating or inhibiting the expression of this psychobiologic disposition. Gender identity, the formation of a female self-representation, and precursors of the maternal ego ideal develop in the context of the girl's object relations (Blum, 1976).

6. Both normal-enough boys and girls enter the Oedipus complex from about two to two and a half years of age on *under the same impetus, by the same general pathway, and for the same reason: to gratify and comply with the first and powerfully expressed heterosexual genital impulses in the libido as well as the child's gender-related ego dispositions.*

7. Parens (1973) owes to Stoller (1973) the view that the little boy becomes attached to his mother, in part, due to pressures of a "primary heterosexuality." Parens (1973) endorses the view that such a constitutionally preprogrammed "primary heterosexuality" exists, but he argues against Stoller's position that it emerges at birth; rather, Parens suggests that such a "primary heterosexuality" seems to emerge at about two to two and a half years of age on and that it thrusts both boy and girl into their Oedipus complex. The present study formally hypothesizes this view.

Now that the data have brought the 1925 postulate into question, a problem in that postulate should be considered. While the 1925 postulate assumes the boy's Oedipus complex to be activated by the emergence of a *psychobiological force—*

innately "programmed" to emerge at its appropriate time (see Freud, 1924 and 1925)—it holds that the girl's entry into that complex is propelled by a narcissistic injury. That is to say, the girl's Oedipus complex is activated by a cognitive (phallic comparison) and a dynamic-experiential event rather than by a biological force. It seems to us that there is a weakness in the postulate that the girl is thrust into heterosexuality by an emotional reaction, by a narcissistic injury, or by a masochistic response to fantasied injury (Blum, 1976). It is not likely that the preservation of the species, which has its first expression in the child's behavior and psyche during the Oedipus complex, is secured by a cognitive, affective or dynamic event.

It is important to point out here that Freud did not assume "true" (adult) heterosexuality or genitality to emerge at the time of the Oedipus complex; he stated that it begins at puberty. The data of direct observation during the protogenital phase, of which the above data presentation is but a very modest sample, reveal the startling degree to which *the little girl's psyche at this phase in development already is dominated by a heterosexual genital drive pressure.* As we noted above, of course, we do not mean that the heterosexuality of the child in the oedipal phase takes the form, or expresses itself, as it will from puberty on, when it emerges in its adult form. The little girl acts like a little girl, not like an adolescent or adult; but there are clearly discernible manifestations of sexual (sensual) drive activity evidenced in her behavior, in object relations, in her play with peers and alone, and we can infer it in her fantasy life (as represented in all the above as well as in dreams, fears, and verbalized thoughts). In other words, we would say that *heterosexuality has an infantile phase and form, and an adult phase and form.*

Summary

Detailed child observational study reveals variable pathways by which the girl enters her Oedipus complex. The data of three normal girls are briefly detailed to demonstrate the path each took. The data reported do not support the generalizability of the 1925 postulate that the girl enters her Oedipus complex by way of her castration complex. It is hypothesized that the girl, as well as the boy, enters the Oedipus complex—given a favorable-enough "expectable environment"—from about two and a half years of age on, compelled by a psychobiologically determined gender-related change in her libido and inherited ego dispositions.

REFERENCES*

Blum, H. P. (1976), Masochism, the ego ideal, and the psychology of women. *This Journal*, 24(5):157-191.

Erikson, E. H. (1959), *Identity and the Life Cycle [Psychological Issues,* Monog. 1]. New York: International Universities Press.

Freud, A. (1958), Child observation and prediction of development: A memorial lecture in honor of Ernst Kris. *The Psychoanalytic Study of the Child,* 13:92-124. New York: International Universities Press.

———— (1965), Normality and pathology in childhood: Assessments of development. *The Writings of Anna Freud,* 6. New York: International Universities Press.

Freud, S. (1919), "A child is being beaten." *Standard Edition,* 17:175-204. London: Hogarth Press, 1955.

———— (1924), The dissolution of the oedipus complex. *Standard Edition,* 19: 173-182. London: Hogarth Press, 1961.

———— (1925), Some psychical consequences of the anatomical distinction between the sexes. *Standard Edition,* 19:243-260. London: Hogarth Press, 1961.

———— (1931) Female sexuality. *Standard Edition,* 21:223-243. London: Hogarth Press, 1961.

———— (1933), Femininity. *Standard Edition,* 22:112-135. London: Hogarth Press, 1964.

Hartmann, H. (1950), Psychoanalysis and developmental psychology. In: *Essays on Ego Psychology.* New York: International Universities Press, 1964, pp. 99-112.

———— (1958), Discussion of Anna Freud's 'Child Observation and Prediction of Development: A Memorial Lecture in Honor of Ernst Kris'. *The Psychoanalytic Study of the Child,* 13:120-122. New York: International Universities Press.

Kris, E. (1950), Notes on the development and on some current problems of psychoanalytic child psychology. In: *Selected Papers.* New Haven: Yale University Press, 1975, pp. 89-113.

Lustman, S. L. (1963), Some issues in contemporary psychoanalytic research. *The Psychoanalytic Study of the Child,* 18:51-74. New York: International Universities Press.

* All references to *This Journal* are to the *Journal of the American Psychoanalytic Association.*

Mahler, M. S. (1972), Rapprochement subphase of the separation-individuation process. *Psychoanal. Quart.*, 41:487-496.

———, Pine, F., & Bergman, A. (1975), *Symbiosis and Individuation: The Psychological Birth of the Human Infant.* New York: Basic Books.

Money, J. & Ehrhardt, A. A. (1972), *Man and Woman, Boy and Girl.* Baltimore: The Johns Hopkins University Press.

Parens, H. (1971a), A preliminary report from the project "Correlations of the Libidinal Availability of the Mother with the Development of Psychic Structure in the Child" (unpublished).

——— (1971b), A contribution of separation-individuation to the development of psychic structure. In: *Separation-Individuation: Essays in Honor of Margaret S. Mahler,* eds. J. B. McDevitt & C. F. Settlage. New York: International Universities Press, pp. 100-112.

——— (1973), Discussion of R. J. Stoller's "Symbiosis Anxiety and the Development of Masculinity." Fourth Annual Margaret S. Mahler Symposium, May 1973, Philadelphia.

——— (1976), *The Development of Aggression.* New York: Aronson (In Press).

———, Prall, R. C. & Scattergood, E. (1970), Project protocol (unpublished).

——— & Saul, L. J. (1971), *Dependence in Man.* New York: International Universities Press.

Spitz, R. (In collaboration with Cobliner, W. G.) (1965), *The First Year of Life.* New York: International Universities Press.

Stoller, R. J. (1968), *Sex and Gender.* New York: Science House.

——— (1973), Symbiosis anxiety and the development of masculinity. Presented at the Fourth Annual Margaret S. Mahler Symposium, May 1973, Philadelphia.

Eastern Pennsylvania Psychiatric Institute
Henry Avenue and Abbottsford Road
Philadelphia, Pennsylvania 19129

THEORETICAL
IMPLICATIONS
IN CURRENT VIEWS
OF MASTURBATION
IN LATENCY GIRLS

Virginia L. Clower, m.d.

IN PREPARING THIS CONTRIBUTION I have proceeded on two assumptions that should be clarified. The first is that analysts
today agree on the meaning of the term "latency." Freud
proposed the concept in 1905 to designate a period of
diminished drive urgency relative to the preceding oedipal
phase. The latency of the drives was viewed as the intrapsychic
resolution of the oedipal conflict in which the ego, confronted
with the reality of the child's immaturity and sexual
inadequacy, is aided by superego condemnation of oedipal
libidinal and aggressive fantasies. As the concept of latency
has been tested, question has arisen as to whether there is an
actual decrease in biological forces. It appears that the
demands of education and socialization, mediated through
relations with the parents, encourage consolidation of ego and
superego function. With better balance between drive and
ego, there is more stable ego function and a relative, not an
absolute, decrease in drive intensity.

The second assumption is that all analysts today realize
that girls in the latency age group do masturbate. By
masturbation is meant stimulation of the genital zone with the

Presented at the meeting of the American Psychoanalytic Association,
December 13, 1974, in New York.

conscious or unconscious aim of self-arousal, characterized by mounting excitement where seeking pleasure predominates over exploring. This assumption may *not* be justified.

Little has been written specifically about masturbation in the human female. A considerable body of literature on autoerotism exists, but clinical observation and theoretical formulation usually has been generalized with the male as focal point. Passing references to masturbation in girls and women are scattered throughout the psychoanalytic literature on child development and female sexuality, and scraps of relevant information may be found in journals and texts on subjects ranging from anthropology to parasitology. It appears that while psychoanalysis has moved from considerations of the psychopathology of masturbation to understanding its role in normal development of boys, there has been a definite lag in corresponding changes in attitudes toward masturbation in girls. Among even the most enlightened and objective physicians, educators, and parents lingers a disposition to feel that masturbation in girls is somehow "not right."

Psychoanalysts are now being accused of holding sexist views, and classical Freudian theory of female sexuality is blamed for reinforcing male chauvinism. Freud believed the discovery of lacking a penis, i.e., being castrated, makes girls turn away from self-stimulation. The clitoris, compared with the larger, more accessible, more focally responsive penis of the boy, is, in his theory, disappointing and disgusting, bonafide evidence of organic inadequacy. To this frustrating inferiority he ascribed inevitable penis envy, less sexual drive, and development of feminine characteristics of masochism and receptivity.

Although Freud himself was never satisfied with his theories of female sexuality, most analysts espoused the initial propositions and continued to discuss the psychology of women almost exclusively in terms of the consequences of the anatomical differences between the sexes and the fate of penis envy, which was seen as a biologically determined phase in normal development. A small group, including Jones (1927, 1933, 1935) and Horney (1924, 1926, 1933), believed penis envy might be secondary, essentially defensive as a flight from the perils of femininity, but this theory gained little serious consideration. Both groups, whether they believed penis envy to be primary or secondary, derived their understanding from clinical work with adult women. Neither group had any information on sexual behavior of the population as a whole or any from basic studies in the anatomy and physiology of sexual response and orgasm. Clinical work with children was only beginning; longitudinal observation of development in normal girls and endocrine studies correlating hormone changes with fantasy and behavior (still insufficient) were nonexistent.

Today, more than 40 years after Freud's original propositions (1925, 1931, 1933), we are still talking about penis envy, female castration, and woman's masculinity complex. In the meantime, we have had the Kinsey Report (1953), the studies of Masters and Johnson (1966, 1970) and a growing body of literature from analysts reporting clinical work with adult women and girls of all ages, as well as direct observation of developing children in clinical and nonclinical situations. Freud, as we all know, revised his theories many times as he accumulated new data and reached fresh insights. Contemporary analysts should do no less. Reconsideration of facts and fantasies about masturbation in latency girls is a case in point.

While it is true that some girls entering latency abandon masturbation altogether, we can no longer insist that this is usual. It is interesting to speculate whether the repression formerly thought normal was ever as common as believed, or whether changing attitudes toward human sexuality have freed subjects and observers to identify masturbatory activity more readily. What *is* true is that girls masturbate *differently* from boys; the focus of genital stimulation and discharge in girls is the clitoris. Masters and Johnson (1966) have pointed out that no organ with the same function exists within the anatomic structure of the male, which no doubt accounts for much confusion in conceptualizing the role of the clitoris in female sexual response. The fact that anatomically it is a true homologue of the penis and that it has been traditionally considered the "female phallus" has obscured understanding of its function, which is totally limited to initiating or elevating levels of sexual tension. The penis has multiple functions: it is the male organ providing for urinary release and deposit of seminal fluid, in addition to operating as the means for discharging sexual tension. The clitoris serves *only* as an erotic focus for sexual stimulation. This capacity is biologically determined, manifest in the preoedipal girl, maintained in latency, reinforced in adolescence, and retained in the mature woman as an integrated part of the genital apparatus.

Masturbation in latency girls typically involves indirect stimulation of the clitoris, and probably the labia minora and introitus, by rhythmic pressure on the perineum and by stretching and bending exercise which uses muscles of the thighs, buttocks, and pelvis. Such activities as jumping rope, playing dodge ball, and folk dancing are characterized by rhythmic movement, counting or chanting to peaks of stimulation, followed by temporary exhaustion and lethargy. Sliding down ropes and bannisters, riding bicycles or horses, afford tactile stimulation, sometimes to climax resembling orgasm.

It is not so common to see girls stimulating themselves manually, although this can be observed in the course of bathing and bedtime. I have talked with many parents, teachers, and pediatricians who report obvious *indirect* masturbation in grade-school girls. Less often do they describe direct stimulation. Accurate information about the incidence of focused manual stimulation of the clitoris in this age group is not now available. Latency is a period under sway of a relatively harsh superego, with tendencies to condemn all instinctual impulse and to project this prohibitive attitude onto the environment. Consequently, adults are rarely the confidants of little girls who are masturbating. Accounts of such activity and information about accompanying fantasies are not easily elicited even in analysis. The literature contains only a handful of pertinent case reports, for no child therapist has the opportunity to work intensively with very many cases of one kind during a professional lifetime. Latency children are notorious for meager free association, few dreams, and limited verbal communication, so that much of what child analysts learn from girls of this age is gleaned from interpretation of fantasy revealed in play, drawing, and storytelling. Phase-specific defenses and transference resistances play a role in limiting exposure of sexual fantasies, and the analyst is often constrained to temper investigative zeal in favor of therapeutic goals.

We do get information when anxiety about the masturbation is severe enough, as in the case of a nine-year-old girl in analysis who had daydreams of being a ballerina and especially enjoyed going with her father to see ballet performances. The middle of three daughters, she was restless, moody, discontented, and in competition both with her fifteen-year-old sister who was father's favorite, and with a seven-year-old sister who was mother's delight. In the beginning of treatment she had trouble getting to sleep at night. She lay rigidly in bed with mounting fear of the dark and of formless, threatening presences. Gradually it became clear that the watchful sleeplessness and rigid posture were adopted to prevent her indulging in the intense excitement provoked by holding a pillow tightly in her arms and rubbing it between her legs. This activity was accompanied by the fantasy of dancing as the star of the ballet, executing spectacular leaps and kicks in a solo performance watched by her adoring father, and her mother and sisters—who were properly humiliated. It culminated in satiation and sleep, but left her feeling vaguely ashamed and guilty. Such clinical findings suggest that oedipal guilt over sexual and aggressive wishes may interfere with focused genital stimulation and with masturbatory gratification. Suppression of specific genital manipulation may lead to familiar displacements: playing with the nose or ears, twirling hair, foot shaking, rubbing, nibbling, or mouthing fingers.

Latency girls who have strong superego prohibitions against pleasure itself, especially those who have not relinquished the primitive oral and anal-sadistic wishes toward the mother, have exceedingly painful conflict over masturbatory urges. Complete repression of masturbation itself can spread to suppression of physical activity and even of fantasy that could serve to discharge sexual and aggressive tensions. Excessive attempts to ward off masturbation may result in symptom formation or in behavioral disturbance manifested as a general restlessness—the girl who is described by parents and teachers as one who can't sit still and doesn't know what to do with herself.

The interest of analysts working with children now centers on understanding masturbation in latency girls in terms of what insight it can give us into the development of the individual girl and about feminine sexuality altogether. Chief among our unanswered questions are where is sexual excitation localized in latency-aged girls, and does sexual excitement follow the same physiological patterns as those of mature women as described by Masters and Johnson.

Selma Fraiberg (1972) has reported on genital sensations in two latency girls in analysis. Both of her cases showed transient anesthesias of the genital, which became "silent or dead" for variable periods of time. This was accompanied by a similar deadness of affect which seemed to be the counterpart of the genital silence. Both girls described a sense of incompleteness in masturbation; both children localized sensations in the genital area, not specifically vaginal. Each was said to have been aware of her own vagina. Very careful inquiry from the analyst, who used a plastic model to clarify confusion about anatomical detail, enabled her to get precise information about the experience each of these girls had in masturbation. Apparently pleasurable sensation came from clitoris, labia, and introitus, less certainly from the vagina, although each girl explored her vagina. Turning away from the genital, coinciding with total loss of erotic sensation, was precipitated by orgastic excitement. This description suggests that a transient loss of ego boundaries, resembling the orgasmic experience of adult women in coitus, may threaten the girl and provoke a repression of genital stimulation and/or discharge of excitement. Fraiberg cites other similar material in the literature. None of these cases reflects a flight from masturbation and genital excitement because of disgust or disappointment in the clitoris. On the contrary, as Fraiberg says (1972), "The analysis of childhood masturbation might . . . include the original flight from the genitals as the result of insupportable, overwhelming excitement and an anesthesia in childhood which was the prototype for frigidity in later years" (p. 474).

Some analytic investigators have found instances of vaginal excitability and fantasies interpreted as coming from vaginal sensation in this age group or earlier; other evidence seems to indicate that before the influence of gonadotropins at the beginning of adolescence the internal genital organs have no mental representation and play no part in masturbatory activity or fantasy. Exceptions to this occur with vaginal irritation from infection or parasites and with premature vaginal entry by sexual abuse, accidental injury, or medical procedures. Greenacre (1950) says, "Vaginal awareness is further increased in those female patients who in infancy have been subjected to repeated stimuli of the rectum and anus" (p. 243). Urethral stimulation is another source of irritability to adjacent vaginal tissues and may encourage rubbing of the external genitals and tentative exploration of the introitus or distal part of the vagina itself.

Reports of deliberate insertion of fingers or foreign bodies into the vagina for pleasure before adolescence are rare. Pediatricians, gynecologists, and urologists note finding a variety of foreign objects in the vagina. However, the published material I am familiar with does not make it clear whether the vagina is the receptacle more often than bladder or urethra, or whether the self-penetration was for pleasure rather than exploration.

The usual spontaneous masturbation of normal latency girls and the mutual sex play, about which we know little, apparently do not as a rule include introducing anything into the vagina. This does not seem hard to understand considering the unreadiness for penetration of the vagina before the hormone-induced changes of puberty. The immature organ has a tissue-thin lining; the vaginal barrel and transcervical diameter are relatively small and inelastic; there is little or no vaginal exudate to provide lubrication in response to sexual excitement; and the lips of the introitus are contiguous, sometimes reinforced by a hymeneal membrane. Intrusion into this structure is painful. In addition, confusion of this orifice with the dirty anus and urethra further discourages vaginal exploration and experimentation.

Recollections of adult women in treatment provide a measure of information about female masturbation in latency. Some may not identify their childhood activity as masturbatory. A characteristic example is a 30-year-old married woman with two children who reported that her only athletic skill as a girl was in gymnastics. She was adept in rope climbing, work on parallel bars, vaulting, and other exercises which either rubbed her perineum directly or stretched it or put pressure on it. She recalled no associated fantasies, but remembered mounting excitement and sensations in the crotch, frequently culminating in a flood of feeling warm all over and transient faintness. She had not thought of this as masturbatory behavior or genital feeling until she analyzed it.

The most serious limitation on deriving insight into

normal childhood development from adult patients is the obvious one: women in analysis are most likely those who have had difficulties in childhood development, and their recollections are either severely repressed and distorted, or what they report is pathological experience. The one adult woman in my practice so far who achieved an almost total recall of her sexual feelings and fantasies from an early age was a mildly neurotic 35-year-old married professional lady who came into psychotherapy to get help with a life crisis. She had no problems with sex. Her first coital experience was at age twenty with a classmate to whom she was informally engaged and deeply committed. Very early in the relationship she began to have orgasm. This affair ended at age 22 when her lover was killed in an accident. Five years later she married and readily established a good sexual relation with her husband.

This patient remembered masturbating from the age of seven. At that time she fell in love with Joe, a boy of eighteen who was an instructor at the ice skating club she attended. Almost every night she masturbated in her bath by directing a stream of water against her clitoris until some kind of spasm and a feeling of satiation occurred. Digital manipulation of the same area did not give the same satisfaction. Her fantasies during masturbation were of Joe. They were skating together, swooping and twirling in a mounting crescendo of speed and excitement. At the end of the turn, Joe would embrace her, and she could in her fantasy feel the warmth and pressure of his arms around her and imagine his kisses. There was no fantasy of genital contact, and she thought she did not have fantasies of vaginal penetration. The skating fantasies continued about two years, although the skating lessons with Joe lasted only a year. At age nine she discovered Gothic romances, and the persistent masturbation was now accompanied by fantasies of herself in the heroine's role, cast into a series of situations where she was helplessly at the mercy of a man who first seemed cold and rejecting or potentially cruel. Eventually he turned out to be a devoted lover. Again, the climax in masturbation coincided with an embrace in fantasy. By age ten she knew all the facts about sexual intercourse and could accept them as pertinent to her own future in some vague way, but without any special feeling. About the same time, she experimented with vaginal penetration: first with a finger, then, after hearing a joke at school, by introducing a candle stub into her vagina about two inches. This was not pleasurable, although it did not hurt. Her vagina felt slick and moist, but penetration was neither exciting nor frightening as she recalled. At age eleven and a half she began to menstruate, and for about a year she masturbated less. Shortly after the menarche she overheard what she interpreted as an erotic interchange between her parents and had a vivid fantasy of their intercourse which made her feel hot all over, curious, and guilty. She also felt a throbbing in the genital area and, for some months thereafter, masturbated with the fantasy of vaginal intercourse with an unidentified man. This was still masturbation using the clitoris primarily, but the patient thought some of the site of both genital excitement and masturbatory climax by midteens was the introitus. This young woman in her late teens had two relationships with men who were physically attractive to her and with whom she had physical contact, including genital manipulation and digital vaginal exploration, with excitement, lubrication, and frequently orgasm without coitus.

In no other one woman have I been able to follow so clearly the shifts in masturbatory activity and fantasy during different stages of development. It was impressive to see that, while masturbatory behavior did not change from early latency to late adolescence, the fantasies changed, and the experience was different in each developmental phase. There was a gradual move from clitoral masturbation—because this is the only genital organ available for discharge in latency— through a stage of wish-fear for vaginal penetration in early puberty, and finally to clitoral masturbation as the trigger and focal point of radiating genital excitement which augments readiness for coitus.

The persistence of masturbation in normal latency girls was long ago recognized by child analysts. As Berta Bornstein (1953) pointed out, there is usually a decline in masturbatory activity at this age in girls *and* boys, but we find that neither masturbation nor capacity for genital sensation is extinguished in the healthy girl in latency. Selma Fraiberg (1972) states that when she can determine with certainty that a latency girl has abandoned masturbation there is reasonable surety that a hysterical (genital) anesthesia exists. My own clinical work, as well as information from direct observation of girls in nonclinical settings, convinces me that any girl who has abandoned genital self-arousal entirely is suffering from an interference with further normal psychosexual development. This finding alone invites re-examination of the early psychoanalytic theory that it is necessary not only for the girl to relinquish her infantile wishes for a penis, but also that she repress awareness of and pleasure in the female organ for genital arousal in order to develop later into a feminine woman.

A recent rereading of Freud's "Femininity" (1933) made me pause and reflect: How culture-bound Freud's patients were, that they led him to adopt such a depressing view of the unattractive alternatives in growing up a woman. He concluded one option is to renounce all sexuality, leading to inhibition and neurosis; another, to deny the fact of being without a penis or to cling to the wish to regain one, leading to a masculinity complex expressed by maintaining clitoral masturbation, thinking of herself as a man and behaving like one to the point of homosexual object choice or—if the penis envy is somewhat modified and sublimated—"to carry on an intellectual profession." The recipe for feminine maturity is to relinquish pleasure in the clitoris, turn love into hate for the mother and hope for a baby from father as a compensation for not having a penis. Freud stated that girls have a hard time maturing. They never reach the heights of creative work and contributions to civilization or the high moral character attained by men, and, by age 30, women are psychically rigid and unchangeable, their libido exhausted by the difficult course of development. One can scarcely escape the idea that if this were indeed all true, no little girl could be blamed for fiercely claiming a phallus as indispensable!

Arresting, too, is that nowhere in Freud's theorizing about female sexuality is attention paid to reproductive capacities as differentiated from the potential for pleasure in the anatomical sex differences. Margaret Mead (1974) has discussed this point. She points out that in Freud's view the vagina is not seen as the entry to the womb, merely as an appropriate displacement from the clitoris. This is refuted sharply by Masters and Johnson (1966), who demonstrated a dual vaginal function: It provides the primary physical apparatus for heterosexual experience and simultaneously acts as a part of the apparatus for conception. In Freud's papers there is no discussion of the girl's discovery of the inside of her body, nor is there any discussion of the boy's anxious response to the development and final painful emergence of his testicles. In fact, Mead says, as babies are seen merely as substitutes for the penis, the entire creative miracle is overlooked, including the paternal contribution. Mead believes that one fallacy of Freud's theory derives from the fact that the entire explanation for sexual differences in development of superego, object love, and search for achievement rested on the high valuation of the penis by both sexes and the denigration of producing a baby. This, because the girl's wish for a child was not regarded as fundamental but only as a substitute, and a second-rate one, for the more highly esteemed phallus.

But why should little girls and little boys, generation after generation in our culture, believe this? Mead comments that in primitive societies all children learn early about male capacity for erection, penetration, ejaculation and female capacity to grow children inside their bodies, to deliver, and to suckle them. There is no more reason for a girl to envy a boy than for a boy to envy a girl. In such cultures the little girl does not perceive herself as a small man until she discovers she is "castrated." She sees herself as a small female who has a womb and will one day be a woman who can bear children. The little boy learns that he has a penis but no womb, that he can never bear a child and must seek achievement in other ways.

Adequate presentation of how a patriarchal society arises is beyond the scope of this paper and outside my competence. Psychoanalysts, however, do understand how cultural influences are brought to bear on developing children through the attitudes and expectations of their caretakers. Kleeman (1965, 1971a, 1975) and Stoller (1964, 1968a, 1968b, 1974) have studied the development of the child's sense of sexual identity. Stoller differentiates the term sex, meaning biological character as determined by chromosomes, genitalia, and hormonal states, from gender, which has psychological and cultural connotations. Both authors report data from studies of developing boys and girls emphasizing that direct observation of normal and disturbed children may confirm or modify theoretical concepts of gender-identity formation derived originally from reconstruction in the analyses of children and adults. Their observations substantiate the view that core gender identity is established for boys and girls before the phallic stage, and they reject Freud's formulation that feminine identity is reached only via penis envy. They stress the impact of the mother's perception of and attitudes toward the sex of her child. As Stoller (1974) puts it, "Anatomy is not destiny; destiny comes from what people make of anatomy." A crucial aspect of what a child makes of its anatomy is what is communicated about it in the earliest stages of development. To the extent that our society continues to educate mothers and fathers who see their female children as biological castrates doomed to inferior psychological, moral, and social development, we will continue to produce women who regard themselves as second class. Many will indeed have intense penis envy, develop masculinity complexes, or fall prey to neurosis as Freud so keenly observed. Some will find a way to relatively nonneurotic feminine maturity, but psychoanalytic theory offers too little about what this is or how it is achieved.

In recollecting the children and adults of both sexes I have seen over the years in clinical or nonclinical situations, I remember many girls and women struggling to separate and individuate from symbiotic ties with the mother, to recognize their sex and affirm their gender, and finally to integrate their fitness for a given biological task into a sense of and belief in an entire identity worthy of self-respect and the respect of others. I remember just as vividly little boys and men suffering acutely with the same developmental problems. Clinical experience demonstrates that the girl's anxiety about being female and becoming feminine is well matched by the boy's anxiety about being male and becoming masculine. Underlying both is the wish for and the fear of a primitive symbiotic union with the mother. The conflict about sexual identity does not begin with the phallic stage in either sex. Study of development shows that separation, individuation, autonomy, capacity for object relations, gender identity, and, finally, the maturity to choose and make a commitment to an adult heterosexual object is a long, slow process which begins in the earliest phases of the mother-child interaction, must be reworked under the influence of progressive and regressive tendencies at every stage of development, and perhaps never ends. In the girl, as in the boy, a certain degree of turning away from the encompassing mother, a rejection of identification with the nurturing mother, may be a necessary transient phase in furthering individuation and autonomy as the task of establishing gender identity emerges. The degree of persistent penis envy Freud postulated as normal and necessary for the girl to achieve femininity is defensive. When it leads a girl in latency to accept herself as literally castrated, to reject her genitals, and to repress satisfying masturbatory activity and fantasy, it is seriously pathological, indicating incomplete resolution of separation conflict and boding ill for future development of mature feminine capacity for satisfying personal and sexual relationships with men. In boys, a comparable degree of severe castration anxiety leading to narcissistic overestimation of the phallus and rejection of any identification with the nurturing mother indicates the same defensiveness. When it leads to the devaluation and exploitation of women, or to the more subtle contempt expressed as spurious gallantry or overprotectiveness, it *can* pass for true masculinity in our society; but it is seriously pathological, interfering with capacity to develop or sustain deep personal and sexual involvement with women (Kernberg, 1974).

Psychoanalysts cannot ignore accumulating data from longitudinal studies of development, clinical work with children, and analysis of adults that is truly scientific and outside a phallocentric, patriarchal point of view. Indeed, it is not necessary to be bound to a theory of human development determined only by biological attributes and vicissitudes of instinct. As Schafer recently put it, "Ego psychology has established as the proper subject of psychoanalytic study the whole person, developing and living in a complex world. . . . We see all aspects of development as being profoundly influenced by learning in a context of object relations that are, on the one hand, biologically essential and biologically directed and, on the other hand, culturally molded and historically conditioned" (1974, p. 459).

Schafer gives a closely reasoned critique of Freud's psychology of women on the basis of illogic and internal inconsistency of the theory. My own proposition is more simple and perhaps more inclusive: a theory is useful to the extent that it offers the best available frame of reference for organizing a set of phenomena. When it no longer serves this function, the theory should be revised. Freud's theory of female sexuality cannot be considered useless because it directed attention to phenomena that might otherwise have been overlooked. Having served this purpose, it needs to be revised.

Summary

Current views of masturbation in latency girls are drawn from direct observation, clinical experience with children, and from recollections of adult women. Reports in the literature and from the author invite re-examination of Freud's original theory that latency girls turn away from clitoral masturbation and develop persistent penis envy as a necessary step in development toward mature femininity.

REFERENCES*

Bornstein, B. (1953), Masturbation in the latency period. *The Psychoanalytic Study of the Child*, 8:65-78. New York: International Universities Press.

Clower, V. L. (1975), Significance of masturbation in female sexual development and function. In: *Masturbation: From Infancy to Senescence*, ed. I. Marcus & J. J. Francis. New York: International Universities Press, pp. 107-143.

Fraiberg, S. (1972), Genital arousal in latency girls. *The Psychoanalytic Study of the Child*, 27:439-475. New York: International Universities Press.

Freud, S. (1905), Three essays on the theory of sexuality. *Standard Edition*, 7:125-243. London: Hogarth Press, 1953.

—— (1925), Some psychical consequences of the anatomical distinction between the sexes. *Standard Edition*, 19:243-258. London: Hogarth Press, 1961.

—— (1931), Female sexuality. *Standard Edition*, 21:223-243. London: Hogarth Press, 1961.

—— (1933), Femininity. *Standard Edition*, 22:112-135. London: Hogarth Press, 1964.

Greenacre, P. (1950), Special problems of early female sexual development. In: *Trauma, Growth, and Personality*. New York: International Universities Press, 1969, pp. 237-258.

Horney, K. (1924), On the genesis of the castration complex in women. In: *Feminine Psychology*, ed. H. Kelman. New York: Norton, 1967, pp. 37-53.

—— (1926), The flight from womanhood. In: *Feminine Psychology*, ed. H. Kelman. New York: Norton, 1967, pp. 54-70.

—— (1933), The denial of the vagina. In: *Feminine Psychology*, ed. H. Kelman. New York: Norton. 1967, pp. 147-161.

Jones, E. (1927), The early development of female sexuality. *Internat. J. Psycho-Anal.*, 8:459-472.

—— (1933), The phallic phase. *Internat. J. Psycho-Anal.*, 14:1-33.

* All references to *This Journal* are to the *Journal of the American Psychoanalytic Association*.

_____ (1935), Early female sexuality. *Internat. J. Psycho-Anal.*, 16:263-273.

Kernberg, O. (1974), Barriers to falling and remaining in love. *This Journal,* 22:487-511.

Kinsey, A. et al. (1953), *Sexual Behavior in the Human Female.* Philadelphia: W. B. Saunders.

Kleeman, J. (1965), A boy discovers his penis. *The Psychoanalytic Study of the Child,* 20:239-265. New York: International Universities Press.

_____ (1971a), The establishment of core gender identity in normal girls. *Arch. Sexual Behavior,* 1:103-129.

_____ (1975), Genital self-stimulation in infant and toddler girls. In: *Masturbation: From Infancy to Senescence,* ed. I. Marcus & J. J. Francis. New York: International Universities Press, pp. 77-106.

Masters, W. & Johnson, V. (1966), *Human Sexual Response.* Boston: Little, Brown.

_____ (1970), *Human Sexual Inadequacy.* Boston: Little, Brown.

Mead, M. (1974), On Freud's view of female psychology. In: *Women and Analysis,* ed. J. Strouse. New York: Grossman, pp. 95-106.

Schafer, R. (1974), Problems in Freud's psychology of women. *This Journal,* 22:459-485.

Stoller, R. (1964), A contribution to the study of gender identity. *Internat. J. Psycho-Anal.,* 45:220-226.

_____ (1968a), The sense of femaleness. *Psychoanal. Quart.,* 37:42-55.

_____ (1968b), *Sex and Gender.* New York: Science House.

_____ (1974), Facts and fancies: an examination of Freud's concept of bisexuality. In: *Women and Analysis,* ed. J. Strouse. New York: Grossman, pp. 343-364.

4733 Reservoir Road, Northwest
Washington, D. C. 20007

ADOLESCENT TO WOMAN

SAMUEL RITVO, M.D

How does adolescence begin and how does it end? We can take puberty as a starting point because the psychological changes of adolescence have to be understood in relation to the biology of puberty. The changes in the body that accompany sexual development and reproductive maturity force a change in the image of the body with far-reaching psychological consequences. With the body changes comes an intensification in sexual and aggressive urges which have little alternative but to come into unwelcome connection with the infantile and incestuous objects. The ties to the infantile objects have to be loosened and shifted to someone in the peer generation. When the adolescent girl loosens the tie to her parents, she loses the support and organization she has drawn from having the parent's ego, ego ideal, and superego as auxiliaries to her own (Lampl-de Groot, 1960). In this vulnerable state the adolescent upheaval, which is necessary and even desirable for the deepening of the personality and for eventual adult independence, is strongly influenced by the history of the childhood conflicts—how they were resolved, what propensity to regression remains and to which early fixation points—what favorite defenses were instituted against anxiety, what character traits were formed. In assessing adolescents, we must look, too, for their progressive, creative potential, their ability to find new solutions for both old and new problems.

How shall we formulate a psychoanalytic perspective on the end of adolescence and the transition from adolescent to woman? In her sexual life the woman will have established or be well on the way to genital responsiveness in a mutually satisfying relationship. She will be capable of entering into, maintaining, and deriving satisfaction from a lasting and stable relationship, capable of surviving the average expectable stresses of daily living. She will have articulated these with a reality-attuned ego ideal, which will include the image of herself as a mother, as well as her own place in the community in whatever other capacity she has chosen and achieved. This is obviously an unattainable idealized prescription, but it will serve as a conceptual guide.

The first line of development I shall consider is the adolescent's feelings about and reactions to the form and image of her own body. Let us start with the impact of the menarche and the bodily changes of puberty. The menarche is an important landmark in early adolescence because it has all the characteristics of a normal developmental crisis. Such a crisis may be a stimulus or an obstacle to the progress of development; aptitudes and abilities may become more available to the personality at the same time as susceptibilities and vulnerabilities may be heightened. It is a time of progression as well as regression. On the regressive side, the menarche tends to stir up old anal and castration conflicts. The girl first perceives and experiences the onset of menstruation as an excretory phenomenon on the model of the old familiar anal and urinary functions. Girls predisposed by earlier neurotic conflicts also perceive it as a damage or mutilation and link it thereby to old concerns about genital injury and castration and dissatisfaction with the body image. The memories of puberty in the analysis of some women show that the experience of the menstrual flow, which, in contrast to the experience with urine and feces, cannot be controlled by voluntary sphincters, contributes to the character traits of helplessness and passivity.

Compliance to a mother who persists in viewing the menarche in terms of anal function may further stifle the girl's ability to find an ego-syntonic and developmentally progressive resolution. This is one way a woman's attitude to her own femininity may be transmitted from generation to generation. In one woman there was an almost continuous connection between the enemas all through her childhood, the mother's anal view of menstruation, her disgust with her own genitalia, and her fantasies of intercourse as an enema. This was one source of her frigidity.

On the progressive side, many girls who previously may have been shy, diffident, and uncertain of themselves show much greater self-assurance and take greater pride in their femininity. Concomitantly they become more assertive and expressive of their own personalities. How the puberty girl feels and behaves is strongly influenced by the ego's response to the original pregenital and phallic instinctual strivings and by the qualities of the object relations to the parents. Shame, fright, and disgust followed by reaction formations may be part of the initial reaction. Girls with earlier intense penis envy and feelings of castration are predisposed to react to puberty—the physical confirmation of their biological femininity—with severe body-image problems.

We have not paid sufficient attention to the effects of the progressive lowering of the age of puberty in our society in recent decades. Some of the most severe reactions occur in girls who start to menstruate at the age of eight or nine. They are likely to react with rage, temper tantrums, shame, and bizarre attempts to conceal the fact of menstruation, treating the soiled clothing as evidence of the failure of sphincter control. The have not had a latency period long enough to establish stable ego structures and to thus maintain a reliable defense against the pregenital drives. The development of the breasts can be either a source of pride and pleasure or a focus for anger and shame, depending on whether the girl's image of her own body is satisfying or acceptable, or whether it is the focus of intense conflict of earlier origin.

Concealment is, I believe, a widespread if not universal

reaction to the menarche. It is a reaction we need to understand more fully because it is important in the psychoanalysis of women. Concealment, particularly of masturbatory fantasies and activities, is more pronounced in the analysis of women than in the analysis of men. This may be a determined, conscious withholding in some instances, accompanied by such declarations as "I will never talk about such things to you, " or "You will never get that from me." Or the concealment may be contained in a blank feeling or state of mind or the patient's declaration that she is thinking about nothing (Lewin, 1948). The attitude of secretiveness and concealment has its earliest roots in the girl's more powerful repression of pregenital strivings, particularly the anal strivings, starting in the preoedipal period and extending all through childhood. A related clinical finding in child psychiatry is the rarity of fecal retention and soiling in girls compared to its frequency in boys. The strong repression of the pregenital strivings in girls is usually attributed to the girls' reactions to the absence of a penis, which is experienced quite regularly as a narcissistic hurt and the focal point for feelings of inferiority and shame, which can be warded off by reaction formations carried out against the anal interests. In neurotic women the reaction formation and the related trait of concealment are intensified in puberty and adolescence in response to the menarche, which is experienced as an uncontrollable soiling that may betray the girl if it is not adequately concealed. These attitudes can exist side by side with feelings of pride, confidence, self-assurance, and adequacy about the new development. The girl's upsurge of erotic interest and genital strivings in adolescence comes close upon the intense threatening resurgence of anality, so that the ego is hard-pressed to cope with both at the same time. A further difficulty arises from the fact that the intensification of the pregenital strivings brings with it a recrudescence of the preoedipal type of object relations with which the pregenital strivings were originally connected. This results in the manifestations of aggressive, anaclitic, ambivalent object-ties and the exaggerated or even pathological defenses against them.

The manner in which the adolescent resolves the issues of her body image and attitudes toward her body is crucial to her sexuality as a woman. The biological maturity that makes reproduction possible also requires that sexual pleasure be experienced directly on the partner's body. Under these new conditions, the adolescent girl's feelings and fantasies about her own body become powerful determinants for the specific conditions under which she will experience sexual pleasure. Feelings of pride, shame, tenderness, envy, hostility have a source in the girl's image of her own body and of the man's body. These feelings are intimately connected with the sexual response. They may enhance or intensify the erotic sexual response or inhibit it to the point of unpleasure, pain, frigidity, and avoidance of bodily contact and exposure. Where the bodily contact is pleasurable, it may also become the basis for strong attachment to the partner on the model of the infantile contact with the mother, producing comfort, solace, and reassurance in addition to erotic pleasure.

Adolescence is also the time when the girl has to bring her masturbation fantasies into a dynamic exchange with the actuality of the sexual relationship. This is the time when sexual unresponsiveness and frigidity become apparent. If the fantasy and actuality cannot be reconciled or integrated by the end of adolescence, the woman may become aware of a fixed neurotic inhibition of her sexuality and have difficulty in establishing lasting, satisfying relationships with men.

Masochistic fantasies containing both the reversal of aggression and the disguised remains of pregenital strivings, with their associated masturbation fantasies, frequently interfere with the establishment of adolescent and adult sexuality, and are a factor contributing to frigidity. The old reactions to the absence of a penis belonging to the phallic-oedipal period may also make an important contribution to the adolescent's difficulties. Reaction to the absence of a penis is universal. Penis envy may simply contribute to the girl's normal development or it may be a major factor in neurosis or in the formation of certain character types, depending on whether the childhood setting in which it first appeared was traumatic for the girl. In some adolescent girls, penis envy combines with a heightened body narcissism to create a provocative, assertive seductiveness in which the sexual arousal of men focuses on the penis. Intercourse takes on a competitive quality, and the girl becomes anxious and frustrated over her inability to achieve orgasm. One successful and satisfying sublimation of penis envy seen particularly in college students is in intellectual functioning and achievement. The mind is looked upon as an idealized part of the body image, and its fine functioning is a source of pride and satisfaction.

Just as the sexual response is constructed piecemeal over a period of time in adolescence, so is the adult form of object relationships constructed from relations with past objects. The adolescent girl has the task of shifting from the original object, the mother, to the man. An early version of this shift occurs in the oedipal period. How the father responded to the little girl's love for him at that time is significant for her adolescent attempts to turn to the man. In any case, the regression to pregenitality in puberty reactivates the preoedipal relation to the mother. In some girls, the regression takes the form of severe eating disturbances, which contain intense aggressive strivings against the mother.

In the severe forms of anorexia nervosa in adolescence, much more frequent in girls than in boys, the rage at the mother, which has been externalized and displaced on to food, has its roots in the repressed oral sadomasochistic conflicts with the mother. The symptoms frequently occur upon separation from the mother when the adolescent goes away from home. It is the introjected mother whom the adolescent is starving for and trying to control and punish. In their milder forms, disturbances of eating of both the bulimic and anorexic variety constitute one of the most frequent complaints among women students in college health services.

When the ambivalent, infantile tie to the mother has to be loosened or broken, the first turning to the man in puberty may be primarily an effort to replace the loss of the mother. The analysis of an adolescent girl provides an illustration.

The patient came to analysis in her late teens because of depression, hypochondriacal symptoms, and concerns about the adequacy of her sexual response. She was free and frank in her social and sexual relations and took great pride and pleasure in her body. Though she had been aware all through her childhood of a slight disgust at smells and feces, she was surprised to discover in the analysis how strong these attitudes were and how many defenses and reaction formations she had erected against them. She was even more surprised to discover that some of these same attitudes existed in connection with her genitals and that her discomfort about her vagina had existed as far back as puberty. At that time she had been very open about her sexual interests and activities with her peers and with mother surrogates but concealed them from her mother, even though her mother's attitude was not prohibitive but more in the mode of laissez-faire. Shortly after the menarche, she and her mother had one of the intense emotional quarrels that punctuated their basically positive relationship. Afterward, she went to her room and wrote a story about a lovers' quarrel. The man leaves after the quarrel, and the woman cannot stay in her lonely bed and goes out crying in the rain to look for him. An adult, unaware of what had preceded the story, commented on the amazing understanding a young adolescent showed for complex adult heterosexual love relationships. The incident ushered in a rapid move over a period of months, in the girl's relations from mother to men. Although the shift from mother to men was made directly and rapidly, the tie to mother and women remained very strong. Indeed, the relations with men had an additional feature in terms of her relations to women. All her life it had been important to her to be special. In adolescence, being special was being unusual and on an adult level in sex. Being important to men would also make her special to women, to both her peers and her mother. Indeed, her sexuality at times was directly competitive with her mother. The sexual relation with men was not fully or consistently satisfying. The more insistent underlying longing was to be held and comforted by the man like a small child. Thus, the relation to the man in early adolescence started as a replacement for the regressive ambivalent tie to the mother, serving at the same time as a way of retaining a special position in the eyes of women, as well as continuing to seek with the man the satisfaction of old longings for the mother. I think this way of shifting from the mother, or woman, to the man with a persistence of mother in the man is a very frequent, if not regular, occurrence. The specific details and features of the process have great individual variations. Much of what is taken to be sexual behavior on an adult genital level among adolescents is actually such a holding and being held. An effort is made to find and provide a feeling of security and intimacy on the model of the old experiences or fantasies with the mother during the strangeness, uncertainty, and anxiety that make up so much of adolescence. If, by the end of adolescence, the woman has not been able to keep the relation to the man free enough of this inheritance from her mother, the probability of establishing a satisfying or viable marriage is considerably reduced.

The wish for a child and motherhood changes during adolescence and in the development from adolescent to woman. The wish for a child, which first appears in childhood fantasy in identification with the mother and as part of the resolution of the Oedipus complex, deepens and becomes more specific with the establishment of the menstrual cycle. It becomes part of the body image. One manifestation of the wish for motherhood and a child appears in the attitude of many girls toward animals and pets. As seen in analysis, the wish for a child is steadily present as a continuing theme, but not as a desire or need that is up for decision or action. As one young woman in her early twenties put it, "When I was fifteen and sixteen, my dream was to marry a farmer, have children, and breed horses, cattle, and dogs." In her twenties she still wanted to be an animal breeder and was developing career plans in that direction, but her neurosis was preventing her from establishing an intimate and stable relationship with a man that would make the wish for a child realizable. The wish for a child was held in abeyance, and she regarded it as a naïve or idyllic fantasy with a lower priority than the analysis of the masochistic, neurotic, and character problems that were impeding her life.

In the adolescent girl, the wish for a child is still strongly tinged with oedipal and pregenital origins. If these remain in the personality with their intense sexual and aggressive qualities directed at the infantile objects, the potential difficulty for the mother-child relation may be grave. In the severe eating disturbances described earlier, if the wishes to devour, destroy, and incorporate are not resolved or stabilized by adequate superego formation and functioning, the psychological peril in childbearing and mothering is great. The child's unconscious wish and fear to devour or be eaten poses a threat to pregnancy and to the mother-child relation. In some women these conflicts intrude quickly in the breast feeding. One mother had to abandon the effort after a few days because she felt the infant was like a rabbit nibbling at her, and she abhorred the messiness. Her own aggression to the child dominated her mothering in the first few years. Another mother gave up the effort, though she was committed to the idea because the erotic feelings the infant stimulated with her suckling were too threatening to the wall of inhibition the mother had established against her sexuality as a result of her own upbringing.

The concept of the ego ideal offers another position from

which to view the transition from adolescent to woman. The restructuring of the psyche with the ascendancy of the ego, which takes place after the turmoil of adolescence, is accompanied by a firmer establishment of the adult ego-ideal—which the adolescent is motivated to realize in order to be loved and approved by the superego. For the purposes of this discussion it is convenient to divide the ego ideal of the young woman into two parts: one more related to the biological side and one that is closer to the social side of her life.

Motherhood as an ideal has early roots in the girl's identification with her mother and the infantile wishes for a child. As Freud said, nothing brings greater pleasure and satisfaction than the fulfillment of an old wish or dream. Many women find it the most moving, enriching and profound experience of their lives. The converse is a question much discussed today: is the experience of heterosexuality, pregnancy, childbirth, and motherhood essential for the completion of the woman's femininity? It is no doubt important for the kind of satisfaction that is close to old dreams and wishes, which in this instance means close to the instinctual drives biologically rooted in the experiences and rhythms of the body. The answer to the question lies ultimately with the capacity of the individual woman for sublimation, a capacity that is related to the qualities and history of her object relations, her identifications, and the degree of fixation as compared to the progressive developmental potential of the instinctual drives.

Another facet to this question serves as a transition to the social side of the ego ideal. The total psychological significance of the experience of motherhood is also influenced by the value, recognition, and prestige society places on motherhood. In a time when a woman's fertility and childbearing functions had high economic value, her prestige and her worth depended very much on her fertility. Woman's fertility does not have that value in our society today. Bearing children is necessary for human survival in an ultimate sense, but in our society it is not necessary for immediate survival or economic well-being as it was in the past. Instead, children are an economic burden. This is an important factor in the reassessment of woman's view of herself and her place in society. If these conditions prevail for an extended time, we may have an opportunity to observe the impact of such external reality factors on unconscious wishes and fantasies.

Among those women for whom the social side of the ego ideal includes a career or profession demanding long preparation and continuing major commitment, the conflict may not be neurotic, but may be between the normal feminine wishes and the demands of reality. The stringencies of the biological timetable are the most unyielding of the various elements the young adult woman must integrate.

From the psychoanalysts' point of view the unconscious wishes and fantasies show no signs of changing. Nor is there any sign that the modern woman has been able to tap new sources of ego strength or flexibility in her effort to adapt to a changed "average expectable environment."

REFERENCES

Lampl-de Groot, J. (1960), On adolescence. *The Psychoanalytic Study of the Child,* 15.97-103. New York: International Universities Press.
Lewin, B. D. (1948), The nature of reality, the meaning of nothing, with an addendum on concentration. In: *Selected Writings.* New York: The Psychoanalytic Quarterly, 1973, pp. 320-322.

Yale University Child Study Center
333 Cedar Street
New Haven, Connecticut 06510

FEMALE AUTONOMY
AND YOUNG   GERTRUDE R. TICHO, M.D.
ADULT WOMEN

BEFORE THE FIRST WORLD WAR, it was extremely rare for a young woman to leave the parental home in order to live by herself. A girl left home only when she married or, in the lower socioeconomic classes, if she went to work, which usually meant going into service. In either case, when a girl left home she moved from one authoritative and protective structure— the family—to another—marriage or employment in a paternalistic setting. The situation changed slowly between the two wars and became the rule rather than the exception only during the last 30 years. An examination of the psychological stresses resulting from this change in social mores can, it seems to me, contribute to a better understanding of female development.

Freud's theory of female psychosexual development, conceived when it was most unusual for a girl in her late teens or early twenties to be living on her own, was decisively influenced by the overriding importance he attributed to the castration complex. Although he made several revisions of his views, such as the significance of preoedipal development and the importance of the mother, his stand regarding the castration complex remained unchanged. It is thus not surprising to find him questioning those who "regard the two sexes as completely equal in position and worth" (1925, p. 258). In his view, the girl's Oedipus complex is made possible and initiated by the castration complex, and, because she has to accept her castrated state in order to develop the positive Oedipus complex, the compelling motivation for its resolution is lacking. Freud states (1925, p. 257), "it [the Oedipus complex] may be slowly abandoned or dealt with by repression, or its effects may *persist far into women's normal mental life*" (italics mine). Later (1940, p. 194), he says, "It does little harm to a woman if she remains in her feminine Oedipus attitude. She will in that case choose her husband for his paternal characteristics and be ready to recognize his authority."

Insofar as Freud considered the superego the heir to the oedipal conflict, his description (1925, pp. 257-258) of women's superego is only a logical consequence of his theory regarding the resolution of the female Oedipus complex: "Their super-ego is never so inexorable, so impersonal, so independent of its emotional origins as we require it to be in men. Character traits which critics of every epoch have brought up against women—that they show less sense of justice than men, they are less ready to submit to the great exigencies of life, they are more often influenced in their judgements by feelings of affection or hostility—all these would be amply accounted for by the modification in the formation of their super-ego. . . ."

In summary, then, the girl's turning to a heterosexual love object is always motivated by her frustrated masculine strivings and penis envy, and her superego does not become an autonomous psychic structure with an internalized and depersonified value system. Such a woman would fare well enough in a paternalistic society in which the only goal for women is marriage to an authoritative husband and the rearing of her children according to the demands of this society.

Freud did not address himself to the subject of the girl's genuine wish for and striving to become a complete woman in her own right and with her own feminine goals and values. This could be overlooked so long as the girl remained in a paternalistic environment and never lived by herself, but we should not forget that Freud on several occasions expressed his doubts about the completeness of his understanding of women. In the concluding remarks of his lecture on Femininity (1933, p. 135), after admitting that his knowledge was "incomplete and fragmentary and does not always sound friendly," he added, "If you want to know more about femininity, enquire from your own experiences of life, or turn to the poets, or wait until science can give you deeper and more coherent information." Science has since certainly taken steps in that direction.

There seems to be little doubt by now that girls do not want to become men, but wish to develop into independent autonomous women. Stoller (1974) has convincingly demonstrated that gender identity is established during the first year of life and from then on remains unchangeable, regardless of later physical or emotional adversities. His findings, although in some aspects contradicting Freud's theories, seem to prove that the parental attitude and the role parents envisage for their children prevail over biological givens. Evidence accumulates in favor of an early sense of femininity with vaginal awareness and excitability (Galenson and Roiphe, 1976; Kleeman, 1971) and whose vicissitudes are determined by the quality of the early mother-child relations and the mastery of the castration complex in all its ramifications, as well as by the development of conflict-free ego formations. Mahler's separation-individuation framework (1975) has added a new dimension to the understanding of early identity formation. The exploration of the development of self- and object representations by Jacobson (1964), Kernberg (1975), and others has emphasized the importance of identificatory processes as a developmental continuum, which depends on the quality of the dyadic relationship and leads to the establishment of a reliable superego formation and an autonomous female identity. Blum's (1976) view of the feminine superego provides a succinct summary: "The feminine superego, including the maternal ego ideal, directs and regulates later feminine trends and interests. Feminine identifications and the ego ideal are of transcendent importance for feminine personality organization" (p. 186). Blum thinks that object relations, social experience, and the cultural surround are also pervasive forces which help to determine oedipal and postoedipal reactions and influence the superego structure and value system.

My work with female patients has convinced me that the turning from mother to father is more complex than hitherto assumed and is crucial for the girl's ability to integrate her genitality with the rest of her personality development. The mastery of this change of object depends, in addition to the vicissitudes of the mother-child relation, on other factors: the quality of the parental marriage, which is a reflection of the parents' idiosyncratic solutions of the Oedipus complex; the father's attitude toward women; and the opportunities and roles society at large provides for women. I agree with the increasing number of investigators (Hartmann, 1958; Jacobson, 1964; Zetzel, 1965, etc.) who see the developmental process as a lifelong phenomenon. There is no doubt that the early mother-child relation has a decisive influence on early partial solutions of the Oedipus complex. These particular solutions provide the thrust and direction for further growth and personality development. It seems to me that a final resolution in the strictest sense, of its being literally "smashed to pieces," as Freud (1925, p. 257) said, does not occur in either male or female. Rather, it is subject to further transformations and new solutions.

For the girl, after the early passing of the Oedipus complex, there will be phases of relative stability and quiescence, as during latency or when she finds satisfaction in a love relationship, and periods of intrapsychic turmoil. Intrapsychic crises may be triggered by biological changes such as puberty, pregnancy, menopause, or serious illnesses. They may also be triggered by environmental demands such as separation from the family, selection of a career or life partner, motherhood, or widowhood. How the girl meets these crises depends upon the availability of sufficient ego strength and of an integrated self to allow a regressive revival of the Oedipus complex to subject its previous solutions to further revisions and transformations. In keeping with this developmental continuum, the reactivation of the Oedipus complex includes all aspects of the incomplete mastery of earlier developmental phases. Pathology consists not only of irreversible regression, but also of permanent incapacity for further development, e.g., if as a result of pathology during the preoedipal phase a severely neurotic solution of the Oedipus complex ensues, one can observe a repetition of this neurotic oedipal constellation during later developmental phases. In spite of further ego development, meaningful object relations and substantial changes in the environment become distorted so as to fit the fixed pathological oedipal situation, which is then relived again and again according to the early solution.

I do not think that a woman who marries at an early age, rears her children, and accepts her husband's authority in all aspects cannot become a mature woman in the sense of genitality. But if no other means for further development of all her faculties beyond procreation are available, her chances to develop into an autonomous woman are diminished. Freuds' statement (1933, p. 134), "A man of about thirty strikes us as a youthful, somewhat unformed individual, whom we expect to make powerful use of the possibilities for development opened up to him by analysis. A woman of the same age, however, often frightens us by her physical rigidity and unchangeability," exemplifies those women whose development came to a standstill at a point of early incomplete resolutions of their Oedipus complex.

Clinical Example

I choose for illustration a case whose pathology is clearly in the neurotic range and does not show too severe a deviation from normal development. Nancy came to therapy at age 23 because of her inability to maintain a meaningful relationship with a man. She was at the time in the midst of a stormy affair with a promising young lawyer. He was sincerely committed to her, and it was at his instigation that she sought help. She professed to liking this man very much, but every so often, particularly after having had satisfactory sexual relations with him, she criticized and derogated him, which led to their fighting. After he indicated his wish to marry her, she began to flirt with another man and behaved so provocatively to her lover that he broke off the relationship. She became depressed soon afterward, regretted her behavior, and told him she wanted him back. But when he willingly agreed to resume their relationship, her love for him diminished and she became extremely self-critical, feeling she had lowered herself by actively seeking him out again. She complained of low self-esteem. She also noticed that a faculty member who had been quite supportive of her suddenly withdrew his interest. Only later did it "dawn" on her that she had been sarcastic and insolent to him.

Nancy was an attractive enough girl, although not particularly neat in appearance. She was in her first year at law school, was doing very well in her studies, and anticipated finding great satisfaction in the pursuit of her career. Her professed goal was to become a renowned lawyer and find a husband with whom she would have a full and sexually gratifying relationship and who would be equally but preferably even more successful in his career. They would have, at most, two children and provide an optimal environment for "the development of their human and intellectual potentials." In her fantasies, she saw herself and her husband providing an atmosphere where the children could grow up without sexual inhibitions and without being hampered by the value judgments of their parents. She mentioned recurrent depressions with thoughts of suicide as a side issue, which would be taken care of if she were able to find and live with a suitable mate. She had elected to start analysis with me because she was convinced that only a "successful" female analyst could help her with her problems.

Nancy's father was a very successful businessman who dominated his wife and two children. Although her mother was an accomplished high school teacher before marriage, she submitted completely to the father's authority, but was chronically depressed. Father ignored her depressions or, when they became severe, expressed his annoyance with her.

The first years of Nancy's life were, so far as is known, without serious incident, with the exception of her mother's chronic depressions. Both parents wanted several children and were pleased by her birth. It is known that mother wished very much for the first child to be a girl.

At the age of about two and a half years Nancy was hospitalized for two weeks because of scarlet fever, and after her discharge from the hospital she developed otitis media. During this time the mother was pregnant, and shortly thereafter Nancy's brother was born.

Mother, together with the maid who had been in the home since Nancy's birth and to whom she was attached, divided their attentions between Nancy and her baby brother, but Nancy violently rejected them and turned to her father who, to everybody's surprise, willingly administered to her needs. From then on, a kind of love affair developed between father and daughter, one of considerable intensity that continued unabated until Nancy was eleven. During latency she loved school, read voraciously, and participated in many extracurricular activities. She developed friendships with several girls toward whom she assumed an active and protective role. She bossed her brother, but enjoyed his and his friends' admiration. Because of her high intelligence, she graduated from high school with honors and without effort was accepted by a leading college. Much to the mother's chagrin, her son was a poor student who, in spite of her efforts to tutor him, remained at the bottom of his class. The father, facing the fact that the boy was intellectually barely average, responded by undisguisedly rejecting him.

The atmosphere of the home was strongly puritanical, with no demonstrativeness or intimacy between the parents. When Nancy reached puberty, she turned against her father because he made it clear that he disapproved of anything having to do with sex. (This was undoubtedly in part because of his unconscious erotic attachment to her.) She felt extremely guilty about her masturbation and denied any sexual interest in boys. Before going to college, she began to pet, which made her feel guilty, but had no serious sexual involvement.

Once away from home, she started to pet heavily, promiscuously, and indiscriminately with other college students and plunged into an eroticized but platonic relationship with a physician ten years her senior. She neglected her studies, and her grades during the first semester were accordingly low, which came as a great shock to her because of the ease with which she had previously achieved excellent grades.

On her first visit home, she turned to her mother, who reacted with empathy and encouragement. Mother, in return, shared with her daughter for the first time the hopes she had had for her own life and her disappointment in her marriage. In a way, Nancy rediscovered mother, and from then on a warm relation developed between the two. Nancy delighted in sharing with mother her scholastic success, her interests in social issues and, in a reserved way, her problems with men. She discovered that mother's attitude toward sexuality was much more lenient that she had assumed, since mother had never dared to express this openly. But in front of father, Nancy pretended that everything was going well in college because she felt too ashamed about her failure. She remained rather distant from him; during later vacations she sometimes provoked arguments with him, pitting her "liberal" views against his conservative ones.

Upon returning to law school after this first visit, she studied conscientiously and her scholastic performance from then on remained superior.

Nancy's analysis showed that the separation-individuation (Mahler, 1975) process started well enough, but during the rapprochement subphase the mother, because of her chronic depression, tried to push the patient into premature independence and was not available when Nancy needed gratification for transient regressive demands. The trauma of the hospitalization for otitis media, together with the arrival of a brother, led to a premature turning to her father, who became idealized and the heir of mother's early omnipotence. Her fantasies showed clearly that she thought that mother had turned her back on her because of her castrated state, although later analytic work indicated that the fantasy of her rejection was projective. The father was rather seductive and showed openly that he preferred his daughter to his wife. Mother accepted this state of affairs, even encouraged it indirectly because of her estrangement from her husband and emotional investment in her son. This attitude made impossible the normal open rivalry between mother and daughter during the oedipal phase. It prevented Nancy from experiencing that mother can tolerate this rivalry and that it did not in reality affect the parents' marriage. Therefore, mother's obliging stance blocked the patient's aggression, which was then partly turned against herself and heightened her unconscious sense of guilt. There were clear signs of guilt feelings and wishes for restitution in relation to mother. If father refused a wish from mother, the girl would beg or charm him into granting mother's request. Because sexuality was taboo, she felt left alone and at the mercy of sadomasochistic primal-scene fantasies. Yet she identified with mother, whose passivity she regarded with contempt, but whom she envied as the object of father's sadistic love, i.e., as the possessor of his powerful but dangerous penis. On the other hand, she identified with an overidealized father.

Jacobson (1964, p. 113) believes that the little girl, because of her castration conflict, develops the nucleus of a true ego ideal even earlier than the little boy and that the building up of this early ego ideal is commonly combined with the establishment of a feminine narcissistic goal: the attainment of physical attractiveness. In this case, we see superego identification with both parents, but the identification with the father is much more intense. Her ego ideal was that of an active, competitive little girl without sexual wishes. Partly because of her high intellectual endowment and father's high estimation of academic achievement, Nancy's narcissistic investment was in learning.

Sexuality was denied and passivity feared. Only after overcoming strong resistances could she remember early clitoral masturbation and vaginal manipulation, which seemed to have occurred infrequently. Father's prohibition of sexuality increased Nancy's already strong guilt feelings about sexual wishes. This made it impossible for her to accept her sexual impulses and to develop a positive sexual identity. To enjoy sexual love became equated with being inferior and unacceptable. Her masturbation fantasies demonstrate the incomplete resolution of the revived Oedipus complex in adolescence. She had two such fantasies. One was to become a brilliant lawyer, held in high esteem by both men and women, who would make important contributions to the improvement of the "oppressed" and to the maintenance of freedom in society. This would turn her into such a desirable woman that an outstanding man would want to marry her. In the other set of fantasies, she was a hard-working attorney mistreated by an unusually competent and successful husband. This mistreatment tied him to her so strongly that he would never seriously injure her because no other woman of equal caliber would ever accept such sadistic behavior. In spite of her turning away from father, she was unconsciously bound to him. Her asexual ideals and self-image were firmly established but still narcissistically overidealized. Her identification with the masochistic mother prevented the establishment of a healthy affirmation as a woman and its ego integration.

The freedom from the family structure led to progressive as well as regressive movements. She was able to permit herself to have sexual experiences which she partly enjoyed and which occasionally led to orgasm, yet her guilt feelings and the upsurge of libidinal and aggressive strivings brought about a temporary regressive breakdown of her conflict-free functions. This also constituted a severe blow to her self-esteem and revived the early preoedipal phase. When she turned to mother, mother's availability and positive response relieved the patient's preoedipal and oedipal guilt. This conveyed to her that becoming an accomplished student and later a professional would destroy neither the mother nor herself. It also enabled her to come to a more mature solution of her oedipal conflicts: her sexuality became more conflict-free, her choice of objects more appropriate, her superego less strict, and her relatively autonomous structures reconstituted. Her goals, although still unrealistically high, became less so. Heterosexual intimacy nevertheless still constituted a threat because of her masochistic identification.

During treatment, the patient maintained a good therapeutic alliance and the transference neurosis focused on her intense hostility to both parents. The father was de-idealized, and her unreliable, diffuse, and personalized value system became depersonified. In keeping with this change, sexuality became acceptable and relatively guilt-free.

To enable her to recognize the good aspects of mother that she had projected onto father was one of the most difficult tasks. She could give up her masochistic identification with mother only after she could work through her hostility and, most important, her love for mother. At this point, a new genital identification with the analyst was possible. This permitted an integration of her female sexuality with the totality of her self-representations.

I am pleased to be able to report that, after termination

of the treatment, she married her young lawyer. I would like to add that follow-up after more than ten years showed that the patient has come fairly close to her original goals. She has to keep a watchful eye on her masochistic tendencies and is aware that she is still vulnerable in the area of not being able to permit herself the normal gratification of interdependent needs in her marriage. She also feels she should be better able to stand her children's hostility. In addition, when one of her children gets sick or hurt she is prone to becoming depressed because she feels guilty for working and not spending her entire time with them.

Discussion

In reviewing this case, one could speculate that without the childhood traumata, particularly mother's chronic depression and the later separation from home because of her illness, the girl would have relived the Oedipus situation under more favorable circumstances in adolescence. After leaving home she would have experimented with the freedom of college life and would have been better able to fulfill goals similar to the ones she described when she started treatment. She would also have been able — as she did during treatment — to reduce these goals to more realistic proportions.

In my experience there are strong indications that preoedipal envy and the resulting aggression toward mother make the "change of object" most difficult. The resulting guilt feelings toward mother also inhibit a libidinal investment and an identification with her. This increases penis envy and makes relations with men difficult.

If there is inordinate preoedipal envy and aggression toward mother, the relation with father in the oedipal phase is then also disturbed, particularly by unconscious guilt feelings about the mother. In order to develop into an autonomous woman, superego identifications with mother and father should take place. Superego identifications so heavily fraught with guilt feelings can lead to severe work inhibitions and/or sexual disturbances. In Nancy's case there was a definite sexual conflict, and her temporary work inhibition, which never occurred again, indicates some problems in this area as well. The work inhibition surfaced during her analysis, but was also connected with her masochism.

Nancy had already developed a closer relationship with her mother before the beginning of her analysis. In my experience, if there is an overt hostile or rejecting attitude toward mother, a certain reconciliation with her should occur in the course of a helpful analysis. Even if the mother is in reality unpleasant, at least some tolerance of her difficulties should become possible. In this regard, Easser's observation (1974) that female patients utilize the female analyst both for purposes of positive identification and to test out their new-found femininity may be of interest. Nancy spent a good part of her analysis doing just that. All of my female patients' relations with their mothers improved up to a certain point, but, as Easser proposes, the mother can never become a model for a revised self-image because of the close link between the girl's former resentment of herself as "second class" with her mother's responsibility for it. Moreover, mother's own residual preoedipal envy toward her own mother every so often is reflected in her relation with her daughter. I have observed this when meeting extra-analytically with a patient and his or her daughter. The fathers were usually unreservedly proud, whereas the mothers' pride in their daughters was invariably mixed with envy.

Easser's observation, with which I agree, should not be mistaken as meaning that in the analysis with a male analyst a revised self-image will not be as complete or more difficult to achieve than with a female analyst. During the course of analysis with a male analyst there will be plenty of opportunities for the female patient to find in her life situation such models for mature female identifications. This material will come up in the analysis and can be analyzed just as well in the transference neurosis with the male analyst. Difficulties may arise with a male analyst who has problems in accepting his feminine identification.

I have nonetheless noticed over the past few years that the number of women, particularly younger ones, who seek out or ask for a female analyst has increased. There seem to be two reasons for this: a search for a model who has accomplished the development of her potentials as well as a certain independence, and fear of male hostility or lack of empathy. It seems that greater freedom creates in these women a mounting fear of male hostility. I am referring not only to the hostility encountered in reality (which I mention later), but also to a fear based on the woman's conscious or unconscious competitiveness with men in both professional and social areas. They are afraid of retaliation. Last but not least, some women are afraid to express their infantile and mature passive yearnings because this makes them in their eyes "inferior" and more vulnerable to male hostility.

I would add that the mother's insecurity and confusion of regarding her female role is transmitted to the girl very early. On the other hand, fathers have more ambivalent feelings about their daughters' striking out on their own.

Last but not least, girls seem to be extremely sensitive to their parents' gratification as they develop into mature women and, at the same time, seem to have the capacity for identifying with their parents in the pain the latter feel at the inevitable separation resulting from this growth. This pain is often aggravated when the girl is the only one or the youngest child, or when the parents' marriage is bad. In such cases the girl's guilt feelings when she leaves home are vastly increased. Very often, girls have the feeling of having left mother in the lurch. Whereas this is sometimes a projection, it may equally well be a correct assessment of reality.

At the present time there is no preformed societal role for women; various choices are available to her. Having to make her own decisions leads to an opportunity for growth and development of autonomy, but also to considerable inner turmoil. The separation from home revives early separation anxieties and unresolved oedipal conflicts. I am sometimes surprised by these young female patients' inner urge for growth: it seems to encourage them to overcome more ominous-looking pathology and help them bring psychic conflicts to healthier solutions.

Added to all these pressures are those imposed by society. The girl who decides to pursue a career may well be acting in accordance with her ego ideal. Too often, however, her real interest in what she is studying is belittled, and she is accused of merely wanting to compete with men. One of my patients, a shy, unassuming physician, came to analysis because of depression and overwhelming anxiety in situations where she had to assert herself. The main problem was her fear of her unconscious aggression. When she was accepted by a prestigious medical school, she was so afraid of failure that she worked very hard. To her amazement, she became the second best student in her class. Some of the male students made sarcastic remarks about competitive women, and from then on, afraid that she would be rejected by her peers and be all alone, she deliberately kept her grades down. Men are often threatened by the young woman's quest for independence, and react with various defensive attitudes: increased aggression, rejection of her as a desirable sexual partner, or withdrawal. Girls experience hostility not only from their male peers, but also, more or less thinly disguised, from members of the faculty. Nor does it help the girl to see bright women being paid less than men in equal positions or finding so few women in responsible leading positions whom she could take for a model.

Unfortunately, a girl who freely chooses not to pursue a career, but marries and becomes a dedicated mother can be hurt in her self-esteem because, in certain circles, to be a "mere housewife" is looked down upon. Some girls recoil from the challenge they have set for themselves by flight into marriage. In spite of some rationalizations, they know preconsciously that they have abandoned an ego ideal. I have seen several young women who asked for help after having dropped out of college and married. Soon after the honeymoon is over they accuse their husbands of looking down on them, are plagued by jealousy of other women who continue the pursuit of their careers, or feel "empty and unfulfilled."

This relatively new crisis in female development has its pathological reverberations in the excesses of women's liberation, in flaunting of homosexuality, and, unfortunately, in an increased suicide rate and need for hospitalization. Freedom for the girl's sexual experimentation until the passing of adolescence is, in our society, still the exception rather than the rule, and sexual intercourse in unmarried young adult women is not as widely accepted as we are prone to believe. This became very clear by the sensation created by Mrs. Ford's remark to reporters about her tolerance of her daughter's sex life. Even in the most liberal homes, the girl gets a double message. She is expected to be discreet in her sexual activities, but active, curious, and adventurous in all other areas. In general, present-day parents still frown on the girl's sexual experimentation as long as she remains at home, but at the same time expect her to become independent and embark on a career. Her male partners feel frustrated and threatened in their masculinity if she is frigid, her self-esteem as a woman is hurt, and she asks herself, "What is wrong with me?" if she is not capable of orgasm. No wonder we are confronted with a new developmental nodal point when the girl leaves the parental home. She now has to fall back on her own resources, cope with the anxiety created by the sudden freedom, and set her own structure.

REFERENCES*

Blum, H. P. (1976), Masochism, the ego ideal, and the psychology of women. *This Journal*, 24(5):157-191.

* All references to *This Journal* are to the *Journal of the American Psychoanalytic Association*.

Easser, B. R. (1974), Panel presentation at the American Psychoanalytic Association on "The Psychology of Women," unpublished.

Freud, S. (1925), Some psychical consequences of the anatomical distinction between the sexes. *Standard Edition,* 19:248-260. London: Hogarth Press, 1961.

—————— (1933), Femininity. *Standard Edition*, 22:112-135. London: Hogarth Press, 1964.

—————— (1940), An outline of psycho-analysis. *Standard Edition*, 23:144-207. London: Hogarth Press, 1961.

Galenson, E. & Roiphe, H. (1976), Some suggested revisions concerning early female development. *This Journal,* 24(5):29-57.

Hartmann, H. (1939), *Ego Psychology and the Problem of Adaptation.* New York: International Universities Press, 1958.

Jacobson, E. (1964), *The Self and the Object World.* New York: International Universities Press.

Kernberg, O. (1975), *Borderline Conditions and Pathological Narcissism.* New York: Jason Aronson.

Kleeman, J. (1971), The establishment of core gender identity in normal girls. *Arch. Sexual Behavior,* 1:103-129.

Mahler, M. (1975), *The Psychological Birth of the Human Infant* New York: Basic Books.

Stoller, R. (1974), Facts and fancies: An examination of Freud's concept of bisexuality. In: *Women and Analysis*, ed. J. Strouse. New York: Grossman.

Zetzel, E. R. (1965), A developmental model and the theory of therapy. In: *The Capacity for Emotional Growth.* New York: International Universities Press, 1970, pp. 246-269.

3052 Garrison St., N. W.
Washington, D. C. 20008

MASOCHISM,
THE EGO IDEAL,
AND THE PSYCHOLOGY
OF WOMEN

Harold P. Blum, m.d.

Models of female development can be surveyed from a number of vantage points, e.g., masochism, passivity, penis envy. I have chosen masochism, proposed as an important dimension of feminine character in the early psychoanalytic literature, as a route to exploring the psychology of women. Special attention to the role of masochism in femininity will lead to reconsideration of psychoanalytic propositions concerning female personality development and structure, and feminine attitudes and values.

Is masochism the normal biopsychological destiny of the human female, or is "feminine masochism" determined primarily by various developmental and sociocultural forces? Are masochistic trends normally synergistic with the female ego ideal? Has the concept of feminine masochism influenced the early psychoanalytic model of female personality development? The answers to these questions depend upon concepts of femininity and masochism. I shall not attempt to elaborate here on the many dimensions of femininity, or on the relationships between masochism and female narcissism or passivity. Masochism is not easily distinguished from passive aggression or self-punishment, and always appears in combination with sadism. Theoretically, one can only speak of sadomasochism, though either masochism or sadism may predominate.

Masochism as used here will refer to pleasure associated with suffering, which is usually a derivative of heightened sexual excitement linked to pain or unpleasure. Masochistic gratifications need not be directly connected with physical pain, but can be associated with mental torture, debasement, or humiliation, or pleasure derived from the induction of anxiety or guilt. The phenomenological description of masochism is on a different level of abstraction from metapsychological formulations and explanations, which relate masochism to the internalization of aggression or the turning around of sadism upon the subject's self, the preservation of the object, libidinization of anxiety, or the erotization of pain. In the masochistic character, as distinct from the overt perversion, the goal of suffering may not be associated with conscious awareness of pleasure or gratification.

Freud's Early Propositions

Freud (1924a) saw masochism and sadism as ubiquitous in man, but presumed the female to have drives with preference for passive aims. He categorized masochism as erotogenic, feminine, and moral. He described masochism as an expression of the feminine nature, stating, "Feminine masochism . . . is the one that is most accessible to our observation and least problematical, and it can be surveyed in all its relations" (p. 161). After introducing the concept, he stated: "This feminine masochism which we have been describing is entirely based on the primary, erotogenic masochism, on pleasure in pain" (p. 162).

Freud regarded the tendency toward the internalization of aggression as a biological basis for feminine masochism. He wrote (1933, p. 116), "The suppression of women's aggressiveness which is prescribed for them constitutionally and imposed on them socially favours the development of powerful masochistic impulses, which succeed, as we know, in binding erotically the destructive trends which have been diverted inwards. Thus masochism, as people say, is truly feminine. But if, as happens so often, you meet with masochism in men, what is left to you but to say that these men exhibit very plain feminine traits?"

Freud uncovered the continuum between the normal and the neurotic and the mutual influences of endowment and environment. Nevertheless, during the early emphasis on the biological and instinctual, there was little focus on the relation between the innate and the acquired, nature and nurture. During early phases of psychoanalytic theory, object relations, the role of reality, the influence of culture and society tended to be in the background, though never entirely overlooked (Schafer, 1974).

During Freud's lifetime, psychoanalytic developmental psychology was in its childhood. Lines of normal and pathological development were incomplete and were sometimes not clearly delineated. Freud's appreciation and understanding of maturation, ego development, and sublimation was not always evenly represented in his own work and was not easily applied and integrated into the thinking of the psychoanalytic pioneers. Primitive fantasies were sometimes related directly to derivative adult character traits, by-passing complex developmental transformations. In addition to the genetic fallacy, which confused mature personality trends and their genetic antecedents, incomplete developmental models tended to influence subsequent theory.

Psychoanalytic considerations of the female personality began with the inception of psychoanalysis. Apart from Freud's self-analysis, his earliest patients, starting with Anna O., were female. Freud, despite increasing experience, remained cautious and uncertain about female psychosexual development. He repeatedly indicated his groping and lack of understanding of femininity, stating, "It must be admitted, however, that in general our insight into these developmental

processes in girls is unsatisfactory, incomplete and vague"
(1924b, p. 179). He referred the psychology of adult female
sexuality as a "dark continent" (1926, p. 212), and his
continued perplexity was manifest in his famous question,
"What does a woman want?" (Jones, 1955, p. 421). Freud was
not dogmatic about his speculations or theoretical propositions, and set an example of changing theory in accordance
with new data and insights. His principal findings remain the
fundamental core of analytic theory and the foundation for
later research and development.

The very complexity of Freud's thinking makes it difficult
to dissect separate strands for independent study or to synthe-
size a detailed overview of his many ideas and coordinate
propositions. His changing and evolving concepts can be seen
in the shift from the claim (1923) that the dissolution of the
Oedipus complex is precisely analogous in girls and boys to a
different developmental line described in "Some Psychical
Consequences of the Anatomical Distinction between the
Sexes" (1925). The early Freudian developmental line of
femininity is more complicated and difficult than for the
male, and perhaps never fully traversed. The early theory
viewed femininity as first emerging from oedipal and
castration conflicts rather than as a preoedipal formation or a
primary developmental tendency. The girl's recognition of
castration "forces her away from masculinity and masculine
masturbation" (Freud, 1925, p. 256). What was emphasized
was the little girl's disappointments, her defeats, and her
deprivation. She was deprived of a penis, disappointed in
herself and her mother, as castrated, and again disappointed
in her oedipal strivings for her father's love, penis, and child.
She was defeated by her oedipal rival, her ambivalently loved
mother. These major disappointments and feelings of damage
led to her need to accept her feelings of bodily and personal
inferiority. Her feelings of bodily injury and loss and the
influence of castration fantasies produced resentment and
penis envy as well as compensatory restitutional longing for a

child. Castration shock was linked to the girl's earlier losses, narcissistic wounds, and envious reactions.

In the over-all perspective, the girl's penis envy and masochistic resignation had their male counterpart in the male's castration anxiety, breast and womb envy, and repudiated feminine identification. However, the early theory did not elucidate either a primary or a positive femininity. The girl's discovery that she was castrated pushed her into the Oedipus complex where she experienced passionate conflict with her parents, wanted impregnation and babies, but was also resigned to future motherhood as a consolation for phallic deficiency.

This view of female development did not by any means meet with monolithic acceptance. Jones (1935, p. 495), for example, objected: "To my mind, on the contrary, her femininity develops progressively from the inner promptings of an instinctual constitution. In short, I do not see a woman — as an 'homme manque' — as a permanently disappointed creature struggling to console herself with secondary substitutes alien to her true nature." Positive gratifying experiences and positive identifications with the mother and nurturant mothering were not elaborated. Nor was the importance of the father, not only in frustrating oedipal wishes, but in confirming his daughter's feminine identity and benevolently supporting the formation of a maternal ego ideal.

The riddle of femininity was compounded by the utilization of, as well as the contrast with, the better-understood male developmental model. Freud (1924a) initially depicted feminine masochism as observed in the male. Here Freud departed from his usual emphasis on constitutional factors, and aberrant male development was an introductory specimen of female masochism. Freud noted that the masochist wants to be treated like a small and helpless child, but particularly like a naughty child. "But if one has an opportunity of studying cases in which the masochistic phantasies have been especially richly elaborated, one quickly discovers that they place the subject in a characteristically female situation; they signify, that is, being castrated, or copulated with, or giving birth to a baby. For this reason I have called this form of masochism, *a potiori* as it were (i.e., on the basis of its extreme examples), the feminine form, although so many of its features point to infantile life" (1924a, p. 162).

It is remarkable that Freud introduced feminine masochism with a male caricature of femininity. The male homosexual specimen of femininity was at the same time a daring and fascinating investigation of femininity in males with excessive bisexuality and feminine identification. Freud, of course, recognized the universality and ubiquity of masculine and feminine trends in all individuals, and he believed in a constitutional bisexuality: ". . . all human individuals, as a result of their bisexual disposition and of cross-inheritance, combine in themselves both masculine and feminine characteristics, so that pure masculinity and femininity remain theoretical constructions of uncertain content" (1925, p. 258). He later (1933, p. 114) additionally commented on bisexuality, ". . . an individual is not a man or a woman but always both—merely a certain amount more the one than the other." Development for both sexes included evolutionary-biological considerations, especially of bisexuality, and could be consistent with an earliest undifferentiated sexuality and one dominant trend and developmental line.

Yet, despite the adherence to innate bisexuality, traditional analytic theory before ego psychology presented a biphasic development of femininity. Female development was originally masculine rather than undifferentiated, mixed, or inherently feminine. Freud (1931, p. 228) observed of girls, "Their sexual life is regularly divided into two phases, of which the first has a masculine character, while only the second is specifically feminine." The little girl's vagina was undiscovered, her clitoris was phallic, and clitoral masturbation was masculine (Freud, 1925, p. 255). This theme appeared in terms of the quality of instinctual energy. Freud

(1905, p. 219) initially regarded libido as masculine, and he supported a male developmental model for both sexes. (This was consistent with his views of a primary masculinity, clitoral maleness, prominent derivation of feminine character, and maternal wishes from penis envy.)

And if libido is masculine, according to Freud, women are also characterized by a weaker sexual instinct as well as a more complicated and difficult sexual development (1908, p. 192). This weaker sexual constitution is amplified by Bonaparte (1953, p 66), "The female organism quantitatively speaking, is in general more poorly endowed with libido than the male." (Today, parallel questions concern whether the female is endowed with less aggression, and her apparently more variable and greater orgastic capacity.) Freud (1933, p. 118), referring to female entry into the phallic phase, observed: "We are now obliged to recognize that the little girl is a little man," but modified his view of (masculine) libido. Refining his earlier association of drive activity and masculinity, he stated (p. 131),

> There is only one libido, which serves both the masculine and the feminine sexual functions. To it itself we cannot assign any sex; if, following the conventional equation of activity and masculinity, we are inclined to describe it as masculine, we must not forget that it also covers trends with a passive aim. Nevertheless the juxtaposition 'feminine libido' is without any justification. Furthermore, it is our impression that more constraint has been applied to the libido when it is pressed into the service of the feminine function, and that—to speak teleologically—Nature takes less careful account of its demands than in the case of masculinity.[1]

[1] The idea of female developmental vulnerability may appear in an early observation of Freud's (1905, p. 191): "In this respect, children behave in the same kind of way as an average uncultivated woman in whom the same polymorphously perverse disposition exists." At the same time, Freud (p. 151) noted the stunting effect of civilized conditions on female erotic life.

The great constraints and complications of female development also referred to Freud's (1933, p. 119) view of the girl's special burdens: "In the course of time, therefore, the girl has to change her erotogenic zone and her object—both of which a boy retains." For Freud, "femininity" decisively emerged with the discovery of the vagina at puberty.

Freud's early and tentative theory allowed little opportunity for developmental mastery of infantile conflicts and attitudes in the female. While he scientifically illuminated the profound civilizing and developmental influence of motherhood, he paradoxically observed that women had little capacity for the sublimation of their instinctual impulses (Freud, 1908, p. 195). Suggesting that women impede cultural development, Freud remarked (1930, p. 103), "Furthermore, women soon came into opposition to civilization and display their retarding and restraining influence—those very women who, in the beginning, laid the foundations of civilization by the claims of their love. Women represent the interests of the family and sexual life. The work of civilization has become increasingly the business of men, it confronts them with ever more difficult tasks and compels them to carry out instinctual sublimations of which women are little capable." This theme was to be repeated and coupled with a supposition of early feminine psychic rigidity (which implied diminished possibility for adaptive transformation). Freud stated,

> We also regard women as weaker in their social interests and as having less capacity for sublimating their instincts than men.... A man of about thirty strikes us as a youthful, somewhat unformed individual, whom we expect to make powerful use of the possibilities for development opened up to him by analysis. A woman of the same age, however, often frightens us by her psychical rigidity and unchangeability. Her libido has taken up final positions and seems incapable of exchanging them for others. There are no paths open to further development; it is as though the whole process has

already run its course and remains thenceforward insusceptible to influence — as though, indeed, the difficult development to femininity has exhausted the possibilities of the person concerned [1933, pp. 134-135].

Freud noted that the female's preoedipal attachment to and her later oedipal rivalry with her mother are intrinsic to her developmental problems; that woman's particularly intense attachment to her father may have been preceded by a phase of exclusive attachment to her mother (1931, p. 225). The preoedipal phase was at first in the prehistoric past of development and confused, in the girl, with the attachment to the maternal love object of the negative Oedipus complex. Freud's (1933, p. 134) observations of these problems included reference to the preoedipal and oedipal phase of maternal identification: "We are no doubt justified in saying that much of both of them is left over for the future and that neither of them is adequately surmounted in the course of development. But the phase of the affectionate pre-Oedipus attachment is the decisive one for a woman's future: during it preparations are made for the acquisition of the characteristics with which she will later fulfil her role in the sexual function and perform her invaluable social tasks." Though Freud noted tendencies toward female oedipal and preoedipal fixation or developmental arrest, this is a very different emphasis from a "first masculine phase," or lack of capacity for sublimation. It augurs the modern formulation of preoedipal determinants of femininity preceding the castration complex of the phallic phase and the relatively conflict-free sources of femininity in the preverbal period. Recent contributions emphasize primary feminine identification with the mother and the important emergence of feminine identity during separation-individuation (Mahler, 1974; Stoller, 1968; Panel, 1970).

In the earlier developmental model, femininity was first discovered to be related to unconscious irrational fantasies of defect and reparation, and disappointment, renunciation, and envy of masculinity. Though the significance of the

negative female Oedipus complex and double identification in
the primal scene was also stressed, feminine oedipal
identification was with a devalued and castrated mother.
These unconscious identifications and the female's biological
role, anticipation of, as well as experience in menstruation,
defloration, penetration, and parturition, all served to excite
and structure masochistic fantasies. Actual genital bleeding at
puberty confirmed the girl's feelings of injury and inferiority.
But the acceptance of menstruation also offered the opportunity of compensatory motherhood and children. (It
should be noted that the female experience of genital bleeding
and pain is all postpubertal and not part of the formative
experience of childhood. This does not diminish the
importance of the child's fantasies, expectations, and
whatever knowledge she may have of adult female sexual
function [and also the positive meaning of menstruation for
fertility and femininity].)

The discovery of the girl's fantasies of mutilation and her
subsequent oedipal conflicts, her reactions of denial, envy,
shame, modesty, compensatory concern for bodily beauty, her
masochistic acceptance of her "inferiority state," or sadistic
revenge for her deprivation, etc., were of extraordinary
importance in the first scientific unraveling of the eternal
enigma of femininity. There was increasing understanding of
the admiration and envy of the mother and her maternal role,
continuing and coexisting with "penis envy." The theory not
only had great explanatory value, but with the gradual
integration of new findings, had increasingly important and
expanding clinical applications. The theory was always
correlated with clinical observation, enlarged with avowed
inference and conjecture. Freud (1933, p. 135) concluded his
lecture on femininity: "It is cerainly incomplete and
fragmentary and does not always sound friendly."

Feminine masochism, an integral part of the early
incomplete analytic theory of female personality development.
was a consequence of drive endowment, of anatomical-physio-

logical sex differences, developmental vicissitudes, and the influence of oedipal fantasies. Insofar as Freud and many of his followers and students emphasized feminine masochism, it must have been prevalent in their patients' fantasies. Fantasies of rape, of being masochistically abused while excited, of sexual enslavement and surrender with mounting excitement are not uncommon in females' conscious erotic daydreams. Furthermore, the superego of the female adolescent also contributes to these fantasies, which simultaneously represent sexual prohibition and punishment for forbidden temptation. Rape fantasies evade guilt over instinctual wishes. Some of these conscious fantasies are derivatives of infantile beating fantasies. Strachey (in Freud, 1919, p. 245) observes that Freud's "study of beating phantasies was especially concerned with the infantile sexual development of girls." Masochistic masturbation fantasies inevitably also reveal prephallic components represented in helpless passivity and omnipotent control, abject submission, and tyrannical power, shameful humiliation and glorified conquest. In addition to the regressive expression of incestuous love and guilt in the "feminine" beating fantasies of girls, Freud (1919) also noted disguised masculine wishes. That the object of the beating was typically a boy additionally represented the girl's penis envy and wish to be a boy. Freud recognized the influence of specific traumatic factors as well as the ubiquity of beating fantasies in both sexes. Uneasy about the comprehension of these masochistic daydreams, Freud (1919, p. 183) further observed, ". . . to a great extent these fantasies subsist apart from the rest of the content of a neurosis, and find no proper place in its structure."

It is problematic whether these unconscious masochistic fantasies of young females are evidence of greater innate masochism than is found in men, where the masochism is generally more disguised and far less ego-syntonic in the manifest content of fantasy. Masochistic perversions are probably more common in males, representing deviant psychopathology. Questions include the defensive role of masochistic fantasies in feminine development and cultural adaptation. Observations of little girls did not record strivings for unpleasure or a greater constitutional masochism in infancy. Freud (1933, p. 118) acknowledged no lag in aggressiveness in the early phases of female drive development, stating "Analysis of children's play has shown our women analysts that the aggressive impulses of little girls leave nothing to be desired in the way of abundance and violence." The roots of later sadomasochism have now been traced not only to pregenital libidinal conflicts, but to heightened aggression associated with infantile trauma and disturbed infantile object relations (Panel, 1956).

It is well to note here that one of Freud's major influences upon the "sexual revolution," a social phenomena that continues to evolve to the present day, was to insist upon the capacity of the female for psychosexual fulfillment (and analytic mastery of infantile conflict).

Freud encouraged in their careers his early female students and collaborators, including his daughter, who became extremely prominent teachers and contributors in psychoanalysis. In no other scientific field has there been such outstanding accomplishment and leadership with the fullest recognition and prestige accorded to female colleagues.

Freud's discovery of the castration complex was an extraordinary event in the history of ideas, and an extremely important discovery for the "liberated" sexual and social role of women. For the first time there was a scientific understanding of the contempt and derision toward women based upon overdetermined irrational, unconscious fantasies. Both boys and girls and their parents unconsciously regarded the female as castrated and, therefore, inferior. The female was not simply oppressed by a male chauvinist society, but was unconsciously identified with her own "damaged and defective" genitourinary apparatus. The disparagement and devaluation of women coexisted with an overidealization and chivalrous overprotection, which was seen as an unconscious psychological consequence of the pitiable injury and castrated state of women. Freud uncovered and brought to the attention of the world the utterly irrational nature of this phallic contempt and derision of women.

Freud's discoveries, so important for the liberation of women and men from the tyranny of unconscious forces, coexisted with other of his ideas which paradoxically outlined a masochistic and incomplete feminine personality. Those particular propositions of a diminished and deficient female psyche will bear fresh scrutiny. The female was then viewed as having a diminished and constrained libido, a weaker and masochistic sexual constitution, an ego with an incapacity to sublimate and a tendency toward early arrest and rigidity, a relatively defective superego, and incomplete oedipal and postoedipal development.

Since Freud regarded the major motive for the formation of the superego as castration anxiety, and the girl was already castrated, she was considered to be lacking in the necessary castration anxiety for autonomous superego formation. Freud stated of women, (1925, pp. 257-258), "Their superego is never so inexorable, so impersonal, so independent of its emotional origins as we require it to be in men. Character-traits which critics of every epoch have brought up against women — that they show less sense of justice than men, that they are less ready to submit to the great exigencies of life, that they are more often influenced in their judgements by feelings of affection or hostility — all these would be amply accounted for by the modification in the formation of their superego. . . ."

Freud (1933, p. 129) further remarked on this consequence of the girl's incomplete oedipal resolution: "In the absence of fear of castration the chief motive is lacking which leads boys to surmount the Oedipus complex. Girls remain in it for an indeterminate length of time; they demolish it late and, even so, incompletely. In these circumstances the formation of the super-ego must suffer; it cannot attain the strength and independence which give it its cultural significance. . ."

Is this an accurate scientific picture of feminine psychic structure relative to masculine psychic structure, an inescapable aspect of the difference between the sexes? Or is this a masochistic model of female personality development? Did the universal myth of the castrated female influence the theoretical conception of feminine psychic structure? Did the analyzed myth reappear as analytic myth? These formulations would not account for the development of feminine pride, self-esteem, self-confidence, and independence.

Freud's genius uncovered the universal unconscious fantasy of men and women that women are castrated. This fantasy pervades institutions and social attitudes and becomes a ubiquitous myth structuralized as a "cultural force."

Freud first analyzed the fantasy, but did not discuss in depth the sociocultural influence exerted by the fantasy of a castrated, inferior female. The probable cultural and developmental influences on Freud's ideas are outside the scope of this paper. His view of women may also be based on a different female population. The women of his time and culture might well have had a different character structure and superego from that of contemporary Western women. Kohut (1959), who affirmed that femaleness cannot possibly be explained as a retreat from disappointed maleness, attributed Freud's views to reliance on the clinical evidence than available rather than to patriarchal bias. Jacobson (1937) proposed that Freud's idea of deficient female superego derived from the study of women prior to female emancipation.

Recent Contributions and
Re-evaluation of Female Development

There are essential differences in psychic structure between male and female just as there are in anatomical structure, in biological endowment, and in environmental response. The early psychoanalytic propositions of a diminished and deficient female psychic structure were tentative and are unsubstantiated by current psychoanalytic data. I would reiterate that they belong to an early phase of psychoanalysis, a historical period when the role of culture was eclipsed by biological considerations, when an understanding of pre-oedipal and postoedipal development was barely in initial outline, and the appreciation of the mother-child relation and the importance of sublimated maternal responsibility and adaptability were insufficiently appreciated.

The preoedipal development of cohesive self- and object representations, of identity and gender identity, and the post-oedipal evolution of a feminine and maternal ego ideal are modern perspectives for female personality development. Pre-phallic genital exploration and masturbation also may contribute to the female body image. The clitoris is probably discovered in infancy, at eighteen months, as an organ of sexual excitement with intentional arousal through apparent repeated self-stimulation (Kleeman, 1975; Galenson and Roiphe, 1976). Clitoral and other genital perception and sensation contribute to feminine body experience and to affective reactions in the little girl and her observing parents. The female body image is also defined by contrast with the male and through maternal identification and education. Contrary to previous theory (Freud, 1925, p. 255), the clitoris cannot be described as masculine, though it may become invested with bisexual meaning.[2] Within the adult psycho-sexual organization of genital primacy and the goal of hetero-sexual union, the clitoris does not "hand over its sensitivity" (cf. Freud, 1933, p. 118), but forms a functional unit with other genital structures. It is questionable whether renun-ciation of clitoral masturbation is either necessary or desirable

---

[2] Freud (1925, p. 254) noted what might be regarded as a feminine-oriented clitoral masturbation, "The child which is being beaten (or caressed) may ultimately be nothing more or less than the clitoris itself..."

for feminine development. The clitoris as a specifically erotic female organ is integrated into mature female sexuality. Some vulva-vaginal sensation and awareness may begin early in life, associated with physical care, infantile masturbation, and possibly nursing and the REM-sleep cycle. Infantile vaginal awareness and sensation might well be repressed before puberty rather than undiscovered (Barnett, 1968).

If the girl has an orgastic potential not found in the boy until puberty, this may have unknown developmental consequences. When does female capacity for orgasm develop? Does earlier puberty, and perhaps an earlier orgastic potential lead to greater defense against female sexual arousal (Fraiberg, 1972)? The inhibition of female masturbation is by no means as frequent in latency as formerly believed, nor does it seem likely that such inhibition is explained entirely in terms of castration feelings and penis envy, which are also found in girls who continue masturbation (Clower, 1976). Constitutional, cultural, and parental influences certainly codetermine the fate of infantile masturbation. In older girls, the often-associated feelings of severe anxiety and guilt are indicative of the powerful influence of the superego.

There is evidence of infantile penis envy and castration anxiety, or precursors of these later reactions, fused with separation anxiety and anal-urethral conflicts at eighteen months of age (Galenson and Roiphe, 1976). However, the preoedipal danger situations with phase dominance are those described by Freud: loss of the object and the object's love. These infantile dangers are associated with parallel fears of dissolution of the body ego and emergent self. The period of life at about eighteen months may represent a developmental nodal point in which there is a confluence of rapprochement crisis, discovery of sex differences, nascent gender identity, and personal identity with use of the pronouns "I" and "me." Between eighteen months and three years the little girl develops and consolidates a relatively irreversible gender identity and a feminine self representation (Stoller, 1976). It is

probable that the girl emerges from separation individuation
with a femininity that contributes to the shape and solution of
her crucial oedipal conflicts (Mahler, 1974). Global maternal
identifications before the phallic phase are associated with
wishes to be a mother, baby, and to have babies. The identifications are fostered by biological role, gender identity, and
the child-rearing and socialization process. With ongoing development the toddler's femininity is not that of the oedipal
phase or of the adolescent or adult female.

The mother's identification with the little girl and the
girl's with her, and the relation with the preoedipal mother
are further defined in the expanding relation to the
preoedipal father and to the family. The contribution preoedipal femininity makes to the onset and outcome of the
oedipal phase has not yet been sufficiently explored. Parental,
especially maternal, sex assignment and rearing practices are
overriding influences in the formation of gender identity
(Stoller, 1968). The child's innate disposition, her body
experience and image, parental influence, and social
learning, all contribute to the development of a feminine self-
representation. Female sex- and gender identity and self-
representation in turn predispose toward later female
identifications. In normal development, both parents foster
and orient the feminine individuation of their daughter, and
the love and approval of both mother and father confirm a
positive feminine identity, body image and ego ideal.

The Ego Ideal and the Female Superego

Freud's concept of the female superego should not be
isolated from his over-all view of the female psyche. The weak
superego he postulated for the female was perhaps fore-
shadowed in his theory of the origin of civilized morality
(1913). The theory of the primal deed of patricide by the
primal horde of brothers led to guilt and morality without

accounting for the origin of morality in women (Muslin, 1972). It is not based upon current clinical observations, nor is it typical of masochism or female depression, usually associated with a sadistic superego. The latency girl shows no lack of superego functioning in prohibition of masturbation and aggressive activity, in demanding social conformity and self-control, in the induction of guilt, shame, and the need for punishment, in industrious work and sublimation.

To explain the girl's entry into the oedipal phase on the basis of castration shock and to explain her deficient superego on the basis of her diminished castration anxiety may constitute an analytic paradox. There is clinical evidence for castration anxiety in women, and that castration anxiety does contribute to, but not singularly initiate, female oedipal development. Oedipal resolution is incomplete in both sexes, with varying effects on superego formation. Girls having felt hurt and disappointed, might well fear new injury. Greenacre (1948) depicted girls as worrisome, already punished for masturbation via castration. Fantasies of castration often coexist with illusory-phallus fantasies. The girl has castration anxiety, but even if she has greater fear of loss of love, the different motives for oedipal renunciation do not predetermine the final superego identifications or the strength of the superego.

It is important to distinguish between superego origins, function, structure, and content. Differences between male and female superego systems are related to biological, cultural, and developmental factors. However, different contents of precepts and values should not be confused with inferior intrapsychic structure or function. If the superego incorporates a cultural ideal of docility and dependency, the strong superego will assert and enforce such values. "Weakness" or compliance could represent a feminine value rather than a deficient structure. Whereas early analytic theory depreciated the female superego, I believe the female superego and maternal ego ideal can now be appreciated as of inestimable importance in the direction and determination of feminine character and interests.

The girl's fear of loss of love is itself a powerful force for superego internalization, related to the subsequent importance of the love and approval of the superego. The bestowal of external and internal approval may reward and foster such "feminine" attitudes as modesty and docility. The postulated rejection of the castrated mother would lead to her possibly being internalized, not only in a defective self-representation, but in an unforgiving, attacking superego. The girl turns to her phallic father from her devalued castrated mother, but also in identification with her loved, admired, and envied mother, and with her mother as aggressor and rival. Actually, the motives and identifications of the little girl and her crucial, continuing relation with her mother need much more detailed elucidation. Girls and boys are both subject to superego precursors, such as sphincter morality, to oedipal rivalry and disappointment, to an elaborate constellation of demands and directives, rewards and punishments; and both identify with the superego of the two parents, and with the ideals of the idealized parents. Jacobson (1964, pp. 112-114) described an earlier nucleus of the ego ideal in the girl than in the boy, which, although vulnerable to regression, could lead to the eventual constitution of a mature maternal ego ideal and autonomous superego. The formation of a feminine ego ideal initiates feminine latency and, with later remodeling, becomes a regulator of feminine interests and aspirations. The female superego is different from the male, but not inferior, even if less rigid and punitive; and feminine values and ideals and masculine precepts are not identical (Schafer, 1974; Jacobson, 1964). An inconsistent or excessively harsh, punitive superego will undermine ego functioning in both sexes. A punitive female superego will inhibit femininity and abort maternal fulfillment, and a "bad mother" introject will interfere with the formation and function of the maternal ego ideal. The maternal ego ideal is an important organization within the female ego ideal, which is a more inclusive and broader structure and value system. The female ego ideal has a maternal core in origin and function, but includes valued representations of all aspects of the mother—active, cognitive, nurturant, sexual, etc.—as well as selected paternal identifications and elements of the ideal self.

Benedek, (1970, p. 139) has described psychological striving for motherhood, first considered in evolutionary perspective as female destiny and role, as rooted in the central organization of receptive and retentive tendencies of the female reproductive drive. Motherhood is, then, a core feminine wish and not secondary or compensatory, but I would emphasize the importance and influence of the maternal ego ideal for maternal wishes and attitudes. More than an id wish, a narcissistic gratification, or a consolation for fantasied castration, motherhood is a most coveted aspiration of the maternal ego ideal.

Wishful fantasies of being a mother are normally organized and integrated at later developmental levels. In latency, the overdetermined maternal attributes are consolidated in the maternal ego ideal. In adult life, the child not only reproduces the archaic self and objects, but represents the bond between the parents and a realization of the mature maternal ego ideal. Maternal ideals and aspirations are deeply rooted in the unconscious feminine superego and contribute to humanitarian concerns and caring responsibility, and the development of discipline and ethics in the succeeding generation.

Internalization of the ideal mother is linked to wishes for an ideal family. More than the desire for motherhood, the vital capacity for motherliness depends upon the psychosexual maturity of the total personality (Benedek, 1970, pp. 157-160), but especially upon the maternal identifications. Cultural attitudes toward motherhood may be in conflict with powerful unconscious maternal strivings. In addition to the familiar prostitution fantasies, the clash of infanticidal wishes and maternal ideals is among the deepest unconscious conflicts of women. Infanticidal conflicts are core conflicts in women with histories of postpartum depression, child abuse, deviant maternal and child development, etc. Full feminine development usually demands motherhood, but this will depend upon the maternal ego ideal, ego interests, and the capacities for sublimation and substitution. The maternal ego ideal has a fundamental regulatory role in motherhood and maternal sublimation.

Masochism and Further Developmental Considerations

The early theory of feminine masochism was buttressed by observable masochistic phenomena in women and by the clinical and theoretical discussions of students of female psychology, e.g., H. Deutsch (1944) and M. Bonaparte (1953). Deutsch, in her many important contributions to the psychology of women, modified some of Freud's hypotheses. She postulated a gradual detachment from the mother rather than a hateful rejection based upon devaluation and envy, as had been earlier proposed (cf. Freud, 1933, p. 121, 127). Deutsch (1944, p. 253) observed: ". . . in favorable cases the process ends with a positive, tender, and forgiving relation to the mother—and such a relation is one of the most important prerequisites for psychologic harmony in later femininity." Deutsch, (1944, p. xiii) however, regarded narcissism, passivity, and masochism as the three essential traits of femininity. She enlarged and emphasized "feminine maso- chism," toward the father, men, and life as a whole (1944, pp. 239-278, 254). Feminine sexuality involved submissive wishes to be castrated and raped by the father. Deutsch (1945, Vol. II, p. 247) wrote, ". . . and some degree of gratification of that primary feminine quality that assigns pain a place among pleasure experiences in the psychic economy, are precious components of motherhood." The conscious erotic desires of women were masochistic expressions of suffering for the lover, of rape, enslavement, and humiliation. Deutsch (1944, pp. 191, 241) also distinguished feminine masochism from the cruelty and suffering of neuroses and perversions, but she believed that masochism was not only normal but desirable and necessary for female adjustment to reality (1944, pp. 276-277).

Excessive masochism could cause women to defend or avoid their femininity, but Deutsch did not clearly distinguish between enduring suffering as the price of love, or in the service of an ego interest or ego ideal, versus masochistic goals. There is a difference between enduring or enjoying suffering—between the goal of motherhood or the goal of labor pains. Persistent fantasies of the primal scene and its masochistic interpretation were regarded as normal rather than neurotic adult female attitudes, although persistent sadistic and castrating attitudes in men were not normally mature. Nor does it follow that girls with fantasied castration would normally seek and enjoy further injury. Deutsch did not question the relative influence of a feminine cultural ideal of devoted sacrifice, that a "mature woman" should assume a masochistic position with contentment and fortitude. Clinically, feminine acceptance of hurts and humiliation might be considered normal rather than neurotic and needing analysis. Further, the masochistic disposition and its transformations and different implications for sexual functioning and for maternal functioning were not explored. I believe there are different developmental lines, though interrelated, for heterosexual partnership, nurturant motherhood, and feminine social roles. The goals of sexual attraction and nurturant mothering are not identical and may be antithetical. Being sexually receptive or nurturant is not equivalent to masochistic submission.

Feminine masochism, in Deutsch's view, was governed especially by feminine narcissism (1944, p. 188). She (1944, pp. 272, 280) also indicated the opportunity for sublimation of feminine masochism, but paradoxically depreciated female intellectual sublimation. She departed from Freud's (1933, p. 117) developmental observation: "One gets an impression, too, that little girls are more intelligent and livelier than boys same age; they go out more to meet the external world and the same time form stronger object-cathexes." (Freud observations here contrast sharply with his comments on female narcissism and passivity.) For Deutsch, empathy and intuition were feminine, but not intellectual activity and exploration, which she regarded as expressive of active-aggressive strivings. Deutsch asserted (1944, pp. 290-291),

> Woman's intellectuality is to a large extent paid for by the loss of valuable feminine qualities: it feeds on the sap of the affective life and results in impoverishment of this life either as a whole or in specific emotional qualities.... Everything relating to exploration and cognition, all the forms and kinds of human cultural aspiration that require a strictly objective approach, are with few exceptions the domain of the masculine intellect, of man's spiritual power, against which woman can rarely compete. All observations point to the fact that the intellectual woman is masculinized; in her, warm intuitive knowledge has yielded to cold unproductive thinking.

The masochistic orientation Deutsch depicted as feminine included the renunciation of intellectuality. Yet, surely the analytic gifts and scholarly contributions of Helene Deutsch contradict her own words.

Gardiner (1955), in a very significant paper, took sharp issue with these views of Deutsch and similar formulations. She argued that except for defloration, intercourse is normally without pain and quite pleasurable for the female; that it could be a passive satisfaction without being a masochistic gratification. The feminine wish for a penis and a child from her love object was not a wish for hurt and humiliation. Gardiner agreed with Bonaparte (1953) that a mature woman must have rid herself of the infantile fear originating in the sadomasochistic conception of coitus and the defensive reactions against sexuality. But whereas Deutsch emphasized pment of the female Oedipus complex, liner's view, was a component instinct which h other partial instincts under genital from the genital phase was more likely to the girl than in the boy. Gardiner differ- ssivity from masochism, rejected normal masochism in mature femininity, but felt that the feminine personality permitted a greater degree of masochistic expression with safety than was possible in the male. She did not regard masochism as necessary for adult feminine sexual fulfillment; the presence of masochistic fantasies or behavior was indicative of unresoved infantile conflicts and fixations. In a panel on masochism (Panel, 1956, p. 536) these ideas were, in effect, supported by Bak who remarked that the masochistic woman was not truly feminine, and by Waelder who commented that masochism was a caricature of femininity. Brenner (1959) depicted masochism as a normal personality component and did not invoke "feminine masochism." Masochistic traits and fantasies are a legacy of infantile, principally oedipal conflicts, with varying importance of the danger situations of early childhood. It would follow from these formulations that whether sexual relations and penetration are regarded as an injurious invasion or a loving union would depend upon psychosexual maturity and object love. The level of object relationship is reflected in the psychological meaning of intercourse and orgasm (Moore, 1968), and intense sado-masochistic fantasy is usually associated with impaired object relations.

The views of female sexual development promulgated by Freud, Deutsch, and Bonaparte were partially rejected by Horney, Jones, Fenichel, and others (Fliegel, 1973). The discussions of feminine masochism and its role in normal and abnormal feminine personality development indicated the lack of analytic dogma. Person (1974) has pointed to the confusion of meaning of clinical themes with developmental causality in the construct of feminine masochism as an inevitable consequence of the anatomical difference between the sexes.

Early dichotomous views of femininity centered, on the one hand, on an emphasis on biological and instinctual forces, and, on the other, on sociocultural factors. Instinctually, the male was predisposed toward sadism, the female toward masochism. The culturalists disregarded biology and unconscious determinants, attributing the masochism and inferiority feelings of the female to adverse environmental processes. They basically disregarded Freud's view of the complemental and interrelated effects of endowment and environment. Horney (1935) and Thompson (1942) attempted to explain female envy of the male and masochism only on the basis of the socioeconomic inferiority of women and as the consequence of their restricted life. Frustration of adult self-realization led to increased dependence, with ambivalently heightened vicarious living through love objects.

With increasing understanding of the importance of early development and of the "facilitating environment," the analysts paid increasing attention to the differences in the rearing of female children and in their socialization. Man's greater size and strength and his visible phallic prowess, which must have figured so importantly in early civilizations, had also been realized in many societies as superior power and prestige. Tendencies toward feminine masochism and penis envy could be reinforced in a reality which favored the prerogatives and privileges of the male. Masochism was the "weapon of the weak," and used for the "seduction of the aggressor." A masochistic and subjugated mother could represent a feminine model of passive self-effacement. The actual relationship between the parents, the position of her mother in the family and society significantly influences the child's later identifications and masculine-feminine attitudes. The psychoanalytic consideration of masochism includes more than drives; it also includes defensive and adaptive functions (Brenner, 1959).

Freud was aware of these problems, observed (1933, p. 116) the social imposition of masochistic attitudes, and warned against underestimating the influence of social customs that force women into passive situations. Freud did not overlook the anchoring of feminine masochism in historical actuality. One of the significant measures of the advance of civilization has been the gradually improved situation of women and children. History was indeed largely his-story and even where women were the power behind the throne, they lacked full authority and responsibility. At the same time, as Freud remarked, women had made few contributions to the discoveries and inventions of civilization. The virtual absence of great female artists and scientists is a fact which appears to have influenced Freud's judgement of their inability to sublimate. Greenacre (1960) has discussed problems of feminine achievement and creativity.

In addition to fundamental biopsychological forces, cultural factors are involved in creativity. The relative lack of great female cultural contributions can be related to questions of a masochistic disposition and to fear of success, as well as failure in competitive situations (Horner, 1972). The girl may be afraid to compete and excel if this is in conflict with feminine goals and ideals. Female education and cultural pursuits were often denigrated. The potential of women for artistic and intellectual sublimation was not always fully admitted or encouraged. Actually, much of woman's creativity may find expression in motherhood, "Certainly there is superb artistic creativity involved in the sound rearing of a child" (Greenacre, 1960, p. 577).

Impetus for man's creativity and "brain children" may be partially derived from his awe, envy, and identification with the active and fertile mother. The full potential of woman's creativity remains to be further evaluated and realized in other disciplines, and compared to their creative contributions to psychoanalysis. (Analyzed women may be especially creative.) The age period of peak maternal responsibility may coincide and compete with certain other forms of creativity which tend to peak at the same age period. With unparalleled educational and social opportunities and encouragement, with freedom from the dangers of uncontrolled, protracted reproduction, there may be new pathways of feminine fulfillment, as well as new conflicts and problems.

It should be noted that the sorrowful, suffering, and martyred mother, the "mater dolorosa," was formerly validated by everyday reality. The young woman of several generations past had experienced the loss of many close female relatives and siblings during her own childhood and could anticipate losses of her own children and possibly of her own health or life in childbirth. Masochistic fantasies and identifications were also based on reality. The early masochistic fantasies of the primal scene and the association of sex and danger are no longer typically validated, nor is there expectation of sick and unwanted children.

The concerned care of children represents both an outlet and a possible impediment for different kinds of feminine creativity. Motherhood need not represent masochistic renunciation, but loving perseverance and the fostering of development in the service of the maternal ego ideal. Commitment to children, despite frustration or deprivation, is not equivalent to masochism or self punishment. Maternal devotion should not be confused with masochistic enslavement or preservation of the object from aggression. Masochism may actually interfere with feminine empathy and predispose toward malformations and pathogenic mother-child conflicts. The child may identify with the mother's masochistic tendencies or may yield to the mother's masochistic provocations with sadistic response or excessive reaction formations and guilt. Maternal self-sacrifice out of consideration and care for the child is not masochism, nor is masochistic provocation of the child mature maternal love. If maternal ambitions and aspirations are masochistic or narcissistic, they will lead the mother to misread the child's cues and will interfere with the child's development through inappropriate gratifications, restrictions, and demands. Mature mothering requires remarkable sublimation and promotes sublimation and mastery in her child. It is impossible to derive maternal devotion and empathy from masochism, narcissism, and penis envy.

Children receive many parental cues for the development of their ambitions and interests, often with major differences for boys and girls. Parental expectations can become internalized, eventuating in self-fulfilling prophecies. Freud assumed parental preference for sons rather than daughters. He stated (1933, p. 133), "a mother is only brought unlimited satisfaction by her relation to a son; this is altogether the most perfect, the most free from ambivalence of all human relationships." Indeed, if control were completely achieved over the choice of the sex of children, would there be a shortage of girls because most couples would prefer boys? The greater love for a son could foster masochism and envy of the male in the daughter. This view of maternal favor of sons was challenged by Deutsch (1944) and Benedek (1970) who called attention to the mother's desire to perpetuate herself and her own mother in her wish for a daughter. Although Freud (1937, p. 252) suggested that repudiation of femininity in both sexes was biological bedrock, his other writings indicated or implied the importance of early developmental influences and the developmental impact of unconscious fantasies and expectations.

The mother is in relative eclipse in Freud's great case histories, both in terms of developmental vicissitudes and their possible repetition in maternal transference. The developmental research that Freud sought and stimulated has now provided new data about early development. Mothers stimulate and respond differently to different children and to children of different sex. Female infants may respond to different kinds of stimulation and may elicit different parental responses (Murphy, 1962). The bedrock of biology precedes the oedipal phase and unfolds in a matrix of object relations. Parental attitudes and fantasies impose a gender identity that may not even be congruent with anatomical and physiological sex (Stoller, 1968). Biology strongly influences, but does not by itself determine, destiny or psychic reality, just as the actual configuration of the body does not necessarily determine the body image.

The vagueness of the female genital area was associated with vague feminine ambitions (Greenacre, 1948) and to problems in abstraction and analytic thinking based upon incomplete body image. Psychoanalytic data confirmed the influence of body image on ego style and ego interests (Keiser, 1956). This is illustrated by Erikson's (1964) concept of "inner space" in femininity and Kestenberg's (1968) concept of the "inner genital." The body ego and biological role of the female indicate the metaphorical significance of both inner space and periodic time. The physiological periodicity represented by the menstrual-hormonal-fertility cycle influences fantasy and personality function (cf. Benedek, 1963). Rhythmicity may be a special component of the feminine personality, especially after puberty. The menstrual cycle, pregnancy and maternity impose unique developmental tasks and are instinsic to the psychobiology of femininity.

The vague and confused external genitals and the invisible internal genitals of the girl are nevertheless also associated with a visible well-defined, and fundamental maternal reproductive role. The uncertain ambitions and goals of the girl may be correlated with her body image and illusory-phallus fantasies, as well as with parental attitudes, sociocultural expectations, and the illusory or real achievements and opportunities in life. Boys and girls show tendencies to have different styles, strengths, and weaknesses, but there is no present scientific basis for any value judgment of a superior sex. Idealization of either parent or either sex, their capacities, functions, or organs is irrational.

Psychoanalytic concepts such as masochism or penis envy should not be invoked or utilized in a simplistic reductionism.

Penis awe, penis envy, and the unconscious depreciation of the female are vastly overdetermined. Penis envy is not a simple biological force or id wish, but a developmental concept related to object relations and identifications. It should not be used as an explanatory platitude isolated from ego considerations, e.g., of the meaning of the penis and of envy, and from earlier preoedipal and narcissistic conflicts. Narcissistic injury and envy may be expressed in terms of phallic narcissism and oedipal disappointment and jealousy. Penis envy is not only a primary development but may also be defensive, and reactive, as noted in the past (Chasseguet-Smirgel, 1970; Horney, 1924). Intractable penis envy may derive from and defend against envy of the preoedipal and oedipal mother. Penis envy is also found in boys and may be discerned in the boy's envy of the larger penetrating and impregnating paternal phallus.

It is necessary to theoretically distinguish between penis envy as a dynamic issue and as a developmental influence. Though very important and ubiquitous, penis envy can no longer be regarded, if it ever was, as the major organizer of femininity. Instead, penis envy might be regarded as the developmental organizer of female masculinity. To derive femininity mainly from penis envy would be developmental distortion and reductionism (although penis envy contributes to feminine character). A feminine identity and self-representation has other important roots. Penis envy may indirectly and adaptively foster a heterosexual feminine orientation, but penis envy is commonly an impediment to femininity.

The feminine superego, including the maternal ego ideal, directs and regulates later feminine trends and interests. Feminine identifications and the ego ideal are of transcendent importance for feminine personality organization.

The awe and admiration of the mother and the cultural expressions of feminine identification may be discerned in such diverse phenomena as initiation rites and *couvade*. The wish to possess, dominate, and control the mother may have become embodied in certain attitudes toward feminine development.

The early fantasy of the omnipotent mother (good and evil) and the dominating phallic mother was covered by the devalued image of the incompetent masochistic woman. This can also be viewed as a reversal of the childhood domination and discipline by the mother, the child's first teacher, and the domination by female teachers during the early years of school. In both sexes, repudiated infantile fears of dependency and symbiosis are additional unconscious factors in the devaluation of women. The circular relationship between unconscious fantasies and sociocultural institutions and interests is related to cultal myths about men and women.

There is no evidence that the human female has a greater endowment to derive pleasure from pain or a lesser capacity for neutralization and secondary autonomy. Masochism is not identical with being passive or receptive, and while it is possible that the human female is more predisposed toward masochism than the male, there are ample, if not necessarily equal, sado-masochistic trends in both sexes. The female's earliest identifications and object relations are of crucial importance for her later sexual identity, feminine role, and maternal attitudes. Not masochism, but a mature maternal ego ideal is indispensable for "good-enough mothering." Masochism invites sadism and suffering, impedes maternal care and empathy, and distorts object love. Sadomasochism is universal in humanity, but I would not regard masochism as an essential or organizing attribute of mature femininity. Hypotheses in which femininity was secondary (to masculinity) in derivation and function were allied to a masochistic developmental model. These antiquated formulations were based on limited analytic data, constructions, and developmental knowledge. The repudiation of femininity is not biological or psychological bedrock, and normal femininity has its own primary developmental lines with its own valued and gratifying features. In both sexes bisexuality not only produces conflicts but contributes to personality organization, and personality harmony requires the integration of bisexual trends. The female superego contributes to this harmonious integration with dominant femininity regulated and supported by injunctions and admonitions, values and ideals.

Summary

Psychoanalytic advances have led to refinement and reformulation of early models of female personality development. Masochism was taken as a point of departure for a study of the psychology of women and earlier hypotheses of a masochistic and inferior female psychic structure. Masochism is a residue of unresolved infantile conflict and is neither essentially feminine nor a valuable component of mature female function and character. Though the female might be more predisposed to masochism, there is no evidence of particular female pleasure in pain. It is important to distinguish between masochistic suffering as a goal in itself, and tolerance for a discomfort or deprivation in the service of the ego or ego ideal.

Initial hypotheses of a diminished female libido, ego tendencies toward arrest and rigidity, relative inability to sublimate, and a deficient superego are imcomplete and obsolete theoretical propositions. The female ego and superego are different from but not inferior to the male.

Female development cannot be described in a simple reductionism and overgeneralization. Femininity cannot be predominantly derived from a primary masculinity, disappointed maleness, masochistic resignation to fantasied inferiority, or compensation for fantasied castration and narcissistic injury. Castration reactions and penis envy contribute to feminine character, but penis envy is not the major determinant of femininity. Penis envy variously impedes and fosters femininity but penis envy is more closely related to the girl's bisexual masculinity.

The female Oedipus complex is central to feminine development, but has significant normative roots in primary and positive feminine identifications and individuation. Contemporary contributions to the psychology of women have emphasized concepts of gender and sexual identity, body image and self-representation, psychosexual response and empathic motherliness, etc. The female superego includes an ego ideal with feminine ideals and values and regulates feminine interests. The maternal ego ideal consolidates overdetermined maternal attitudes, guides the formation and integration of maternal attitudes, and directs the developmental achievement of "the ordinary devoted mother." Conflicts between the maternal ego ideal and infanticidal impulses are ubiquitous and clinically significant.

Current theoretical amendments conceptualize mature female autonomy, pride, and self-esteem. Female creativity may be exemplified in many and new forms in addition to motherhood. The capacity to sublimate and to foster sublimation in children is a prerequisite for normal motherhood. Femininity evolves under the influence of parents and culture, with unique developmental challenges and transformations, and a universal psychobiological core linked to functions and roles that should be neither idealized nor devalued.

REFERENCES*

Barnett, M. (1968), "I can't" versus "he won't": Further considerations of the psychical consequences of the anatomic and physiological differences between the sexes. *This Journal*, 16:588-600.

Benedek, T. (1963), An investigation of the sexual cycle in women: methodologic considerations. *Arch. Gen. Psychiat.*, 8:311-322.

———— (1970), Motherhood and nurturing. In: *Parenthood: Its Psychology and Psychopathology*, ed. E. Anthony & T. Benedek. Boston: Little, Brown, pp. 153-166.

———— & Rubenstein, B. B. (1939), The correlations between ovarian activity psychodynamic process. In: *Psychoanalytic Investigations*. New York: Quandrangle, 1973, pp. 129-223.

Bonaparte, M. (1953), *Female Sexuality*. New York: International Universities Press.

Brenner, C. (1959), The masochistic character: genesis and treatment. *This Journal*, 7:197-226.

* All references to *This Journal* are to the *Journal of the American Psychoanalytic Association*.

Chasseguet-Smirgel, J., ed. (1970), *Female Sexuality*. Ann Arbor: The University of Michigan Press.

Clower, V. (1975), Significance of masturbation in female sexual development and function. In: *Masturbation: From Infancy to Senescence*, ed. I. Marcus & J. Francis. New York: International Universities Press, pp. 107-143.

———— (1976), Theoretical implications in current views of masturbation in latency girls. *This Volume*, 24(5):109-125.

Deutsch, H. (1944, 1945), *The Psychology of Women*, Vols. I, II. New York: Grune & Stratton.

Erikson, E. (1964), Womanhood and the inner space. In: *Identity, Youth and Crisis*. New York: Norton, 1968, pp. 261-294.

Fliegel, Z. (1973), Feminine psychosexual development in Freudian theory: A historical reconstruction. *Psychoanal. Quart.*, 42:364-384.

Fraiberg, S. (1972), Some characteristics of genital arousal and discharge in latency girls. *The Psychoanalytic Study of the Child*, 27:439-475. New York: Quandrangle Books.

Freud, S. (1905), Three essays on the theory of sexuality. *Standard Edition*, 7:125-243. London: Hogarth Press, 1953.

———— (1908), "Civilized" sexual ethics and modern nervous sick. *Standard Edition*, 9:179-204. London: Hogarth Press, 1959.

———— (1913), Totem and taboo. *Standard Edition*, 13:1-161. London: Hogarth Press, 1955.

———— (1919), A child is being beaten. *Standard Edition*, 17:177-204. London: Hogarth Press, 1955.

———— (1923), The ego and the id. *Standard Edition*, 19:3-66. London: Hogarth Press, 1961.

———— (1924a), The economic problem of masochism. *Standard Edition*, 19:157-170. London: Hogarth Press, 1961.

———— (1924b), The dissolution of the Oedipus Complex. *Standard Edition*, 19:173-179. London: Hogarth Press, 1961.

———— (1925), Some psychical consequences of the anatomical distinction between the sexes. *Standard Edition*, 19:243-258. London: Hogarth Press, 1961.

———— (1926), The question of lay analysis. *Standard Edition*, 20:179-258. London: Hogarth Press, 1959.

———— (1930), Civilization and its discontents. *Standard Edition*, 21:59-145. London: Hogarth Press, 1961.

———— (1931), Female sexuality. *Standard Edition*, 21:223-243. London: Hogarth Press, 1961.

———— (1933), Femininity. *Standard Edition*, 22:112-185. London: Hogarth Press, 1964.

———— (1937), Analysis terminable and interminable. *Standard Edition*. 23:216-254. London: Hogarth Press, 1964.

Galenson, E., & Roiphe, H. (1976), Some suggested revisions concerning early female development. *This Journal*, 24(5):29-57.

Gardiner, M. (1955), Feminine masochism and passivity. *Bull. Phila. Assn. Psychoanal.*, 5:74-59.

Greenacre, P. (1948), Anatomical structure and superego development. In: *Trauma, Growth, and Personality*. New York: International Universities Press, 1969, pp. 149-164.

_____ (1960), Woman as artist. In: *Emotional Growth*. New York: International Universities Press, 1971, pp. 575-591.

Horner, M. (1972), Toward an understanding of achievement-related conflicts in women. *J. Social Issues,* 28:157-175.

Horney, K. (1924), On the genesis of the castration complex in women. In: *Feminine Psychology*, ed. H. Kelman. New York: Norton, pp. 37-53.

_____ (1935), The problem of feminine masochism. In: *Feminine Psychology*, ed. H. Kalman. New York: Norton, 1967, pp. 214-233.

Jacobson, E. (1937), Wege der weiblichen Über-Ich-Bildung. *Internat. Zeitschr. Psychoanal.*, 23:402-412.

_____ (1964), *The Self and the Object World*. New York: International Universities Press.

Jones, E. (1935), Early female sexuality. *Internat. J. Psycho-Anal.,* 16:263-273.

_____ (1955), *The Life and Work of Sigmund Freud*, Vol. II. New York: Basic Books.

Keiser, S. (1956), Female sexuality. *This Journal,* 4:563-574.

Kestenberg, J. (1968), Outside and inside, male and female. *This Journal,* 16:457-520.

Kleeman, J. (1975), Genital self-stimulation in infant and toddler girls. In: *Masturbation: From Infancy to Senescence*, ed. I. Marcus & J. Francis. New York: International Universities Press, pp. 77-106.

Kohut, H. (1959), Introspection, empathy, and psychoanalysis. *This Journal,* 7:459-483.

Mahler, M. (1974), Symbiosis and individuation: the psychological birth of the human infant. *The Psychoanalytic Study of the Child,* 29:89-106. New Haven: Yale University Press.

Moore, B. (1968), Psychoanalytic reflections on the implications of recent physiological studies of female orgasm. *This Journal,* 16:569-587.

Murphy, L. (1962), *The Widening World of Childhood*. New York: Basic Books.

Muslin, H. (1972), The superego in women. In: *Moral Values and the Superego Concept in Psychoanalysis*, ed. S. Post. New York: International Universities Press, pp. 101-125.

Panel (1956), The Problem of Masochism in the Theory and Technique of Psychoanalysis, M. Stein, reporter. *This Journal,* 4:526-538.

Panel (1970), The Development of the Child's Sense of His Sexual Identity, V. L. Clower, reporter. *This Journal,* 18:165-176.

Person, E. (1974), Some new observations on the origins of femininity. In: *Women and Analysis,* ed. J. Strouse. New York: Grossman, 1974, pp. 250-261.

Schafer, R. (1974), Problems in Freud's psychology of women. *This Journal,* 22:459-485.

Stoller, R. (1968), The sense of femaleness. *Psychoanal. Quart.*, 37:42-55.

_____ (1976), Primary femininity. *This Volume,* 25(4):59-78.

Thompson, C. (1942), Cultural pressures in the psychology of women. *Psychiat.,* 4:331-339.

23 The Hemlocks
Roslyn Estates, New York 11576

PENIS ENVY:
FROM CHILDHOOD
WISH TO
DEVELOPMENTAL
METAPHOR

WILLIAM I. GROSSMAN, M.D.
and WALTER A. STEWART, M.D.

NONE OF FREUD'S THEORIES of female sexuality and psychology has been subject to more severe criticism than
his concept of penis envy. The persisting controversy over this
issues suggests that the basic theoretical questions have not yet
been clarified. And because the theory lacks clarity, its clinical
application does not always produce the results expected. Our
presentation centers on two such instances, offering clinical
vignettes wherein problems in the interpretation of penis envy
are demonstrated.

Both patients were in second analyses. In both first
analyses, because the patients expressed envy of men and an
inability to accept femininity, both analysts interpreted the
unconscious penis envy to their patients. Both patients
accepted the interpretation with apparent conviction, yet the
analyses became stalemated. Freud's (1937) famous dictum
that, ". . . with the wish for a penis and the masculine protest
we have penetrated through all the psychological strata and
have reached bedrock, and thus our activities are at an end"
(p. 252) seemed at first to have been vindicated.

Neither of the second analyses, however, confirmed this
view. In the second analyses of both patients it became clear
that the central conflicts involved a sense of identity,

193

narcissistic sensitivity, and problems of aggression. These conflicts were expressed in terms of a general envy, a sense of worthlessness, inadequacy, damage, and deprivation. The patients apparently easily accepted the reductionism of the interpretation of penis envy in the first analyses primarily because it fitted into their own tendency toward this type of understanding. They regularly explained any unhappiness they experienced as due to some unfair deprivation. This led, of course, to a constant state of envy. The inexact interpretation (Glover, 1931) — or at least the incomplete interpretation — of their penis envy reinforced their sense of being defective and deprived and increased their sense of injustice.

As we hope to show in our clinical examples, *the interpretation had an organizing effect, but not a therapeutic one*. The interpretation, in our view, functioned like a delusion: it brought order into what was otherwise a type of "free-floating envy" or a ready tendency to become envious. The idea of a wish for a missing and unobtainable organ provided a concrete and understandable explanation for dissatisfaction.

Case Presentations

The first patient, Mrs. A., diagnostically a narcissistic character, began her first analysis when she was 21 years old, shortly after she had graduated from college. In the last few months of her college career she had developed an obsessional concern with the meaning of words. This symptom, plus an intense shyness and depression, led to her treatment. She was the first child, four years older than her sister. She described her father as a shy man, successful in business and impatient with and critical of women. He was undemonstrative and objected to being touched. He patronized women and disliked what he considered their hyperemotionality. He was a chronic tease. The patient wanted to impress him and often entered into long aimless arguments with him, which ended in her feeling defeated and running away in tears. Her mother was preoccupied with appearances and hid her anxiety under an aggressive, dominating façade. Insensitive to the feelings of others and often given to sudden enthusiasms for various life styles, she was self-indulgent and was indulged by her husband. Both drank considerably, and dinner often ended in angry recriminations.

The mother constantly criticized the patient for her shyness, her poor posture, and general awkwardness. The mother found these faults particularly irritating because she set such high value on popularity and social success. She liked to recall her social life abroad and recount the number of proposals she had had. Neither the father nor the mother felt there was any reason for a woman to acquire an education; they had no intellectual interests and never had any open discussions about ideas.

The avenue toward a successful feminine development was partly closed by the patient's feeling she couldn't compete with her mother. The mother's craving to be indulged and her self-indulgences meant she wanted to have and had all the advantages of being fed and catered to that belong to babyhood.

Little is known about the first analysis except that the analyst felt that the patient's penis envy was the central issue. In fact, it became so central an obsessional preoccupation that the patient seriously considered going to Denmark for a transsexual operation in which she expected the transplant of a penis could be accomplished. This bizarre response notwithstanding, the patient appeared to have benefited from the first analysis. For the first time in her life she was seeing a man her parents found acceptable. Partly to gain their further approval, she impulsively decided to marry him. Because of this decision and with some satisfaction with the apparent improvement, the analyst decided to terminate the analysis— a decision the patient accepted. The analyst later mentioned to one of us that he felt pleased that the analysis had led the patient to give up her Bohemian ways and to marry a respectable man of her own class.

After the marriage, the patient adopted the role of the upper middle-class "devoted wife and mother with healthy outside interests." This role-playing did not prevent her from becoming progressively more depressed and dissatisfied. She returned to analysis for short periods of time over the next ten years. Her dissatisfaction finally reached such a pitch, she wanted to separate from her husband. She felt he was totally self-absorbed and that their sexual life was an empty ritual. She decided to re-enter analysis, and, because her first analyst was not available, he referred her to one of us.

In the first few sessions she complained that her husband dominated all social gatherings so that by comparison she felt totally unimportant and neglected. He became an overnight expert on a wide variety of subjects, particularly any in which she showed an interest.

In retrospect, she felt the marriage had been a mistake, that she had married because her analyst seemed to approve. She recalled that soon after the termination she felt a sense of surprise and anger that the relationship with the analyst had ended. It seemed that in her mind the marriage was meant to make her more acceptable to the analyst; that he would continue to see her, protect her, and recognize her true but hidden values. Later she came to feel that she had too readily and indiscriminately accepted the interpretation that she wanted a penis.

Mrs. A. was a shy woman who spoke in clichés. She tended to see all issues in black or white, and as having cosmic implications which were not clear to her. Similarity implied an identity, and difference of tastes, opinions, or interests implied a total misfit. Because she disliked a picture in the analyst's waiting room, she felt she and her analyst were so different and incompatible that he would never understand her or be able to analyze her. She saw herself as a radical and a feminist and felt her difficulties stemmed primarily from the social discrimination against women. She saw the analyst as an uncritical disciple of Freud's who would only see her social protests as penis envy and would attempt to influence her to return to the kitchen and find fulfillment in submission to a man. She felt that, if she agreed to anything the analyst said, she would have to agree to everything.

It became apparent that she had taken the interpretation of her "penis envy" in the first analysis simply as the "proof" of her worthlessness. She had not seen it as an interpretation, but rather as an accusation and a confirmation of her worst fears that she was in fact hopeless and worthless. To the extent that she admired any quality in a man, she became depressed and felt despair. The only solution she could envisage was that she should admit and accept her degraded state.

Her emotional responses were positive and negative extremes. Her affection became infatuation, her admiration, idealization. In the analysis, her sense of worthlessness and her need for love and admiration were central issues. She was rivalrous with and envied both men and women.

The admiration-rivalry conflict reminded her of her feelings for a male cousin who lived with the family when she was in her early teens. She loved and admired him and was impressed by the fact that he could go to the village and date girls there. She looked up to him, but felt he could never be interested in her. She felt awkward, shy, and inarticulate in his presence. This awe of men was still present when she entered the second analysis. She admired men "who could travel to Chicago on business." The patient's awe of men and her sense of relative worthlessness led to the analysis of her masochistic trends, which took the form of spanking fantasies and fantasies of anal rape. The focus of her complaints about being a woman dealt more with the fear of humiliation and ridicule than with the sense of castration—that is, anal and masochistic features were the most prominent. Since admiration always led to rivalry and envy, and sexual interest to aggression, the only permanent tie to the object was of a sado-masochistic nature. She chose the masochistic role and the defense of a mild paranoid attitude. Indeed, the "helpless acceptance" of the penis envy interpretation in the first analysis seemed masochistically gratifying.

Even to interpret her masochism posed the threat that the interpretation would be experienced as a "put down" and gratify her masochistic impulse; all interpretations, if not narcissistically gratifying, gratified masochistic wishes. They were felt as attacks in which her worthlessness, her defectiveness, and her aggression were unmasked. The analysis threatened to become interminable, one in which the relationship to the analyst was maintained, but only at the price of an analytic stalemate.

Over many years the patient was able to recognize her need to be a mistreated little girl, rather than to face her disappointments as a grown woman. The emphasis on the male-female dichotomy gradually lessened and focused more on the problem of her status. As she increasingly experienced the positive values in being a woman rather than a victimized child, she became less clinging, more outgoing, and her sense of humor increased. The sadistic impulses behind the masochistic submission have become clear to the patient. Finally, interpretations were experienced as illuminating and helpful. The case is now in a terminable phase.

In summary, the issue of wanting a penis never came up in that form. Rather, the conflict appeared more widely narcissistic in terms involving the patient's importance and value, although it was expressed chiefly in terms of the disadvantages of being a woman. When, in the first analysis, an interpretation of her penis envy was offered, she took the interpretation quite literally and concretistically, as shown by her plan to go to Denmark for a transsexual operation. Her envy of men was only one aspect of an envy that dominated her life. Her complaints were that in all situations she had been cheated. Her sister got her mother's breast. Her mother had the baby, was loved and indulged by the father, and had everyone's love and admiration, even the patient's. Mrs. A. felt doomed to be the one who has nothing, and has no claim to love or fame.

She could not do what many of our patients can do: see the emotions and experiences that lie behind this way of expressing their conflicts. *As analysts we may also on occasion have similar difficulties in knowing how concretely the metaphors of development are to be understood.*

Our second case, Mrs. B., a 28-year-old married secretary, had begun her analysis with a woman analyst. She stated, with seeming unconcern, that she was homosexual and alcoholic. She subsequently reported a doll phobia. She had been married for one and a half years when she confessed her homosexual interests and activities to her husband. He insisted she see the family physician, who referred her for analysis.

The patient was the oldest of three children and the only girl. Her brothers were two and a half and five years younger. The father was an angry, anxious man. The patient said that if he looked at a lovely view, the only thing that caught his attention would be the garbage dump. The mother was a flirtatious woman, the life of the party. She paid little attention to the patient except when the father was away, when she would take the patient into bed with her. The patient recalled lying in "spoon position" next to her, stiff with fear. Mrs. B. had had almost no direct contact with the father, all communications being routed through the mother. The father's father had been an improvident man with many get-rich-quick schemes. She recalled with a great sense of loss and guilt that he had taken her sledding, caught pneumonia, and died. She had felt she would be accused of murder. This grandfather had three children, the patient's father being the youngest. There were two older sisters, both of whom had been promiscuous, possibly prostitutes, and certainly alcoholic. The father held up his sisters as bad examples of what would happen to the patient if she ever did anything of which he disapproved.

During adolescence, she recalled "playing dead," for a long period of time and frightening her playmates. She also remembered cutting her wrists, which she claimed was in order to get attention, thinking it was the equivalent of the injuries boys got when they played football. She had always had the wish and expectation of becoming a priest, ignoring the fact that, at that time, this was not possible. She had consciously wished to be a boy because boys had greater freedom and companionship. Her dreams had a bizarre quality and were full of injuries and bleeding. In one dream she became radioactive and was therefore a threat to all who came near her. In another dream a young man had his tongue cut out.

The first analyst felt the patient was identified with men and that she was pretending to be a man. When asked if she really wanted to be a man, the patient replied, yes, she did, but then added, "Of course, not consciously." She felt her brothers were better off, being stronger, able to win medals and admiration. A dream stating that "All people should have medals that no one was stupid!", along with other material, convinced the first analyst that the patient resented being the "only one in the family who did not get a penis."

The first analyst interpreted the patient's penis envy to her. The patient quickly agreed that this was the issue and, in fact, the only reason for her coming into analysis. Since her wish could not be fulfilled, there was no point in her continuing the analysis. A sadomasochistic impasse developed in which the patient felt the analyst treated her as if she were a criminal. In response, the patient refused to listen to anything the analyst said or to tell her anything meaningful about herself. This was the situation after one year; in the face of this impasse, she was referred to one of us.

Mrs. B. was a short, stocky woman who looked younger than her stated age. She was obviously under great tension, which she handled by acting in a pseudotough manner. When asked about her feelings at suddenly being transferred to a new analyst, she said she felt it was "just in time," and that she was "lucky to get out alive." She "interpreted" this to mean that in her "unconscious she must be murderously angry," and then added, "but this is only one interpretation. . . there may be others."

It was apparent that in the first analysis Mrs. B. had experienced all interpretations, including the one of penis envy, as accusations and as an assault. During her second analysis she recalled that her younger brother by two and a half years, had had severe colic as a baby and had cried constantly. On one particular occasion, he was left to "cry it out" in the patient's room. She recalled being afraid of her wish to strangle him. When he finally stopped crying and fell asleep, she was afraid he was dead or, even more frightening, that he had crawled out of his crib and was snaking across the floor, creeping toward her with the intention of eating her up.

Her dreams and associations suggested that she was the illegitimate daughter of one of the father's sisters. This suspicion was confirmed, and then the fact of her extra ordinary early neglect emerged. Her biological mother, the more delinquent of the two sisters, had been totally incapable of taking care of her. The patient had been so severely neglected, she had to be hospitalized in a starved condition. She remained in a Catholic home between the ages of fourteen and eighteen months. In an eerie manner she recalled a number of experiences from this time, and one particularly traumatic event. She recalled an evening when a child in the crib next to her was crying inconsolably. She refused to stay down in the crib and had to be tied down. When the patient woke next morning, she saw that the girl in the crib had died, having suffocated in her own vomitus. This was the incident screened by the memory of the brother's crying and was the major contributing experience to her doll phobia.

The diagnostic category of borderline seemed quite clear when she reported that she bathed each evening because she might meet the analyst in her dreams. This type of thinking also illustrated the patient's inability to distinguish between the reality of an experience and its possible symbolic meaning. On one occasion, when at the beach with her nieces, she wanted to keep them warm by wrapping the terry cloth robe she was wearing around them. She felt she could not do this because it would signal her wish to be pregnant and she couldn't afford to let anyone know of this.

In the analysis, the central issue was the patient's fear of aggression. The pseudotough demeanor and the conscious wish to be a man were her defenses against her fear of the man's aggression. This in turn was based, of course, on the projection of her own aggressive and destructive impulses which she quite correctly felt she couldn't control. As a consequence she was constantly tense, frightened, and on guard. When her mother once asked about her analysis and if her analyst was handsome, the patient had a fantasy that the mother would storm into the analyst's office, break up the furniture, and either kill or seduce the analyst.

The patient's "wish to be a man" was in part a response to her father's feeling that most women were dirty and unable to exert any self-control. It was also an effort to overcome some envy of her brothers. Of much more significance was the role of the "penis envy" as a defense against castration. In regard to the man's phallic aggression, penis envy represented an identification with the aggressor. But the patient was afraid of impulses from all stages of psychosexual development. She was perhaps most afraid of being devoured and of her own cannibalistic impulses. These fears were based, of course, on the early neglect and frequent abandonment. The early neglect contributed to poor ego boundaries and poor self-object differentiation. The consequent projective identification is clear—in her fear of her brother's cannibalistic impulse, the aggressive sexuality of all men, and the firm belief that she was lucky to have "gotten away alive" from her first analyst. Her chronic panic was also illustrated by her fear of being close to or touched by her mother. One can say that she lived in a perpetual state of panic that she would be eaten, beaten, or penetrated. The fantasy of being radioactive, dangerous, and not to be touched was one defense. The other was to depersonalize. The alcoholism was a way of diminishing the panic, as was also the homosexuality, in which she took the male role, since men appeared to be less vulnerable.

The interpretation of the penis envy exploited a metaphor, which seemed to represent both her fears and her defense against them. It created a type of delusional formation that brought order into her thoughts. It is reminiscent of Schreber's (Freud, 1911) delusional system, which also involved homosexuality and self-transformation, and which was intended to act as a defense against aggression.

These two cases help to explain why a woman's "wish for a penis" or "envy of the penis," whether inferred and interpreted as an unconscious wish during analysis or stated openly by the patient, must be treated—like the manifest content of a dream or a screen memory as a mental product. It is not to be regarded as an ultimate, irreducible, and even genetically necessary truth, impenetrable to further analysis. This is most obviously true in patients who come for analysis having interpreted their own dissatisfactions as "penis-envy." It is particularly and more significantly true in patients such as ours, whose envy is conscious and where the narcissistic injury and fear of aggression are more central to the illness. In these cases, the "wish for a penis" is but one highly condensed representation of these critical concerns. We have been told of other cases in which the interpretation was made that what the patient "really wanted was a penis, a penis of her own," in which the envy of men hid a sense of deprivation, worthlessness, and fear of abandonment. These feelings and the experiences that led to them were the critical issue. The interpretation of penis envy, even when it referred to real experiences, reduced the multiple sources of dissatisfaction to a single cause. Whether intentionally or unintentionally, a clinical metaphor was thus created.

Discussion

For over 50 years the role of penis envy in feminine psychosexual development and in pathology has been questioned. For Freud, the discovery of the anatomical distinction between the sexes marked the real beginning, or more accurately, the nodal point, in the differences between male and female psychosexual development. He regarded libidinal development prior to this moment as essentially similar in boys and in girls and did not concern himself with other factors — for example, the effect on development of the different ways in which parents treat their sons and daughters. Freud may not have recognized the importance of these particular environmental determinants in psychosexual development or, more likely, he may have been primarily interested in reconstructing the *typical* ways in which the child's distorted understanding of reality influenced his development. In any event, he seems to have focused on the route by which object relations developed out of narcissism and how the succession of libidinal goals resulted from the transformation of instincts. He saw the little girl's observation of a penis as marking a turning point in her psychosexual development, observing that girls react to this discovery with a feeling of damage, deprivation, and envy. Their response is a narcissistic injury and an envy that is concerned with genital differences and often focuses on the penis. Freud felt the wish for a penis had to be transformed into a wish for a baby if normal feminine development was to be accomplished. More precisely, he stated that the wish for a penis added to the wish for a child, which originated in other sources (1917, 1933). The optimal solution to the penis-baby transformation, in Freud's view, was one of the *forces* that led to the change from the girl's preoedipal attachment to the mother to the oedipal attachment to the father.

Freud's formulation of the girl's development was based on a comparative approach to the development of both boys and girls. It seemed to highlight the ubiquitous factors common to both sexes (Freud, 1931), while sharply contrasting the differences entailed in the development of masculinity and femininity. Freud's examination of early female sexuality led him to emphasize certain aspects of the preoedipal period. He stressed the role of early dissappoint-ment, narcissistic injury, fixation, and penis envy in the development of women's psychosexual pathology. He thought that the failure to resolve in an optimal way the developmental challenges posed by penis envy would of necessity impair the change of object and the change of leading genital zone. Character disorders, neurosis, genital inhibition, and the rejection of femininity would almost inevitably be the result.

In contrast to these views was a series of papers by Horney which led to an apparently irreconcilable difference between the two. She (1967) acknowledged an early "narcissistic" penis envy, but discounted its importance in pathology. In her view, penis envy did not promote development, but was the result of the girl's disappointment in her naturally developing attachment to her father. Penis envy could help to repress the little girl's fears of penetration of the vagina by the large penis of the father. Horney's approach thus had the value of pointing to the need to clarify the origins of penis envy, its defensive function, and its role in early object relations.

We shall not pursue here the ramifications of this interesting controversy. The important point for clinical and theoretical understanding of penis envy is that we need to resolve the false antithesis generated by the apparent disagreement. "Penis envy" and the "denial of the vagina," "early narcissistic injury" and "disappointment in object relations," are different facets of the same issues of normal and pathological development. The overemphasis of one facet or the other promotes the tendency to reductionism in clinical interpretation, as occurred in the first analysis of each of the patients we presented.

Freud and Horney agreed that penis envy could occur during development on a narcissistic basis and as a result of oedipal disappointment. They differed with regard to which type was more important for pathology. The differing views can be reconciled with an epigenetic approach, an approach that enables us to recognize that the child's awareness of the genital differences is an important organizer of experiences at many levels of psychic differentiation and integration (Grossman, 1975).

We suggest that, of the two distinctly recognizable phases (see Greenacre, 1953), in the earlier phase, the awareness of the genital differences becomes meaningful in terms of the child's sense of her worth and in terms of her attempt to differentiate herself from her mother. Narcissistic needs and self-object differentiation are then the critical developmental issues (Galenson and Roiphe, 1976; Mahler, 1975; Mahler et al., 1975). In the later phase, the relationships to both parents as a function of the sexual difference is the important issue and leads to the familiar fantasies of the phallic stage and the oedipal period; conflicts having to do with object relations and drive impulses are central, along with the formation of the ego ideal and superego. Once the genital differences are discovered, and once penis envy appears, the latter becomes enmeshed in those relations that give it meaning. The working out of the oedipal relations will have an important influence in determining to what extent both conscious and unconscious penis envy come to stand as the representation of earlier and later conflicts.

Thus, to the child, the meaning of the discovery of the "anatomical distinction" will depend on a complex variety of preparatory experiences. The timing of this discovery will be important, since the child's cognitive and libidinal levels will naturally play a part in his interpretation of this new information. Narcissistic conflicts and the child's relations to both parents will determine the final result. Parental attitudes toward the sex of the child, toward their own genitals and sexual relationships, will aid or disrupt the child's integration of the awareness of the genital differences.

We think the awareness of the importance of these factors, which is forced upon us by the clinical examples we have presented, helps to resolve some current criticisms of the penis envy concept.

Finally, it follows from our discussion that, in the clinical setting, the emergence of "penis envy" must be treated as a manifest content, the significance of which will only emerge in the analysis. Narcissistically fixated patients, for example, when they confront the fact of the genital differences, will experience this awareness as a further narcissistic injury. To narcissistically oriented patients, "penislessness" can at any time in the psychosexual development become a prime example of deprivation, and they experience this in the same way as when they were eighteen months old. A severe disturbance in the narcissistic development will create a traumatic vulnerability to the discovery of the genital differences and to all experiences of deprivation. Thus, the primal scene, too, will be traumatic because, as another instance of stimulation without gratification or resolution, it is experienced as a narcissistic affront.

Clinically, the problem is to distinguish penis envy as it represents an attempted regressive solution to oedipal conflicts from penis envy as part of a general narcissistic character disorder. As in the cases we have presented, the penis envy is apt to be merely one means of representing the narcissistic injuries of all levels of development.

Whether penis envy is, in a particular instance, a contributing factor in the development of narcissistic character pathology, or whether it is a consequence of this pathology or otherwise implicated in it, the attendant ego disturbances present technical problems. We have observed other patients similar to those presented and have recognized certain factors making the analysis of "penis envy" difficult. Commonly found factors include global identifications and the associated fears of merging and abandonment, domination-submission conflicts, fear of overwhelming aggression, masochistic fantasies, primitive defenses, and extreme sensitivity to narcissistic injury. Patients with narcissistic character disorders also responded in a remarkably similar way to any interpretation of "penis envy" or their "wish for a penis" in particular. They seemed unable to distinguish fantasy, metaphor, or symbolic representation from reality. This is very clear in Mrs. B.'s fear of warming her nieces by wrapping them in the terry cloth bathrobe she was wearing—not permissable because it meant a wish to be pregnant. The original wish to warm the children was totally ignored because the symbolic meaning of the act became the only "reality."

The patients clearly did not respond to the interpretation of their "penis envy" in a way that was useful to them. They heard it as a final immutable truth. Although they readily agreed to the interpretation, it was with a feeling of despair—for it confirmed their worst fears of being worthless.

Is the problem of interpretation one of technique, in the sense that the interpretation was, for example, incorrect or poorly timed? Or is the stalemate that occurred in these cases due to a lack of clarity in our clinical theory?

We believe that the interpretation of the penis envy was correct in the sense that it described the patient's defensive effort toward the resolution of an inner conflict, and, yet, in some sense it must be incorrect, since it was not helpful (mutative) to the patient.

Perhaps the issue can be more clearly seen from another perspective. We wish to focus on the way theoretical constructs and developmental models are sometimes applied to clinical situations. Certainly, examples such as ours can serve only as illustrations. Furthermore, our understanding of these cases can be enriched if countertransference and other technical problems are considered as well. Still, there is a problem of the application to interpretation and reconstruction of theory and developmental understanding. The analyst's understanding of his patient is informed by psychoanalytic theory, especially conceptions of drive and defense and their role in development. We have a shorthand for describing patients' conflicts that we use in presenting cases, and penis envy is part of that shorthand. When we speak of penis envy we may be referring to a number of things simultaneously, including experiences, fantasies, wishes, derivatives, and so on. In this sense, then, the concept of penis envy may be said to be a metaphor belonging to the theory, since the concept derives its name from a specific experience. To classify clinical material under the heading of penis envy is to "interpret" the case, according to one way we use the word interpretation.

What about the patient's "wish for a penis"? It may be conscious from the start of treatment as an intellectualization. It may, as in the cases presented, be a conscious wish as the result of a prior analysis. In that instance, it needs to be analyzed, for it is a conscious mental content whose unconscious meaning must be understood.

We are suggesting that in these cases, the analysts lent the patients their theoretical metaphor and the patients accepted it. In these cases, too much that was important in the patient's conflicts was condensed under this heading. For them, the metaphor was an apt one in that it represented one of their desires and sources of dissatisfaction. However, the wish for a penis was not their own developmentally derived metaphor, their own unconscious shorthand for representing their childhood disappointments. Nor was the disappointment over the discovery of the genital difference the starting point of the derivatives later to be interpreted as penis envy. The misapplication of the theoretical metaphor to the clinical situation was a confusion of theory and clinical situation which reduced the patient's conflicts to the "bedrock" of a concretely apprehended metaphor. We believe that, in development as well, the wish for a penis may also become the unconscious concretely apprehended metaphor for childhood disappointments that are associated with the recognition of the genital difference.

The tendency to use theoretical formulations directly in clinical interpretations, in a sense, like a theoretical cliché, undoubtedly arises with the failure of clinical understanding. It is a misuse of theory that is common and to which theory easily lends itself. The analyst may then explain his lack of success as due to the fact that the interpretation involves the "bedrock" wish, or that there is faulty reality testing, a thought disorder, or other defect. Thus he explains the "immutability" of the wish.

The interpretation of the patient's wish for a penis is correct in that it makes conscious the metaphoric representation of the conflict. It offers a frame of reference from which the patient can look at the experience. It is incorrect as a clinical interpretation because it forces a theoretical impersonal form onto the material. It has only an organizing function; not a therapeutic one. This miscarriage of the purpose of an interpretation seems to have characterized the analytic approach in the first analyses of the patients presented.

Some patients, primarily those with neurotic conflicts, are not misled by the metaphor and will make the interpretation meaningful and therapeutic. These patients, quite unlike the category of patients our examples illustrate, generally resist the interpretation at first. Indeed, it takes hard and time-consuming analytic work to convince the neurotic patient that the unconscious fantasy of possessing a penis is derived from childhood, but is active as a determinant of her current life activities and the nature of her object relations. We think these clinical differences can be accounted for if the early narcissistic syndromes of penis envy are distinguished from the later object-related forms.

We believe this distinction rests on and also supports the theoretical formulations presented earlier in the paper. Finally, we hope the theoretical distinction helps in understanding why the early controversy concerning penis envy and the current criticisms of the concept have not been resolved.

Summary

Two phases of penis envy are considered. The first regularly occurs early in development and is registered as a narcissistic injury which can be resolved under optimal conditions and can contribute to female psychosexual development. If, however, it is not favorably resolved or, even more significantly, if the basic character disorder is of a narcissistic type, the awareness of the genital difference becomes one of many narcissistic traumas.

A later phase of penis envy usually represents a regressive effort to resolve oedipal conflicts. In the past, these two phase-oriented forms of penis envy have not been adequately distinguished.

Two clinical examples are presented in which the envy of men was only part of a tendency to envy in a narcissistic character disorder. In the analysis, the interpretation of the penis envy offered a metaphor around which all of the "free-floating" envy could coalesce. The cases illustrate the necessity to consider penis envy as the manifest content of a symptom that needs analysis, rather than as "bedrock" or ultimate conflict.

REFERENCES*

Freud, S. (1911), Psychoanalytic notes upon an autobiographical account of a case of paranoia. *Standard Edition,* 12:3-82. London: Hogarth Press, 1958.
_____ (1917), On transformations of instinct as exemplified in anal eroticism. *Standard Edition,* 17:126-133. London: Hogarth Press, 1955.
_____ (1931), Female sexuality. *Standard Edition,* 21:223-243. London: Hogarth Press, 1961.

* All references to *This Journal* are to the *Journal of the American Psychoanalytic Association.*

_____ (1933), Femininity. *Standard Edition,* 22:112-135. London: Hogarth Press, 1964.

_____ (1937), Analysis terminable and interminable. *Standard Edition,* 23:216-253. London: Hogarth Press, 1964.

Galenson, E. & Roiphe, H. (1976), Some suggested revisions concerning early female development. *This Journal,* 24(5):29-57.

Glover, E. (1931), The therapeutic effect of inexact interpretation; a contribution to the theory of suggestion. *Internat. J. Psycho-Anal.,* 12:397-411.

Greenacre, P. (1953), Penis awe and its relation to penis envy. In: *Drives, Affects, Behavior,* ed. R. M. Loewenstein. New York: International Universities Press, pp. 176-190.

Grossman, W. I. (1975), Discussion on "Freud and Female Sexuality." *Internat. J. Psycho-Anal.,* in press.

Horney, K. (1967), *Feminine Psychology,* ed. H. Kelman. New York: Norton.

Mahler, M. S. (1975), Discussion of "Some suggested revisions concerning early female development" by E. Galenson and H. Roiphe. Presented at the New York Psychoanalytic Society, 11 February 1975.

_____ , Pine, F. & Bergman, A. (1975), *The Psychological Birth of the Human Infant.* New York: Basic Books.

Montefiore Hospital and Medical Center
Department of Psychiatry
111 E. 210 St.
Bronx, N. Y. 10467

REGRESSION AND REINTEGRATION IN PREGNANCY

JUDITH S. KESTENBERG, M.D.

I N RECENT YEARS, PSYCHOANALYSTS HAVE BEEN CHALLENGED to revise Freud's concept of femininity and to construct a new one that would be based on standards of female rather than male development. Many authors have contributed significantly to our understanding of childhood precursors of feminine identity, especially those influenced by parental attitudes. However, there is a universal reluctance to search for an answer to the baffling question: *What are the endogenous sources of femininity and how do they manifest themselves in childhood?*

Few doubt that the oedipal yearning for the father is the childhood prototype of female heterosexuality. Clinicians confirm that the prevailing interest in the external genitals comes to a peak in the early phallic phase, is accompanied by penis envy and a desire to fill the role of the father in relation to the mother. No doubt, the high value placed on the phallus facilitates the feminine-oedipal wish to be penetrated and impregnated. But the idea that the girl's productive inside plays no role in her development other than to provide a receptacle for the penis, is not backed by clinical experience.

Anna Freud (1965) pointed to the confluence of matura-

Dr. Kesternberg is Director of Child Development Research, an organization which sponsors the S. L. Green Prenatal Project, conducted in the L. I. Jewish Medical Center, New Hyde Park, N. Y. and in the Center for Parents and Children, Port Washington, N. Y.

tional changes which express themselves in phases and relationships that structure and help unfold maturational advances. In the boy's development there is a peak phase which prepares him for manhood. The phallic phase confirms his phallic identity and enforces his identification with the father. Is it conceivable that in the epigenetic ground plan there is no phase in which maturation brings about development toward womanhood, based on inner genital wishes and interests? Such a phase must be one through which both sexes pass, a phase in which the not-yet-functioning reproductive organs are primed in both sexes and both sexes identify with the childbearing mother.

Some twenty years ago I described (1956a, 1956b) a preoedipal, maternal phase (later renamed "inner-genital") which I consider the cradle of maternality in both sexes. The phallic-oedipal phase that follows brings out phase-specific heterosexuality. Girls and boys vacillate between the negative and positive aspects of the Oedipus complex, but the oedipal triadic wishes to give or receive a child are new editions of the preoedipal, inner-genital urges to create and nurture a child in a dyadic relationship.

In previous papers I have described the childhood antecedents of pregnancy and parenthood. Here I shall attempt to pursue the genetic continuity between these antecedents in the inner-genital phases in childhood and adolescence and the vicissitudes of feminine development during pregnancy. I shall review the principal psychoanalytic theories about early and later wishes to have a child and the bearing they have upon the upheavals of pregnancy. I shall then recapitulate my own views about inner-genital phases and try to demonstrate that pregnancy is not generally experienced as a substitute for a missing penis. In my view, it is an adult inner-genital phase which revives problems from the two earlier inner-genital phases, one in early childhood and the other in early adolescence. I shall examine the phases of regression and progression or reintegration that are triggered by local and organismic changes in the expectant mother. Finally, I shall give some data in support of the thesis that pregenital regressions, which follow no detectable order during earlier inner-genital phases, during pregnancy tend to follow a sequence organized by the predominant psychosomatic constellation of successive trimesters. The result is a new organization which affirms the inner-genital position of the woman and reinforces her right to motherhood.

Pregnancy represents a culmination of wishes which began in childhood and fluctuated in intensity, to reappear in full force at the time when fulfillment was possible, that is, during the generative stage of adult development (Erikson, 1953). In the nine months of gestation, fantasies evolving from childhood and elaborated in adolescence become integrated with current representations and adult points of view. New sensations and moods accompany the progressive changes in the body that underlie the transformation of the body image of the pregnant woman. In regressing to earlier phases of child-expectation, each pregnant woman has a new chance to resolve the conflicts between herself and her mother who—in fulfillment of an old wish will no longer bear children while the young woman will become a mother, at last.

Review of Literature

In his early writings Freud showed a consistent interest in the symbolism of pregnancy in dreams (1900, pp. 400-401), symptoms (1905), impulses (1920), primary-process communication (1909b), and in acting out (1917). He discovered early that a child was unconsciously equated with feces (1909a) and with a genital, male or female (1900). Concurring with Rank (1912) that urinary and genital excitations or both give rise to water dreams, which express a pregnancy wish, he implied the equation of urine, semen, and the amniotic fluid. The wish to repeat the mother's experience during childbirth related not only to the birth of siblings but also to one's own rebirth (1900).

Freud stressed that both sexes had a "passionate desire" to bear a baby which repeats itself in transference (1920). Despite the abundance of data about the preoedipal and prephallic sources of the wish for a child in both sexes, Freud consistently assigned its derivation to an oedipal desire to be impregnated by the father and to receive a child in lieu of a penis (1933, 1940).

Deutsch (1924), collaborating unofficially with Freud, confirmed his belief that the vagina is not awakened until menarche and even then derives its qualities from other organs: its passive attitude from "oral, suckling activity" and its active components from its being identified with the penis. Only when it becomes a receptacle, not of a penis, but of a child, does ". . . the *vagina* . . . itself *represent* [*s*] *a child*" (p. 198, italics mine). By giving up the claim of the clitoris to represent a penis, woman establishes the maternal function of the vagina. Incorporating the father, she makes him into the child of her pregnancy. Coitus becomes a pleasurable act "owing to its role as a beginning of pregnancy." Despite her subordination of female sexuality to a motherhood based on the incorporation of the paternal phallus, despite her idea that the vagina rather than the uterus is a receptacle for the child, Deutsch discovered the role of the vagina as symbol of the child and transmitter of maternal feelings. However, she was not able to trace inner-genital impulses and their sublimation into maternality from their early beginnings (Kestenberg, 1956a, 1956b), and never could grant the girl a time when her body image developed independently from the father.

Deutsch's presentation of pregnancy phases has remained a psychoanalytic classic and source book (1944-1945). She divided pregnancy into two periods. In the first, she claimed, the heightened narcissism is maintained through great quantities of pregenital libido being drawn to the mother-child unit. In the second period, when quickening is felt, the hitherto pregenital relation to the child becomes phallic and the libido, once withdrawn from the primary object and transferred to the sexual partner, flows back as secondary narcissism. In the first period, the act of incorporation (fertilization) induces a regression, already evident in coitus. Vomiting represents the wish to expel the child and is then counteracted by anal retention. Because vomiting usually ceases after the first trimester, this view implies that orality is followed by anal regression in the second trimester. In the period after fetal movements have been felt, the ego ideal, modeled after the father, becomes embedded in the unborn child, who at the same time represents a "psychological neoplasm" as part of the punitive superego (1924, p. 203). Parturition repeats the birth trauma and becomes a masochistic orgy. This was confirmed by Bonaparte (1935, 1953) who looked upon all feminine functioning as masochistic. During lactation, the equation breast-penis compensates for the feeling of emptiness after parturition (Aleksandrowicz & Aleksandrowicz, 1973) and reverses the act of possession of the vagina by the penis. Thus, despite her great clinical acumen, Deutsch derived every successful and positive maternal function from the ever-present phallic prototype.

Freud acknowledged his debt to women analysts who helped him understand the 'pre-Oedipus phase' which, he said, lasted well into the third or fourth year in some girls (1931, p. 226). Collaborating with Freud, Brunswick (1940) traced the child-wish from an "asexual oral" source and from an anal passive desire to receive a baby from the mother. Transforming the passive into an active wish, the girl wants a penis so that she can give a baby to her mother. This active penis-wish transforms once more into a passive one when the oedipal girl wants to receive the father's penis to initiate impregnation and childbirth. There is a great deal of confusion between the negative oedipal phase of the girl (Lampl-de Groot, 1928) and Freud and Brunswick's preoedipal-phallic phase (1940), which was recently renamed "phallic-narcissistic" by Anna Freud (Edgcumbe and Burgner, 1975).

Freud spoke of the little girl's doll play—not as an

expression of her identification with her mother in the "pre-Oedipus phase"—but simply as turning from passivity to activity in the "undisturbed phallic phase" (1933, p. 128). This view seems especially significant, inasmuch as he consistently equated activity with masculinity and consistently looked upon maternal activity as masculine. Concurring with Freud and Andreas-Salomé (1916), Brunswick assumed that early vaginal sensitivity, reported by many authors[1] was of an anal origin (1940, p. 278). Femininity, with its various functions was said to be derived from pregenital or phallic wishes until it was legitimized as a genital-masochistic attitude by the maturation of reproductive organs and centers (Freud, 1924).

Greenacre (1950) showed in great detail how early vaginal sensations fused rectal and bladder tensions and could be mistaken for them. Reconstructing from adult analyses, she discovered that clitoric interest developed later and was often isolated from feelings in the vagina. I have looked upon the preoedipal phase which precedes the phallic, negative-oedipal constellation in the girl as an inner-genital, maternal phase (1956a, 1956b, 1966, 1967, 1968b, 1975, in press). Repeated in adolescence in a new edition, the inner-genital phases anticipate the adult developmental phases of women (Erikson, 1950; Benedek, 1959).[2] While the mother and later the father play the role of external organizers in the development of sex-specific identity, this function in adulthood is assumed by new love objects and by children of both sexes. Jackel (1966; in press) discovered that pregnancy wishes and actual impregnations occur as reactions to object-loss, which may be repeated in response to separations from the analyst. The study of these data reveals not only the various levels of restitution of the lost object in pregnancy, but also the importance of the external

---

[1] See Horney, 1926; Lampl-de Groot, 1928; Sachs, 1929; Muller, 1932; Brierley, 1936; Jacobson, 1937; Eissler, 1939; Greenacre, 1950; Kramer, 1954; Kestenberg, 1956a, 1956b, 1967, 1968a, 1975; Bradley, 1961; Barnett, 1966; Fraiberg, 1973.

[2] See pp. 222-227 below for a summary of my views.

love object's organizing function, which helps convert mourning for one's lost childhood into the creation of a new child (Kestenberg's discussion of Jackel's paper [in press]).

Discussion of Selected Data from Interviews and Observations

Interviewing expectant parents and cross-cultural information[3] brings into focus the universal conflict between the wish for the child's survival and the wish for his death during pregnancy. The husband's good will appears to be a frequent safeguard against the perils of sterility and infanticide. Klein et al. (1950) interviewed 27 primiparas and found that good marital relationships counteracted typical pregnancy fears. The proper initiation and completion of the fetus is felt to be dependent on the husband's repeated fertilization (Ferenczi, 1924; Mead, 1963) or nourishment given to the wife (Laurentin, 1963). Perhaps to gain protection against the destructive wishes of the husband or herself, the pregnant Bororo wife leaves her husband to stay with her parents for two years (Dupire, 1963). In Iran the husband may not kill any living being during the wife's pregnancy. Fears that the mother or envious women will take away the child are often transferred to the husband (see also Rumpelstilskin) where they may strike a responsive chord of pregnancy and child-envy.

Each culture provides its own safeguard against the temptation to hurt or kill the weakened parturient woman and her helpless baby. Each culture has its own failures in this respect. Perhaps the mechanization of sterile obstetric care, which deprives the modern woman of emotional support (Bibring, 1959; Bibring et al., 1961) represents a failure of an original safety measure. The success of brief treatment, administered by Bibring's team to pregnant women suffering from seemingly major disorders, may have been due to the therapist's

[3] I am indebted to Janet Amighi for the anthropological data and for a critical discussion of current attitudes toward pregnancy.

providing the protection and good will in lieu of parents, husbands, and obstetric attendants. Chertok et al. (1969), in an extensive study on maturational crises of pregnancy and delivery, found that preparation for delivery and the encouragement of husband participation (Lamaze, 1956; Friedman, 1975) made deliveries easier. Through emphasis on activity and self-reliance, the modern woman is frequently challenged to achieve rather than regress. This may hinder the optimal use of pregnancy regression. Modern authors who follow Deutsch (1944) recognize the adaptive aspect of pregnancy regression and regard pregnancy as an integrative crisis (Chertok et al., 1969; Racamier, 1950). No doubt, a balance between regression and integration must be tipped in favor of the latter to help woman face the adult tasks of childbearing and child care.

There is a prevailing trend now to study the manifestations of stress in three phases (trimesters) of pregnancy (Chertok et al., 1969; Jessner et al., 1970). Clinical examples indicate the predominance of certain conflicts in each trimester. For instance, Jessner et al. quote typical fears of early pregnancy months: ". . . she did not want to be devoured by a jackal—her image of a child" (p. 218). The joyful recognition of the fetal movement in the second trimester frequently gives rise to a new ambivalence, with the woman feeling that she is ". . . at the mercy of the unborn, [of] having no control over the growing creature within" (p. 222). Yet she is convinced that her actions have a profound influence over the fetus. Even though problems of domination and being dominated are generally recognized as anal-sadistic in nature, Chertok et al. (p. 31) describe the general tone of the second trimester as oral and suggest that it is the third trimester that brings out conflicts between retention and expulsion, derived from anal tendencies (see Deutsch's view referred to above). Chertok et al.'s interpretation of third-trimester stress may be due to their lack of distinction between different forms of holding and releasing) see description of urethral phase below). Jessner et al. are more specific in their descriptions of third-trimester concerns when they say: "Most women [at that time] experience the fetus as an enemy, who is injuring the kidneys or the womb" (p. 223). Time is of the essence and there is an increasing "impatience to get it over with" (p. 224). These conflicts appear more genital-urethral in nature than anal. Despite their emphasis on conflicts and fears during various phases of pregnancy and during delivery, all authors, with the possible exception of Rheingold (1964) concur that the revival of regressive conflicts should not obscure the undisputed fact that each step in the attainment of motherhood enriches the feminine ego (Erikson, 1964), with the increased narcissism becoming a ". . . store house for waves of tenderness that will radiate into the outer world" (Jessner et al., 1970). Benedek (1970) puts special emphasis on oral regression in pregnancy, but lists other common pregnancy fantasies, many of which are concerned with the content of the womb (p. 146). Although she goes too far afield postulating a special instinct for survival that underlies child wishes, she brings an order into modern thoughts on femininity by demonstrating that the "penis-in-the-womb" fantasy does not make pregnancy a substitute for a missing penis. It is used for "   the integration of the two phases of the female reproductive drive, the heterosexual drive and the tendency to receive and retain, i.e., conceive" (p. 147). No doubt, the inner-penis fantasy prepares the girl not only for conception but also for the acceptance of a male baby (Jacobson, 1937; Kestenberg, 1956a). However, Benedek does not make a link between the early and later child-expectations. Looking upon pregnancy as an extended luteal phase and less concerned with other physical changes, she cannot trace the antecedents of pregnancy feelings and wishes further than puberty. Neither does it become clear, in the many formulations of the integrating effect of pregnancy, how the massive regressions of this stress period facilitate the reorganization of the feminine ego into an adult maternal ego. We may begin to understand better how these processes evolve when we look back at the developmental line toward motherhood.

Preparation for Childbearing—From Childhood to Adulthood

There is a tacit understanding among modern students of development that psychoanalytic phases are not merely libidinal (Kestenberg, in press). To each phase belongs a dominant psychic organization, with the soma providing the internal and the caretakers the external organizers of a given developmental task (Kestenberg, 1967). This brief review will take both organizers of motherhood into account.

A girl is destined to travel a full cycle from sharing the placenta with the mother in a truly symbiotic union to creating a new one in adulthood. The newborn girl's large and succulent container and passage for a baby as well as her congested external genitals (Pratt's "genital crisis of the newborn," 1954) leave somatic imprints in the child and provide her caretakers with clues about her female gender. Mother and baby daughter probably can feel a sameness, born of similar rhythms of movement. This may make it harder for the girl baby to distinguish between the external space provided by the mother and her internal space, which conveys feelings of fullness and pleasure. Gradually the primal cavity (Spitz, 1955) extends deeper into the body, encompassing the sphere of the mouth, intestines, anus, and the pelvic organs, opening to the outside. Because of the special type of innervation of internal organs, localization is difficult and the child has to depend on sometimes vague kinesthetic cues to feel what is inside and how one functional organ-set differs from another. It is likely that inner-genital congestions play a special role in the development of the girl.

In the oral phase, the rhythms of incorporation and ejection, and of acceptance and rejection, merge with maternal rhythms of lactation and associated inner-genital waves of excitations. When they clash they aid differentiation between the child and the mother (Kestenberg, 1975). Emerging as a baby girl who feels a sense of belonging to the mother, the little girl begins to share and communicate. In the anal phase she develops a feeling of ownership which is firmly rooted in her newly won stability and feelings of possession. She feels what is inside herself and carries herself as well as external objects, which she holds and holds on to. She vies with her mother for domination, especially with regard to the accumulation and retention of things. Everything is hers. She wants her father's and brother's penis and, if her mother is pregnant, she relocates the baby into her own tummy. Her interest in babies intensifies her need to hold and to carry. She practices and learns to differentiate what is hers from what is her mother's, what she can keep from what she must return. In the urethral phase (Kestenberg et al., 1971; Mahler et al., 1975), the two-year-old becomes aware of the pressure of her bladder, and she tries to coordinate her mobility with a new way of retaining and releasing. She senses her fullness and feels how she lets go, which is different from the straining rhythm of holding and expelling feces. Her struggle for autonomy is different as well. She is now concerned with making time her own and gaining initiative. She drops people and things, ignoring and letting go when she wishes, and resumes where she left off in her own good time. She becomes increasingly interested in achievement rather than possessions. She values those who can direct their urine at will and can perform locomotor stunts. Thus, she wants a penis as a tool for control rather than an organ of pleasure. If her mother is pregnant, she expects the baby to come out with the urine, which prompts her to experiment with bladder control. Her play is becoming maternal-directive. She decides when to feed, bathe, and dress dolls—and herself as well.

Overlapping these tendencies, but more clearly observable at the age of three, the taking, holding, carrying, filling, and their counterparts, giving, ejecting, expelling, and letting go, become endowed with a new quality. All functions of the body become subordinated to inner-genital feelings which are not easy to localize or understand. There is a languid surrender to a sensuous welling up and radiating from inside outward and vice versa. The vying of regressive pregenital components with one another and with inner-genital tensions creates a disequilibrium between the progressive forces of growing up and the regressive pull to be a baby once more. The integrative task of the girl in the inner-genital phase is to establish a primacy of the generative feminine inside over the alimentary and excretory organs and functions. Inner-genital impulses give rise to fantasies. In a primary-process type of thinking, the girl creates a baby out of food, feces, urine, and all that can be used as raw material for generation and regeneration. Excited, full, feeling an elastic, expandable, enlarging, and contractile tissue within her, the girl feels the baby inside. When the feeling becomes more than she can cope with, she nags her mother. Regressively, she combines the nagging with an irritable demandingness, with vying for power, and with simultaneous refusal of and impatient asking for help. When the nagging feeling inside goes away, she feels nothing and becomes concerned with the fear that she had lost her baby. By externalizing inner-genital impulses, the three to four-year-old girl learns to sublimate sexual wishes into maternal fulfillment. Phallic wishes may appear in this still preoedipal period, but they are not dominant. Identification with the mother helps to establish the little girl as an intuitive and understanding "play-mother." The baby within her is created in the image of herself and the mother. Her mother and the mother's accessory—the father—shrink in fantasy while the girl expands and grows on the inside and on the outside. When she can no longer maintain the dual role of child and mother and has to acknowledge her childlessness, the little girl becomes angry and depressed. Her imaginary baby seems to die. The related conflicts and fears anticipate the feelings of pregnant women who doubt the reality of the baby and at the same time are afraid that the fetus was lost or died. Angry at the baby-hoarding mother and full of murderous impulses against the unreal baby inside of her, the little girl erects reaction formations which give rise to generous wishes to give mother a real baby.

The four-year-old girl's renunciation of her baby ushers in a denial of her creative inside and her entry into an active negative-oedipal, phallic phase. This subphase of the phallic phase is identical with what Edgcumbe and Burgner call "phallic narcissistic" (1975). Intense penis envy and identification with the oedipal father give rise to fantasies of growing a phallus that can be converted into a baby and presented to the mother as a gift. Feelings of being filled with a tremendous inner penis (Jacobson, 1937) help eradicate the inner cavity and permit no entry. They presage the fear that an enormous baby will rip the mother during delivery. Veering from negative to positive oedipal wishes, the child practices identification with both parents. The inner-genital, preoedipal identification with the mother fostered maternal behavior; during the positive oedipal development, the child identifies with her mother as a rival for the father's affection. This is the cradle of feminine heterosexuality (Lampl-de Groot, 1928). Penetration and impregnation by a highly valued penis is in the center of fantasies. Reopening the previously closed-up feminine inside, the girl makes her father responsible for the hole she has. Masochistic fantasies of being injured by him or the phallic baby, left inside, merge with wishes to be protected by him as successor to the preoedipal mother. The father's approval of the girl's productive inside, which he "creates" during the oedipal-phallic phase, helps her to postpone her pregnancy wishes in a benign transition into latency. However, recreating mother and father in children remains a powerful latent wish in the girl's life. The hoped for baby girl retains the quality of the preoedipal mother and the phallic baby son is a replica of the oedipal father or his substitute, a brother.

There is some evidence that small quantities of hormones play a role in childhood sexuality. A central inhibition of their release in greater quantities in latency parallels the massive repression of pregnancy wishes at that time (Kestenberg, 1967). An ongoing sublimation of inner-genital drives exerts an integrative influence on the formation of ideals of motherhood and ideal children, which become incorporated into the superego (Kestenberg and Robbins, 1975). With the breakdown of latency organization, the young adolescent girl is faced with a new edition of inner genitality. A massive regression to preoedipal, pregenital, and inner-genital trends, as well as a revival of negative and positive phallic-oedipal strivings, make it possible for the girl to reorganize these trends into her adolescent feminine genitality. Fertilization through overeating and masturbating is a typical prepuberty idea, which follows the general trend of displacing upward. Preoccupation with breasts may be due to orophallic distortions of pregnancy and lactation fantasies. Menstruation becomes associated with fecal masses or bloody urine, with castration, and with the loss of the generative inside. A renewal of the painful feeling of "losing the baby" generates resentment against the mother and the offending organ. A wish to actively expel or injure what is inside combines with masochistic fantasies of bleeding as a result of rape, becoming impregnated, and delivering a phallic product of an oedipal union. The integrative influence of menstruation and of more mature inner-genital sensations acts in unison with the integrative influence of parents and peers to bring order out of the chaos. The adolescent inner-genital phase ends with a reintegration in which the menstrual cycle becomes coordinated with ideas of impregnation, pregnancy, and delivery. These gain a meaningful representation via identification with the mother.

In later adolescence the increased progesterone production goes hand in hand with the appearance of uterine cramps and blood clots. This and other new phenomena make the girl aware of the inner genital as a dynamic center of the inner feminine space. The Oedipus complex is revived, and there is an increasing need to fantasize impregnation by the father. The ongoing transformation of sensuous into affectionate relationships facilitates the sublimation of masochistic fantasies. Pain becomes an aid for the sharpening of body boundaries, and feminine masochism becomes elevated into the capacity for tolerance of pain, self-sacrifice, and endurance (Kestenberg, 1961, 1966, 1968a). The reward of being loved as wife and mother with the approval of the pre-oedipal and oedipal mother becomes the core of the feminine superego. Its flexibility allows the young woman to react sensitively to changes in her body (later in the child's body) and to regress without losing sight of her role as organizer of progression.

Entering her first adult developmental phase (Erikson, 1959), the young woman seeks intimacy with a new permanent object and is not ready for a new triangular relationship. Once the.partners have become accustomed to the fact that they cannot be mother and father to each other, there is partial disillusionment and a renewal of the search for ideal closeness. Too much closeness breeds aggression, yet separation is not the solution. Planning a child, the young woman renews her position as a potential mother. By consenting to have a child, the husband reclaims the role of a masculine protector and can also sublimate his own wish to be a mother. For him, the seed that perpetuates his father and himself is no longer wasted. For the prospective mother, her inner genitals receive a confirmation and an enlargement of scope, comparable to that of the pregnant mother of her childhood. The conception-coitus revives oedipal feelings in both partners and allows for a reworking of the adult superego vis-à-vis the previously forbidden actions that lead to pregnancy. The new pregnancy is a common enterprise, but the woman's role in it is central, that is, she does the major share of work, with the husband assisting the organization of her new development.

Phases of Pregnancy

Research based on longitudinal studies, group discussions, and observations,[4] and on examples given in literature

[4] I am grateful to the parents of the Center for Parents and Children, 1972-1976, and to the doctors and nurses in the Long Island Jewish Medical Center who assisted our research group. My special thanks go to Mrs. Janowitz, the head nurse of the Neonatal Unit.

suggested to me that there was a considerable regression during pregnancy, with a tendency for oral conflicts to predominate in the first, anal in the second, and urethral in the third trimester. I had no data to support the view that the second part of pregnancy was experienced as a fulfillment of phallic-oedipal wishes. To examine regressive and progressive organizations during pregnancy from the psychoanalytic point of view, I read and classified eight psychoanalytic case histories before, during, and after pregnancy. Among these were one verbatim transcript, five complete week-by-week accounts, one in which the period of pregnancy and termination was summarized extensively, and one that did not extend beyond the first trimester.[5]

Methodology

Evaluating data from analyses conducted by other analysts posed many questions. In order to assemble a sufficient number of cases whose study would warrant generalization, I had to read and evaluate written reports by different analysts. By removing myself from the personal therapeutic experience, I could extract data about pregnancy which—for various reasons—could not be subject to scrutiny by the analyst. Most analysts did not link up the patients' associations and dreams with pregnancy changes unless the patients themselves brought them into sharp focus. Despite the fact that most analysts did not analyze defenses against and derivatives of urethral or inner-genital wishes, my own interpretations rarely contradicted theirs, but rather included them within a larger context of dominant themes. Some analysts chose not to interpret material about pregnancy in order not "to disturb the psychic equilibrium or the developing cathexis of the

[5] I am indebted to all analysts who made this material available to me. To preserve their patients' anonymity I must refrain from acknowledgements by name My special thanks go the the New York Psychoanalytic Institute and its Clinic Director, Dr. George E. Gross.

fetus." This was suggested to me by a thoughtful analyst who graciously put at my disposal the verbatim record of the case that will be described later in the paper. In this instance, I submitted to the analyst my own interpretations, asking for an evaluation of my views.

In order to assess the nature of pregnancy changes without mistaking them for individual predilections or for regressions due to analysis, I read and scored the entire history of each case. Systematic scoring made it quite apparent that typical changes occurred regularly during pregnancy, regardless of the nature of the patient's problems. Perusal of accounts from analyses of expectant fathers did not show the same or similar trends. In the majority of cases studied, patients referred to their pregnancy rather infrequently, but typical regressions were evident in the material, sometimes even before pregnancy progressed enough to be established by tests. To objectify these over-all findings, I took random two-week samples (excluding only those before and after vacations) from the beginning and/or end of treatment and from each pregnancy trimester and compared the respective qualities and rates of regression and the general themes emerging at those times (for an example of scoring see Table, p. 232). In all cases, current inner-genital experiences exerted a regressive pull toward earlier inner-genital modes of wishes, conflicts, fears, and defenses, but special circumstances would bring out one component more than another. A few examples will illustrate how individual variations influenced the course of typical pregenital regressions, which were embedded in the over-all inner-genital organization of pregnancy.

A hysterical patient who was generally preoccupied with orophallic oedipal fantasies became beset by oral problems in the first trimester. The latter continued to overshadow the now increasing anal conflicts way into the second trimester.

A compulsive patient had overt dreams about dirt in the second trimester. Moreover, her quest for domination in transference, her need for stability, and an increase in her reaction formations against soiling were dominant in the second trimester.

Defensive silence would appear in the third trimester as a method to ward off urethral wishes to "let go." Two patients who had been bedwetters in childhood could not tackle this problem until it became dominant in the third trimester. The relative overloading of my sample with enuretic patients might have skewed my findings. However, we must also keep in mind that individual predispositions were strengthened in those trimesters in which such trends usually increased.

Scoring and Evaluation

Guided by categories listed in Anna Freud's metapsychological assessment, especially the developmental lines of various activities and fantasies (1965) and by the scoring methods developed for movement profiles (Kestenberg, 1975), I classified the recorded sessions in accordance with their regressive features. Noting shifts and combinations, I evaluated the components as dominant, equivalent, or subordinated to others. The mode of regression was deduced from wishes, fantasies, and dreams; from ego attitudes, defenses, acting out; from typical fears, conflicts, and relationships that repeated the central challenge of earlier developmental phases. Progression was noted when a new organization emerged after a resolution and working through of regressive and new conflicts. Table I shows my method of scoring.

Findings

To put my findings into proper perspective one must keep in mind: the relative smallness of the sample, the newness of my scoring method, the fact that I was the only scorer, and the difficulty inherent in delimiting and quantifying data from analyses. For these and other reasons, the findings must be viewed as preliminary and subject to revision and reformulation.

As expected, there was a sequence of predominantly oral anal, and urethral regressions in the first, second, and third trimesters respectively. The unexpected finding is at considerable variance with the original proposition. The pregenital regressions do not seem to stem from pregenital phases directly, but from inner-genital phases, which are regularly initiated by regressions. All regressions were subordinated to inner genitality and organized by this progressive trend toward femininity. In contrast to pregenital regressions, phallic-oedipal regression seemed to predominate during impregnation and attempts to refertilize. Because most patients returned to analysis long after delivery and were then preoccupied with baby care, it was not possible in this sample to study the immediate impact of delivery on psychic functioning.

The over-all regression to inner-genital phases in childhood and/or adolescence promoted a type of regression that had occurred at those times. Current inner-genital drives facilitated a reintegration on a higher level and organized pregenital regressions in a sequential order quite unlike that encountered in earlier inner-genital phases. While the early regressions are diffuse or dictated by previous fixations, the specific inner-genital changes during pregnancy seemed to give direction to a sequentially organized progression which seemed relatively independent from previous findings. Phallic-oedipal fantasies were interwoven with others, but—except in special cases (see Table I)—did not seem to play a dominant role during pregnancy proper. At times, it was evident that thoughts about the oedipal father were used to disguise preoedipal yearnings for the mother and the baby.

The end of each trimester (approximately) brought on a special ego-gain which facilitated the acceptance of the fetus through incorporation, the maintenance of stable maternal attitudes through retention, and an anticipation of delivery via the mechanism of "letting go," in this order. The repetition of the past gave the pregnant women a new chance

TABLE I

SCORING OF RANDOM TWO-WEEK SAMPLES FROM BEGINNING OF TREATMENT AND FROM THREE PREGNANCY PHASES OF A PATIENT, DIAGNOSED AS OBSESSIVE

Components	Before pregnancy		First trimester		Second trimester		Third trimester	
		%		%		%		%
oral	o 7	20	12	32	3	14	1	4
anal	a 15	44	6	16	11	50	4	16
urethral	u 3	9	5	13	0	0	4	16
inner-genital	i 3	9	9	23	4	18	10	40
phallic	p 6	18	6	16	4	18	6	24
Combinations with inner-genital components	ia- 2	66	io- 5	36	io- 2	33	io- 2	18
	ip- 1	33	ia- 3	21	ia- 3	50	ia- 2	18
			iu- 3	21	ip- 1	17	iu- 3	28
			ip- 3	21			ip- 4	36

Combinations with phallic components	pa- 3 80 pi - 1 20	po- 3 30 pu- 2 20 pi - 3 30	pa- 3 80 pi - 1 20	po- 1 10 pa- 2 20 pu- 3 30 pi - 4 40
THEME	Conflict over dominance	Dependent — seeks support to accept baby	Withholds aggressively — stands up against mother to defend baby	Sees delivery as achievement — competes with doctors

The letters stand for the various components. Numbers indicate frequency of occurrence in two-week sample.

This scoring includes not only the libidinal components, but various other characteristics (such as aggression or defenses) of the developmental phase to which the patient was regressing at the time.

To appraise changes in the constellations of the three pregnancy phases one cannot confine oneself to simple comparisons of percentages. Special circumstances in the life of this particular patient increased phallic wishes in the third trimester. This would have obscured the substantial increase in urethrality had it not been revealed through a separate computation of pregenital components alone (before pregnancy: o 28%, a 60%, u 12%; first trimester: o 52%, a 26%, u 22%; second trimester: o 21%, a 79%, u 0; third trimester: o 18%, a 41%, u 41%). Another consideration is the influence of previously established fixations which, in this case, can be seen before pregnancy and in the second trimester (a 44% and 50% respectively).

to resolve their old conflicts with primary objects, especially the mother, and to prepare for the establishment of a new family in continuity with the old one.

The First Trimester. This is the period of transition in which nidation is accomplished, an embryo is created and transformed into a fetus. It seems that the pregnant woman reacts to the physiological inner-genital and systemic changes without knowing what they are. Thus, she relives the onset of earlier inner-genital phases, becoming confused by sensations and feelings she can neither locate clearly nor understand. Alterations in the oral and gastric mucosa may trigger off odd tastes, nausea, and cravings. Changes in the breast are likened to premenstrual swellings. These phenomena facilitate a shift upward,similar to that which initiates adolescence.

There is a gradual rise of estrogens and progesterone with the developing placenta taking over as the major source of their secretion.[6] Chorionic gonadotrophine, produced by the trophoblast (Guttmacher, 1960) is held responsible for the nausea of the first trimester. The trophoblast digests and liquifies uterine tissue with its "... cells not only burrow[ing] into the uterine lining and eat[ing] out a nest for the ovum," but also through "... quivering, finger-like projections ... extend[ing] greedily into the blood-filled spaces" (Eastman and Russel, 1970, p. 30).

Thus the placenta is formed as an organ of primary somatic communication between mother and fetus (Green, 1958).

The softening of the uterus and the venous engorgement of the vulva, vagina, and cervix in beginning pregnancy may evolve into sexual excitement. Because of its displacement upward, this theme may be overshadowed by nausea and fantasies of oral conception and ejection of the fetus.

---

[6] Data on physiology have been compiled from Burnett, 1969; Eastman and Russel, 1970; Fuchs and Klopper, 1971; Guttmacher, 1960; Ingelman-Sundberg, 1966; Lipkin, 1974.

Underneath is the conflict between the acceptance and rejection of the excited, generative inner-genital. The acceptance of the fetus as real hinges on the woman's feelings of having something worthwhile inside and not needing to suffer rejection because of it.

A patient, Mrs. Y., a bed wetter in childhood, was fixated in the phallic-oedipal phase, and had a propensity for oral dependence on the analyst. In the first trimester she complained that her mother and father did not care about her, but did not mention any physical symptoms when she said that it made her sick to her stomach thinking about her rejection. Looking at her father "regurgitated" her, especially when people told her that she had sexual feelings for him.

Mrs. Y. used the phrase "sick to the stomach" as a metaphor which expressed the wish to eject the feeling of being unwanted (= not cared for = not fed properly, making the oral cavity sour instead of sweet and being eaten instead of eating). It also expressed the wish to incorporate the father's penis. Above all, the father became the procreator while she remained the rejected baby. Within this context the father seemed to represent the patient's pregnant mother as well as the patient herself.

Throughout this phase, Mrs. Y. behaved like a girl in the inner-genital phase who can no longer cope with inner-genital tensions and gets angry at her nagging inside which, in the language of the unconscious, represents herself, the mother, the mother's baby and her own. Externalizing her impulses, projecting her aggression on the analyst, and shifting from below upward, she used oral representations to integrate conflicting anal and phallic ideas with the all-pervasive inner-genital drives and interests. Representing the analyst in a dream as a huge black bug ready to claw her, she condensed in this imagery the fetus with the vagina dentata, and the oedipal father with the phallicized, pregnant mother. Despite the invasion of many regressive components into her ideation, the oral-sadistic regression figured most prominently within the prevailing inner-genital orientation. Her total demeanor in transference pointed to her need to be a very little, dependent, and cared-for baby girl who was pregnant herself. She condensed her wishes to bite the phallus off with nagging in an argumentative manner, similar to that displayed by the dissatisfied three-year-old who regresses when frustrated.

Most striking was her need to be loved and accepted even though she was full of bad sexual feelings and pregnant. She felt like exploding from sexual, inner-genital tension, and she was sorry for the little girl in her who felt helpless. Her anger culminated in a wish to hurt her mother, which led her to become aware of sexual feelings.

Through repeated working through of fears and through trying various ways of resolving conflicts between accepting and rejecting her genital, the pregnant woman can also reconcile herself with her mother. After complaining about her mother's cruelty and rejection in a repetitious and nagging manner, the patient reminisced about her sister's delivery and became depressed. But soon she recalled an episode in her childhood in which she had touched a hot stove and burned herself. At that time her mother not only picked her up to comfort her but was very loving. In this touching screen-memory one could recognize the integrative influence of the mother who not only accepted her daughter's "hot" femininity but forgave her for touching herself. After a passing fear that she will burn her older child, the patient began to accept herself as the incubator that holds and comforts the lonely fetus inside. The identification with the loving preoedipal mother paved the way for hopes of acceptance by the father. She dreamed about refertilization as a mode of making herself acceptable to the two sides of the father: one engulfing, yet protecting, orophallic oedipal father and the other weak and in need of mothering himself, a preoedipal accessory to the mother. Repeating the reconciliation with her mother, she remembered how tender her father could be. By becoming both his baby and his mother, she could escape the sadistic attacks of oedipal men as well as her own perilous identification with the sadistic intruder, which forbode injury to the baby. Now she could regain trust in her husband, the real father of the baby who cared for her and their children.

The first trimester usually ends with the acceptance of the baby and a reaffirmation of the expectant mother's new identity. With nidation accomplished and the placenta established, the inner genital becomes the center of narcissistic enrichment and the husband can be drawn into the magic circle of the new dual existence as protector, as provider for and defender of the mother and the fetus.

Second Trimester. The expectant mother carries the fetus in a shockproof container, with a built-in temperature control, a metabolic vascular exchange system and a self-regulatory hormone production which guarantees the well-being of the child and the mother. She can no longer hide her pregnancy and can carry the baby proudly, acknowledging its autonomy, especially when she feels movement. As the fetus grows, stretches, and shifts positions, the pregnant woman readjusts her posture and her gait to achieve stability on the basis of a new balance. She can — in some measure — explore what the fetus is doing, and her radiant happiness is similar in many ways to that of the toddler who discovers the world and loves it. But her world is inside herself. She may not know it, but she feels how the uterus displaces her intestines to the side and upward, coming closer and closer to the intercostal rim.[7] She may mistake the first fetal movements for intestinal rumblings. Yet, in the center of her experience is not the belly, full of feces and gas, but an inner fulfillment, a filling and stretching of the inner space that affirms and expands on previous recognitions of having something stable, yet changeable and malleable inside.

----

[7] In the fifth month of her pregnancy, one very sensitive mother dreamed that she was carried upside down with her intestines moving in the direction of her chest. In the first trimester she had repeated dreams about food, and she initiated her second trimester by a dream about "making." (Data from the Center for Parents and Children.)

Anal-sadistic regressive trends seem to dominate this pregnancy phase and taint other pregenital and phallic components, but they are not usually direct descendants of their predecessors in the second year of life. They are rather new editions of regressions that occurred in the inner-genital phases of childhood and adolescence.[8] This becomes evident in dreams, fantasies, habits, in dealing with separation-individuation of the self and the fetus, and in the reintegration of relationships to the preoedipal mother and her accessory, the preoedipal father (Kestenberg, 1975). Being trapped in a house or enclosed in water is a typical pregnancy dream in which the dreamer identifies with the fetus and pictures the surround of his habitat. In the second trimester these themes combine with preoccupations with dirt, with scoptophilic wishes to look and reach inside the body and with anal-sadistic struggles with the mother, expressed in nagging and arguing. They are derivatives of similar exchanges of the three to four-year-old girl and of their revival in early adolescence.

In the fifth month of her pregnancy, Mrs. X. dreamed that she was trapped in a house, then was in water where someone tried to touch her. In another dream the water was slimy and dirty, and she became overwhelmed by a desire to beat a child. As she related this to the analyst she wanted to scream, and accused the analyst of being evil. She began to nag the analyst, asking him, in a not-too-well-disguised manner, to get inside of her and feel what is there. She recalled that she had seen her parents naked and blamed them in an argumentative way for letting her see things she should not have seen. Her need to get inside of herself to make sure that there was a real baby inside of her became evident in the next session. She reported that she saw a little girl on the street and it came to her mind with great clarity that the child was real. She was surprised by this

---

[8] As seen in Table I, an anal-sadistic fixation may make the inner-genital orientation in the second trimester less prominent, while the anal-sadistic regression predominates.

unexpected thought. From here on, the anal-sadistic regression became evident as it invaded the inner genital and phallic-oedipal masturbatory concerns and wishes. She reminisced about her parents and described how the father was "killing and dirtying" her mother. One would expect that she would now speak of anal impregnation and its result, an unreal fecal child. Instead, another feature of the early anal-sadistic phase came into the foreground. She experienced stranger anxiety in relation to the analyst—he became unreal to her. She asked: "What are you like? What do you want?" She was surveying the analyst as if he were a stranger, like the fetus. A few sessions later she dreamed about an image representing the fetus moving inside of her. At no point did she speak directly about experiencing the fetal movement, but she began to feel for her lonely baby and identified with the fetus. She wanted to get on someone's lap. Disappointed in the analyst who would not carry her, she turned to her husband for sympathy. Reassured and certain that he would protect her, she became more maternal and protective of herself as well. She assured the analyst that she would not let herself fall apart (a typical fear of both inner-genital phases). Then, in an effort to become stronger and less dependent, she reversed roles with the analyst and her mother.

She accused her mother of being weak and "crawling" while she, the patient, planned to stand up for herself as a "big, beautiful, and strong mother."[9] The next session she renewed her depreciation of herself. Her excited vagina felt dirty, and she had a new urge to put things into it. She complained naggingly that the analyst had taken her wonderful feelings away from her and had "thrown them against a wall." Here, she seemed to externalize the sensations of being thrown by the fetus or feeling that something in her is throwing the fetus against her abdominal wall. She acted as if she were tempor-

[9] Note the expressions "crawling," "standing up," borrowed from the experiences of the toddler, and followed by the reversals of the three-year-old girl who hopes to grow into motherhood at the expense of the mother who shrinks into a baby and changes places with the toddler.

arily out of balance and had to regain a new equilibrium to once more feel strong and steady.

In succeeding sessions the patient worked through her attempts to become a mother rather than a baby by looking at her father and the analyst as helpless people dependent on her for support. She began to feel compassion for her father whom —she thought—wanted to creep back into his mother's womb and be a baby himself. The fetus inside her has begun to take shape: in the image of herself as a helpless baby and her mother as well as father all reborn in her womb and formed into better people.

To become the tenderly cared-for and idealized baby, the fetus must be purged from associations with malevolent objects and the mother's transgressions or wishes which might soil and deform her inside, making it dirty and falling to pieces rather than an indestructible mother-child unit. The externalization of inner-genital feelings and projection of fears of self-destruction to parents must be worked through so that the parents can lose their malevolence in the external world and become idealized, protective grandparents to the child. For the process of transformation to become circular, with the inner genital (= baby) radiating good feelings toward parents, analyst, and husband so they in turn can approve of the baby and aid in its shaping, the fetus must become differentiated from discardable contents of the body. These are food, feces, urine, vaginal secretion, and the phallus that must be given up. In the second trimester they frequently become condensed under the heading of dirty excrements which change shape and fall into pieces to be flushed away. It is necessary to differentiate the forbidden touching of the anus and the genital from trying to look inside and looking at the baby. By looking inward kinesthetically and figuratively or through the wall by touching what is inside of her uterus, the pregnant woman forms an image of the baby as clean and whole and benign. She can now transfer a great deal of her narcissistic libido, which she had withdrawn from objects, to a new, albeit still internal object — the baby.

Third Trimester. The third trimester prepares the prospective mother for relinquishing of the cherished internal baby so that she can redirect her motherliness to an external, unattached child.

Estrogens, as they are needed for the activation of stronger uterus contractions and for the well-being of the fetus and the newborn, are now increasing. Pregnandiol excretion has been rising in the first and second trimester. At birth, however, the ratio between pregnandiol and estriol equalizes. The plasma testosterone, which rose early in pregnancy, rises again in the last month. Fetal movements are becoming more frequent, of longer duration, and fluttering in nature. They are often identical with urethral rhythms (Kestenberg, 1975). Urinary frequency is common, as is bladder pain, both probably due to the displacement of the bladder by the uterus.[10] Other organs, such as the vagina, may become painful, and some women complain that the fetus kicked them there. Former bed-wetters are embarrassed more than others, but most women at that time identify with the urinating fetus inside. Pleasure is mixed with anger. The fetus who grows rapidly and triples his weight in the last three months is becoming a burden, pulling the inside down, rather than a load to be carried. Waiting is a chore, but there is also a fear of losing control and losing the baby. Dissatisfied with her clumsiness and her mounting anger at the fetus, the woman in the third trimester becomes increasingly weary of expressing her feelings and ashamed of her wish to get rid of the baby. As in previous phases, many pregenital and phallic components come under the dominance of inner-genital interests. In some instances the phallic

[10] Urinary frequency (not pain) is frequent in early pregnancy as well. At that time it is usually a welcome sign of pregnancy and its significance is absorbed in the oral-genital organization prevalent at that time (see first trimester in Table I).

elements are more clearly attached to the now prevailing urethral inner-genital sphere of regression (see third trimester in Table I).

The revival of urethral regressions, typical for earlier inner-genital phases, combines with the anticipation of "breaking water," to give rise to a dread of premature delivery during urination. During the last months of pregnancy the fear of losing the baby and dying is strongest. Dripping of amniotic fluid may be mistaken for urine, and fear of drowning the baby is connected with the dread of a floodlike eruption of the amniotic fluid. The adolescent equation of milk, urine, and ejaculation is revived in association with current breast changes. These and similar fears and ideas may be obscured by long silences (Chertok et al., 1969), which represent a shift upward, with the closed mouth equated to the closed urethral sphincter. Defensive accounts of achievements and competition with men, which revive urethral penis envy, are as frequent as excessive interest in mobility and means of transportation. Riding over water in dreams signifies the exodus of the baby, who is pictured as walking or running out like a toddler. This is more prominent in analyses of former bed-wetters.

In the seventh month of her pregnancy, Mrs. Y. dreamed about a lot of activity. In all her dreams, people were moving and things were displaced all over. In one such dream she was going to the seashore, and, on reaching it, she thought that she had to work hard while others enjoyed themselves. Having to work alluded to her labor and her duties as a mother, with the analyst standing by idly and enjoying himself. This was followed by a repetitious nagging of the analyst and complaining that she could not express her feelings. Whether by insight or by intuition, the analyst told her that she was "blotting" them out (= drying them). The patient reacted by a fear that she would become wild if she let herself go. While worrying that she was crazy, she felt like "moving toward" the analyst. This led to an avalanche of genital feelings and oedipal fantasies. Projecting her self-depreciation upon the analyst, she accused him of looking down on her as a worthless "piddling" creature, but her desire to wet herself and her fear of incontinence did not reveal itself until the following session. She reported a dream in which she was bleeding from her wrists and hands, associating this imagery with forbidden sexual feelings. Then she denied having such feelings with a simplicity reminiscent of the regressed three-year-old child who can say "I do" and "I don't" without feeling a contradiction. When the analyst remarked: "You know you have them", she lapsed into silence. When asked to speak, she talked about her stomach, but soon began to laugh in an embarassed manner and confessed sheepishly that she had the desire to wet her pants right there and then. "Having to go" also released her inner-genital sensations. Ashamed of her babyish wishes, she projected her urethral-genital impulses upon the analyst whom she described as "squirming, giggling, and embarrassed" by what she said. First the patient and then the analyst became the squirming, wetting baby who was trying to get to the sea-shore.

In the following months the patient worked through her conflicts over wetting and drowning the baby. Toward the end of her pregnancy she became increasingly afraid of the delivery and dreamed about movement under water again. Preoccupied with vehicles pulling through clear water, with skating on clear ice, and with fishing, she made no connection to her fear of doctors who would be pulling the baby out and getting it to move out from her inside. However, she did fear their interventions on a conscious level. Dreading the separation from the analyst, she behaved like a little girl in her rapprochement phase (Mahler et al., 1975). Feeling abandoned and needing her mother, she thought about the time her mother had gone to the hospital to deliver a sibling. Identifying with her, she seemed to forgive her and understand. On leaving her analysis before delivery, she resolved to give up the fantasies which where important in analysis and turn to reality. Soberly, she remarked that her older child and her husband needed her. She became a good mother and wife before she could deserve a good delivery of a healthy new baby.

In the last months before delivery, women worry a great deal about prematurity, injury to the child, and the pain inflicted upon them. A great deal of this worry is expressed in terms of losing control, drowning the baby, and losing the inner genitals, which will fall out with the outpouring of blood. The underlying aggression has a chance to become transformed into the activity involved in delivery. In analysis, they seem to reorient themselves, directing their thoughts to the practical aspects of their life and away from looking inside and introspection. A new wave of identification with the mother, who gave birth to her daughter and to siblings, counteracts fear of death. A recognition of maternal interest in the new baby, which contrasts with previous denials and prohibitions of childbearing in childhood and adolescence, allows for a resolution of old conflicts and giving up of sadomasochistic fantasies related to delivery and baby care. In transference, a new ability to detach herself from the analyst goes hand in hand with the parturient woman's readiness to detach herself from the fetus. Becoming capable of letting go without loss of control, she is ready to terminate her pregnancy.

In the last weeks of pregnancy there is an anticipation of the three phases of stress during labor and delivery (Friedman, 1975). The impending separation from the fetus revives separation and stranger anxiety and evokes fears of the hospital. The second stress, which comes to a peak during the greatest stretching of the cervix, is anticipated in fears of being injured by the baby's movement. The third stress, most prominent during delivery proper, concerns the loss of the genital that would come out with the baby. Under optimal conditions of pregnancy, conflicts regarding inner genitality and procreation have been resolved, and a way has been paved for the joyful acceptance of parental responsibility. The aid of the husband makes the conquering of stresses into an adaptive, creative task for both parents. Under those circumstances, regression transforms into progression and both parents can experience the long period of child expectancy as an adult inner genital phase.

Summary and Discussion

A review of psychoanalytic literature reveals the still prevailing assumption that the wish for a child is derived either from pregenital or phallic drives. Generally, femininity does not seem to exist before puberty. The regression in pregnancy is looked upon as a revival of pregenital and phallic-oedipal wishes which serve procreation. There is a conspicuous lack of interest in or denial of the role of the inner genitals in early and later phases of child expectancy.

The present study of pregnancy phases is based on my previous classification of development toward parenthood (1956b, 1975). I postulated that an inner-genital phase follows the pregenital and precedes the phallic phases. Its beginning is marked by a massive regression to pregenital interests, which allows for a reintegration of these components with the now prevailing inner-genital orientation. There is a confluence between an intense identification with the preoedipal mother and an externalization of inner-genital impulses in maternal activities. Penis envy is marked in the phallic, negative-oedipal period, during which the girl identifies with the father. Positive-oedipal-phallic wishes promote an attachment to the father, an aggrandizement of his phallus, and a need to be penetrated and impregnated. The inner-genital phase is essentially maternal; the positive-oedipal-phallic phase is the cradle of feminine heterosexuality. Adolescence begins with a new edition of an inner-genital constellation during which regressive pregenital and phallic trends become subordinated to the new adolescent genitality. Triggered by physiological changes and supported by a lasting identification with the preoedipal and oedipal mother, a progressive acceptance of inner genitality forms the basis for the adolescent push toward adulthood.

For the present study, I read and classified psychoanalytic case histories of expectant parents. Type of regression was established on the basis of revivals of developmental tasks from an earlier phase. This developmental framework proved to be a verifiable and heuristically fruitful tool for the organization of data obtained from psychoanalyses.

On the basis of nonanalytic observations and examples from literature, I expected to find an oral regression in the first, an anal in the second, and a urethral regression in the third trimester of pregnancy. Instead, I found that the prevailing regression in pregnancy drew on earlier inner-genital phases in which pregenital regressions occurred. Their orderly sequence during pregnancy does not duplicate the manner in which regression occurs in childhood. It is most likely directed by the sequence of physiological changes to which pregnant women react with a special sensitivity. This constitutes an aid in the transformation of earlier forms of child expectancy into an adult form. During the nidation in the first trimester, oral incorporative trends reflect the attachment of the fetus to the mother. With the formation of the placenta, a true symbiotic state is established. During the time the pregnant woman carries the now securely attached fetus in the second trimester, anal retentive trends facilitate and aid the recognition of the fetus as a separate object, a host of the uterus.

During the preparation for giving up the fetus in the third trimester, urethral "letting-go" trends act as an aid for the anticipated conversion of the internal into an external object — the child.

A phallic-oedipal regression seems to be dominant during the initiation of pregnancy. No data had been obtained regarding the psychological meaning of delivery.

My over-all findings indicate that *pregnancy repeats and reorganizes all earlier forms of child-expectation. Far from being a pregenital or phallic state, it appears to be a new inner-genital phase in feminine development.*

REFERENCES*

Aleksandrowicz, M. & Aleksandrowicz, D. (1973), Obstetrical pain-relieving drugs as predictors of infant behavior variability. *Unpublished.*

Andreas Salomé, L. (1916), "Anal" and "sexual." *Imago,* 4:249-273.

Barnett, M. C. (1966), Vaginal awareness in the infancy and childhood of girls. *This Journal,* 14:129-141.

Benedek, T. (1959), Parenthood as a developmental phase. *This Journal,* 7: 389-417.

⸻ (1970), The psychology of pregnancy. In: *Parenthood,* ed. E. J. Anthony & T. Benedek. Boston: Little, Brown, pp. 137-152.

Bibring, G. L. (1959), Some considerations of the psychological process in pregnancy. *The Psychoanalytic Study of the Child,* 14:113-121. New York: International Universities Press.

⸻ Dwyer, T. F., Huntington, D. S., & Valenstein, A. F. (1961), A study of the psychological process in pregnancy and of the earliest mother-child relationship. *The Psychoanalytic Study of the Child,* 16:9-72. New York: International Universities Press.

Bonaparte, M. (1935), Passivity, masochism and frigidity. *Internat. J. Psycho-Anal.,* 16:325-333.

⸻ (1953), *Female Sexuality.* New York: International Universities Press.

Bradley, N. (1961), The doll. *Internat. J. Psycho-Anal.,* 42:550-555.

Brierley, M. (1936), Specific determinants in feminine development. *Internat. J. Psycho-Anal.,* 17:163-180.

Brunswick, R. M. (1940), The preoedipal phase of libido development. In: *The Psychoanalytic Reader,* ed. R. Fliess. New York: International Universities Press, 1948, pp. 261 284.

Burnett, C. W. (1969), *The Anatomy and Physiology of Obstetrics.* London: Faber & Faber.

Chertok, L., Bonnaud, M., Borelli, M., Donnet, J. L., & Revault d'Allonnes, C. (1969), *Motherhood and Personality.* Philadelphia: Lippincott.

Deutsch, H. (1924), The psychology of women in relation to the function of reproduction. In: *The Psychoanalytic Reader,* ed. R. Fliess. New York: International Universities Press, 1948, pp. 192-206.

⸻ (1944-1945), *The Psychology of Women,* Vols. I & II. New York: Grune & Stratton.

Dupire, M. (1963), The reputation of Bororo women. In: *Women of Tropical Africa,* ed. D. Paulme. Berkeley: University of California Press, pp. 47-59.

Eastman, N. J. & Russel, K. P. (1970), *Expectant Motherhood.* Boston: Little, Brown.

Edgcumbe, R. & Burgner, M. (1975), The phallic-narcissistic phase. *The Psychoanalytic Study of the Child,* 30:161-180. New Haven: Yale University Press.

Eissler, R. (1939), On certain problems of female sexual development. *Psychoanal. Quart.,* 8:191-210.

Erikson, E. H. (1950), *Childhood and Society.* New York: Norton.

⸻ (1953), Growth and crises of the healthy personality. In: *Identity and the Life Cycle* [*Psychol. Issues,* Monogr. 1]. New York: International Universities Press, 1959, pp. 50-100.

* All references to *This Journal* are to the *Journal of the American Psychoanalytic Association.*

_____ (1959), *Identity and the Life Cycle* [*Psychol. Issues*, Monogr. 1]. New York: International Universities Press.

_____ (1964), Reflections on womanhood. *Daedalus*, 2:582-606.

Ferenczi, S. (1924), *Thalassa: Theory of Genitality*. Albany: Psychoanalytic Quarterly, 1938.

Fraiberg, S. (1973), Some characteristics of genital arousal and discharge in latency girls. *The Psychoanalytic Study of the Child*, 27:439-475. New York: Quadrangle Books.

Freud, A. (1965), Normality and pathology in childhood: Assessment of development. *The Writings of Anna Freud*, 6. New York: International Universities Press.

Freud, S. (1900), The interpretation of dreams. *Standard Edition*, 4 & 5. London: Hogarth Press, 1953.

_____ (1905), Three essays on the theory of sexuality. *Standard Edition*, 7:125-248. London: Hogarth Press, 1953.

_____ (1909b), Notes upon a case of obsessional neurosis. *Standard Edition*, 10:5-149. London: Hogarth Press, 1955.

_____ (1909b), Notes upon a case of obsessional neurosis. *Standard Edition*, 10:153-318. London: Hogarth Press, 1955.

_____ (1917), A childhood recollection from *Dichtung und Warheit*. *Standard Edition*, 17:145-156. London: Hogarth Press, 1955.

_____ (1920), Beyond the pleasure principle. *Standard Edition*, 18:3-64. London: Hogarth Press, 1955.

_____ (1924), The economic problem of masochism. *Standard Edition*, 19:157-172. London: Hogarth Press, 1961.

_____ (1931), Female sexuality. *Standard Edition*, 21:223-243. London·.Hogarth Press, 1961.

_____ (1933), New introductory lectures on psycho-analysis. *Standard Edition*, 22:5-182. London: Hogarth Press, 1964.

_____ (1940), An outline of psycho-analysis. *Standard Edition*, 23:141-207. London: Hogarth Press, 1964.

Friedman, D. (1975), Conflict behavior in the parturient. *Transactions of the 4th International Congress of Obstetrics & Gynecology*. Basel: Karger, pp. 373-375.

Fuchs, F. & Klopper A., ed. (1971), *Endocrinology of Pregnancy*. New York: Harper & Row.

Green, W. A. (1958), Early object relations, somatic, affective and personal. *J. Nerv. Ment. Dis.*, 126:225-253.

Greenacre, P. (1950), Special problems of early female sexual development. In: *Trauma, Growth and Personality*. New York: International Universities Press, 1952, pp. 237-257.

Guttmacher, A. F. (1960), Hyperemesis. In: *Medical, Surgical and Gynecological Complications of Pregnancy*, ed. A. F. Guttmacher & J. J. Rovinsky. Baltimore: Williams & Wilkins, pp. 166-169.

Horney, K. (1926), The flight from womanhood. In: *Feminine Psychology*, ed. H. Kelman. New York: Norton, 1967, pp. 54-70.

Ingleman-Sundberg, A. (1966), *A Child is Born*. New York: Dell Publications.

Jacobson, E. (1937), Wege der weiblichen ueber-ich-bildung. *Internat. Zeitschr. f. Psychoanal.*, 23:402-412.

Jackel, M. M. (1966), Interruptions during psychoanalytic treatment and the wish for a child. *This Journal*, 14:730-735.

_____ (in press), Object loss and the wish for a child. To appear in volume commemorating the 25th anniversary of the Division of Psychoanalytic Education, Downstate University, Brooklyn, N. Y., ed. M. Kanzer.

Jessner, L., Weigert, E., & Foy, J. L. (1970), The development of parental attitudes during pregnancy. In: *Parenthood,* ed. E. J. Anthony & T. Benedek. Boston: Little Brown, pp. 209-244.

Kestenberg, J. S. (1956a), Vicissitudes of female sexuality. *This Journal,* 4:453-476.

_____ (1956b), On the development of maternal feelings in early childhood. *The Psychoanalytic Study of the Child,* 11:275-291. New York: International Universities Press.

_____ (1961), Menarche. In: *Adolescents,* ed. S. Lorand & H. I. Schneer. New York: Hoeber Press, pp. 19-50.

_____ (1966), Rhythm and organization in obsessive-compulsive development. *Internat. J. Psycho-Anal.,* 47:151-159.

_____ (1967), Phases of adolescence with suggestions for a correlation of psychic and hormonal organization, part I and II. *J. Amer. Acad. Child Psychiat.,* 6:426-463; 577-614.

_____ (1968a), Phases of adolescence with suggestions for a correlation of psychic and hormonal organization, part III. *J. Amer. Acad. Child Psychiat.,* 7:108-151.

_____ (1968b), Outside and inside, male and female. *This Journal,* 16:457-520.

_____ (1975), *Children and Parents: Psychoanalytic Studies in Development.* New York: Aronson.

_____ (in press), Notes on parenthood as a developmental phase. To appear in volume commemorating the 25th anniversary of the Division of Psychoanalytic Education, Downstate University, Brooklyn, N.Y., ed. M. Kanzer.

_____ Marcus, H., Robbins, E., Berlowe, J., & Buelte A. (1971), Development of the young child as expressed through bodily movement, I. *This Journal,* 19:746-764.

_____ & Robbins, E. (1975), From early rhythms of socializaton to the development of community spirit. In: *Children and Parents: Psychoanalytic Studies in Development.* New York: Aronson, pp. 443-460.

Klein, H., Potter, H. W., & Dyk, R. B. (1950), *Anxiety in Pregnancy and Childbirth.* New York: Paul Hoeber.

Kramer, P. (1954), Early capacity for orgastic discharge and character formation. *Psychoanalytic Study of the Child,* 9:128-141. New York: International Universities Press.

Lamaze, F. (1956), *Qu'est-ce-que l'accouchement sans douleur par la Méthode Psychoprophylactique? Ses principes, sa réalisation, ses resultats.* Paris: Savoir et Connaitre.

Lampl-de Groot, J. (1928), The evolution of the Oedipus complex in women. In: *Psychoprophylactique? Ses principes, sa realisation, ses resultats.* Paris: Savoir et Connaitre.

Laurentin, A. (1963), On Nzakara women. In: *Women of Tropical Africa,* ed. D. Paulme. Berkeley: University of California Press, pp. 121-178.

Lipkin, G. (1974), *Psychological Aspects of Maternal-Child Nursing.* St. Louis: C. V. Mosby.

Mahler, M., Pine, F., & Bergmann, A. (1975), *The Psychological Birth of the Human Infant.* New York: Basic Books.

Mead, M. (1963), *Sex and Temperament in Three Primitive Societies.* New York: Morrow.

Muller, J. (1932), A contribution to the problem of libidinal development of the genital phase in girls. *Internat. J. Psycho-Anal.*, 13:361-368.

Pratt, K. C. (1954), The neonate. In; *Manual of Child Psychology*, ed. L. Carmichael. New York: Wiley, pp. 190-254.

Racamier, P. C. (1950), Les nourrissons avec leur mère à l'hôpital psychiatrique. Quoted in Chertok et al., 1969.

Rank, O. (1912), Die symbolschichtung im wecktraum und ihre wiederkehr im mythischen denken. *Psychoanal. Psychopath. Forsch.*, 4:51.

Rheingold, J. C. (1964), *The Fear of Being a Woman.* New York: Grune & Stratton.

Sachs, H. (1929), One of the motive factors in the formation of the superego in women. *Internat. J. Psycho-Anal.*, 10:39-50.

Spitz, R. A. (1955), The primal cavity. *The Psychoanalytic Study of the Child*, 10:215-240. New York: International Universities Press.

30 Soundview Lane
Sands Point, L. I., New York

SOME OBSERVATIONS ON WORK INHIBITIONS IN WOMEN

ADRIENNE APPLEGARTH, M.D.

F ROM THE EARLIEST DAYS OF ANALYSIS, work has been recognized as one of the most important aspects of human life. Although occasional articles have been addressed to the theory of work or to disturbances in performance (Hendrick, 1943; Menninger, 1942; Oberndorf, 1951), and learning inhibition in the normal or even superiorly endowed child has been the subject of a number of papers (Halpern, 1964; Hellman, 1954; Mahler, 1942), the subject of work inhibition in women has been neglected. This neglect might be expected during the years when psychoanalysis was young, inasmuch as the number of women in the professions and in business, the group from which most analytic patients are drawn, was then relatively small. Nonetheless, as the numbers of women in these occupations have increased, analytic observations have lagged. Social preconceptions and parts of analytic theory undoubtedly play an important role in this finding: Because it has been regarded as less natural for women to seek careers, the wish to do so may be interpreted as pathological, representing too strong an identification with the father, or pathological penis envy—in short, a representation of misplaced masculine strivings.

It would seem appropriate, therefore, to focus on these disturbances in women, both because the subject has been neglected and because such problems are appearing in some profusion. This profusion may be accounted for by the fact that increasing numbers of women are attempting to establish careers, as well as by the diminution of reality obstacles in recent years. When severe obstacles exist in the outside world, they serve to screen from view the presence of internal problems. Moreover, not only internal and external obstacles may divert women from careers, but also the very gratifying alternative pathway of marriage and motherhood, which enjoys intense societal support as well. Both the obstacles on the outside and the gratifications of the alternative can be used defensively to disguise internal disturbances.

Perhaps I should clarify what I mean by a work or learning disturbance. I am referring to a relatively definite and localized disturbance in this function in particular and do not include patients whose disturbance is only part of a larger and more serious ego disruption. The patients I have in mind are actually seeking a career or are already in one, sought because of their own interest, and one which they intend to pursue indefinitely. They are to be distinguished from a fairly large group of women who work to help with the family finances, but who do not have a career goal in mind for themselves. Of course, this group of today contains many of tomorrow's work inhibitions, as many difficulties become evident later when these same women attempt to resume interrupted careers or establish new ones after their children have grown older.

I have had an opportunity to observe work inhibition over several years in patients both in analytic psychotherapy and analysis. Their career choices included medicine, law, psychology, social work, teaching, administrative work, and business. I would like to attempt to summarize and to categorize some of my observations and also to offer some clinical examples which may highlight some of the categories. It will be immediately apparent that the examples will also contain dynamics from other categories as well, since complicated factors naturally enter into the production of these phenomena. Nor can I claim to be making an exhaustive exposition of the dynamics, since, as I have said, my observations stem from my own experience, which is naturally incomplete. In addition, I would like to stress that the basic causes of many inhibitions are the same for both men and women, and that I am not making a claim to uniqueness in outlining them. Certain factors, however, have different weight and some may seem different in kind.

In the studies of work and its vicissitudes already mentioned, there has been ample elaboration of the inhibitions produced by instinctualizaton, either aggressive or libidinal, of the whole of the work function or any of its parts. Also, the important distinction between work as a sublimation and as a reaction formation and the greater liability of the latter type to subsequent breakdown has been discussed (Reich, 1949; Hendrick, 1943). My aim is to fill in the picture by delineating other influences leading to work inhibition, especially those most important in women.

I shall pass quickly by the disturbances in work that are so often found in schizophrenics, severe depressives, and even borderline states. All activities, both mental and physical, may be so filled with sexual and aggressive meaning in such a disruptive way that work is only one of many activities grossly interfered with.

More specific disturbances can be attributed to the influence of pathological narcissism. The pattern produced will depend upon the level of the narcissistic conflict. In general, narcissistic patients may have great difficulty learning because of their preoccupations with the risk of failure, or even the risk of mistake—which seems to them to be much the same thing. This leads them to avoid situations in which they do not have some degree of certainty that they can succeed and, indeed, succeed from the very outset. They are usually driven by unrealistically high expectations and ambitions, while simultaneously reproaching themselves bitterly for failing to live up to these. They frequently attempt to pursue their ambitions to a certain point, only to withdraw just before the moment of real testing—they may withdraw their applications to prestigious schools before being turned down, or fail to complete papers or dissertations, or manage not to take their examinations. Most often, this action seems to them to be motivated by a sudden and puzzling disappearance of their interest in what up to then had seemed to be a most engrossing pursuit.

Typically, their interest in their chosen endeavors seems to be characterized more by ideas of narcissistic gain — an illustrious career, being admired, etc. — than by the sort of pleasure in function and satisfaction of derivatives of libidinal and aggressive drives one hears about from other types of patients. Narcissistically oriented patients often have the idea that those who can do things well were somehow born able to do them, and they seem to lack the concept that skill is not inborn but can be acquired by practice. They therefore view their difficulties as evidence of some grievous basic defect in their make-up which they feel powerless to remedy. Also, as part of their narcissistic entitlement, these patients resent any discomfort, including the discomforts of experiencing difficulties in a task, and they respond with rage and the feeling that something unfair is occurring. This further undermines their motivation for attempting to surmount their difficulties, because they more or less consciously feel that they should not be expected to put up with such problems. They therefore appeal to fate, or await other outside interventions, or attempt to discover tricks that will make the difficulty disappear.

Very different family backgrounds may be associated with such constellations. One patient grew up with a single parent, the mother, who continually emphasized to this only child how perfect she was and how extraordinarily talented. It was clear that the mother needed to feel that she had produced a perfect being and that, together, they formed one unit of perfection and mutual admiration. The result was that the child was never able to carry through any project past the point to which unpracticed talent would take her, inasmuch as settling down to work at anything would show at once that she was as yet some distance from perfection, however promising she might be. This would be unbearably disillusioning for both mother and child. Needless to say, the patient had devastatingly low self-esteem.

A more expectable family background is one in which the child was frequently derided and little was expected. Berger and Kennedy (1975), have reported interesting studies along these lines. They found that the mothers of children presenting with a picture of pseudo backwardness were characterized by very low feelings of self-worth and regarded themselves as defective. The mothers seemed to view the child in question as sharing these attributes, a view the children complied with in order to preserve the maternal bond. At least one patient of mine fell into such a category: Her family expected little in the way of achievement or independence, and she grew up feeling she was in some way defective and that the only safety lay in a close connection with the family or, later, with a man. Because of her feeling of defectiveness, she was most intolerant of any difficulties experienced in the course of learning. Another constellation is seen in the patient who experiences herself as being a narcissistic fulfillment for one or both parents. This constellation is, I think, more frequently seen in men, where the boy fulfills ambitions for the mother, who sees him as a part of herself, usually her missing penis. Gifted girls, however, may play a similar role for the mother and may then refuse to employ their gifts, both as a way of establishing separateness from her and for purposes of revenge. Halpern (1964) has commented on the feature of rebellion as a motivation for learning disabilities in children.

The higher-level narcissistic disturbance produced by penis envy deserves detailed consideration because of the seriousness of the problems produced and because it disables women mainly, although feelings of inadequacy of the penis in respect to other men is certainly a troublesome concern for many men. Penis envy and other aspects of the psychology of women have been surrounded by controversy from the early days of psychoanalysis, and these topics have been the focus of additional attention in recent times. The concept of penis envy in particular has come under heavy fire from a number of quarters, especially from the women's movement. At this point I would like to outline what I consider to be the observations which are to be grouped under this heading, because, in my opinion, whatever one's ideas are about the genesis of the phenomenon, the findings themselves are very clear. Under the heading of penis envy I place both direct, ultimately conscious, envy and also a group of what seems like easily identified derivatives of it. I am referring to those women who present with a picture of general doubt as to their capacities, even to the point of conviction that some essential feature necessary for success is missing. This missing feature is most often localized in the brain, and these women have a conviction that men have something that they do not. No matter what success they achieve academically or in work, they tend to think of themselves as having fooled people or gained their position through some fraudulent means. Many of them feel that they can only attain their ends through some special manipulations by means of their sexual charms or by capitalizing on their "weakness." They experience a strong sense of having been deprived or injured, and insist upon redress of their grievance. They admire men, even to the point of worship, and are generally contemptuous of women. However, the presenting conscious attitude may for a long time be a hostile and contemptuous one toward men, because consciousness of the worship and envy produces intense rage. Their contemptuous devaluation often centers around activities in which men are considered to be especially masculine, e.g., sports, interest in cars, hunting. Many women, spurred on by these feelings, develop high achievement and therefore do not fall within our group, although they may share with the others painful feelings of being fraudulent or having stolen their success. This feeling seems to be related to the attribution by these women, together with the rest of society, of a masculine character to achievement, especially in certain fields—science, medicine, mechanical facility, etc. Some women are quite clear in their annoyance at men's valuing their penises and are conscious of some envy of the penis itself. Some women are aware of feelings that a magic power or splendor attaches to it.

These, then, are the observations to be explained, and they are very common observations, indeed, in women patients. I believe the essential differences of opinion occur around the explanations of these findings. As is doubtless well known, Freud considered that penis envy is a phenomenon which can be observed in little girls directly, a finding with which all child observers appear to agree, and he attributed it to the girl's envy of anything more than she had, together with her supposition that she had a less adequate organ for masturbation, and, furthermore, was not equipped to carry out her phallic strivings with her mother. In short, these are essentially internal factors in the girl. Freud tells us little about the factors that influence the outcome of penis envy, that is, whether it takes a normal direction and is more or less submerged, or takes a pathological turn toward the masculinity complex with homosexuality as its extreme. By way of explanation he invokes constitutional variations in the strength of aggressive drive, which then alters the degree of activity in the girl.

Everyone is familiar, of course, with his further idea (1924) that the absence of the penis is compensated for by the fantasy of having a baby, later realized in fact. Other analytic writers of the time, most notably Horney (1967) and Jones (1927, 1933, 1935), took issue with Freud's explanation of penis envy, though not with his observations. Horney considered that the phenomenon was not as self-evidently explained as Freud assumed, although she did find grounds for some envy on the basis of greater availability of the penis to the boy, since touching was permitted in the course of urination. Also the penis permitted narcissistic pleasures in urinating contests, etc. However, she felt that none of this would account for the strong influence of penis envy in women were it not for other accentuating factors which were added to it simultaneously. She laid heavy emphasis on the effects on the little girl of the vastly superior position both in valuation and powers enjoyed by the boy and man both in the family and in society at large. In addition, she pointed out how many more restrictions were placed on the girl's instinctual life, both sexual and aggressive. The girl's envy would tend to center on the penis itself because that was the significantly different feature which to her mind would explain the different way she was regarded. In addition, Horney felt that initial penis envy was strengthened to the degree that the heterosexual wishes of the oedipal phase were regarded as especially dangerous and therefore retreated from in the form of the envy of, or the wish to be, a man instead. Freud's formulations also rested on the concept of penis envy as an important explanation of the differences in intellectual life, capacity for sublimation, and quality of object relations.

Today, whatever one's theories about female sexuality, more stress would certainly be laid on the importance of identifications, various ego and superego factors, and the influence of family and society in general. Even the wish for a baby is considered to represent far more than simply a compensation of penis envy. These ideas about female strivings' representing compensations for penis envy have, I think, been in part responsible for some of the neglect of work inhibitions I mentioned earlier, for such a view must regard career aspirations as, by definition, rather pathological, as compared with the same strivings in men.

The consequences of penis envy in the life of the woman can be far-reaching. I have been impressed with the relatively low self-esteem of women as a group compared to male patients. Men, of course, have troubles with their self-esteem, but, in women, the degree of doubt of capacities in comparison with others seems to be of a different order of magnitude. These women seem to have resigned themselves to being unable to achieve except in traditional female fields, or may react to early attempts that run into difficulties with an intense feeling of humiliation at having their defectiveness once again demonstrated. They may subsequently shrink from similar attempts and generally limit their horizons. Their feeling that their career activities are masculine arouses fears that they have lost or will lose their sexual identity as women, to say nothing of their conviction that they will no longer be attractive to men. There is enough reality in this to make resistances around it difficult to analyze, for many men do have problems with women who actively use their intelligence. A typical adaptation to these narcissistic problems has always been open to women—namely, to be in a close relationship to an admired man who is successful for her and in whose company she feels at last complete, having finally managed, by some sort of fusion with him, to acquire the penis to which such magic qualities are attributed. Another adaptation has, of course, been to have a child who is idolized and fused with in much the same way. Such adaptations have exacted a heavy price, both from the woman and the man or child, in the form of intense pressures on the other person to succeed in behalf of the woman's narcissism. Another result of penis envy is an intense feeling of resentment for being deprived and defective, a resentment that first settles on the mother and may even be distributed more widely. Because these patients feel that lack of a penis blocks their progress, they have an unconscious plan of waiting until one is furnished, whereupon, they imagine, all their difficulties will vanish. It is startling, in fact, to see the extent to which they overvalue men and imagine that men have no difficulties and uncertainties similar to their own.

As I have worked with these cases, I have been struck by the difficulty with which the conviction of female inferiority is given up. One might imagine that revelation to a patient of such a conviction and some exploration of the basis for it might be greeted with relief and pleasure and that she might turn readily to the task of shedding an apparently unservicable belief. However, this is not the case. Freud remarked (1937) that one of the most difficult problems was to induce a woman to give up her envy of the penis and her insistence upon obtaining one. I agree with his observation, but confess that I do not feel that I yet understand completely why this is so. Women will hasten to prove to me in additional ways that they indeed lack certain faculties and will supply abundant evidence that men do have them. Certainly, if a woman is strongly oriented toward redress of grievance, or revenge on men or on the mother, she does not lightly give up the conviction of damage. Or if she avoids competition by assuming an inferior position, it is essential for her to maintain it. The persistence of the phallic wishes toward the mother is also an important influence. Interpretation of all these currents does not always produce as ready a resolution as is seen in other symptomatology. However, it is also true that few neurotic convictions receive as much outside support as does this one, since society continues to restrict certain freedoms and opportunities for women, who are devalued in many ways and from whom less is expected.

I should not leave the subject of narcissism without mentioning that its effects on work are of course not all detrimental. Disturbances in narcissism may act as a great stimulus, and certain occupations may afford strong narcissistic compensations. One patient was an outstandingly dedicated and capable physician partly because of her omnipotent strivings, which were highly gratified when she could prevent suffering and death and which led her to make superhuman efforts in behalf of her patients.

Having considered the relation of narcissism to certain work disturbances, let us turn now to the way conflicts around aggression may ·produce problems in achievement. To consider aggression introduces as well the topic of activity and passivity and the relative quantities of each of these that is normal in men and women. There would, I think, be fairly general agreement with the observation that girls and women tend to be less physically aggressive and active than boys and men, but disagreement begins when the basis for this is considered. Constitutional differences have been invoked, and, certainly, animal studies tend to support the idea that there are important innate differences in the amount of overt aggressive behavior to be observed in males and females. In man, however, the innate, is much altered by experience, and it is clear that much pressure is exerted on girls as they grow up to be less aggressive and less physically active than boys. But as a further complication, we must consider mental as well as physical processes in the light of activity and aggression, and these do not seem to stand in a simple relationship to one another. The pattern of physical activity sometimes seems to pervade mental life as well, but, often enough, aggressiveness and activity in these two spheres exist in an inverse relationship to one another. Also, consider the aggressiveness and activity of a woman when her children are threatened. Whatever the reasons, the patterns of aggression and, most important, women's attitudes toward it are somewhat different from men's. However, I would first like to mention some features which are more similar than different.

In men, we see many work inhibitions centering around conflicts over aggression, with intense and paralyzing guilt being provoked by what is seen as highly destructive activity, stemming from either the oedipal or pregenital level. Women may also present with the same major constellations, but the triumph more often involves surpassing and showing up the mother as weak, stupid, and only a woman. A real oedipal triumph may lie in the close sharing of intellectual and other career pursuits with the father, to the mother's total exclusion. Sometimes a masculine identification also results, but this seems by no means to be the rule. An example of pregenital inhibition is afforded by a patient successful in her profession, who could not enjoy her successes because they made her feel immensely powerful and sadistic, making her feel that she had crushed all those around her. She would then become very much afraid of their reaction and have to retreat from certain aspects of her work. A higher-level and more complicated example that of an extremely successful business woman who struggled constantly to avoid the consciousness that she was more active, energetic, and capable than her husband—who was, indeed, remarkably passive. She was afraid she would damage him through her very capability, to say nothing of her contempt and anger. As a result, she struggled to inhibit her capability and to limit the horizons of her ambition. She had grown up the favorite of an unsuccessful father who had been nagged and criticized by the mother, who was at the same time apparently jealous of the patient's successes. The patient resolved not to repeat this pattern and married a man she considered to be the opposite of her father, only to have it turn out, as is so often the case, that he was essentially the same.

The differing attitudes toward aggression in men and woman are reflected in work. Women often complain of themselves in treatment that they are aggressive and competitive, with the clear feeling that these are entirely bad traits and not consistent with the ideal they have of themselves. Especially, they may complain that they are competitive with men, and their internally-arising fears find much reinforcement from society and even from the side of misused analytic theory according to which women are labeled castrating whenever they are competitive. Obviously, some serious difficulties exist in the work area when a woman shrinks from competition if her chosen field happens to be one in which competition is a feature. Many girls in high school give up academic excellence for just such reasons. A related superego attitude of importance is the attitude toward curiosity, exploration, and, especially, toward internal self-regulation—that is, following the dictates of one's own conscience and one's bent. All of these tend to be held up as desirable and admirable for men, but usually not for women, who have been systematically taught that it is desirable that they please others and conform to the expectations of others. Curiosity and exploration, besides being superego matters also carry with them the element of danger, not only fantasy dangers, but real ones as well. In both the physical and mental world, one is indeed more apt to get into trouble venturing onto unknown paths alone than by remaining at home, and men and women are encouraged toward different ideals with respect to danger. Narcissism demands in men that they attempt to suppress fear, while women allow themselves far more yielding to it without shame, and in some interesting cases even wear their fearfulness as a badge of distinction. Some women feel consciously that they must emphasize their weakness in order to build up the self-esteem of the man, and fall into the group of those who suffer guilt over their strength and capability. Others seem to regard fearfulness as another sign of their having been injured. They can display it in a martyred way and exact recompense for it in the way of special consideration.

It has been of interest to me to observe a frequent problem women have in a closely related area, namely, the problem of being alone, especially of doing things alone. Men, of course, do not like being alone either, but the concern over this seems much higher in women. They feel incomplete, not a in a libidinal sense, but a narcissistic one, having the feeling that they lack the essential connection which gives them status or simply a feeling of importance and meaning. They are afraid to undertake tasks alone, assuming their incapacity and that unknown dangers will overtake them if the magic of the protective man is not present. For many such women, the shadow of the strong mother of early childhood can be easily seen in this invulnerable image of the man. The fear of venturing out alone physically is these days usually rationalized by invoking the real dangers on the streets, but a little investigation easily reveals that the problem is far more fundamental and basically of internal origin. Such an attitude toward being alone in a physical sense also has it reflections in the mental sphere, and produces a tendency to be quite circumscribed in the range of their minds, especially in permitting originality. All of the attributes of the superego and ego ideal mentioned handicap the successful pursuit of the more rough and tumble fields where originality and aggressiveness are needed.

At this point, having mentioned some difference in super-ego content, I should like to digress slightly and take up the matter of the supposed differences in the superego in men and women, since this is a concept which has led to a good deal of unrest concerning psychoanalytic theory. Freud's attributing different superego qualities to men and women arises quite naturally from his theory of the origin and resolution of the Oedipus complex in the two sexes. Essentially, he reasoned that, since the girl already lacks a penis, she does not fear castration as the boy does, and therefore the strongest motive for giving up the oedipal attachment to the father is missing, with the result that girls resolve this complex less completely. Because superego formation proceeds out of the resolution of the Oedipus complex, it must follow that the girl's superego cannot be as well formed. Freud expressed his impression of the difference as follows: "I cannot evade the notion (though I hesitate to give it expression) that for women the level of what is ethically normal is different from what it is in men. Their super-ego is never so inexorable, impersonal, so independent of its emotional origins as we require it to be in men" (1925, p. 257). I believe that Freud may have failed to distinguish clearly enough between superego content and basic superego structure or function. As I mentioned earlier, women often seem to have as a superego content the value that they should be responsive to the wishes and opinions of others and should not be too strongly guided by their own ideas or pursue their own paths. Such a value system will certainly result in behavior that will at first glance appear to reflect, as Freud says, a less inexorable, independent superego. Furthermore, the areas that men and women regard as matters for the superego vary somewhat. For example, women seem to have stronger strictures against aggression in its more extreme forms and also against sexuality. It simply has not been my observation that women are less governed by guilt or that they show relative superego weakness. Theoretically, if one were to alter one's ideas about the formation of the superego in the two sexes and consider that essentially it is the same in both, then how is this to be reconciled with the supposed differences in resolution of the Oedipus complex? Doubt has been cast in many quarters, beginning with Horney (1924), on the idea that the girl does not fear castration. Actually, much evidence is at hand that girls fear injury and mutilation to the genitals as a result of their oedipal strivings in a way analogous to the boy, and it seems consistent with observation to suppose that this, together with the frustration imposed by the parents, brings the Oedipus complex to its resolution in much the same way in both sexes. Certainly Freud's observations must have been correct that girls remain much more closely tied to the family than boys, but in his day such a pattern was supported and encouraged by the family, while discouraged for the boy, and therefore a kind of seduction was offered by the father which surely would interfere with full resolution of the Oedipus complex.

These considerations bring us to yet another source of inhibition of work, namely, problems around the dependent gratifications. Being taken care of has been, over the years, one of the prime rewards for women, inducing them to acquiesce in their position. For many women it may represent an important narcissistic pleasure, in the sense of being highly valued, to be so protected and provided for. Moreover, it certainly satisfies passive, oral needs. Some women hesitate to undertake careers because of their conviction that to do so would jeopardize their opportunity to be gratified in this way. Although such a constellation can arise out of very early oral fixations, I have been more impressed with a strengthening of these wishes and a justification of them arising out of the feeling of having been injured or deprived through not being men, so that important things are owed them in return. If they did not continue to assert their incapacities to do for themselves and indeed began to move on in work of their own, they would give up their claim to reparations. What I am saying only rounds out the more familiar picture of regression from the dangers of activity and the assumption of the prerogatives of adulthood.

Until now, I have been discussing mainly internal influences at work in women who seek careers and experience inhibitions in that function. However, the problem of the legitimate competition between the demands of motherhood and a career remain as a complex amalgam of real and internal forces. Even distinguishing between these may be difficult at times. Children, especially small ones, need a great deal of attention from mothers, and we are still in the process of learning to what degree this attention can be provided by others without significant detriment to mother or child. Alternative child-rearing practices will provide useful information, especially around the question of how much of the early child care can be done, instead, by the father. All of this is becoming more urgent, for modern education and society are probably going to produce women who will be less well adapted to staying home with young children. The woman who was raised to be pleasing, nonassertive, giving to others even to the point of martyrdom, dependent, possibly timid, and centered on family was probably better adapted to the task of mothering young children, but that was in a day when more women died young and indeed the life span for everyone was shorter. Today, the price of such character formations on the family and children can be seen in the empty-nest syndrome when a woman of 35 to 40 is no longer needed in the same way by her now adolescent or older children and she faces another 34 to 40 years without the goals that had been so significant until now. Sometimes problems for these women cause such guilt and other interference with the children at that later time as to make one wonder if what earlier seemed like a favorable mothering for young children is really such a fruitful adaptation seen from the broader viewpoint. It seems probable that what is good for both at one time may be bad at another stage of life or what is good for one party may not be for the other, and our opinions may ultimately be guided by what is a reasonable compromise — which may disappoint our hopes for an ideal solution. Certainly the whole picture is greatly complicated by various neurotic factors. Many women who wish to pursue work of their own are tormented by guilt even in the wish, feeling that proper mother love does not permit the straying of attention. Others may suffer echos of their own separation anxieties as children and hesitate to be away from their own children lest something harmful befall them. All the identifications with the parents come to the fore and produce additional complications. But this is a familiar subject and has been written about a good deal.

In these remarks I have also not focused at all on the ways in which special realistic obstacles still remain in the path of women attempting to follow careers, even though a considerable effort is being made to smooth the way. Old attitudes and needs die hard, even though conscious attempts are made to react differently. However, when we act as clinicians, we see that the presence of such obstacles can be used as a formidable resistance to the exploration of inhibitions in areas of achievement and also in the area of women's strong feelings of their own inferiority. Effectiveness in treatment, I believe, rests on focusing on these resistance functions, whatever we may decide to do as private citizens about the realistic outside obstacles.

REFERENCES

Berger, M. & Kennedy H. (1975), Pseudobackwardness in children: Maternal attitudes as an etiological factor. *The Psychoanalytic Study of the Child,* 30: 279-307, 1975. New Haven: Yale University Press.

Freud, S. (1924), The dissolution of the oedipus complex. *Standard Edition*, 19:
    172-179. London: Hogarth Press, 1961.
_____ (1925), Some psychological consequences of the anatomical distinction
    between the sexes. *Standard Edition,* 19:243-258. London: Hogarth Press,
    1961.
_____ (1937), Analysis terminable and interminable. *Standard Edition,* 23:209-
    255. London: Hogarth Press, 1964.
Halpern, H. (1964), Psychodynamic and cultural determinants of work inhibition
    in children and adolescents. *Psychoanal. Rev.,* 51:173-189.
Hellman, I. (1954), Some observations on mothers of children with intellectual
    inhibitions. *The Psychoanalytic Study of the Child,* 9:259-274. New York:
    International Universities Press.
Hendrick, I. (1943), Work and the pleasure principle. *Psychoanal. Quart.,* 12:311-
    330.
Horney, K. (1924), On the genesis of the castration complex in women. In: *Femi-
    nine Psychology,* ed. H. Kelman. New York: Norton, 1967, pp. 37-53.
_____ (1967), *Feminine Psychology,* ed. H. Kelman. New York: Norton.
Jones, E. (1927), The early development of female sexuality. *Internat. J. Psycho-
    Anal.,* 8:459-472.
_____ (1933), The phallic phase. *Internat. J. Psycho-Anal.,* 14:1-33.
_____ (1935), Early female sexuality. *Internat. J. Psycho-Anal.,* 16:263-273.
Mahler, M. (1942), Pseudo-imbecility. *Psychoanal. Quart.,* 11:149-164.
Menninger, K. (1942), Work as a sublimation. *Bull. Menninger Clinic,* 6:170-182.
Oberndorf, C. P. (1951), Psychopathology of work. *Bull. Menninger Clinic,* 15:77-
    84.
Reich, W. (1949). *Character-analysis.* New York: Orgone Press.

1610 Scott Street
San Francisco, California 94115

PARENTAL
MISLABELING OF
FEMALE GENITALS AS A
DETERMINANT OF   HARRIET E. LERNER, PH.D.
PENIS ENVY AND
LEARNING INHIBITIONS
IN WOMEN

AS CHILDREN GROW UP THEY ARE TAUGHT that boys have a penis and girls have a vagina. That the little girl is taught she has a vagina, an internal organ difficult to examine in reality, but is not told she has a vulva that includes the clitoris and labia, may be a critical factor in her psychosexual development. Significantly, this incomplete labeling of female genitals is an almost ubiquitous phenomenon: If one interviews parents, or reads literature on sex education it is evident that the girl child is told that she has a vagina and nothing else. Even literature written for an adolescent population typically communicates this same undifferentiated picture of female genitals. "A girl has two ovaries, a uterus, and a vagina which are her sex organs. A boy's sex organs are a penis and testicles. One of the first changes (at puberty) will be the growth of hair around the vaginal opening of the girl" (Taylor, 1972, p. 47).

The author expresses her gratitude to Drs. Paul Pruyser, Stephen Lerner, Marie R. Badaracco, and Peter C. Novotny, for their helpful comments and suggestions.

269

Such an incomplete, poorly differentiated and anatomically incorrect picture of female anatomy may have its most critical effect during the preoedipal and early oedipal phases of development when the girl discovers her clitoris as the prime source of sexual stimulation and gratification. In my opinion it is of serious psychological consequence to the child that she discovers an organ of pleasure that frequently is not acknowledged, labeled, or validated for her by the parents, and which is thus inevitably experienced as "unfeminine" (i.e., only boys have something on the "outside"). More specifically, I believe this miseducation to be one contributing factor to penis envy in women and I would speculate that penis envy is not simply the wish for a penis (i.e., one wants to have what boys have), but rather may reflect the wish to validate and have "permission" for female sexual organs, including the sensitive external genitals. I would suggest that at a deeper level penis envy is a symptom that may, in certain women, express an unfulfilled wish to have permission from mother to be a sexually operative and responsive female. This idea, is in keeping with Torok's (1970) suggestion that penis envy is the girl's unconscious pledge to a jealous and possessive maternal imago that she will not achieve genital fulfillment and will deny herself pleasure with the penis for mother's sake.

Clinical Example

The following case presentation illustrates how the mislabeling of female genitals may contribute to penis envy as well as to symptomatic learning inhibitions. Ann was a married professional woman with children, whose initial decision to enter intensive psychotherapy was precipitated by a number of accumulating internal and external stresses. Three of her symptoms, which proved to be dynamically interwoven, will form the focus of the treatment fragment presented here.

The first symptom that Ann reported was sexual

inhibitions with her husband. While she experienced vaginal sensations during intercourse and felt that she "liked" her vagina, she had feelings of disgust, shame, and anxiety about her external genitals that greatly interfered with her capacity to experience sexual pleasure. She was unable to allow her husband to look at her vulvar area, and similarly was unable to examine herself, thus maintaining some uncertainty about her own anatomical realities. She referred to her external genitals as "my outside stuff" and was unable, during the early part of treatment, to say the words clitoris, labia, and vulva without experiencing an acute sense of anxiety and humiliation.

Ann's second major symptom was a tendency to become confused and "stupid" in areas that related to what she called "time and place." For example, despite very superior intellectual ability, she would typically become disoriented in regard to time sequences — "Is fall before autumn, or are they the same thing? I can't remember." "Today could be Monday or Friday. Now I can't say which it is without stopping to figure it out." "If someone says to me, 'I went last spring,' I get confused. I may have to say the months and seasons to myself to place it in time." Ann was similarly disrupted in her thinking when it came to geography and spatial relations. She had difficulty picturing the location of a country, or relationships among countries or continents. She complained of having no "internal map" of the city in which she had lived for many years, and was characteristically confused about directions. In fact, she would often look at her wedding ring in order to distinguish with confidence the difference between left and right. The contrast between the degree of helplessness and confusion she experienced in these areas of functioning, and her otherwise rich and highly differentiated style of cognition was indeed striking.

Ann's third symptom was penis envy: her envy and idealization of male genitals was at times only thinly disguised. She was unable to comfortably assume the top and more active position in intercourse—a reluctance she later understood as reflecting the confusion she would experience in this position as to "who had the penis" and her conflicted wish that it be hers.

An important theme that became elaborated during the course of Ann's treatment was her confusion about what her own genitals looked like—a confusion she later linked with her inability to comprehend temporal and spatial structures or relationships. She spoke of the incomprehensible complexity of her external genitals: "What's between my legs is like a clock. A clock is simple on the outside. It has numbers and two hands. But if you look beyond the surface, the intricacy of a clock is too much to figure out. It's the same with me. If you look superficially, it's like having a crack like you see on statues. But if you really really look, then there's a lot of confusing parts. It seems like too much to figure out." Often, in a sequence of associations, she expressed her sense of helplessness about "figuring out" her genitals, followed by similar expressions of helplessness about her inability to comprehend her physical environment: "It's crazy, but I don't think I can ever comprehend where things are at [referring to her genitals]. I don't think men know either. They're always fumbling around. Sometimes my husband can't find my clitoris. It's like he needs a roadmap or something. When I direct him, I feel like a traffic cop. I'm not sure of my way around either." Ann used much the same language to describe her confusion about finding her way around the city: "It's like I don't have a map in my head no matter how often I've seen it or been there. It seems too confusing, almost hopeless, to try to figure out how everything is placed. It's always like seeing a place for the first time."

As Ann began to link her confusion about her anatomy to her temporal and spatial disorientation, she also began to associate her envy of the penis with the fact that the male organ is "neat and simple," "easy to figure out," and "without confusing or hidden parts." It was "validated" by others, whereas her external genitals were "unspeakable." "Everyone knows that men have a penis and everyone can say the word—even at parties. But the only word that people will say to describe what women have is 'vagina'."

With the progression of the treatment, the connection among these three themes (disgust and confusion about her external genitals, disorientation of time and place, and her envy of the penis) became clearer as I began to understand the salience of the word "permission." Ann sometimes experienced surges of anger or depression when referring to a vaguely defined feeling of "not having permission" for her external genitals, which she claimed had been "invalidated" and "denied" to her. Her sexual difficulties as well as her spatial and temporal confusions indeed proved to be symptomatic of her conflict around "having permission to have what I have."

Ann's feeling of "not having permission" achieved various expressions in her relation with me. When I was absent for two weeks, she experienced increased feelings of disgust about her vulva and a decreased ability to enjoy sexual relations or even physical contact with her husband. On my return she complained at length about how the disruption of treatment had exacerbated her sexual difficulties. Later, she had a fantasy that I was secretly pleased by this course of events; her increased sexual inhibitions were a "gift" to me—an implicit statement that my presence and the treatment I offered were of "number one" importance. Having sexual pleasure in my absence was not permissible because it might make me feel irrelevant, pushed out, and even unhappy.

Similarly, Ann insisted that I wished to deny her pleasure with her clitoris. Armed with the information that I was a "Freudian," she became angrily preoccupied with the idea that I wanted her to be "totally vaginal" and that, as far as I was concerned, she only had permission for her internal genitals. When Ann understood the genesis of her feelings of "not having permission" her symptoms were significantly attenuated.

Two critical developmental events were linked to Ann's fantasy, "I do not have permission to have what I have." One was early punishments she received from her mother for masturbating, which, for Ann, meant that having pleasure with her genitals (and wishing to have sexual pleasure with father's penis) was destructive to mother. The second was her early education that "boys have a penis and girls have a hole where the baby comes out." Ann's experience of discovering her external genitals and having pleasure with her clitoris and vulva was not solely prohibited by a masturbation taboo. More importantly, the incomplete information she received about her anatomy was for her "a message that I didn't have what I had." As she said, "What I had that felt good didn't have a name. It wasn't supposed to exist. Only boys had something on the outside. So I couldn't have my clitoris and still be a girl. No one can deny the penis to a boy. No one could not give it a name or make it into a secret. To have a penis is to have permission to have what you have."

Ann's inability to comprehend the "geography" of her genitals or of her external world was really a promise to mother that she would "not look." Looking meant that she would see something (her vulva, especially her clitoris) that wasn't supposed to be there for mother's sake. Penis envy, in Ann's words, was ". . . a wish to have permission for what I really *did* have, which was more than a vagina where babies come from." Penis envy not only expressed Ann's wish to have her own sexuality "validated," it also served to block this forbidden wish by preventing sexual fulfillment, thus reassuring a prohibitive maternal imago that she (Ann) would not become a fully sexually responsive woman who took pride in femininity.

Discussion

It is hardly necessary to stress that this treatment fragment is not intended to account for the complexities of feminine body image or to provide a comprehensive explanation of the symptoms of penis envy and disturbed cognition. Clearly, penis envy often has other meanings than that illustrated by Ann's case (Moulton, 1973)[1] just as a breakdown in sharply focused and differentiated perception and cognition may reflect a range of intrapsychic and cultural determinants (Shapiro, 1965; Lerner, 1974a).

Nor do I wish to imply that the inaccurate and incomplete labeling of female genitals will invariably convey to the girl child that she should deny herself sexual pleasure for mother's sake. The context of the parent-child relationship in which the sexual misinformation is conveyed is of considerable importance. In Ann's case, for example, there were additional aspects of her development that led to the internalization of a jealous maternal imago who did not want her to achieve genital fulfillment. Parental failure to label the components of female anatomy will have its most pathogenic effects when it occurs in the context of other sexual or oedipal prohibitions impeding normal development.

I would speculate, however, that even in the best of parent-child relations, the failure to explicitly acknowledge and label the girl's external genitals, especially the clitoris, cannot help but have pathogenic consequences. This idea is in keeping with the suggestion that vague information regarding one's sexuality and sexual differences is an important etiological factor in disturbed reality testing and severe psychopathology (Bellak and Benedict, 1958, p. 29). One consequence is to impair the girl's capacity to develop an accurate and differentiated psychic representation or "map" of her genitals and to impede her in the difficult

---

[1]Despite widely divergent views regarding the meaning of penis envy, there seems to be an evolving agreement that this symptom does not have its primary roots in objective anatomical realities. Recent writers are stressing that penis envy frequently has its origin in the dyadic relation between mother and daughter and is a symptom reflecting the child's difficulties in identifying with and achieving differentiation from a mother who is experienced as jealous, intrusive, or castrating (Chasseguet-Smirgel, 1970; Torok, 1970).

developmental task of differentiating the internal from external genitals (see Kestenberg, 1968). The fact that the girl's own exploration of her genitals is not corroborated or paralleled by information from her environment may lead to anxiety, confusion, and shame regarding her sexuality. *Because neither sex is informed that the clitoris is part of "what girls have," this organ will be cathected as a small and inadequate penis rather than as a valid and feminine part of the girl's sexuality.*

Of even greater dynamic significance is that this mislabeling will carry with it an implicit or unconscious communication to the girl child. In Ann's case, parental failure to label the external genitals was perceived as an unconscious message that she was to deny herself sexual pleasure and genital fulfillment for mother's sake. While the unconscious message may vary in differing interpersonal contexts, something along the following lines will be communicated: the vulva (including the clitoris) is not important, must not be spoken of or thought about, or should not exist.[2]

Torok (1970) has emphasized the forbidding of masturbation as a central determinant of penis envy. She writes that the girl idealizes and envies the penis in order to reassure the possessive and intrusive mother that she will never achieve genital fulfillment, that she will abandon her desire to have pleasure with the penis, and that she will live out her days in unfulfilled longing for an unattainable object. According to Torok, the mother who forbids masturbation communicates that she would lapse into bitter emptiness and envy if the child could achieve satisfaction without her.

I believe that the forbidding of masturbation with a

---

[2]Unlike boys, who characteristically masturbate by focused and specific genital manipulation, girls are reported to more commonly engage in nonspecific, indirect forms of masturbation (Clower, 1976). I suspect the avoidance of focused manual clitoral stimulation may in part reflect the failure to acknowledge and label this organ for the girl child.

known and recognized body part is a more benign message to the child to relinquish female sexuality than is the neglect to "validate" and give a name to the girl's sensitive external genitals. I would further speculate that the ubiquity of the female "castration complex" does not stem primarily from the fact that the clitoris is a smaller (and thus inferior) organ compared to the penis. Rather, the girl's feeling of being "cheated" may reflect parental failure to explicitly acknowledge that the vulva (especially the clitoris) is an important aspect of "what girls have." It is interesting to note that in Freud's time, the words clitoris, vulva, and labia were not included in the dictionary and, in this country, the only word in Webster's dictionary to refer to female genitals was vagina. One might question how pride in femininity could flower at a time when our language did not include a word for the part of female anatomy most richly endowed with sensory nerve endings and with no function but that of sensual pleasure.

While the appropriate additions to Webster's dictionary have since been made, little has changed, linguistically speaking, since Freud's day. Not only do parents fail to tell their daughters that they have a vulva which includes a clitoris, but my interviews reveal that the very idea of such communication produces a curious reaction of embarrassment and discomfort in the parent. In addition, it is surprising how many educated parents report never having heard the word vulva (including a large number who think the term refers to a Swedish automobile). Many of these parents think the word vagina means both the internal and external genitals. In our professional circles, as well, the avoidance of the word vulva is striking, even when the context specifically calls for it.[3]

[3]In Martin Mayman's Rorschach scoring manual, which is used by clinical psychologists at The Menninger Foundation, the word vagina is repeatedly misapplied to Rorschach percepts of the external female genitals. Similarly, patients who take this test frequently report seeing "vaginas," although subsequent inquiry, as well as the stimulus attributes of the inkblot, demonstrate that it is the female external genitals that are being perceived. The appropriate term *vulva* is very infrequently used even when residents, medical students, and professional staff are tested.

Although failing to appreciate the significance of parental mislabeling of female genitals, psychoanalytic theorists have been particularly sensitive to the complexities and difficulties that female anatomy presents to the growing girl. It has been noted, for example (Moulton, 1973) that while boys have "... the obvious advantage of possessing a neat, visible organ ..." (p. 213) which can be handled without reprimand during urination, the girl's genitals are less accessible to either visual or manual inspection. Attention has also been given to the unconscious vagina-mouth equation, which may cause the girl or woman to fear this organ because of its fantasied castrating oral-devouring and destructive potential. In addition, the external genitals may be frightening because they may be perceived as resembling a wound, an idea that is reinforced by menstrual bleeding (Abraham, 1920). Simone de Beauvoir (1953) has written: "The sex organ of a man is simple and neat as a finger; it is readily visible and often exhibited to comrades with proud rivalry; but the feminine sex organ is mysterious even to the woman herself, concealed, mucuous, and humid, as it is; it bleeds each month, it is often sullied with body fluids, it has a secret and perilous life of its own..." (p. 386).

It must be stressed, however, that the "mysterious" and concealed nature of female anatomy does not necessarily prevent the girl child from discovering the components of her genitals. She will inevitably discover her external genitals, including the clitoris, in the course of masturbation and maternal care. Further, vaginal activity and possibly orgastic potential may exist during infancy and childhood. Vaginal stimulation may occur in early infancy during sucking (Brierley, 1936), during infant toilet training (Greenacre, 1950; Moulton, 1973), and in a variety of indirect ways during child care (Kestenberg, 1968). In addition, the child's clitoral masturbation may lead to intense sensations in the inner -genitals via nervous and vascular connections. In contrast to Freud's belief that the vagina is nonexistent until puberty

(1905), pediatric reports suggest that little girls may begin vaginal masturbation at a very early age. More important, those children who are "ignorant" of their vagina as a tangible organ that can be examined and explored, may still discover their vagina in terms of deep coenesthetic sensations.

All things considered, however, it seems to be a relatively more difficult task for the female child to achieve a comfortable, accurate, and differentiated appreciation of her genitals than for the boy. Whether the girl's greater difficulty reflects anatomical realities, or whether it stems primarily from parental failure to corroborate the girl's own sexual explorations and genital sensations, is a question deserving careful investigation. Clearly, many intrapsychic and cultural factors may combine to prevent the growing girl from achieving a full understanding and appreciation of her own sexuality.

Concluding Remarks

Before Masters and Johnson (1966) published their research findings, the clitoris was literally considered to be a vestigial organ in adult sexuality; clitoral stimulation was considered "masculine" or "phallic" and was written off as a manifestation of penis envy or sexual immaturity. Psychoanalytically speaking, the adult woman was given the same message as the little girl: the most physiologically sensitive part of her anatomy, which has no function other than that of sensual pleasure, is "unfeminine," of "masculine character," and should be denied—i.e., it does not or should not exist. Whereas it is now recognized that the intensity of clitoral sensations never cease (although the role of the vagina achieves primacy), we have only recently acknowledged that the clitoris is a valid and important organ of adult sexuality.

Partially under the impact of the current feminist movement, psychoanalytic circles have given increased attention to the "phallocentric" bias of our theorizing, with attempts being made to correct certain misconceptions about femininity (Lerner, 1974b) and female sexuality (Chasseguet-Smirgel, 1970). In our eagerness to re-evaluate Freud's theories about women, we may bypass an equally significant theoretical task, which is to make dynamic sense of those distortions and misconceptions that have, in fact, been established and maintained. Giving the clitoris its rightful role in female sexuality is no more important a task than gaining dynamic understanding of why the clitoris and the external genitals have been "denied" to begin with—a denial well illustrated by current parental teachings, our own past theorizing, and, in its most extreme form, by the custom of excising the clitoris and ablating the labia, which has been practiced on millions of women in certain cultures (Ploss et al., 1965). Clearly, this denial must stem from powerful feelings of anxiety and dread that both sexes share regarding the external female genitals. Perhaps it is a symptom of this anxiety that so much psychoanalytic attention has been directed, instead, to the fear of the internal genital, the vagina.

It is not accurate, however, to say that psychoanalysis has ignored the terror associated with the external female genitals. Technically speaking, castration anxiety in males does not occur from seeing the vagina (which is hardly accessible to visual inspection), but rather from seeing "the hairy maternal vulva" (Lederer, 1968, p. 3) and the vulva of the young girl. It is the vulva and not the less visible vagina that may give the appearance of a "wound" and it is the clitoris that may arouse or reinforce men's fears that their penis can indeed be lost, reduced in size, or drawn into their body. Freud himself (1940) recognized the horror that the vulva inspires and recalls a passage from Rabelais in which the exhibition of a woman's vulva puts the devil himself to flight.

Perhaps it is not so much that the fear of the vulva has been ignored by psychoanalytic theorists, but rather that the consequences of this fear have not been fully appreciated. Parental failure to label the girl's external genitals may be one important symptom or manifestation of this fear, although it is unlikely that this neglect derives solely from anxieties which have their origin in the anatomical structure of female genitals. My interviews with parents suggest that additional factors are at work as well, such as the parents' anxieties about acknowledging the female child as a sexual individual who has pleasure with her genitals. (As one mother explained: "It's easy to talk about the vagina because it's a reproductive organ, but telling my daughter about her clitoris seems like telling her to go masturbate.") More careful and systematic investigation is necessary to further elucidate the dynamics underlying such parental discomfort, and failure to acknowledge and name the girl's sensitive external genitals.

In conclusion, it is relevant to note that the clitoris is only one aspect of female experience that has been denied or invalidated by nonrecognition or by application of the label "masculine." Some women have been inhibited in exciting aspects of personal development and achievement by their conscious and unconscious fears that ambitious, competitive, self-seeking strivings are "masculine." Having valued aspects of one's self-experience labeled as gender inappropriate may lead not only to conflicts and inhibitions, but to cognitive and intellectual impairments as well. It is a challenging task for psychoanalysis to seek greater understanding of the unconscious meanings of femininity and of the labeling of specific traits, strivings, and behaviors as "masculine" or "feminine," and to further assess both the adaptive and pathogenic implications these labels may have for the growing child.

Summary

A survey of sex education literature confirms parents' self-reports regarding sex information imparted to their children. With relatively few exceptions, young children (and even teenagers) are taught that "boys have a penis and girls have a vagina," without further linguistic distinctions made regarding the sensitive external genitals of the female child. It is suggested that this incomplete, undifferentiated, and often inaccurate picture of female genitals prevents the growing girl from achieving pride in femininity, and may lead to anxiety and confusion regarding her sexuality. A case is presented in which the failure to label the girl's external genitals was a contributing factor to penis envy, as well as to conflicts about "looking" which led to symptomatic learning inhibitions.

It is suggested that the ubiquity of the female "castration complex" may not stem primarily from the fact that the clitoris is a smaller (and thus inferior) organ compared to the penis. Rather, the girl's feeling of being "cheated" may reflect parental failure to explicitly acknowledge that the vulva (especially the clitoris) is an important aspect of "what girls have." Because visible and sensitive aspects of the girl's genitals are not labeled for her, the girl may feel that she does not have "permission" to develop into a sexually responsive and complete woman. As in the case presented, penis envy may be a symptom expressing the wish to have one's female sexuality "validated," but which also serves to block this forbidden wish by inhibiting sexual responsiveness and pride in femininity.

REFERENCES[*]

Abraham, K. (1920), Manifestation of the female castration complex. In: *Selected Papers.* New York: Basic Books, 1953, pp. 338-369.

Beauvoir, S. de (1953), *The Second Sex.* New York: Knopf.

Bellak, S., & Benedict, P. K., eds. (1958), *Schizophrenia: A Review of the Syndrome.* New York: Grune & Stratton, 1966.

Brierley, M. (1936), Specific determinants in feminine development. *Internat. J. Psycho-Anal.,* 17:163-180.

Chasseguet-Smirgel, J. (1970), *Female Sexuality.* Ann Arbor: Univ. of Michigan Press.

Clower, V. L. (1976), Theoretical implications in current views of masturbation in latency girls. *This Journal,* 24(5):109-125.

Freud, S. (1905), Three essays on the theory of sexuality. *Standard Edition,* 7:125-244. London: Hogarth Press, 1953.

[*] All references to *This Journal* are to the *Journal of the American Psychoanalytic Association.*

_____ (1940), Medusa's head. *Standard Edition*, 18:273-275, London: Hogarth Press, 1955.

Greenacre, P. (1950), Special problems of early female development. In: *Trauma, Growth, and Personality*. New York: International Universities Press, 1969, pp. 234-258.

Kestenberg, J. S. (1968), Outside and inside, male and female. *This Journal*, 16:457-520.

Lederer, W. (1968), *The Fear of Women*. New York: Grune & Stratton.

Lerner, H. E. (1974a), The hysterical personality: A "women's disease." *Comprehensive Psychiat.*, 15:157-164.

_____ (1974b), Early origins of envy and devaluation of women: Implications for sex role stereotypes. *Bull. Menninger Clinic*, 38:538-553.

Masters, W. H. & Johnson, V. E. (1966), *Human Sexual Response*. Boston: Little Brown.

Moulton, R. (1973), A survey and reevaluation of the concept of penis envy. In: *Psychoanalysis and Women*, ed. J. D. Miller. New York: Brunner-Mazel, pp. 207-230.

Ploss, P., Bartels, M., & Bartels, P. (1965), *Femina Libido Sexualis*. New York: The Medical Press.

Shapiro, D. (1965), *Neurotic Styles*. New York: Basic Books.

Taylor, K. (1972), *Almost Twelve*. Wheaton, Ill.: Tyndale House Publishers.

Torok, M. (1970), The significance of penis envy in women. In: *Female Sexuality*, ed. J. Chasseguet-Smirgel. Ann Arbor: University of Michigan, pp. 135-170.

The Menninger Foundation
Topeka, Kansas 66601

SLEEP ORGASM

IN WOMEN

Marcel Heiman, m.d.

I N SUMMARIZING THE LITERATURE of the past hundred years regarding sleep orgasm in women, the findings of the non-
psychoanalytic writers (Rosenthal, 1875; Kisch, 1907; Heyn,
1924; Imielinski, 1961; Winokur et al., 1959; Gebhard et al.,
1970; Kinsey et al., 1953) are as follows:

1. Sleep orgasm may be the result of psychic stimuli
proceeding from the brain.

2. Sleep orgasm is the expression of a normal sexual
drive, and neither the cause nor the result of neurosis.

3. Sleep orgasm may occur prior to the experience of
wakeful orgasm, and the memory of it may have become
repressed.

4. Sleep orgasm may be the result of sexual abstinence.

5. Sleep orgasm may be the result of anxiety.

6. Sleep orgasm may take place—exceptionally—prior to
the onset of menarche.

7. The person in the dream accompanying sleep orgasm
may or may not be an incestual object.

Although some of these findings also hold true for men's
sleep orgasm, the differences are even more significant. It is
beyond the scope of this paper to expand on these.

The early psychoanalytic writers, mainly Rank (1912),
Freud (1900), and Ferenczi (1925), considered undisguised
dreams of sexual content a rare occurrence, and thought of
them as being the result of unacceptable pregenital and/or
incestual wishes. More recently Lewin (1946), Eissler (Panel,

285

1969), Sarlin (1963) arrived at a similar view regarding awake orgasms, i.e., that the genital apparatus may be used to discharge pregenital impulses. Therefore, despite superficial similarities, orgasms differ regarding their sources. Mention should be made of Money's (1960) observations on some paraplegic women who experience "phantom orgasm" in their sleep. His observations are important regarding the part repressed memories play, and also because they touch on the question of an interplay of psychological and physiological stimuli in producing sleep orgasm.

Case 1

From the time she finished college until she arrived at my office at the age of 29, the patient, the youngest of three sisters, moved from action to action to avoid confrontation with her problems of feeling depressed, empty, lonely, being nothing, the fear of being homosexual, of breaking down and becoming schizophrenic like her next older sister, and of not being a woman.

She met her husband on a trip to Europe and performed fellatio while still a virgin. Within a year, she was engaged and married and back to Europe on her honeymoon. While still on the boat she became pregnant: this resulted in feelings of guilt and intense panic, and she felt she had to have an abortion. She had an illegal abortion accompanied by terror and torment, which brought little relief and increased her guilt. When she gave birth to a baby boy a year later, she hoped that everything would be settled and her guilt reconciled.

With the arrival of the baby, she became attached to the child and distant from her husband. She now felt dissatisfied with him sexually. By the time she entered treatment three years later, she was firmly established with a lover with whom she had experienced orgasm for the first time. She was constantly occupied with the thought of leaving her husband

and, less intensely, with the thought of marrying her lover. The roles she assigned unconsciously to each man made it impossible for her to make a decision and brought her into treatment.

The first dream orgasm took place in the setting of the approaching summer vacation—the first to occur during her treatment. The analytic material dealt with her fear of separation and her wish not to lose me. The day preceding the dream she had started to menstruate. In the evening she had intercourse with her husband, after which she flowed more freely. She recalled that, after he had pulled out, she had felt a taste of blood in her mouth: "It was a kind of 'aftertaste.' "

The dream: While kneeling with her torso upright as if praying, she feels the penis of a man who is somewhere in the room approaching her. Just before the penis gets inside her vagina, she puts some contraceptive jelly on her diaphragm. Then she has an orgasm twice and wakes up.

The associations referred to the Communion and getting the Body and the Blood of Christ—"as a taste"—placed on the tongue. The patient was raised as a Catholic and had left the Church some time prior to her marriage to her non-Catholic husband. Her mother is a Church-going Catholic, and so the Church has always been Mother-Church.

She felt depressed. The concern of losing her analyst worried her: If she can't get enough mothering now, what is she going to do, she wonders, when her mother will be dead and she herself will reach menopause? "I will need mothering then even more, because there will be no mother to mother me, and I won't be able to have a baby to mother it." She resents that she had a menopausal mother who either had no milk or not enough milk or her milk wasn't good enough. But on the other hand, she had a nursemaid for many years who was all her own and who was her substitute mother. The nurse and the patient were "one"; they loved each other without any feeling that they used each other—a description also applicable to her relationship with her lover. In addition, the nursemaid had lost her own mother, and so they were mother to each other. Just as she had to go outside the family for love when she was a child, so has she now to go outside the marriage for a lover.

For some time she had been severely depressed by the prospect of her analyst's approaching vacation, complaining of an empty, hollow feeling in the pit of her stomach. On one of these occasions, following the first session upon his return, she presented a dream she had had while visiting her parents: "I had a baby and the baby was nursing at my breast. It was a wonderful feeling. Exactly what I needed."

At one time during the treatment, when she had been having rather little sex, she felt that her breasts had become smaller, that they "were drying up" because there had been so little sex, so little loving, so little fondling of them. She felt that, as the suckling baby keeps the breasts large and in milk, so does her lover's fondling of her breasts. And just as the breasts dry up if there is no fondling, so does she dry up if there is no affection. We can understand that she perceived sexual intercourse as being fed, as satisfying her need for being mothered.

This woman showed wide fluctuations from reality-attuned feelings and behavior to fairly deep regressions. As, for instance, the following incident of identification with her unborn baby: "I can remember in the palms of my hands and in my belly—outside and inside of me—*that* feeling when the baby moves; I can still feel it. Nothing makes you realize it more than when you put your hands on the belly." Her memory of being pregnant and longing for a baby becomes fused with her longing to be a baby, to be unborn: The day before, after leaving the office, she had come back and knocked on the door (something she had done at the beginning of her treatment rather frequently, but not lately). She seemed quite moved when I showed her the connection and, in a tiny voice, says: "Yes, I don't like being borne out of this room." My office is her mother's womb in which she feels secure. For a long time she had assumed a fetal position — both in the chair and on the couch.

One day, upon leaving a session and wanting a cigarette but not having one, she had the following sensation while walking down the street: "My mouth was watering for that cigarette and the taste in my mouth was sweet." At this point she remembered that she had felt that taste twice: "Once, when I had an orgasm for the first time, and I was so surprised and the taste was so sweet; and the second time" — at this point she stopped and she seemed blocked: "This is unrememberable." But then she continued: "It was when I started to nurse my baby, and I remembered thinking, it tastes sweet, and I was surprised."

The patient then added: "When I nursed, I would feel contractions in my uterus. It is comparable to an orgasm and that is where I am mixed up: because *in having an orgasm I am nursing* — I am the mother and the child.

We may assume, therefore, that through identification with her baby in the nursing situation she is able to recapture the distant echo of what she called the unrememberable mouth-experience when she was a baby and nursing. Perhaps this in turn allows us to assume that, in the situation of being left by a mother figure, the patient's dream orgasm is a (fantasied) wish-fulfillment of having the nipple in her mouth. Indeed, confirming this assumption, it was in a state of frustration — "her mouth watering for a cigarette" — when she felt the sweet taste in her mouth. As a child of a menopausal mother, nursing might very well have been a frustrating experience for her.

In having an orgasm she feels she is nursing, and in nursing she feels she has an orgasm. She fantasies man and woman in intercourse as a mother and child in the nursing situation, where she is in the position of the mother and child, in the position of the man and woman, or of both at the same time. Perhaps this woman, more so than for others, felt primal-scene fantasies more directly as a mother-child situation, leading to her feeling a need for something in her mouth.

There is some clinical evidence that this patient differentiated either poorly or not at all the bodies of the lovers and the bodies of mother-child: they are one, and fused with each other. As she says, "The child does not know what is mother and what is baby—just as a mother feels that a baby is part of her." "When I nursed, I had a sweet, contented smile: the nursing smile of the mother is related to the nursing-sucking motion of the baby."

She perceives sex as satisfying her sexual needs both as a grown-up woman and of the child in her: "I wouldn't need to be a little girl." Being satisfied sexually by the man permits her to mother the man, since through intercourse she has gained his strength.

Discussion

Why does the patient not dream—as she had once—that she had a baby nursing at her breast and finds her wish fulfillment in that way? Why does the dream change the oral wish to a genital experience?

Some of the patient's waking sensations may contribute to the understanding of her dream orgasm. Once when she was in the middle of her period, "bloody and dry," she had the sensation of feeling the shape of her vagina, and felt the vagina to be hungry like an empty stomach. At such times she dreamed of herself as a wild animal wanting to devour. Lorand (1939) describes a patient's hunger sensations of a sucking nature in the vagina; another of his patients called the vagina a monster constantly hungry. It is important that the dream mentioned earlier took place during menstruation. In addition to mobilizing castration anxiety, menstruation has been found to mobilize aggressive-cannibalistic impulses on various levels (Heiman, 1956). In our patient, we find these impulses predominantly on an oral level. Her hallucinatory sensation of a bloody "aftertaste" belongs here. This

experience took place after her husband withdrew his penis
when they had intercourse during her menstrual period the
evening before the dream. Knowing that the patient had a
strong tendency to identify mouth and vagina and to displace
from one to the other, we can assume that she responded to
the withdrawal of the penis from her vagina as if the nipple
was withdrawn from her mouth. We need to remind ourselves
here that fellatio was her first sexual experience, performed on
her own initiative.

A preliminary study on the nature and source of orgasm
in a hundred women has shown that some of them derived
strong sexual excitation from fellatio, even to the point of
orgasm. Freud (1905), in a footnote added in 1920, refers to
the confessions of a grown girl in "Das Lutscherli" [The
Sucker], which he had read in 1919, who "represents the
satisfaction to be gained from sucking as something
completely analogous to sexual satisfaction, when this is
obtained from a lover's kiss" (p. 181). The description given of
absolute satisfaction, of other-worldly bliss, resembles our
patient's experience. I have described (Heiman, 1963) a
similar observation:

> This woman found it very difficult to look at me dur-
> ing her sessions. When she finally did look, the hour
> ended with her having an orgasm. Four months earlier
> she had given birth to a baby girl. 'When I feed baby,
> with her sitting on my lap and sucking milk from a
> bottle, I get sexually aroused.' Perhaps the most diffi-
> cult thing for her to speak of was that she still 'sucks'
> liquids from a glass 'as if through a nipple,' and this
> arouses her sexually. She 'sucked' the tongue of the
> first boy who kissed her and felt the sexual arousal in her
> vagina. In a dream in which her baby had drowned she
> recalled that one could restore life by manipulating the
> baby's tongue in a rotating fashion (!). This woman pre-
> ferred masturbation to intercourse. She masturbates by

manipulating her nipples, which leads to orgasm" [p. 382].

The "after-taste" of blood in the patient's associations to the orgasm dream is the only evidence that the withdrawal of the need-satisfying object caused frustration, aroused anger, and mobilized biting and cannibalistic impulses. Our assumption that the patient wished to separate the penis from its body by force, just as she felt forcibly separated from her analyst (feeling "borne" out of the office), finds some confirmation in the dream orgasm at the time before his vacation. In the dream, the penis—as if moved by a supreme, magical force—becomes separated from the man's body, approaches her, and finally enters her body through her vagina; then she has two orgasms. "One for the body and one for the blood of Christ," as the patient added whimsically. The dream in its manifest content was completely bloodless. Only in the association do we find the blood: the body and the blood of Christ is placed on her tongue—"As a taste," she said, a parallel to the "after-taste" of the evening before. As a result of the exquisite dream work, there is no bloody specter in the manifest dream.

We may now attempt to answer the question why the dream changes the oral wish to a genital experience, and we may attempt an interpretation of the orgasm dream in our patient.

When strong oral, biting, devouring, cannibalistic impulses are present, triggered by the loss or threatened loss of the (part) object, the dream deals with them by displacing the scene from the mouth to the vagina, and by changing the desired nursing situation on mother's breast to a genital one resulting in orgasm. *In the sexual act, the aggressive, destructive, incorporative pregenital impulses may be placed in the service of the sexual act and may be utilized for the production of an orgasm.* The dream orgasm is used to ward off and to disguise unacceptable pregenital wishes. This is analogous to her thought that sexual intercourse satisfies her needs as a woman and the needs of the child in her. We may also recall here that she experienced her first orgasm with her lover, who represented her nursemaid, her good mother. We may wonder if she felt her mother to be as frustrating orally as she felt her husband to be frustrating sexually.

The patient described how her sexual needs and her needs for mothering (her oral needs) were being satisfied through sex. Being the man and the woman in the sex act as well as the mother and the baby in the nursing situation, the patient expressed the total satisfaction by saying: orgasm is nursing—and nursing is orgasm. The orgasm represented total satisfaction and fulfillment on several levels.[1]

Kestenberg (1956, p. 258) discussing the question of assumed early vaginal participation in female development, cites Freud's paper on Leonardo (1910): "A mother's love for the infant she suckles and cares for is something far more profound than her later affection for the growing child. It is in the nature of a completely satisfying love-relation, which not only fulfills every mental wish but also every physical need; and if it represents one of the forms of attainable human happiness, that is in no little measure due to the possibility it offers of satisfying, without reproach, wishful impulses which have long been repressed and which must be called perverse" (p. 117).

The total satisfaction is hypothesized as being the result of the patient's identifying with her baby in the nursing situation. This assumption sees the mother and the female infant in the nursing situation fused as far as objects and part-objects are concerned. It further assumes parallel

---

[1] There might be a genetic link for our patient to be able to feel to be both mother and baby in the nursing situation, and man and woman in the coital act, as I have pointed out (Heiman, 1963, p. 370), following the lead of Deutsch (1925, p. 192). This thought would be in line with Kubie's (1974) assumption that the two "drives," i.e., being child and adult, and being woman and man, might be related.

experiences in mother and infant—in the oral and in the vaginal cavities, in this case.

There are clinical observations indicating that the infant's sucking evokes oral sensations in the mother—regardless of whether the baby is breast- or bottle-fed. In addition, it has been reported that the infant's sucking may stimulate the mother's genitals. (It is, of course, possible that this might be an abnormal maternal response—a regressive failure of maternal sublimation). What needs to be added, in order to make this "mystical" union complete, is the contention that the infant also experiences genital sensations, that the infant's sucking also stimulates it's own genitals.

This hypothesis is based on two conditions. One, that the female infant—from birth—is capable of genital excitation (and discharge); and, two, that the nursing process as a result of fusion of objects and part-objects might provide such a simultaneous stimulation of oral and vaginal cavities of both mother and infant. One is as difficult to prove as the other.

Kestenberg (1956) referring to both Brierley (1932) and Payne (1935), who "thought in terms of spontaneous overflow of excitation from the oral to the vaginal zone," considers it feasible that a local response of vaginal "sucking" may develop in association with oral sucking (p. 261).

Barnett (1968) contends—without giving the basis for her assumption—"that girls are anatomically capable of having vaginal sexual activity from birth and, unlike boys, are capable of orgastic release" (p. 590). And later: "The capacity for genital discharge is the normal condition in girls, with such discharge occurring in consequence of the child's own needs..." (pp. 594-595).

Fisher (1975), on the basis of recent sleep-dream research, has suggested the possibility that in the female infant, as in the male, a cycle of sexual arousal during REM or dreaming sleep may be present, but states that the evidence for such an endogenous source of sexual stimulation is not yet definitive. In fact, he suspects the possibility that there may be a true sex difference, that the nocturnal penile thrust characteristic of the male infant may not have an analogue in the female.

Greenacre (1950) had expressed the view that vaginal sensations may precede clitoral sensations (p. 240). In a later paper (1954) she speaks of genital orgasm as early as in the eighth month "in situations of stress" (p. 54). She sees such an orgasm as a spontaneous discharge for which the genitals serve as a channel.

Kleeman's (1976) observations deal with genital self-stimulation in infant and toddler girls. Among his recommendations for further study is "The impact of stress overstimulation on genital sensation or discharge of tension through genital channels" (p. 102).

The "sensuous interaction" which Galenson and Roiphe (1976) place during the early rapprochement phase may be seen as a bridge between the earliest such interaction, i.e. the nursing situation, and later developmental phases.

If our interpretation of the patient's sleep orgasm in the situation of being left by a mother figure is correct, the sleep orgasm may be the result of dealing with the loss of the object or part-object and the resulting frustration. She separates the nipple-penis from the body and incorporates it orally and vaginally. This is one of several versions of what I call the "portable analyst": when the analyst leaves, she retains what she wants most.

Now we can better understand why, following her analyst's return, the patient had the blissful dream of having a baby at her breast: the need-satisfying object (part-object) had returned, she was united again with mother at her breast—blissfully sucking: no frustration, no anger, no violence, no aggression: neither in the manifest dream content nor in her associations. The next step would be Lewin's blank dream.[2]

Money's (1960) findings might be useful for our

---

[2] The blissful feeling in the dream is like the "sweet, contented smile" the patient felt while nursing her baby. Indicating her identification with her baby, she related the nursing smile of the mother to the nursing-sucking motion of the baby. At one time, she compared the "nursing smile" to the smile of the Mona Lisa.

discussion: since women who never experienced orgasm before their spinal injury did not have orgasm dreams, Money wondered whether, for the orgasm dreamers, "sex was a matter of memory." This might be applicable to our patient, where, apparently, a non genital memory was one element entering into the dream work.

The resulting sleep orgasm might not only serve to disguise a pregenital experience—as I suggested earlier—it might in addition be the expression of such a nursing experience, when oral and genital sensations were felt simultaneously and possibly could not be discriminated.

Case 2

Ferenczi (1916) has written of a dream of anal intercourse that disguised the shameful experience of defecating on the floor the night preceding the dream. The importance of anal drive derivatives' contributing to sexual dreams leading to orgasm was observed in another patient at a time in her treatment when she finally was able to feel anger and was beginning to express it. This woman, prior to her marriage, had a number of induced abortions. She came for treatment because after marriage she could not carry to term. The first dream to be reported occurred when, during therapy, she perceived pregnancy and delivery in anal terms with fears of bursting. She also had angry memories of defecating in the presence of her father while he was taking a shower in her full view, and recollections of her first pregnancy following marriage when she was preoccupied with her anus, which was full of sensations, and when she wanted anal intercourse for the first time in her life. She was especially angry at her mother who had "squeezed" her out of the womb and had thereby hurt some of the patient's "plumbing." Observations by Galenson and Roiphe (1976), the significance of which is still under study, might be mentioned in this context. Galenson and Roiphe saw the emergence of ambivalent feelings to the mother, in girls between seventeen and twenty months of age, after they had seen their father's penis and seen him urinate. An awareness of the difference between the sexes also is manifest in girls of this age.

Dream: She feels a compelling urge to masturbate, the urgency having the sensation of immediacy: She was drawing a sketch of a man sitting on the toilet with his pants down. Suddenly, she is seized by sexual excitement and a wish to masturbate. She wakes up with an orgasm, her back arched.

Galenson (1971) and Galenson and Roiphe (1976) describe how one of their subjects, Ruth at age eighteen months "began to draw" following her discovery of the anatomical differences between the sexes.

The next dream was produced in the context of the parent's rage at everyone connected with and perhaps responsible for another miscarriage which occurred at that time during treatment. Her husband came in for a special measure of anger—"she could have kicked, punched, and strangled him"—because he lost her contact lenses (i.e., her eyesight) while she was in the hospital, which she perceived as a castration. More realistically, she was angry at the physician who had examined her vaginally and whom she accused of having infected her and thus of having caused the miscarriage. She dreamed of a baby "with shit all over the face," and she marveled at how wonderful it is that girl babies can sit in their shit without getting an infection in the vagina. So it might be the anger—"the shit"—that kills her babies.

Dream (again with the compelling urge to reach an orgasm quickly): She dreams of masturbating, "squatting against a toy lion with a furry head!" At the point of orgasm she wakes up lying on her stomach with a Kotex pressed against her genitals. She sadly recalls that after every miscarriage she has a dream with orgasm. Because all her associations have to do with anger at mother and mother figures, the orgasm might be the result of her anger—an "anger-orgasm"—probably at her mother who is made responsible for the miscarriage—another castration—experienced unconsciously on an anal level.

Discussion

The intense anger described by this woman, flooding the organism to an intolerable degree, presents one of the situations in which an immediate discharge is imperative. Greenacre (1954) considers such an explosive genital discharge a "stress orgasm." I have described (Heiman, 1959) another orgasmic response of the genital organs that is not unlike the stress orgasm: the sudden uterine bleeding in situations of severe stress or fright. It represents a special form of functional uterine bleeding ("fright-bleeding").

Schur (1955) dealt with this problem: the greater the degree of anxiety the ego experiences, the more predominantly the ego utilizes nonneutralized (aggressive) energy. At its height, anxiety reaches "panic with an abundance of somatic phenomena up to shock," at which point the ego will operate "exclusively" with nonneutralized energy." At such times, also, nonneutralized libido will be utilized by the ego—the discharge phenomena being orgasm (p. 125).

Her orgasm dream—after experiencing an abortion—as a culmination of masturbating with a furry toy animal, could be linked to Galenson and Roiphe's (1976) observation of little girls' using toy animals for masturbation after being confronted with the anatomical difference between the sexes, and their attempt to deal with the resulting castration anxiety. The anger the patient feels at her mother is strong enough to allow us to assume that it has its root in early childhood.

Returning again to the first patient, I would call attention to the similarities between the clinical observations of Fliess (1956) and Lewin (1946) to my own. Fliess's patient had one of her "orgastic dreams" during analysis after having had lunch with her mother. According to him, she reincorporated her mother's breast by seeing her. This reminds us of my patient who had an orgasm after looking at me. Lewin's patient had a blank dream with orgasm, stimulated directly by contact with the mother, which reproduced for her a union with her mother at nursing. Lewin's description of the meaning of separation—such as the impending vacation, the end of the analytic hour or the canceling of an hour—for these patients is almost identical with what I have described in my patient.

The earliest narcissistic bliss, in other words, the satisfaction at the mother's breast and in her care, fulfills the infantile need for security. Rado (1926) postulates an "alimentary orgasm" as following upon nursing, a prototype for the future genital climax. Even though Rado's assumption of a nursing orgasm needs to be understood metaphorically rather then literally, Lewin leaves no doubt regarding his views. This view is in harmony with the hypothesis presented here. Also in agreement is the idea that the metaphorical nursing orgasm represents the prototype for the future genital climax.

Lewin (1950) describes a patient who equated vaginal with oral activity: "The fantasied nursing is displaced downward so that the contractions of labor stimulate or reactivate the process of suckling, with the baby's head substituting for the breast" (p. 115). My own observations demonstrate that the displacement downward holds true even more regarding the actual nursing situation which, as I pointed out, may enhance sexual feelings both on a physiological and psychological level (Heiman, 1963). Our patient—feels contractions while nursing. But, in addition, in this woman, functions and organs are interchangeable, leading to confusing sensations. while nursing she feels she has an orgasm—and in having an orgasm she feels she is nursing.

Lewin's patient, who equated the head of the baby with the breast she was sucking as a baby, and the delivery of the head of the baby with the withdrawal of the breast, is again very similar to our patient: she equates mother and baby in the nursing situation to the point of fusing them. This becomes apparent, for instance, when she recalls tasting the sweet taste of the milk in her own mouth when she started to nurse her baby. Thus, it might be the fusion that causes the confusion.

It is the interchangeability between oral and genital, between mother and child in the nursing situation, and between woman and man in the coital situation that becomes manifest to such a degree in our patient. The reactivation of the early mother-child relation during both nursing and coitus cannot be described accurately and completely as a displacement downward. There are, in addition, elements of fusion and identification for which we have to assume a high degree of regression and a consequent blurring and even disappearance of the boundaries of the representations of self and object (Sarlin, 1963).

The hypothesized sensations in the genital organs in the female infant during the nursing situation—while not a universal phenomenon—might in some instances form a prototype on which genital sensations in the subsequent years would be built. Separation- and castration anxiety might mobilize the memory traces laid down during the nursing experience. Handling the genital organs, including mastur-bation, could, when considered from this point of view, during the second and third years of life provide satisfaction for the female child on both the genital and oral levels. This view would hold true regardless of the means used for masturbation.

But we might also consider the possibility that in situations of tension—sexual tension, anger, or anxiety—the genital organs are available as a channel for discharge. The urgency for genital discharge—and its explosive nature—as observed in the second patient was seen to be linked to anal drive derivatives, confirming observations of early psycho-analytic writers. I described the dream orgasm of the patient as an anally derived "anger-orgasm." We may assume the possibility that it is built on the basis of earlier nursing sensations in the infant's genitals, associated with frustration.

Early sexual stimulation of the genital organs, possibly including orgasm, might be assumed in those instances where sleep orgasm is experienced prior to awake orgasm. Apparently these early sexual experiences are repressed deeply enough not to find access to consciousness during wakefulness. The exceptions are those women who on account of their psychopathology are quite orgastic.

Observations of sleep orgasm occurring in paraplegic women favor the view that, at least in those instances, sexual excitation up to and including orgasm is initiated by a dream and is experienced by the sleeping woman as an orgasm. Further studies are needed to establish the occurrence of such processes in women not physically handicapped. In the latter instances, however, we may assume that the pelvic organs become stimulated secondarily. Upon awakening, some women might not be able to differentiate where the orgasm originated. Observations made in the past and by the author (unpublished) on women whose sleep orgasms are akin to hallucinatory experiences of coitus ("incubus") very likely belong in this category. Such considerations permit us to speak of "orgasm dream" as well as of "dream orgasms."

Our clinical data seem to confirm earlier psychoanalytic observations that sleep orgasm may serve to disguise unacceptable pregenital and/or aggressive impulses. It is not unlikely that these impulses may, in some instances, contribute to the formation of sleep orgasm. Further studies are needed to establish a similar mechanism for awake orgasm. After all, we do not know yet whether dream orgasm mirrors awake orgasm, and if so, with what degree of accuracy.

Summary

Some of the recent most challenging contributions to our knowledge of female sexuality were provided by direct observations as early as during the second year of life concerning genital self-stimulation and masturbation in girls. Other investigators have advanced the proposition that girls are capable of vaginal masturbation and possibly of experiencing vaginal sensation and stimulation very early in life.

Our own clinical study on sleep orgasm, based mainly on data obtained from the analysis of one woman, leads to formulating the hypothesis that in some instances the nursing situation may provide sensations in the genitals (vagina), not only for the mother, but also for the baby.

We assume that such sensations in the genitals of the infant female are not the result of mechanical stimulation of the genital organs—as described during the second year and later—but are the result of a "resonance" phenomenon whereby the infant's genitals, including the vagina, are stimulated from within.

The observations of orgasm made by others and by the author should be considered the first tentative steps toward an understanding of the complex nature of female orgasm. Eventually, further studies might lead to distinguishing more clearly a sexual orgasm in a narrower sense from a sucking orgasm, from an anger orgasm, and from a stress orgasm—i.e. an unspecific genital discharge. Sleep orgasm can represent gratification of unacceptable disguised sexual wishes and can therefore occur after intercourse and orgasm experienced when awake. The study of sleep orgasm might be of value in relation to the general problems of female orgasm.

I would like to close with a reminder that some of the formulations presented in this paper are quite obviously largely speculative.

REFERENCES*

Barnett, M. (1968), "I can't" versus "he won't." *This Journal,* 16:588-600
Brierley, M. (1932), Some problems of integration in women. *Internat. J. Psycho-Anal.,* 13:433-448.

*All references to *This Journal* are to the *Journal of the American Psychoanalytic Association.*

Deutsch, H. (1925), The Psychology of women in relation to the functions of reproduction. In: *The Psychoanalytic Reader*, ed. R. Fliess. New York: International Universities Press, 1948, pp. 165-179.

Ferenczi, S. (1916), Pollution without dream orgasm and dream orgasm without pollution. In: *Further Contributions to Theory and Technique of Psycho-Analysis*. New York: Basic Books, 1952, pp. 297-304.

———— (1925), Psycho-analysis of sexual habits. In: *Further Contributions to the Theory and Technique of Psycho-Analysis*, New York: Basic Books, 1952, pp. 259-297.

Fisher, C. (1975), Discussion of paper by Galenson, E. and Roiphe, H. on "Some suggested revisions concerning early female development" (unpublished).

Fliess, R. (1956), *Erogeneity and Libido*. New York: International Universities Press, p. 91.

Freud, S. (1900), The interpretation of dreams. *Standard Edition*, 5:402-403. London: Hogarth Press, 1953.

———— (1905), Three essays on the theory of sexuality. *Standard Edition*, 7:125-243. London: Hogarth Press.

———— (1910), Leonardo da Vinci and a memory of his childhood. *Standard Edition*, 11:59-137, London: Hogarth Press, 1957.

———— (1915), A case of paranoia running counter to the psycho-analytic theory of the disease. *Standard Edition*, 14:261-272. London: Hogarth Press, 1957.

Galenson, E. (1971), A consideration of the nature of thought in childhood play. In: *Separation-Individuation: Essays in Honor of Margaret S. Mahler*, eds. J. B. McDevitt & C. F. Settlage. New York: International Universities Press, pp. 41-60.

———— & Roiphe, H. (1976), Some suggested revisions concerning early sexual development. *This Journal*, 24(5):285-304.

Gebhard, P., Raboch, J., Giese, H. (1970), Female sexuality. In: *The Sexuality of Women*, Vol. I, New York: Stein & Day, pp. 18-20.

Greenacre, P. (1950), Special problems of early female sexual development. In: *Trauma, Growth and Personality*. New York: International Universities Press, 1969, pp. 237-258.

———— (1954), Problems of infantile neurosis: Contribution to a discussion: In: *Emotional Growth*. New York: International Universities Press, 1971, pp. 50-57.

Heiman, M. (1956), Psychological influences in functional uterine bleeding. *Obst. & Gynec.*, 7:240.

———— (1959), Separation from a love object as an etiological factor in functional uterine bleeding. *J. Mount Sinai Hospital*, 26:57.

———— (1963), Sexual response in women. *This Journal*, 11:360-385.

Heyn, A. (1924), Uber Sexuelle Träume (Pollutionen) bei Frauen. *Arch. Frauenkunde*, 10:60-69.

Imielinski, K. (1961), Uber den nächtlichen Orgasmus bei Frauen. *Psychiat. Neurol. med. Psychol.*, 13:390-392.

Kestenberg, J. (1956), On development of maternal feelings in early childhood. *The Psychoanalytic Study of the Child*, 11:257-291. New York: International Universities Press.

Kinsey, A. et al. (1953), *Sexual Behavior in the Human Female*. Philadelphia: W. B. Saunders, pp. 192-193.

Kisch, E. (1907), *The Sexual Life of Women in its Physiological, Pathological and Hygienic Aspect*. Transl. N. Paul. New York: Allied, 1910.

Kleeman, J. (1976), Genital self-stimulation in infant and toddler girls. In: *Mastur-bation: From Infancy to Senescence*, ed. I. M. Marcus & J. J. Francis. New York: International Universities Press, pp. 77-106.

Kubie, L. (1974), The drive to become both sexes. *Psychoanal. Quart.*, 43:349-426.

Lewin, B. (1946), Sleep, the mouth and the dream screen. In: *Selected Papers*. New York: Psychoanalytic Quarterly, 1973, pp. 87-100.

_____ (1950), *The Psychoanalysis of Elation*. New York: Norton, p. 87.

Lorand, S. (1939), Contribution to the problem of vaginal orgasm. *Internat. J. Psycho-Anal.* 20:432-438.

Money, J. (1960), Phantom orgasm in the dreams of paraplegic men and women. *Arch. Gen. Psychiat.*, 3:373-382.

Panel (1969), The theory of genital primacy in the light of ego psychology, M. Berezin, Reporter. *This Journal*, 17:969-987.

Payne, S. (1935), A conception of femininity. *Brit. J. Med. Psychol.*, 15:18-33.

Rado, S. (1926), The psychic effects of intoxication. *Internat. J. Psycho-Anal.*, 7:396-413.

Rank, O. (1912), Die Symbolschichtung im Wecktraum und ihre Wiederkehr im mythischen Denken. *Jb. psychoanal. psychopath. Forsch.*, 4:51.

Rosenthal, M. (1875), Klinik der Nervenkrankheiten. Stuttgart, Verlag von F. Enke, p. 469.

Sarlin, C. (1963), Feminine identity. *This Journal*, 11:790-816.

Schur, M. (1955), Comments on the metapsychology of somatization. *The Psychoanalytic Study of the Child*, 10:119-164. New York: International Universities Press.

Winokur, G., Guze, S. B. & Pfeiffer, E. (1959), Nocturnal orgasm in women. *Arch. Gen. Psychiat.* 1:180-184.

1148 Fifth Avenue
New York, New York, 10028

Burness E. Moore, m.d.

T HE STUDIES BY MASTERS AND JOHNSON (1966) of human sexual behavior by means of direct observation and physiological techniques have evoked a re-examination of theories about
male and particularly female sexuality derived largely from
psychoanalytic observations. In a lengthy paper, based primarily on the work of Masters and Johnson but also including
data from embryological, anatomical, primatological, and
endocrine studies, Sherfey (1966) presents conclusions that
appear to contradict some of the long-held views of psychoanalysts. She develops three major theses: (1) that Freud's
concept of bisexuality is outmoded and no longer useful in understanding female sexuality; (2) "that there is no such thing
as a psychopathological clitoral fixation" on the basis of anatomical and physiological evidence that vaginal orgasm as distinct from clitoral orgasm does not exist; and (3) that woman's
sexuality is insatiable and civilization has resulted from the
need to subjugate it.

The physiological observations of Masters and Johnson
are recorded, are reproducible, and may be confirmed by
others. Though the evidence is less easily presented, it is also
true that psychoanalytic interpretations regarding the vicissitudes of female sexuality have been confirmed many times
and are well established. It is my belief that we must regard

---

This article is a modified version of one that appeared in the *Journal of the
American Psychoanalytic Association* (1968), 16:569-587.

both sets of data as valid and attempt to integrate our understanding of female sexuality on the basis of both. Sherfey has
made a worthwhile attempt at integration of information
from many disciplines, but her conclusions about female
orgasm itself are, in my opinion, ambivalent and therefore
ambiguous, and her views about the nature of female sexuality
too sweeping and far-reaching in respect to cultural evolution.
Benedek (1968) has answered Sherfey's first contention, and
Orr (1968) responded to the third. In this paper, dealing with
the second, I shall attempt to reconcile the apparent dis-
crepancies between the physiological observations and psychoanalytic theory which led Sherfey to her conclusions by a
consideration of the role of psychic representation in determining sexual responsivity and the experiential nature of
orgasm in the human female.

     At this point it will be useful to summarize the findings of
Masters and Johnson that are significant for the purpose of my
discussion:

     1. The basic physiological responses of the human body
to sexual stimulation are vasocongestion—widespread, but
concentrated mainly in the pelvis and genitals—and generalized increase in muscle tension.

     2. In the female, stimulation applied directly or indirect-
ly to the clitoris—manually, with an artificial penis, or in coitus—increases pelvic venous congestion, involving the plexi
surrounding the lower third of the vagina, the vestibular
bulbs, the labia minora—and labia majora in multipara—
anterior commissure, and the uterus. To a lesser degree, the
shaft and glans of the clitoris are also engorged.

     3. At a critical level of tension, contraction of certain
muscles of the pelvic floor surrounding the lower third of the
vagina (the bilateral bulbocavernosi, transverse perineals, external anal sphincter, rectus abdominus, levator ani, and the
ischiocavernosi) is triggered, discharging the vasocongestion in
rhythmic contractions that are experienced subjectively as
orgasm. The extravaginal muscles contract against the cir-

cumvaginal venous chambers and not against the vaginal wall, which does not itself participate. The same type of discharge occurs with any form of sexual arousal or coital position and whether or not there is anything in the lower third of the vagina to contract against. The inner two thirds of the vagina lengthens and distends as sexual excitement increases and remains expanded and relatively immobile during the orgastic experience. There is, therefore, little opportunity for any stimulation of this upper section of the vagina by penile thrusts. Sherfey has added that the two portions of the vagina clearly show different embryonic origins.

4. Although the mucosa lining the lower third of the vagina appears to be an erotogenic zone during the thrusting action in coitus, the degree of its sensitivity is unknown, and it appears intimately connected with the clitoral-labial complex.

These and other physiological observations by Masters and Johnson of human female orgasm were introduced to psychoanalysis by Marcel Heiman (1963), who correlated them with various pyschoanalytic observations. Fliess (1956) and Lorand (1939), for example, had postulated a division of the vagina into a proximal two thirds, representing a new erotogenic zone acquired by the pubescent girl, and a distal third, which is "anatomically vestibular and pleasure-physiologically phallic." My own review of the psychoanalytic literature (Panel, 1961) had led me to believe that the importance of vaginal rather than clitoral sensation had been exaggerated and that so-called frigidity in some instances did not seem primarily related to psychic conflict. At the same panel, Helene Deutsch made a definitive statement based on 40 years of psychoanalytic study of the sexuality of women. The similarity of her conclusions and those of Benedek (1961), based on psychoanalytic observations, to the findings of Masters and Johnson, based on direct observation, represents a remarkable example of the almost simultaneous convergence of knowledge from different scientific fields described by Spitz (1955). To make more explicit the similarity, I would like to quote briefly from Helene Deutsch's (1960) remarks at that time. She expressed her conviction that

> the female sexual organs consist of two parts with a definite division of function: the clitoris is the sexual organ, the vagina primarily the organ of reproduction. All waves of sexual excitement, often very strong and urgent in women, flow into the clitoris, and only subsequent, more or less successful, communication of this excitement to the vagina secondarily incorporates this organ into the sphere of sexual experience. Originally the vagina was endowed with the dynamic forces of reproduction. The erotization of the vagina is a job performed by way of the clitoris and by the active intervention of the man's sexual organ.
>
> This central role of the clitoris is not merely the result of masturbation, but is a biological destiny. The muscular apparatus of the vagina is in the service of reproduction and may or may not become involved in the orgastic activity [p. 360].

Her description of the movements of the vagina as having the character of sucking in and relaxing, with a rhythm adjusted to the rhythm of the male partner, is a fair clinical approximation of the rhythmic muscular contractions observed in the lower third of the vagina as described by Masters and Johnson.

Although Sherfey quoted the view of Benedek and Deutsch as late exceptions to generally held psychoanalytic views, she apparently discounted their clinical conformity to the new physiological information because of Benedek's and Deutsch's—to her, puzzling—continued adherence to the clitoral-vaginal transfer theory. She raises the question of whether much of the sexual neuroses in women today could be, in part, iatrogenic, produced by erroneous assumptions of vaginal and clitoral responsivity. If so, she concludes that these erroneous concepts must be dispelled from the minds of psychoanalysts and psychiatrists . . . [by] *indisputable* proof that *the vaginal orgasm as distinct from the clitoral orgasm* does not exist and whatever does exist instead is compatible with the many observations on female psychosexuality we know to be true. If such proof is forthcoming, the psychoanalytic theory may not be refuted but will require amendations [p. 36]. However, the dilemma does not lie in the overimaginative theorizing of psychoanalysts, as many critics imply. The theories offered in place of the psychoanalytic ones are inadequate or say the same thing in different ways. More importantly, none of them deals with the biological realities: all women *do* have a seemingly rudimentary penis; it *is* the primary source of maximum sexual arousal in childhood; its very presence and functioning *are* the result of genetic, evolutionary adaptations; and clitoral fixation very obviously can, and very often does, interfere with vaginal functioning. The dilemma lies in the erroneous basic premises supplied to psychiatry by biology, a significant part of which has been corrected only in the past few years. None of the alternative theories to the psychoanalytic one has made use of this new biological information [pp. 42-43].

In a detailed presentation of the work of Masters and Johnson, supported by little-known embryological, anatomical, primatological, and endocrine studies, Sherfey establishes fairly convincingly her thesis that vaginal orgasm as distinct from clitoral orgasm does not exist *physiologically*. She submits the observation of Masters and Johnson that clitorally induced orgasms may be, and often are, as intense or more so than vaginally induced ones, and multiple orgasms are more likely to occur. There may be, therefore, some validity to her conclusion that "The common idea that clitorally induced orgasms are confined to the clitoris and are necessarily less satisfying *physically* than vaginally induced orgasms is mani-

festly erroneous" (pp. 98-99). Although she herself is inconsistent in its use, Sherfey's substitution of "coital orgasm" for
what has previously been called "vaginal" may be desirable in
the light of the recent physiological studies, since it describes
the situation without anatomical implications. But her statement that "These findings force us to the conclusion that *there
is no such thing as psychopathological clitoral fixation; there
are only varying degrees of vaginal insensitivity and coital frigidity*" (p. 101) is not consistent with her own admission that
"clitoral fixation very obviously can, and very often does, interfere with vaginal functioning" (p. 42). She states that she
has left the psychological forces operative in the development
of coital frigidity to another paper, and so far has not demonstrated the compatibility of her interpretation of the
physiological findings with "the many observations on female
psychosexuality we know to be true" (p. 36).

Despite the paramount importance of the clitoral system
physiologically in respect to orgasm, Sherfey concedes that
most women clearly prefer vaginally induced orgasms, "but
not because the sheer physical pleasure is greater, either in intensity or frequency of orgasmic release" (p. 107). The crux of
the matter seems to be the issue of physical versus psychic satisfaction. As in the case of her objections to the role of bisexuality in female sexuality (see Benedek, 1968), so also in regard
to clitoral and vaginal erotogeneity, Sherfey overlooks the
truth that the anatomical and physiological facts, though important, are of less consequence clinically than their psychic
representation. Hysterical anesthesias do not conform to the
anatomical distribution of nerves but to the patients'
erroneous concepts of the body. Distortions of previously
learned anatomical facts about the genitals are frequently observed in analytic practice, and the facts Sherfey marshals
have been, she says, previously unknown, or in some instances
curiously ignored or neglected even by biologists. Could more
be expected of patients? Evidently there is a strong need in
both sexes to cathect the vagina as the organ of mature sexual

pleasure, promoting conclusion of the sexual act with ejaculation intravaginally. This situation is essential to reproduction, and preference for vaginal or coital orgasm, as opposed to that stimulated by external manipulation of the clitoral system, has obvious adaptive advantage biologically. Our interest, however, is in how psychic representation of her sexual organs comes about in the human female, and its consequences for the issues under discussion: coital frigidity or acquisition of the capacity for coital orgasm.

Genital organization of the libido ("the combination of the component instincts and their subordination under the primacy of the genitals") is accomplished through the maturation of the ego, which, as Freud (1923), Schilder (1935), and many others have shown, is largely related to body structure and function. The child's perceptions of body sensations gradually build up self-representations which are finally amalgamated into a sense of self (Jacobson, 1964). Sarlin (1963) has described in detail how a feminine identity is ultimately established in relation to woman's anatomy and her species characteristics of maternal lactating function and intrauterine gestation of the fetus. He believes that woman's destiny as a mammal determines a greater role of orality in female psychosexuality than in male, agreeing in this with Brierley (1932) and others. He suggests that clitoral erotism and phallic erections are associated with the passive mouth-breast stimulation by the erect nipple of the mother's breast during actual feeding of the infant and that fantasy substitution of the clitoris or penis for the erect nipple contributes to the unconscious equation of "clitoris-nipple (breast)—penis".[1] He adds,

---

[1] Evidence that a neuroanatomical and physiological basis exists for this unconscious equation has been presented by McLean (1962, 1973). Stimulation of various parts of the limbic system, including the cortex, in the squirrel monkey evoked penile erection. Points of stimulation eliciting facial, oral, and alimentary responses cluster in the amygdala region, while those eliciting genital response are concentrated in the medial septopreoptic region. They unite in the anterior hypothalamus in a region of converging nerve fibres involved in the expression of angry and defensive behavior. Because of the close neural relationship between parts of

The human infant in the mutually satisfying, sensual experience at the breast shares with the mother the first
physical erotic experience of a love relationship out of
which eventually evolve the adult capacities for genital
love and its associated psychic manifestations in the form
of consideration and affectionate devotion [p. 799].

The "primal scene" of the phallic period, the observation of sexual relations between the parents, is superimposed upon an earlier and more basic primal scene at
the oral level in which the infant at the mother's breast
was an active participant in an overtly erotic relationship
and not an outside observer [p. 798].

This hypothesis would help to explain the oral material associated with primal-scene fantasies and dreams in analysis. A re-
enactment of this original primal scene takes place in the foreplay of the adult in erotic kissing and mouth-breast stimulation. In this connection a number of analytic, behavioral, and
physiological observations confirm the intimate relationship
between the breast-nipple and the clitoral system. Brierley
(1932) found evidence of vaginal contraction (we would now
assume of the lower third) in infants during happy suckling or
during a time of acute frustration at the breast, and Marie
Langer (1951) and Lorand (1939) postulated that frigidity is
related to frustrated orality. Masters and Johnson (1966) have
demonstrated nipple erection and breast engorgement during
sexual excitement, whether or not they are directly stimulated. Many of their subjects have experienced erotic excitement, three of them to orgasm, while nursing, an observation
previously reported by analysts. Women who nursed their
babies returned more quickly to sexual activity postpartum

the limbic system, excitation of one part readily spills over into another. This
relationship is exemplified in the association of penile erection with feeding in
babies and animals. These neurophysiological findings contribute to an understanding of the primitive nature of the interrelation of oral and genital behavior
as well as their connection with aggressive behavior. This was conceptualized
long ago by Freud in terms of a fusion of libidinal and aggressive instinctual drives.

and exhibited a greater interest in and capacity for orgastic release.

On the basis of observations of penile erections during nursing, I would postulate that stimulation of the penis, and presumably the clitoris as well, must occur on a neurophysiological basis. This experience—the beginning of erogenous sensitization—would be accompanied by the psychic representation of a primitive part object—expressed in the concept "body-nipple (breast)"—and the actual loss of that part object contributes to the differentiation of the self from the object. This representation develops further in the growing child as a result of the mother's physical ministrations to his body, and the complex of interrelated representation is reinforced by direct clitoral stimulation. Generalized skin erotogeneity becomes linked with that of the clitoris or penis and may conceivably aid the ego in acquiring the concept of whole as opposed to part object. The superficial vasocongestive sex flush, observed during the preorgasmic phase in three quarters of the female and one quarter of the male subjects in Masters and Johnson's studies, provides evidence of a physiological basis for these associations in psychic representation, which, during the phallic phase, take the form of the unconscious equation, "body-phallus." (The greater incidence and more extensive distribution of the skin flush in female than in male subjects is another indication of the more diffuse erotogeneity of the female. It suggests a basis for the impression of a greater significance of the body-phallus equation in females than in males.) Observation of the differences between the sexes produces consequences for this ego organization of self-representations in the female child that are too familiar to require description: I refer, of course, to continued clitoral hypercathexis, penis envy, and the development of the masculinity complex in varying degrees of severity.

That the vagina does not acquire psychic representation comparable to that of the clitoris was at first attributed to the absence of vaginal sensation in the little girl. Phyllis Greenacre

(1950) has reviewed the extensive literature presenting evidence to contradict this supposition, but it is agreed that vaginal sensations in the young child are vague, diffuse, amorphous, and poorly differentiated from those of the surrounding pelvic organs, especially the anus, with which the vagina shares a cloacal origin. In addition to the role of tactile, proprioceptive, and pain sensations, Keiser (1956) gives prime importance to the visual experience in building the mature body image. The relative invisibility of the female organs limits their perception and hence their inclusion in psychic representation. So also does sight of the boy's penis, for the affects of envy and jealousy and the wish and defence against the wish for a penis produce inevitable distortions. Shifting libidinal cathexes at various stages of development alter the various parts of the body image, but with a time lag that contributes to further distortion. Added to this is the effect of oscillations of libido described by Helene Deutsch (1925). Not only do later stages of libido development contain elements of the earlier phases, but, conversely, constituents of the later phases are also interwoven with earlier ones on the path of regression. Keiser believes that the unbounded and ill-defined nature of her genital representation, as well as the distortions mentioned, result in a sense of incompleteness about her body image that is reflected in woman's feeling about herself. Fearful fantasies of penetration and destruction are influenced in part by sadistic components derived from fusion of vaginal representation with that of the anus. Also, the fantasy of castration represents a rent in her body ego, which she constantly tries to repair. Penis envy may fuse with a wish to complete the body image—to do away with the opening in the body schema. I might add that the resulting dynamics would constitute a special example of the ego's defensive functions operating in the service of the id by contributing to the wish for intercourse.

The vaguely perceived vaginal sensations and tensions are experienced passively by the ego, in Kestenberg's (1956) opinion. But "Passivity promotes haziness of boundaries, stimulates fantasies, and thus acts adversely upon reality testing" (p. 458). Only through active experiences can an organ image develop fully, she says, and the girl child often attempts to discharge vaginal tensions on an outside object, the baby doll, over which she can attain active mastery. Externalization of the vagina in doll play,[2] based on identification with the phallic mother and the feces-child equation, is a means by which the ego not only actively seeks to achieve psychic representation of the vagina, but also does the same thing for the concept of motherhood.

Barnett (1966) has provided further understanding of the problems of psychic representation posed by the vagina and their effect on its cathexis. She believes that penetration and loss of body contents are threats to body integrity. These contribute to fears that interfere with the conscious cathexis of cavities, unless such threats can be minimized or mastered by the development of voluntary, intrinsic motor control. Such control quickly develops for the oral and anal orifices, but the vaginal introitus lacks the muscular means. Moreover, there are no animate or inanimate substances or objects available that can be viewed as part of herself with which to fill the cavity and help define its shape, form, and function or to provide discharge of tension by the passage of contents. Vague awareness of a cavity without such protection or definition gives rise to anxiety and a need to repress awareness of the organ. A return to clitoral masturbation, with accompanying defensive clitoral hypercathexis and penis envy, helps achieve and maintain repression of conscious vaginal sensation. To

---

[2] This equation of the vagina with the baby doll has been described by Helene Deutsch (1925) as a regressive psychic phenomenon in the adult woman during the sexual act. Through a process psychically analogous to sucking and incorporation, which repeats in regard to the penis the earlier experience at the breast, the vagina becomes the receptacle for the original part object subsequently represented by the whole body. The vagina itself now represents the child and "becomes the 'second ego,' the ego in miniature, as does the penis for the man."

these factors contributing to vaginal decathexis is added the fact that the clitoris is a more dependable organ than the vagina for the discharge of sexual tension in the phallic phase. This can be understood in terms of the current physiological studies. The greater tendency to orgastic release after pregnancy is attributed by Masters and Johnson to the development of the venous plexi in the pelvic structures and cryptic clitoral organs. In the absence of such development in the phallic phase, even that produced by hormonal influences during puberty, clitoral stimulation would be sufficient only to cathect that structure itself. Though possible, orgasm is rare, and perception of sensation from the clitoral system surrounding the lower third of the vagina must be minimal. What clitoral sensation there is helps to assuage the feeling of "nothingness" accompanying the little girl's evaluation of herself as inferior to those around her. We may assume that the clitoris, like the penis, is originally stimulated during nursing and that symbolically it becomes a nipple substitute and later "a little penis" in identification with father. With pubertal enlargement of the breasts, erotism of the nipple itself is established, and the association between the nipple and clitoral system is reinforced, with the consequent increase in clitoral cathexis. The pelvic changes related to the hormonal influences during puberty and the onset of menstruation have, at the same time, redirected the girl's attention to her vagina and her lack of control of this organ. The conflict over masochistic fantasies described by Deutsch (1930) is intensified, and Barnett suggests that there is a renewed need to displace and deny her vulnerability, which might help explain the increase of phallic-aggressive activity on the part of girls during this stage.

From birth onward, the penis is visible, easily manipulated, rewardingly responsive to stimuli, and readily capable of discharging erotic tensions. There are therefore relatively few problems about its psychic representation and permanent cathexis as the organ of sexual pleasure. Male sexual function has, as a result, a focused quality reflected to some degree in ego functioning. In contrast, the female organs, though stimulated early, undergo tremendous changes during development. Their diffuse distribution, small or concealed nature, and the uncertainty of the origin of stimuli interfere with psychic representation and contribute to greater cathexis of varying parts at different periods. The ego's effort to achieve mastery over these organs and define their location, boundaries, and functions continues throughout life. It seems improbable that a complete psychic representation of female structure and function can occur until after the anatomical and physiological changes of puberty, the development of the venous plexi of the pelvic organs, stimulation by the penis in coitus, and pregnancy and parturition. Even then, it cannot be expected that an anatomically precise differentiation between the vagina and the cryptic clitoral structures will be made. The latter are intimately connected with the clitoris itself, but also partially envelop the lower third of the vagina. Vicissitudes in individual development will determine whether sensation from the cryptic structures involved in orgasm are associated with the clitoris or the vagina in the psychic experience. Greenacre (1950, 1952) has discussed the varying preoedipal configurations with respect to the two zones of genital reactivity resulting from accidental or forced premature functioning at different developmental levels.

Orgasm itself must achieve psychic representation, and while that representation may be modified by the biological maturation mentioned above, which enhances the potential for an experience conforming to what has been described as "vaginal" orgasm, the outcome appears to be psychically rather than physiologically determined. With the same physiological phenomena, orgasm may be experienced as occurring in various genital and even nongenital locations, regardless of the site and means of stimulation (Masters and Johnson, 1966). Preference as to modes of stimulation and the site of the orgastic experience seems to be dependent on cathexes reflecting conflicts and compromises between the ideal sexual self-representation and defensive needs.

Even after relatively normal psychosexual development, with its long history of clitoral cathexis and repression of vaginal sensations, inadequate or discontinuous sexual stimulation and vaginal intercourse before a platform of arousal has been achieved may contribute to an unwillingness to give up the certain pleasure of orgasm by direct or indirect clitoral stimulation externally for the uncertainty and often disappointment of vaginal intercourse. Despite the varying degrees of clitoral and vaginal cathexis caused by the factors mentioned and the extravaginal source of coital pleasure suggested by Masters and Johnson's observations, it is the vagina as the organ and coitus as the act that are ultimately cathected as a nearly universal ideal for maturity in female psychosexual development. Perhaps for the woman it is fulfillment of the ego's need for mastery of an ill-defined genital self-image — to fill the cavity — as well as its indispensability for the purpose of reproduction that determines this vaginal cathexis. Sherfey herself admits that "we all want the vaginal orgasm to exist and the clitoral orgasm not to exist." Regrettably, because of discordant drive development, interferences with psychic representation and the orderly progression of shifts in cathexes, and conflicts in identificatory processes, this ideal is often not attained.

It needs to be emphasized that this viewpoint does not represent a continued adherence on my part to Freud's clitoral-vaginal transfer theory. Sherfey is right that this part of Freud's theory must be modified. But I believe she exaggerates the psychological significance to be attached to the primary role of the clitoral system, physiologically, in female orgasm, and her emphasis in this regard may serve to perpetuate the oversimplification of a dichotomy of the female genitals. We should not replace a vaginal myth with a clitoral myth. My emphasis in this paper has been on the development of self-representations and a body image consistent with mature female functioning. For the reasons given, both sensation and cathexis of the different parts of the female genitalia will vary during different developmental periods. While the clitoris retains cathexis and major significance for erotic arousal and discharge throughout life, there is, during development, an expanding representation and cathexis of other parts, including the labia and introitus. This fact seems to be defended against by a common tendency to refer to both external and internal genitalia as the "vagina," encouraging the denial of pleasure in other parts. For mature sexuality, the clitoral cathexis is not relinquished, but rather becomes integrated psychically with a total erogenous response, as suggested by Masters and Johnson's observations of nipple arousal, skin flush, vaginal secretion, and muscular movements, preparing for intromission and orgasm (see Benedek, 1968; Panel, 1961).

The integration of erotic cathexes occurs *pari passu* with structural organization as influenced by primary objects. It is generally recognized that preoedipal and oedipal conflicts may interfere with identification with a female object and result in disturbances in drive organization and ego regressions that may seriously impair the capacity for mature genitality. But even earlier factors may affect drive organization. There are indications that the androgenic hormone increases both the capacity for orgastic release and the expression of aggression (Money and Ehrhardt, 1972). Elsewhere (Moore, 1975), I have postulated that the differentiation of the libidinal and aggressive drives from the undifferentiated instinctual energies, stimulated by frustration, aids in the process of separation-individuation, provided means of aggressive discharge are available by which separation can be actively achieved by the child himself. But cultural influences, in addition to possible biological ones, tend to inhibit or modify the expression of aggression in girls and women. With such limitations of aggression and separation experienced passively, there may be a proclivity for continuing fusion of self- and object representations. Conversely, too early differentiation of the aggressive drive, as a result of traumatic mothering or other factors, could give rise to an extreme degree of ambivalence, premature and unstable organization of the ego, including its defensive functions, and a split in objects and the self (Rubinfine, 1962). Under either circumstance, the regression occurring during the sexual experience and orgasm may threaten the drive and self-object differentiation achieved, and contribute to sadistic and masochistic wishes. Depending on the resolution of conflicts, such wishes may contribute to fantasies facilitating orgasm or to defenses precluding it.

Inherent in woman's diffuse erotogeneity is the possibility for an ego organization different from that of the man, not inferior, but specifically adapted to her role in reproduction and motherhood, since the ego is modeled to some degree on the body and its functions.[3] A certain type of ego diffusion, based initially on the diffusion of erotic cathexes, might facilitate some primary-process tendencies, such as displacement, and alter the nature of secondary-process achievement and general ego integration as well (Panel, 1961).[4] Added to this, an instability of the body image connected, on the one hand, to loss of object during separation-individuation and, on the other, to the lack of an external, easily controllable genital sufficiently cathected because of the pleasurable discharge it affords, often leads to the use of transitional objects. These provide the opportunity for internalizing mother by projecting the self onto the transitional object, facilitating introjective-projective mechanisms, the capacity for empathy, the splitting of self and objects into good and bad, and the differentiation of drives, so that distancing and integration on a higher level can

[3] I also subscribe to the view that there are superego differences between the sexes, though I do not believe they are of the nature described by Freud or that they have the implications he ascribed to them. A full discussion of these differences and those of the ego ideal are beyond the scope of this paper.

[4] These speculations are necessarily incomplete and unsubstantiated except by clinical impressions. They are offered as a possible stimulus to further inquiry. The structural differences, even if they can be reliably established, must be subtle and are made even less apparent by the psychological bisexuality of humans. Both sexes may demonstrate the same traits, and there are wide variations within the same sex.

be achieved. Consistent with these developments, it seems to me that attention cathexes are shifted more readily from one object to another by women, and there is a greater capacity for simultaneous attention to various tasks—preparation for the roles of motherhood implicit in the maternal ego ideal. The result is, I believe, that women may be more object directed and social than men (see Benedek, 1968).

But apropos our subject, if there are advantages in such ego organization for woman's role, there may also be disadvantages from the standpoint of orgastic potential. Women seem to have greater difficulty in bringing together their dispersed erotic cathexes to adequate intensity and focus to achieve orgasm. Masters and Johnson (1966) have demonstrated that continuous stimulation is necessary, and arousal is easily lost with any interruption. For some women, simultaneous stimulation of two or more erotic areas, such as the mouth, nipples, or anus, as well as the clitoris and vagina, is necessary to achieve a summation of excitement and trigger orgasm. Impulses, conflicts, and defenses also appear to be similarly dispersed in many psychic representations, so that they remain isolated, but predispose to a threatening dissociation of affects. Conscious fantasies may also be dissociated from specific genital cathexes. Thus, girls often have vague romantic fantasies, but do not relate them specifically to the excitement of the genital area, though some women are able to trigger orgasm by a summation of psychic and bodily stimulation through fantasies, often of a masochistic nature, during intercourse. I suggest that the effect of this diffusion is to limit the ego's aid to orgastic gratification or even to divert its efforts into defensive channels as a result of conflict within the ego, based on its inherent nature. Orgasmic dysfunction, or frigidity as it used to be called, has been attributed by many to a defense against the threat of ego dissolution.[5]

_____

[5] I do not mean to imply that the female ego is more vulnerable than the male. Factors inherent in the physical attributes and development of the male child influence his psychic structure with equal potential for adaptation to the male role or liability in sexual performance. In fact, in males, deficiencies of mothering in the

In both sexes gender identity is influenced by identifications with both parental objects as well as by continuing cathexes of preoedipal and oedipal objects. In the sexual act there are regressive reactivations of such object cathexes and of narcissistic cathexes through projection of an idealized self on the partner. In this situation the role of current as well as past objects is of course significant. In view of a somewhat tenuous capacity for orgastic release, however, I submit that a certain degree of narcissistic withdrawal, with focus on the erogenous zones and the mounting erotic tension, is necessary in some cases. This is balanced by a concern with the sexual object, and some women achieve orgasm in identification with their partners, but for others the degree of narcissistic concentration necessary may elicit unconscious fear of object loss; in defense they may be unable to focus adequately on their own arousal and attainment of orgastic release. In any event, even if orgasm is achieved, these multiple factors may help to account for not only the site of the experience of orgasm, but also for its intensity and the pleasure derived. The psychic pleasure experienced is not necessarily correlated with the physiological activity.

Narcissistic and object-relation conflicts and the resulting total structural integration therefore contribute to shifts in cathexis attached to various parts of the female sexual apparatus during the course of development.[6] This paper therefore reaffirms the possibility that persisting clitoral hypercathexis may interfere with satisfying sexual relations with the opposite sex. In clinical practice, however, there has been a tendency to

separation-individuation stage may also result in a lack of cathexis of the entire self, which is later experienced as an inadequacy of the genitals. As Benedek (1968, pp. 445-446) states, "Transient ego regression is a constituent of the orgasmic capacity in both sexes.... unconscious fear of ego regression may impede the orgasmic capacity of men as well; this, however, happens more frequently in women."

[6] That there are similar shifts, during development, of the cathexis attached to various parts of the male genitals, some serving defensive purposes, is indicated by the work of Bell (1961, 1965).

equate cathexis, a psychic phenomenon, and its derivative manifestations with psychic sensation. Thus, it has been widely assumed, by analysts as well as others, that Freud's clitoral-vaginal transfer theory was dependent on erotic sensation, and that it implied for mature female responsiveness the necessity of an orgasm experienced in the vagina itself. It is true that the description of orgasm by many women does coincide with this expectation, and analytic treatment has sometimes resulted in the development of the capacity for vaginal or coital orgasm. The too rigid definition of frigidity by Hitschmann and Bergler (1936) — absence of "vaginal" orgasm — contributed to an overemphasis on this concept of transfer of erotic *sensation* from the clitoris to the vagina. Because their definition appeared to be supported by observations relating to penis envy and the masculinity complex, it was largely accepted by psychoanalysts, although clinical experience continued to confirm the importance of the role of the clitoris in orgasm described by Freud in 1905. Aberrations in successive phases of drive and ego development were adduced to explain the inability of some women to achieve "vaginal" orgastic release. Psychoanalytic experience strongly supports the view that the nature of orgasm as well as frigidity are, like all behavioral phenomena, the result of multiply determined factors, including specific resolutions of conflict. Disturbances accompanying various stages in female psychosexual development obviously did disrupt orderly development and cause impairment in the erotic life of some women, but in others such developmental vicissitudes had apparently not given rise to conflict. This fact was sometimes overlooked, as well as the possibility that in some instances "vaginal" orgasm might have pathological implications. Certain aggressive, masculine women, using the vagina like an "illusory phallus," unconsciously deny their own penisless state by an orgasm that seems to vie with that of men. Despite such neurotic and psychotic women who experience intense "vaginal" orgasm and the loving, giving, maternal, and happy women who do not -- even though they feel fully gratified—"vaginal" organ became accepted as the hallmark of sexual and psychological normality and the goal of the supposedly well informed. Clinical experience to the contrary was either ignored or attributed to failure of analysis. This is an instance, quite common in the application of psychoanalytic knowledge, in which the validity of some analytic concepts has outweighed the uncertainty of other assumptions.

The demand for female orgasm, similar and equal to that of the male but differently located, affords an interesting example of the ambivalent feelings of mankind about the differences between the sexes. To be realistic, we must take recognition of the fact found by virtually all investigators, including Masters and Johnson, that there is a far greater variation in female sexual response and orgasm than in male, even though the same physiological reactions occur in all women. Instead of insisting on a particular type of orgasm as the norm —one involving erotic sensation and orgasm experienced within the vagina—I believe that we should consider cathexis of coitus as the *sine qua non* of a mature feminine attitude.

Despite such a mature and favorable feminine attitude, women may not achieve orgasm all the time for a variety of reasons not necessarily psychopathological. Various factors, including identification with an active-erotic mother, for example, may make it necessary for certain women, if they are to achieve coital orgasm, to have a degree of activity in the love act that is inhibiting to their male partners. I think it is conceivable that an impaired orgastic response in such a woman may be a more mature, realistic, and adaptive reaction to her sexual mate than an overwhelming orgastic reaction that would be threatening to him and impair a tenuous but in other respects gratifying object relationship or satisfactory marriage. Therefore, to the bases for so-called frigidity inherent in the psychosexual development of the individual woman, we must add the psychological problems of her sexual partner, their emotional interaction, the adequacy of stimulation, the influence of hormones, the circumstances under which intercourse takes place, and various social and cultural attitudes toward sex. While none of these factors can be or has been neglected in the psychoanalytic view, psychoanalysis is a therapy of the individual and cannot modify external factors except by influencing their psychic representation and reducing the conflicts that interfere with action appropriate to change them. In this fact there is an inherent limitation to what can be accomplished by psychoanalysis in the treatment of human sexual dysfunction, however much the total functioning of the patient may be benefited.

Other determinants may also limit success in the treatment of sexual dysfunction. It is obvious that the human sexual act is a profound and complex phenomenon. It is often initiated by nonverbal cues, preferably in a situation of emotional closeness as well as physical intimacy—i.e., an affecto-motor state similar to that which exists between mother and infant. The foreplay preceding genital union reawakens cathexis in earlier stages of psychosexual development, building up and fusing erotic tension derived from each. Ideally, the regressively achieved tension has a genital discharge, an orgastic culmination in an ecstatic fusion with the partner that symbolically repeats the earliest blissful state of union with the mother. This regressive-progressive reverberation of the drive expressions in the sexual act, in which narcissistic and object-directed libido and their aggressive counterparts are intermingled with defensive functions, reflects the entire history of object relations of the individual. Events or human relationships which traumatize the child at particular stages of development help account for the variations we see, and it is on this basis that analysis provides the best approach to the solution of sexual problems. Orgasm, however, is the result of a complex interaction of physiology, affect, fantasy, and behavior which expresses the ego's organization of pregenital and genital experience. The degree of condensation involved, the relation of these factors to physiological mechanisms, and their relative inaccessibility to analysis have inescapable consequences. The modes of sexual interaction and their progression to orgasm have, I believe, some of the inflexibility of somatizations or the relatively fixed nature of character traits. This does not mean that they cannot be influenced by analysis, but it does imply that the actual physical experience of orgasm is less subject to change by analysis than the psychic meaning of the sexual act.

The possibility of sexual differences in treatment response, whether based on differences in ego organization similar to the superego differences we recognize or based on biological differences between the sexes, has important implications for the goals of psychoanalysis and evaluation of its therapeutic success, especially in regard to orgastic response. In the treatment of frigidity it may be that we shall have to recognize innate obstacles as well as the limitations of analytic technique if we are not to find ourselves pursuing a will-o'-the-wisp. In evaluating the results of treatment in cases of frigidity, therefore, I suggest that we base our judgment on intrapsychic change rather than on the apparent physical nature of orgastic response. In that case, the objectives outlined by Deutsch (1960) might be accepted as the criteria for success in the analytic treatment for frigidity. These include a signficant lessening of the unfavorable influences of pregenital and pre-oedipal development; the solution of oedipal problems; the resolution of bisexuality; the development of control over the main source of sexual inhibition, feminine masochism; and the attainment of a postambivalent affective position in object relations.

It needs to be stressed that the attitudes that are relevant to the attainment of these objectives permeate the entire object relationship and marital situation and are not confined to the sexual act alone. If the total object relation has been significantly improved and the sexual act is a mutually loving one that is brought to a happy end with relaxation and a sense of complete gratification, I believe that this coital culmination will be sufficiently cathected, and the localization and intensity of orgastic discharge should assume less significance than it is currently given.

Just as the direct observations of childhood phenomena have enriched the theoretical concepts we have arrived at through analytic reconstructions, it is to be hoped that the direct observations of sexual behavior and physiology by Masters and Johnson will add a new dimension to our understanding of human sexuality. Already, their work has helped to clarify some of the important but hitherto obscure aspects of human behavior. It must be recognized not only that these phenomena cannot be interpreted solely on physical or psychological bases, but also that it is misleading if observations derived from one field are applied too concretely to another. Continued careful correlation of studies is indicated. At this stage, however, instead of being inconsistent with data derived from other disciplines, psychoanalytic hypotheses about female sexuality, based on psychic derivatives rather than direct observation, appear to have an approximate if not precise anatomical verification and a psychic reality that transcends the physical.

Summary

This paper examines questions about the validity of the clitoral-vaginal transfer theory arising from anatomical and physiological evidence that vaginal orgasm, as distinct from clitoral, does not exist. Psychic rather than physical satisfaction seems to determine the preference of most women for coitally induced orgasm, despite the fact that clitorally induced orgasms may be equally or more intense. This preference, biologically adaptive, is the result of an ego maturation influenced by self- and object representations which contribute to a feminine identity based on woman's anatomy and species characteristics of lactation and intrauterine gestation of the fetus.

The hypothesis is offered that erogenous sensitization of the clitoris, perhaps on a neurophysiological basis, begins during the nursing experience, accompanied by the psychic representation of the nipple-breast as part object. Loss of this part object contributes to the differentiation of the self from the object and, together with other factors, aids in the establishment of a complex of interrelated representations which form the basis for the well-known unconscious equation "body-nipple (breast)-phallus" and a continued cathexis of the clitoris. Although there is evidence that early vaginal sensations occur, the sensations are ill-defined, and, the invisibility of the female organs limits their perception and inclusion in psychic representation. The ego reacts passively to vaguely experienced sensations, and its passivity contributes to fantasy and poor reality testing in respect to the boundaries of the organs. Lack of ego control over the vaginal opening and inner organs also gives rise to anxiety and a need to repress awareness of the vagina, with a return to clitoral masturbation, defensive clitoral hypercathexis, and penis envy. Pubertal changes reestablish erotism of the nipple itself, with a reinforcement of clitoral cathexis until menstrual function, intromission of the penis, pregnancy, and parturition complete the psychic representation of female structure and function. These vicissitudes of development contribute to greater cathexis of varying parts at different periods and determine whether sensation from the cryptic structures involved in orgasm are associated with the clitoris or the vagina.

Correlation of observations from other disciplines with those of psychoanalysis offers the possibility of expanding understanding of behavior only if a clear distinction is made between the psychic experiencing and objective observations of phenomena. If metapsychological factors are taken into account, instead of inconsistency, there is a remarkable concurrence between current psychoanalytic theory and recent anatomical and physiological studies in respect to female orgasm.

It is suggested that cathexis of coitus and the achievement of intrapsychic change sufficient to significantly improve the object relationship be substituted for preconceptions about the desirable intensity and localization of orgastic experience as the criteria for improvement in cases of frigidity treated by psychoanalysis.

REFERENCES*

Barnett, M. C. (1966), Vaginal awareness in the infancy and childhood of girls. *This Journal*, 14:129-141.
Bell, A. (1961), Some observations on the role of the scrotal sac and testicles. *This Journal*, 9:261-286.
———— (1965), The significance of the scrotal sac and testes for the prepuberty male. *Psychoanal. Quart.*, 34:182-206.
Benedek, T. (1968), Discussion of Mary Jane Sherfy: "The evolution and nature of female sexuality in relation to psychoanalytic theory." *This Journal*, 16:424-448.
Brierley, M. (1932), Some problems of integration in women. *Internat. J. Psychoanal.*, 13:433-447.
Deutsch, H. (1925), The psychology of women in relation to the functions of reproduction. *Internat. J. Psycho-Anal.*, 6:405-418.
———— (1930), The significance of masochism in the mental life of women. *Internat. J. Psycho-Anal.*, 11:48-60.
———— (1960), Frigidity in women. In: *Neuroses and Character Types.* New York: International Universities Press, 1965, pp. 358-362.
Fliess, R. (1956), *Erogeneity and Libido.* New York: International Universities Press.
Freud, S. (1905), Three essays on the theory of sexuality. *Standard Edition*, 7:1-243. London: Hogarth Press, 1953.
———— (1923), The infantile genital organization. *Standard Edition*, 19:141-145. London: Hogarth Press, 1961.
Greenacre, P. (1950), Special problems of early female sexual development: In: *Trauma, Growth and Personality.* New York: International Universities Press, pp. 237-258.
———— (1952), Pregenital patterning. *Internat. J. Psycho-Anal.*, 33:410-415.
Heiman, M. (1963), Sexual response in women: a correlation of physiological findings with psychoanalytic concepts. *This Journal*, 11:360-387.
Hitschmann, E. & Bergler, E. (1936), *Frigidity in Women: Its Characteristics and Treatment.* New York: Nervous and Mental Diseases Monograph, Series No. 60.
Jacobson, E. (1964), *The Self and the Object World.* New York: International Universities Press.
Keiser, S. (1956), Female sexuality. *This Journal*, 4:563-574.
Kestenberg, J. S. (1956), Vicissitudes of female sexuality. *This Journal*, 4:453-476.
Langer, M. (1951), *Maternidad y Sexo.* Buenos Aires: Editorial Nova.

* All references to *This Journal* are to the *Journal of the American Psychoanalytic Association.*

Lorand, S. (1939), Contribution to the problem of vaginal orgasm. *Internat. J. Psycho-Anal.,* 20:432-438.

Masters, W. H. & Johnson, V. E. (1966), *Human Sexual Response.* Boston: Little, Brown.

McLean, P. D. (1962), New findings relevant to the evolution of psychosexual functions of the brain. *J. Nerv. Ment. Dis.,* 135:289-301.

―――― (1973), *A Triune Concept of the Brain and Behaviour.* Hincks Memorial Lectures, ed. T. J. Boag & D. Campbell. Toronto & Buffalo: University of Toronto Press.

Money, J. & Ehrhardt, A. (1972), *Man and Woman, Boy and Girl.* Baltimore & London: Johns Hopkins University Press.

Moore, B. E. (1964), Frigidity: a review of psychoanalytic literature. *Psychoanal. Quart.,* 33:323-349.

―――― (1975), Freud and female sexuality: a current view. *Internat. J. Psycho-Anal.,* 57:287-300.

Orr, D. W. (1968), Anthropological and historical notes on the female sexual role. *This Journal,* 16:601-612.

Panel (1961), Frigidity in women, B. E. Moore, reporter. *This Journal,* 9:571-584.

Rubinfine, D. (1962), Maternal stimulation, psychic structure, and early object relations; with special reference to aggression and denial. *The Psychoanalytic Study of the Child,* 17:265-282. New York: International Universities Press.

Sarlin, C. N. (1963), Feminine identity. *This Journal,* 11:790-816.

Schilder, P. (1935), *The Image and Appearance of the Human Body.* New York: International Universities Press, 1950.

Sherfey, M. J. (1966), The evolution and nature of female sexuality in relation to psychoanalytic theory. *This Journal,* 14:28-128.

Spitz, R. A. (1955), The primal cavity. *The Psychoanalytic Study of the Child,* 10:215-240. New York: International Universities Press.

150 East 73 Street
New York, New York 10021

PROBLEMS IN FREUD'S PSYCHOLOGY OF WOMEN

Roy Schafer, ph.d.

EGO PSYCHOLOGY HAS ESTABLISHED as the proper subject of psychoanalytic study the whole person developing and living in a complex world. No longer is ours a theory simply of instinct-ridden organisms, turbulent unconscious dynamics, and the like. We see all aspects of development as being profoundly influenced by learning in a context of object relations that are, on the one hand, biologically essential and biologically directed and, on the other hand, culturally molded and historically conditioned. We also emphasize the clinical as well as theoretical dangers to psychoanalytic understanding represented by any simple and immediate reduction to infantile dynamics.

On this basis, ego psychology has helped establish lively two-way interchanges between psychoanalysis and modern biology, psychology, anthropology, history, linguistics, philosophy, aesthetics, and other disciplines. Proceeding with justified caution, psychoanalysis has been moving within the history of ideas, of which it is itself, of course, a significant part. And within the history of ideas, sooner or later it comes to pass that well-established answers are found to require reconceptualization or replacement by new answers, framed to deal with different and possibly better questions.

My work on this paper was generously supported by the Old Dominion Fund and the Foundation for Research in Psychoanalysis.

This article originally appeared in the *Journal of the American Psychoanalytic Association* (1974), 22:459-485.

331

Consequently, psychoanalysts who genuinely appreciate ego psychology will not shrug off the current great discussion of the making, warping, and exploiting of women in our society. In this discussion, fundamental Freudian propositions about psychological development are being challenged from all sides while the entire psychoanalytic enterprise is being widely discredited as the child and now the servant of the male-dominated social order. Simply interpreting these criticisms as militant rationalizations of penis envy being put forth by neurotic females and their male supporters is a flagrant instance of reductionism and intellectual isolationism and is equivalent to shrugging off this discussion, which, it should be noted, concerns the allegedly distorted development of men as well as women. We should be prepared to rethink the concept as well as the role of penis envy in female development. This we can do without dismissing or minimizing our many findings concerning its psychological importance.

My focus here will be on some problems in Freud's theoretical generalizations concerning women's development and characteristics. These generalizations deal with typical conflicts and typical rational and irrational attempts to solve the conflicts. They have, of course, been of incalculable value both in understanding the varieties of female development and, through clinical psychoanalysis, in greatly alleviating neurotic disturbances in individual instances. But there are problems, and my strategy in getting at them is to focus on the type of theorizing Freud used in this connection. I shall examine the logic and internal consistency of his ideas; I shall try to sort out the preconceptions that went into the making of the theory, the empirical evidence it deals with, and the rules by which this evidence was established, and, additionally, to identify the confusions between these three features of the theory. These are the theoretical features and the confusions that determine what will be certified as fact, how the facts will be related to each other, and whether and where there will be factual errors and failures to make sense.

It is legitimate to begin by limiting the discussion to Freud alone. One warrant for doing so is that much of the current criticism is directed specifically against Freud and relies heavily on allegedly representative quotations from his writings. Another warrant is this: although many major theoretical and technical advances beyond Freud have been made by his psychoanalytic descendents, his basic assumptions, indeed the very mode of his thought, are still very much with us in modern psychoanalysis. Consequently, one may concentrate on Freud without being ahistorical. At the same time, one must bear in mind that over the years Freud modified many of his ideas. We must ask, therefore, whether he modified his psychology of women.

It seems that he did. Not only did he finally emphasize how little, after all, he really understood female development (1931, 1933); additionally, he began to emphasize, along with the vicissitudes of penis envy, the major and continuing influence of the girl's active preoedipal attachment to her mother. But Freud was not altogether consistent in making this change, for, in his final discussions of the subject (1937, 1940), he pretty much reverted to his earlier, simpler, and patriarchal viewpoint (1923b, 1925). To put it plainly, this is the viewpoint from which female development appears to be both second best and second-rate — second best in the experience of the girl and woman and second rate in the judgment of patriarchal spokesmen of civilization at large. Freud never did consolidate and develop a fundamental change in this regard. From this fact follow many of the problems in his psychology of women.

I shall be discussing some major and representative problems under three headings: The Problem of Women's Morality and Objectivity; The Problem of Neglected Prephallic Development; and The Problem of Naming. The three headings simply correspond to how my analysis of the material worked out; they do not imply a coordinated or consolidated critical plan.

The Problem of Women's Morality and Objectivity

What sense, if any, could Freud have been making when he characterized women as being less moral than men? Consider what he said:

> . . . for women the level of what is ethically normal is dif-
> ferent from what it is in men. Their super-ego is never so
> inexorable, so impersonal, so independent of its emotion-
> al origins as we require it to be in men. . . . that they show
> less sense of justice than men, that they are less ready to
> submit to the great exigencies of life, that they are more
> often influenced in their judgements by feelings of affec-
> tion or hostility—all these would be amply accounted for
> by the modification in the formation of their super-
> ego . . . [1925, pp. 257-258].

Freud was well aware that many or most men manifest serious deficiencies in conventional moral rectitude. He saw this in their personal lives: think of the men in the Dora case (1905a). He saw it in their professional lives: consider the scandalous way in which he was treated by his colleagues in medicine and psychiatry. And he saw it in the lives of men as citizens: recall his remarks on the First World War (1915b). More than once he expressed plainly his low estimate of the morality of most people in the world he knew. Consequently, in his generaliza-tion about women's morality, he could not have meant *most* men, at least not in *that* sense of the word moral.

In one respect, he seemed to be referring to a certain quality of moral rigidity characterizing men more than women. Men's moral stands seemed to him much less easily swayed by emotional appeals or so-called subjective impres-sions than those of women. Men seemed more consistently to affirm and abide by abstract and so-called objective prin-ciples. Although it could be argued effectively that the idea of this quantitative sex difference rests on a selection of criteria that is biased in favor of men, and so more or less begs the question, I shall by-pass this issue in order to stay close to Freud's line of thought, and I shall grant, though only for the sake of critical analysis, that this difference is real. Most psychoanalysts would, I think, infer from the "fact" of this quantitative difference that men have a greater capacity for isolation of affect. Like many others, Freud did estimate that hysterical proclivities are more commonly encountered in women and obsessive proclivities in men, and he did portray isolation of affect as a peculiarly obsessive mechanism (1926). Consequently, it seems to follow from Freud's generalization that obsessive natures are more moral than hysterical natures. But the proposition makes no sense, and this for two reasons. One is that, although obsessives differ from hysterics in at least certain aspects of their morality, it is meaningless to suggest that it is possible to measure such differences on a single scale or indeed on any scale, for these are no scalar quantities that are in question; they are modes of response or configurations of attitude and behavior. One would only be imposing a value judgment in the guise of making an empirical quantitative comparison. Apparently following the conventional patriarchal approach of his time, Freud was *in this sense* confusing values and observations. (In another sense, which is irrelevant here, there can be no value-free observations.)

In addition to this logical objection to the invidious comparison, there is a psychoanalytic objection to be raised. Even assuming this isolation and this rigidity to be true differentiae, a psychoanalyst could never accept the obsessive as a more definite morality or a firmer one. This is so because obsessive morality is founded on intellectualization, reaction formation against anal-sadistic tendencies, irrational and savage unconscious guilt, and much devious immorality for which atonement must be continually made or which must be "magically" undone; additionally, obsessive tendencies toward scrupulosity serve as unconscious equivalents of masturbation and torture. The obsessive model is, according to psychoanalytic understanding, a poor model of morality, indeed.

And if one were to argue on behalf of milder or more neutralized versions of this morality, one would still have to compare them with milder or more neutralized versions of hysterical morality, and so one would still have to face the other problems I have just raised. The charge of reductionism or genetic fallacy would have to be made against *both or neither* of these references to the infantile psychosexual prototypes of morality.

Thus far, Freud's quantitative comparison of the morality of men and women does not seem to stand up. Let us therefore examine it from another viewpoint. Freud also seemed to be assuming that holding to moral stands once taken, regardless of consequences in one's personal relationships, is a sign of firmer morality, and that men clearly surpass women in this regard. There are additional grounds for entertaining this interpretation of Freud: he did think the predominant danger situation in the lives of women is loss of love, whereas that position in the lives of men is occupied by castration (1926); and since castration anxiety is considerably more narcissistically detached a concern than fear of loss of love, in its being more remote from the immediate vicissitudes of love relationships, it provides a more impersonal foundation for moral activity. In Freud's final theory of development, this castration anxiety is the chief incentive for the renunciations and identifications that constitute the influential superego organization (1923a). Freud concluded that girls, already believing themselves to have been castrated, lack of the same incentive as boys to become moral, and consequently seek solace and restored self-esteem in being loved by men and receiving babies from them (1925).

In this context Freud was clearly not appreciating two factors, one being the part played in the girl's development by the example of the active, nurturant mother who has her own sources of pride and consolation, and the other being the part played by the great variety of positive environmental emphases concerning girls and women. His attention was fixed on the

decisive part played in the girl's development by one set of unconscious equations: my lost penis = father's actual penis = the
baby given me by father's penis.

Freud's conclusion seems inevitable: it is not only that
women crave unconsciously to be loved, invaded, and impregnated, but that they bend their morality all too readily in
order to fulfill these cravings; their fear of disapproval often
overrules whatever independent sense they may have of what is
right for them and others. No Freudian psychoanalyst would
deny the applicability of these propositions to many segments
of the significant problems presented in analysis by typical
neurotic women in this culture. But surely every such analyst
would affirm as well that, whatever the castration anxiety of
men might have to do with superego structuralization, typically that anxiety is so unresolved, so persistent, and so intense
that it continuously incites men to violate conventional morality. When Freud cautioned against overestimating the degree
of true superego formation in people in general, he must have
meant men in particular.

More remains to be said about superego morality. For
Freud, the unconscious infantile superego was the foundation
of individual morality and established its character. His immediate *developmental* concern in working out his superego
theory was to give an account of how and why the incest taboo
is established and secured. He did not address himself particularly to the concept of reality-attuned, organized, adaptive
moral codes as, later on, Hartmann was to do (1960). That
Freud had some definite ideas along this line is suggested in
many places in his writings. These ideas are also implied in the
dictum that, according to Hartmann, he was fond of quoting:
what is moral is self-evident. But in his psychoanalytic writings, he did not sharply distinguish between superego and
moral code.

Generally speaking, the consequences of drawing this distinction have been insufficiently appreciated. One such consequence is a radical alteration of our idea of superego, for now

we are able to see that superego is not morality at all, nor can morality grow out of it alone, for superego is fierce, irrational, mostly unconscious vindictiveness against oneself for wishes and activities that threaten to bring one into archaically conceived, infantile danger situations. As Freud described it, unconscious superego is mostly a demonic aspect of mind;[1] and as he developed this theory of it, it is his Death Instinct enshrined in psychic structure (1923a, 1930). This is the sense of Freud's conclusion that one aim of therapeutic analysis is to reduce superego influence on ego functioning (1933); by this, he did not mean any reduction of morality.

This severe authority does generally enforce respectful observance of certain fundamental personal, familial, and societal taboos. In this respect, it is a powerful set of primitive prohibitions and policies of self-punishment. But at the same time Freud also demonstrated that this authority may be subversive of people's achievements, their love, and even their moral codes, for, like any harsh and arbitrary authority, it continuously incites rebellion, hatred, and self-destructiveness. Superego can even make criminals of people. Whatever superego does contribute toward eventual morality requires considerable tempering before that morality can be secured, and certainly superego cannot temper itself; it cannot achieve its own independence of its being and its emotional origins.

It follows that Freud may have drawn exactly the wrong conclusion from his theory. If, on account of her different constellation of castration concerns, a girl does not develop the implacable superego that a boys does, then at least in this respect she might be better suited than a boy to develop a moral code that is enlightened, realistic, and consistently

---

[1] I say of unconscious superego that it is *mostly* demonic, for Freud also pointed to a benign, loving aspect of superego (Schafer, 1960). But that aspect, too, is archaic in its magical, grandiose, and absolute attributes, and so cannot amount to a moral code; like the punitive aspect, it can only constitute part of the history of that code.

committed to some conventional form of civilized interaction among people. And perhaps that is the truth instead and the basis of another widely held view of women that Freud ignored in this connection: women as the guardians of civilized conduct and morality.[2] Probably no one factor or description could state the whole truth in this regard. One remains dissatisfied both with Freud's estimate of men's and women's moralities and with his assuming that one may measure and generalize in this respect.

Can one be satisfied with Freud's related view that women are less objective, lucid, and acute in comprehension than men (1920)? Here, Freud was implying that, as well as less superego development than men, women manifest less ego development (though when he said this, in 1920, he had not yet formulated his structural theory; but see also his paper of 1931). The derivation of this generalization is the same one I presented of Freud's estimate of women's morality: briefly, that an already castrated being's incentive for development is weaker than that of a being fearful of castration; that castration anxiety is the greatest spur of all to ego development, as to superego development.

If we again agree provisionally that there are or may be sex differences in ego development, how are we to construe them? As in the case of morality, I suggest that these are not measurable differences in degree of development. Certainly one can measure the degree of development of single skills or functions according to the rules for applying specific scales to performances elicited by standardized methods. And certainly

---

[2] I shall not argue here for or against the logical inevitability or empirical truth of either of these conclusions or of any other. Before doing so, one would have to scrutinize various types or styles of moral code—the assumptions, articulation, flexibility, scope, and applications of each; that would be to have studied qualitative differences as such. Also, one would have to compare the developmental sequences of relaxing initially severe superego policies against consolidating a moral code despite initially insufficient superego formation. Clinically, we see both sequences.

one can make informal estimates of this circumscribed sort, with the naked eye as it were. But, taken as a whole, differences between men and women in ego functioning are qualitative, corresponding to *modes* of functioning rather than *amounts*. Contrary to Freud, there can be no final authority on the question of whether one mode of functioning is superior to another, for the question makes sense only in a context of values. Modes may be described, and different modes may be contrasted, but only a taken-for-granted patriarchal value system could lead to Freud's unqualified statement about women's relative mental incompetence.

Furthermore, there are contradictions to be noted. For example, if women are, as Freud believed, more intuitive and keenly empathic than men, are they not thereby manifesting another *kind* of acute comprehension? The difference then would not lie in acuteness at all, but in the judge's estimate of worth. Additionally, there hovers over all these considerations the major questions of whether or in which respects these differences do exist, and, if they do, whether they are inevitable or are enforced or at least exaggerated by methods of rearing and educating boys and girls differently in and for a phallocentric world. There is also the hard question posed by wide individual differences *within* the sexes.

Here I should point out that Freud's social critics are close to Freud in a fundamental sense. Freud, too, presented the world as phallocentric, though he had in mind the world as it exists in psychic reality, whereas his critics are referring to the actual formative and normative environment. And yet, what of it? Let us grant the primary or tremendous importance of psychic reality: then we would expect it to shape the comprehension of social reality, to constitute a significant part of the social reality one encounters as other people, and, historically, to determine much of the content and organization of social reality—to all of which real adaptations would have to be made. Consequently, the child's sexual identity would be defined by that "complemental series" of inner and outer influences that Freud regularly invoked in his developmental propositions. Additionally, Freud relied heavily, in his final theory of ego and anxiety, on the idea of the infant's prolonged helplessness and the consequent importance of the environment, both as it really is and as it is in psychic reality; this means that external reality and psychic reality shape each other. In this light, one may view Freud's more thoughtful feminist critics as exploring the following questions concerning sexual identity: To what extent does societal indoctrination shape psychic reality and regulate the development of skills, attitudes, and ideas and values about oneself in relation to others? And how are any such societal influences mediated by family roles, schooling, and the actualities of later existence as well as by anatomical-physiological differences between the sexes? These questions are not alien to Freudian inquiry, especially when it is informed by ego psychology and adaptive considerations. What is problematical is the patriarchal bias in Freudian conceptualization and emphasis, a bias involving taken-for-granted models of masculine and feminine roles in our society.[3]

One must conclude that Freud's estimates of women's morality and objectivity are logically and empirically indefensible. In large part these estimates implement conventional patriarchal values and judgments that have been misconstrued as being disinterested, culture-free scientific observations.

---

[3] In some early and illuminating Freudian papers on female sexuality, Karen Horney (1924, 1926, 1932, 1933) identified patriarchal bias in the then-existing psychoanalytic literature on the sexes. And yet her mode of thought continued the patriarchal tradition of formulating sweeping generalizations about the sexes. It is the mode of the authoritative scientist laying down definitively the properties of a species. It is unlike the nonpatriarchal mode of that exciting and evocative mixture of observation, impression, discovery, perplexity, and reservation that one encounters throughout Freud's case studies and clinical papers, that part of his *oeuvre* which, patriarchally, Freud seemed to regard as merely his "novels" or preliminary scientific data (one might almost say, in his terms, the feminine side of his work). Here I can only allude to the idea that phallic prototypes and values play major roles in our traditionally esteemed modes of knowing.

The Problem of Neglected Prephallic Development

This is the problem created by Freud's having tried to account for women's personality characteristics and problems mainly in terms of the phallic phase. It is necessary to put this problem in theoretical perspective before coming to the problem itself. Accordingly, I shall first discuss in some detail certain general features of Freud's theorizing that seem to account for his having based so much of his theory of psychosexual development on anatomical genital factors.

The problem of neglected prephallic development was introduced into Freud's theorizing, and thus into his comparative views on men and women, by his adhering to a biological, evolutionary model for his psychology (Schafer, 1970). This model requires a teleological view of the propagation of the species (see, e.g., Freud, 1933, p. 131). That is to say, it requires the assumption that individual human beings are destined to be links in the chain of survival. This assumption necessarily implies the idea that genital sexuality is the culmination of psychosexual development, and that idea, in turn, necessarily implies that anything else is an arrest of development and so must be, in some sense of the so-called natural order of things, unnatural, defective, or abnormal. Accordingly, pregenital pleasures, being nonprocreative, belong at best to foreplay in adult sexual life; otherwise they are perversions. And homosexuality, being similarly nonprocreative, is to be viewed not as an alternative to genital heterosexuality but as a so-called inversion. One observes in this entire line of thought the operation of an implicit but powerful *evolutionary value system.* According to this value system, nature has its procreative plan, and it is better for people to be "natural" and not defy "the natural order." The propositions are not neutral.

Here is one of the great ironies in the history of psychoanalysis: even after Freud gave up the idea of an instinct of self-preservation and in general de-emphasized his ideas about very specific instinctual drives, he continued to adhere to this line of thought and valuation, and in so doing, contradicted his major clinical observations and conclusions. Clinically, even as early as his "Three Essays in the Theory of Sexuality" (1905b), he had come to realize that genital heterosexuality is a difficult, imperfect, more or less precarious achievement, and that this is so because it is a psychological as well as a biological eventuality. Biology provides chiefly the stimuli, especially the insistent and potentially painful stimuli of bodily needs, and the sensuous zones; it is experience in human relationship that defines and emphasizes specific aims and objects. The attainment of genital primacy is therefore very much a matter of the child's learning certain lessons about sexual pleasures and dangers, and its developing some type and degree of mastery of both of these. This learning and striving for mastery will, of course, involve many animistic, illogical, unrealistic, and symbolic infantile mental processes; these processes, usually ignored or underestimated by the cultural revisionists, are among the phase-specific features of early psychosexual development. And this learning will be very much under the influence of bodily experience in the context of some caretaking presence. But however crude, it *is* learning.

In effect, Freud has shown that for human beings there is nothing inevitable about propagating the species. This is truly a revolutionary discovery; because we know only societies that, owing to various combinations of need and tradition, are geared for creating children, we tend to take it for granted that procreativity is a central and inevitable aspect of human beings, as of other animals. It need not be argued here that, in crucial respects, human beings differ fundamentally from other animals, and it was Freud's clinical contributions that made it possible to realize in how many ways and how insistently societies steer children from their infancy toward procreative male and female roles. However imperfectly, we are continuously preparing children in our society to become fathers and mothers in nuclear families. Freud also showed, and especially emphasized, that, from the standpoint of the child, this indoctrination impinges on, and to a large extent is understood in terms of, the child's own wishes to be in the procreative role; these are wishes based on the child's identifications, rivalry, love, infantile fantasies, sensuous desires, and other variables familiar from clinical work. But there is no sense of assuredness among the members of our society that the child's own procreative wishes would or could by themselves finally establish their own primacy; and so, implicitly and explicitly, we plan the child's psychosexual development. We turn out men and women who will have children in nuclear families, too, and who, in turn, will prepare their children to continue this pattern and will think it good and natural to do so and live so.

Although it is fruitless to speculate about how children would develop in this respect if left to their own devices, we can further consider the place of learning in procreative genitality because there are other and real types of control situations. For instance, in our society we often observe children and adults who have been indoctrinated by parents to hold ideal conceptions of sex roles other than the traditional procreative ones. These are the psychologically masculinized daughters and psychologically effeminized sons. Moreover, procreation is not an inevitable consequence of the pleasures of sexual excitement and orgasm; nor is heterosexual genital intercourse the only route to these pleasures.

Considerations such as these highlight the centrality of learning in the human being's movement toward procreativity. Consequently, we need not and should not assume a self-fulfilling instinctual drive toward propagation of the species. Nor is it logical to argue that some drive of that sort has to be operative, even though it is not amenable to our isolating it and studying its action, for if we cannot study it, we have no right to speak of its existence or to build it into the foundation of our theories, as Freud did.[4]

---

[4] That it might have a place in preliminary or informal speculation, which might then lead to significant discovery, is another matter altogether. I have discussed logical problems in psychoanalytic theory elsewhere (1972, 1973a, 1973b).

Finally, with regard to *unlearned* influences on psycho-sexual identity, it must be noted that Freud never really inte-grated his references to constitutional differences in the strength of masculinity and femininity with his psychological propositions about sexual development. Furthermore, he did not—indeed, could not—demonstrate that he regularly en-countered these differences in the neurotic people with whom he was working.

Thus, it is one great consequence of Freud's discoveries that our psychoanalytic explanations may no longer presup-pose any natural or pre-established culmination of human psychosexual development. Another consequence, corollary to the first, is that psychosexual outcomes other than repro-ductive genitality are called illnesses and arrests in develop-ment *only from the standpoint of the values and associated child-rearing practices common to most members of a society.* In speaking of perversions and inversions and their cure, we are operating in the realm of societal value systems concerning taken-for-granted evolutionary obligations; we are not operating in any realm of biological necessity, psychobiologi-cal disorder, or value-free empiricism. There is no established relation between these value systems and psychoanalytic in-sights, though there may be between these value systems and religion or existential choices. None of which is to deny, of course, that clinical psychoanalysis can and does often greatly reduce profound and painful conflicts in these areas, or that it may be legitimate or even inescapable to define illness in terms of value systems. But we should know that this is what we are or may be doing.

The argument may be pursued by emphasizing Freud's helping us to understand the socially widespread intense re-vulsion toward, and derogation and persecution of so-called sexual deviants. He showed that these violent reactions are founded on three factors: a degree of precariousness in the heterosexual genitality attained by most nondeviant people; a greater or lesser dread common to these people of succumbing to modes of gratification that would disconfirm their heterosexual genitality; and some readiness on their part to project their repudiated desires onto others and then persecute them. This *precariousness* expresses various unconscious fixations on and regressions to homosexual and pregenital pleasures, and this *dread* and *persecution* reflect the intense, partly incorporated social pressures against assuming these deviant sexual roles. These pressures have, of course, impinged on the child's archaic fantasies of pleasure, destruction, castration, loss of self and others, and loss of love and security; and they have been understood in terms of these fantasies and gained much of their great power from them. Along the same line, Freud helped us to see through and beyond our society's many hypocritical moralistic attitudes toward pleasure of all sorts and its usually excessively confining sense of decorum, especially with regard to sexuality. But this understanding of sexual development and sexual attitudes must be predicated on the proposition that human sexuality is indeed *psycho*sexuality. The concept psychosexuality excludes a sexuality of blind instincts culminating in propagation of the species, as in nonhuman organisms (though even for them this simple statement is no longer really acceptable); and it excludes a sexuality simply of erotic techniques and orgasmic adequacy. Psychosexuality means mental sexuality, that is, a sexuality of meanings and personal relationships that have developed and been organized around real and imagined experiences and situations in a social world.

Freud disregarded this consequence of his own revolutionary clinical discovery. He persevered with the biological, evolutionary model and value system. Just as his doing so greatly confounded his metapsychological theorizing (Schafer, 1973a), it limited his clinical view of development prior to the phallic phase; thereby, it interfered with his developing an altogether satisfactory developmental psychology of girls—and of boys as well. The fact that psychoanalysts, in following Freud, tend to regard and name these early phases the *pre-*

genital and *pre*oedipal phases betrays the relevant bias and limitation in traditional thinking.

In Freud's major systematic statements, he repeatedly indicated that real mental development begins and is crystallized during the time of the passing of the Oedipus complex, which is the very time when the foundations of procreative genitality are being decisively laid. For example, Freud spoke of the ego as at best a rudimentary organ before this time. Also, he seemed to underestimate the influential fantasies of incorporated parental figures and other "presences" that seem to abound during the very early years and to persist to some extent thereafter. Further, Freud held that it is not only the superego structure which is established during the resolution of the Oedipus complex, but the structured and structuring ego as well (1923a); for only then, on the strength of its new identifications and the desexualized energy now available to it for sublimated activity, does the ego begin to function as an organized, independent, and influential agency.

In his structural theory of mental development, Freud provided no fully adequate and integrated treatment of the acquisition of language, habit training, oral and anal fantasy life, consolidation of narcissism, rudimentary character formation, and many other early factors. Despite his tremendous discoveries concerning just these prephallic factors, Freud still put the phallus, oedipal fantasies, castration anxiety, and procreation in the center of his developmental theory. And yet one can only begin to comprehend the development of the phallic phase and the Oedipus complex and the possibility of their coming to any resolution whatsoever on the basis of considerable prephallic ego development (Schafer, 1968b).

The centering on ultimate procreative genitality explains some of the imperfections of Freud's psychology of women. The essential point may be developed through consideration of Freud's having pretty much taken for granted the girl's catastrophic response to her discovering the anatomical difference between the sexes and her basically implacable envious attitude thereafter. Freud was remarkably incurious about the background of these reactions. He did refer (almost in passing, it seems) to speculative ideas put forward by others concerning the girl's being primed to respond thus catastrophically by prior losses of breast and feces; otherwise, he was silent. Similarly, with regard to the danger situations of loss of love object and loss of love, which precede the era of castration concerns, Freud's comments remained schematic as well as isolated from considerations of the extremity of the girl's reaction to the anatomical difference.

We encounter the same problem even in Freud's major revisionary efforts in 1931 and 1933. Although there he stressed the pregenital girl's activity, her mother's "sexual seduction" of her through bodily ministrations, the girl's natural ambivalence toward her mother and her struggle with her over masturbation, he did not present these variables as the foundations of the castration shock. These variables remained isolated. Soon they would be superseded by the beginning of the "feminine [phase] to which she [the girl] is *biologically destined*" (1933, p. 119, emphasis added). Here there is no sense of developmental continuity.

To mention only one more problem: Freud was too quick to favor the designation penis envy for the complex array of feelings, wishes, and fantasies of which penis envy is, after all, only a part, though often a most intense and consequential part. Here, the influence of phallocentrism can hardly be overlooked.

Insofar as it is the hallmark of psychoanalytic investigation, and particularly of Freud's thinking, that it always presses its questions further and further in the interest of establishing the fullest understanding possible of the particularity of response on the part of individuals in specific circumstances, especially when these reactions are intense, disturbing, profoundly formative, and enduringly influential, it is all the more remarkable that at this point there are virtually no questions forthcoming. It is as if it is sufficient just to know that girls assume they are phallic in the way boys are, and that they pursue active as well as passive aims until the terrible time of revelation, mortification, and envy. But it is not sufficient. The psychoanalytic clinician as well as theorist must remain curious and so must go on to ask: Why *is* the girl so extremely mortified and envious? Her mortification and envy are not explained by the fact of her simply seeing the difference; nor are they explained by her having previously maintained unchallenged her assumption that she and the boy are anatomically alike. To begin to answer the question at all satisfactorily, one must assume that, before the time of mortification and envy, it was already terribly important to the girl that there be no differences between herself and boys. And to make that assumption is to land smack in the middle of so-called pregenital mental development. At this point, this phasic location can no longer seem quite so *pre*genital, in any case. In effect I am arguing that we cannot have a simple, self-evident *shock theory* of the girl's extreme mortification and consequent penis envy. That the girl reacts this way indicates that she is already heavily invested in and worried about genital comparison and intactness. Freud's consistently restricted view of these developments is evident in the way he contrasted to the boy's initial "irresolution and lack of interest" the girl's response to having to face the anatomical difference: "She makes her judgement and her decision in a flash. She has seen it [the penis] and knows that she is without it and wants to have it" (1925, p. 252).

The problem of the readiness for castration shock is not the whole of the difficulty. In his quest for particularity of explanation, the psychoanalyst must also ask about the apparent precariousness of the girl's self-esteem in the face of the genital discovery, however and whenever it is made. Indeed, in Freud's theory this precariousness is presented as so great that the collapse of self-esteem in the context of the castration fantasy is held to be a decisive and permanent influence on the woman's entire mental development and organization. As

Freud was to put it much later on, penis envy was the "bed-rock" of her neurotic problems (1937). But, again, where are Freud's questions in this regard? It was he, after all, who taught us how to establish through psychoanalysis the historical background and determination of psychological traumata.[5]

Even after making allowances for due restraint on speculation, one may still argue that Freud was in a logical and methodological position to at least raise these questions about the readiness for mortification and envy and the precariousness of self-esteem. The answers, about which I shall have more to say later, would have to center on the girl's relationship with her mother during the first years of her life, and they would establish the profound importance of this relationship throughout the remainder of the daughter's existence — as of the son's. *That Freud did not raise these questions seems to be in large part an expression of his being preoccupied with the organs of reproduction, in consequence of his commitment to an evolutionary model and value system.* On this account, Freud neglected to a noteworthy degree two interrelated psychological variables, one being manifestations of mind prior to the time of the phallic phase and the Oedipus complex, the other being the powerful role played by learning in the development of sexual attitudes, roles, and subjective experience. Far more than it should have, anatomy had become Freud's destiny.

Anatomy and reproduction, and anatomy and mind: the links were forged. Despite Freud's keen awareness of early mental functioning, he developed no *psychological* way of taking it into account. Mostly he biologized the early mental

⟩

---

[5] Methodologically, Freud was wise not to press his questions too far. He cautioned against formulating propositions concerning mental processes during the earliest phases of development, for, typically, the relevant data from clinical analysis are, at best, extremely fleeting, fragmentary, and ambiguous, and it is primarily through analytic work proper that developmental propositions are to be framed and tested (1931).

processes by relegating them to instincts, instinctual energy, processes, and principles, such as the pleasure principle, the primary process, and the repetition compulsion; and he viewed each of these as seeking to gratify its own aims in its own way; thereby he anthropomorphized them, that is, reintroduced psychological propositions by the back door of biology (Grossman and Simon, 1969; Schafer, 1972, 1973a, 1973b).

A psychological approach to the prephallic period must center on the girl's primary, mind-formative, certainly intensely and complexly physical, and ultimately indestructible relationship with her mother. Freud, however, was mostly concerned to explain the girl's turning *from* her mother *to* her father as lover and sire of her children. In this effort, he portrayed the girl has having simply turned against her mother and, together with that, against her own identification-based active orientation and her clitoris. But, to be consistent with psychoanalytic propositions and findings, one must see the girl and, later, the woman as being in a profoundly influential, continuously intense and active relationship, not only with her real mother, but with the idea and imagined presence of her mother, and with her identification with this mother; one must also see her as integrating her clitoris firmly into her sexuality. Whatever the girl's narcissistic vulnerability at the time of the castration shock, it would have its history and find its meaning in this matrix. Although Freud approached this consistency in some of his later papers, he did not achieve it.

Freud's value-based interpretation of his investigations is further evidenced in a limitation of his approach to the problem of the analysis of transference. Typically, he construed the transference he had observed as based on the ambivalent tie to the father of early childhood. Even in his paper of 1931, in which he was reconsidering his psychology of women and beginning to emphasize the importance of the pregenital relation to the mother, he suggested that it would be *female* analysts particularly who would be the ones to work out the child's early relation to the mother. Thereby he continued to neglect the essentially androgynous role of the psychoanalyst in the transference; for the male analyst this means his female as well as male identity in this central aspect of his work. There is little evidence of Freud's having been alert to or impressed by maternal transference to the male analyst—or, for that matter, by maternal countertransference on the part of the male analyst.

It is not inaccurate to attribute to Freud a relative neglect of bisexuality, even though that concept and the relevant observations are such central elements in his theory of development. This neglect is evident in his discussions not only of transference, but of resistance, ego and superego formation, and other topics as well (Schafer, 1973b). He was preoccupied with the father's position in a way and to a degree that stunted his conception of the mother's status in the family and thereby her stature in his theory. Again, for his theory of development the important thing was to get the girl to become *feminine* and ready to receive love and babies *passively* from an active man, thereby to continue to propagate the species. For this, Freud thought he needed a sustained phallic perspective. But that perspective is not inclusive enough for his own psychoanalytic discoveries.

The Problem of Naming

Now we must consider how such designations as feminine, passive, and active behave in descriptive and explanatory propositions. This is the problem of naming.

To designate is also to create and to enforce. By devising and allocating words, which are names, people create entities and modes of experience and enforce specific subjective experiences. Names render events, situations, and relationships available or unavailable for psychological life that might otherwise remain cognitively indeterminate. Consequently, whether or not something will be an instance of masculinity or femininity, activity or passivity, aggression or masochism, dominance or submission, or something else altogether, or nothing at all, will depend on whether or not we consistently call it this or that or consistently do not name it at all, hence do not constitute and authorize its being. Similarly, to the extent that we link or equate such names as, for example, femininity and passivity, we exert a profound and lasting formative influence on what it is said to be like to be feminine or passive. Logically, there is no right answer to the questions, what is masculine and what is feminine and what is active and what is passive. There are no preconceptual facts to be discovered and arrayed. There are only loose conventions governing the uses and groupings of the words in question. And these conventions, like all others, must manifest values.

For example, in our society we often merge words pertaining to social values such as status and so-called breeding with words pertaining to sexual identity. To be a lady in the sense of a fine lady and to be feminine may be set up as equivalents, with the consequence that a woman who does not act ladylike, according to a certain conception of that word, may be said to be not feminine. In this instance, not feminine might mean rude, loud, socially too forward, sexually too adventurous, intellectually too serious, or cosmetically too casual or vivid. Thus, to say that a woman is not feminine is often a way of saying that she does not act or look like a woman "ought to" act or look. An additional part of this poor lesson is the implicit idea, "She is bad." In this way, verbal conventions that implement value judgments are passed off as simple and unequivocal facts — and are so learned by children (Hartmann, 1960).

Clinical psychoanalysts have much occasion to observe and modify the disturbing influence of cultural, familial, and individual conventions regarding the valuative use of words or names and of their groupings and equations, especially in the case of words pertaining to sexual identity, aggression, and personal worth.

In this third and final (and all-too-brief) section of my discussion, I shall concentrate on one strategic problem of naming: how Freud used the words active and passive in relation to the words masculine and feminine. Freud showed some awareness in this regard that he was using and devising verbal conventions. In one place he said, "Maleness combines [the factors of] subject, activity and possession of the penis; femaleness takes over [those of] object and passivity" (1923b, p. 145). In another place he said, "we call everything that is strong and active male, and everything that is weak and passive female" (1940, p. 188). Except for his reference to the penis, which, being an empirical rather than a defining proposition, is out of place in the first statement, Freud seemed to know that he was not making empirical assertions about how women really and necessarily are. In many places he even insisted that women come in all kinds, as do men. What was wanted was merely a suitable rubric for such personal characteristics as weakness and passivity. The names he chose were masculine and feminine (or male and female), and so, within this verbal convention, a woman is masculine to the extent that she is active and strong, and so on (see, e.g., 1933, pp. 114-117).

Whatever one's criticisms of this choice of names, such as that it both implies and enforces a derogation of women, it seems thus far that Freud was proceeding logically. In fact, however, he repeatedly lost his bearings and did not keep definition distinct from observation. Freud's logical sophistication did not stop him from making all sorts of conventional patriarchal statements about what women are actually like and should be like (e.g., submissive to their husband's authority). Such statements suggest that all kinds of "right" answers about sexual identity are being dictated by a pair of biological principles—the masculine and the feminine. Freud's repeated remarks about constitutional strength of masculinity and femininity reveal this to be so.

One may trace this same confusion developing in the

course of Freud's "Female Sexuality" (1933). What was masculine and feminine, like what was moral and objective, seemed to be self-evident to him. His attempt at definitional rigor succumbed to this complacency. For Freud, then, feminine comprised passive, submissive, and masochistic; it meant the willing object of the man's biologically natural sexual and aggressive activity. It does sound as if now the continuation of the species has been scientifically guaranteed. So, incidently, has the continuation of the patriarchal social order, which, in his theories at any rate, Freud seemed to take uncritically as Reality. To put it another way, normative links were assumed between, on the one hand, female-feminine-passive-submissive-masochistic, and, on the other hand, male-masculine-active-dominant-aggressive; this being so, a change of any one term would necessarily imply a change of all the others linked to it.

In trying to explain how women get to be as they allegedly are, particularly in terms of their attempts at resolving their penis envy, Freud made many fundamental and grand discoveries. Nevertheless, he was begging the question in at least two different ways. One was his presupposing that in fact women get to be *essentially* passive, submissive, and masochistic. The other was his presupposing that it is their psychobiological destiny to get to be as he said they are. Consequently, he worked with a simplified view of women, and he paid scant attention to the questions whether and to what extent girls are continuously being seduced and coerced into being "that way" by members of a society committed unconsciously, if not consciously, to guaranteeing that outcome.

Much of the argument turns on the meaning of passive. For Freud, masochism is the passive complement of sadistic aggression; submission is the passive complement of dominance; being loved, of loving; being looked at, of looking; and being impregnated, of impregnating (see, e.g., Freud, 1915a). If all these passivities add up to femininity, we had better be clear about how Freud was using the word passive. The trouble is that Freud was not clear or consistent in his use of that word. At times he was even self-contradictory. First of all, he confused phenomenological passivity with passivity in the eyes of the psychoanalytic observer of behavior (Schafer, 1968a). A clear example from psychoanalysis is the so-called fate neurosis in which, phenomenologically, one repeatedly experiences oneself as the unfortunate passive victim of circumstance, while the psychoanalytic observer of behavior sees the person in question as actively bringing about his or her own misfortunes, say as symbolic castrations or incestuous wishes or as abandonments in punishment for unconscious oedipal triumphs. Secondly, when Freud generalized about women's passivity, he neglected such factors as unconscious identification with the partner in any significant relationship. These are factors whose importance he had been the very one to establish through his psychoanalytic method. In this connection, for example, the masochist is understood to be also unconsciously identifying with, and thereby vicariously enjoying the activity of, the sadistic partner; and to this one must add that moral masochists, at any rate, not only actively seek out and provoke the abuses they seem to suffer passively, but use their suffering to torment others. Thirdly, Freud repeatedly demonstrated how extraordinarily subtle and complex the interweaving of active and passive themes can be in any one person's life, from which it follows that one-sided or simple characterizations of any significant project as active or passive hardly makes sense, once one knows a given person and situation well enough. Yet Freud was not deterred from generalizing on the basis of such simplistic characterizations. Again, he dealt inconsistently with his own discoveries and conceptual perspective.

Perhaps most fundamental to the analysis of this problem of naming is that, in many crucial instances, the decision whether to speak of behavior or of aims or attitudes as active or passive is like the decision whether to say of a certain glass of water that it is half full or half empty. For example, to be exhibitionistic one must find a real or imagined audience and show oneself off, which is to be active; and it is to be looked at, which is to be passive. Another example: to be loved is to be passive, and yet there are so many ways of getting to be loved and of receiving love, all of which are forms of being active. One more example: does the penis penetrate the vagina or does the vagina receive the penis? Here I should point out that, immediately after the sentence I quoted earlier in this section, in which Freud grouped subject, activity, and possession of the penis as the referents of maleness, he went on to say, "The vagina is . . . valued as the place of shelter for the penis; it enters into the heritage of the womb" (1923b, p. 145): one must ask whether a place of shelter can be passive and whether a womb can be passive, or, to put it in terms of persons-in-relation, which are the proper ones, one must ask whether it makes any sense to say of a woman engaging in sexual intercourse that she is simply passive and whether it makes any sense to say of a mother that she is simply passive. Although Freud raised this last question (1933, p. 115), he did not draw its consequences for his general theory.

That Freud was not prepared to think about mothers very far is, as I noted earlier, evident from how little he said directly about them and about relationships with them, and, correspondingly, how little he said about how they appear in the transference, the resistance, and the formation of the ego and superego systems. Additionally, in his writings he showed virtually no sustained interest in their subjective experience — except for their negative feelings about their own femininity and worth and their compensatory cravings to be loved and impregnated, especially with sons. Consequently, Freud dealt with the feminine trends in men chiefly in terms of the two factors of castration and passive homosexuality, and he failed to consider in depth and systematically what more is entailed by being a woman and feeling like one in our society and how it might be different under other conditions. It seems that he knew the father and the castrate in himself and other men but not the mother and the woman.

To return to the idea of a fine lady: there is a Victorian precept that in sexual relations "a lady doesn't move." The modern psychoanalyst has to recognize this role, not as passivity, but as a desperate form of activity—a drastic inhibition required to play this inactivated part. The inhibiting may be carried out unconsciously and supplemented by conscious aversion, and the groundwork for this behavior would have to have been laid in early childhood, but it is activity nonetheless, at least as much as anything else is. It is from Freud particularly that we have learned about this unconscious activity. Yet, although Freud the clinician was ever alert to the many forms unconscious activity takes in the lives of women, Freud the theoretician, when dealing with the development of sexual identity, named this inhibition passivity and made it the crux of femininity.

Concluding Remarks

Freud was working within a nineteenth-century biological-medical tradition that was not of his making. He merely applied and extended the conventions that constituted that tradition. That tradition was marked by a fusion of mechanistic and evolutionary modes of thought and patriarchal complacency. It based itself on ruling principles of nature, such as survival; great natural polarities or dichotomies, such as activity-passivity and masculinity-femininity; and other broad generalizations designed to take nature by the throat. Additionally, it was a tradition of belief in the idea of value-free empiricism and of pride in the achievements of the utterly objective scientist, and so was philosophically too immature to appreciate what is better established today—namely, the pluralistic, relativistic, linguistic, and inevitably valuative aspects of the various forms of knowledge. Against these odds, Freud's achievement is all the more impressive. Nevertheless, at this historical moment we are obliged to identify and clarify the problematical aspects and limitations of Freud's contributions to the psychology of women. Much remains to be said on this subject, and on the correlated subject of the fear that haunts the lives of men, pervading their relationships with women as well as with men: the fear of being second best and second-rate themselves.

Summary

Freud's ideas on the development and psychological characteristics of girls and women, though laden with rich clinical and theoretical discoveries and achievements, appear to have been significantly flawed by the influence of traditional patriarchal and evolutionary values. This influence is evident in certain questionable presuppositions, logical errors and inconsistencies, suspensions of intensive inquiry, underemphasis on certain developmental variables, and confusions between observations, definitions, and value preferences. Under three headings—The Problem of Women's Morality and Objectivity, the Problem of Neglected Prephallic Development, and The Problem of Naming—I discuss Freud's generalizations concerning ego and superego development in boys and girls, penis envy, biologically predestined procreativity, the role of the mother, the fateful linkages male-masculine-active-aggressive-dominant and female-feminine-passive-masochistic-submissive, and other topics as well. In general, it is argued that Freud's generalizations concerning girls and women do injustice to both his psychoanalytic method and his clinical findings.

REFERENCES

Freud, S. (1905a), Fragment of an analysis of a case of hysteria. *Standard Edition,* 7:3-122. London: Hogarth Press, 1953.
———— (1905b), Three essays on the theory of sexuality. *Standard Edition,* 7:125-243. London: Hogarth Press, 1953.
———— (1915a), Instincts and their vicissitudes. *Standard Edition,* 14:109-140. London: Hogarth Press, 1957.
———— (1915b), Thoughts for the times on war and death. *Standard Edition,* 14:274-300. London: Hogarth Press, 1957.

_____ (1920), The psychogenesis of a case of homosexuality in a woman. *Standard Edition*, 18:140-172. London: Hogarth Press, 1955.

_____ (1923a), The ego and the id. *Standard Edition*, 19:3-66. London: Hogarth Press, 1961.

_____ (1923b), The infantile genital organization. *Standard Edition*, 19:140-145. London: Hogarth Press, 1961.

_____ (1925), Some psychical consequences of the anatomical distinction between the sexes. *Standard Edition*, 19:243-258. London: Hogarth Press, 1961.

_____ (1926), Inhibitions, symptoms, and anxiety. *Standard Edition*, 20:77-174. London: Hogarth Press, 1959.

_____ (1930), Civilization and its discontents. *Standard Edition*, 21:59-145. London: Hogarth Press, 1961.

_____ (1931), Female sexuality. *Standard Edition*, 21:223-243. London: Hogarth Press, 1961.

_____ (1933), New introductory lectures on psychoanalysis. *Standard Edition*, 22:3-182. London: Hogarth Press, 1964.

_____ (1937), Analysis terminable and interminable. *Standard Edition*, 23:211-253. London: Hogarth Press, 1964.

_____ (1940), An outline of psycho-analysis. *Standard Edition*, 23:141-207. London: Hogarth Press, 1964.

Grossman, W. I. & Simon, B. (1969), Anthropomorphism: motive, meaning, and causality in psychoanalytic theory. *The Psychoanalytic Study of the Child*, 24: 78-114. New York: International Universities Press.

Hartmann, H. (1960), *Psychoanalysis and Moral Values.* New York: International Universities Press.

Horney, K. (1924), On the genesis of the castration-complex in women. *Internat. J. Psycho-Anal.*, 5:50-65.

_____ (1926), The flight from womanhood: the masculinity complex in women as viewed by men and by women. *Internat. J. Psycho-Anal.*, 7:324-339.

_____ (1932), The dread of woman. *Internat. J. Psycho-Anal.*, 13:348-361.

_____ (1933), The denial of the vagina. *Internat. J. Psycho-Anal.*, 14:57-70.

Schafer, R. (1960), The loving and beloved superego in Freud's structural theory. *The Psychoanalytic Study of the Child*, 15:163-188. New York: International Universities Press.

_____ (1968a), On the theoretical and technical conceptualization of activity and passivity. *Psychoanal. Quart.*, 37:173-198.

_____ (1968b), *Aspects of Internalization.* New York: International Universities Press.

_____ (1970), An overview of Heinz Hartmann's contributions to psycho-analysis. *Internat. J. Psycho-Anal.*, 51:425-446.

_____ (1972), Internalization: process or fantasy? *The Psychoanalytic Study of the Child*, 27:411-438. New York: International Universities Press.

_____ (1973a), Action: its place in psychoanalytic interpretation and theory. *The Annual of Psychoanalysis:* 1:159-196.

_____ (1973b), The idea of resistance. *Internat. J. Psycho-Anal.*, 54:259-285.

New York Hospital
525 E. 68th Street
New York, New York 10021

THE MASCULINE ENVY OF WOMAN'S PROCREATIVE FUNCTION

DANIEL S. JAFFE, M.D.

WHILE THE ROLE of penis envy in female psychology has been given adequate recognition and discussion in the psychoanalytic literature, the concept of an analogous envy in the male of feminine parts and functions has encountered some resistance.[1] There have been several communications[2] on the subject before and since Boehm attempted a definitive formulation in his paper "The Femininity-Complex in Men" (1930), but at this time a review seems desirable in order to integrate certain data concerning early developmental phases, the adult phase, and cultural and anthropological considerations relating to procreative organs and functions.

To envy, according to Webster, is "to be discontent at the possession by another of what one would like for oneself." It could readily be argued that the man has no wish to possess what the woman has, on account of castration anxiety. In this

---

Clinical Professor of Psychiatry, Georgetown University School of Medicine, Washington, D.C.

This article originally appeared in the *Journal of the American Psychoanalytic Association* (1968), 16:521-548.

[1] This has been pointed out by Zilboorg (1944), Jacobson (1950), Bettelheim (1954), and others. The obscuring by overcompensatory valuing of penis and intellectual power has been referred to by Chadwick (1925), Landauer (1931), Fromm (1943), and Klein (1928). Fenichel believed the boy in fact avoids envy of childbearing comparable to the girl's penis envy because of his ability to get pleasure from the penis (1945, p. 83).

[2] Those not mentioned elsewhere in this essay are Eisler (1921), Faergeman (1955), Groddeck (1923), Khan (1965), and van Leeuwen (1966).

connection, it may be recalled that Freud (1937) believed that it is not the passive or feminine attitude per se that is repudiated by men, but passivity toward another male, which betokens castration. Furthermore, Freud had recognized the necessity of accepting the feminine tendency (Erikson, 1955), as he had himself done in his transference to Fliess, where submissiveness, dependence, receptiveness, and gestative qualities marked the creative struggles from which his psychological products emerged (Erikson, 1954).

Procreativity as such is an adult function, and Erikson suggests that the task of achieving the sense of generativity contributes to the nuclear conflict of middle age. In his view, the distinguishing characteristic of generativity is the ability to lose the self, via the ascendency of mutuality and genitality, with progressive ego investment and libidinal cathexis of the product that has been generated (1950). In order to achieve this goal, the adult male must overcome whatever anxieties he has attached to feminine identification during his earlier development. The biphasic nature of this problem makes it necessary to examine the phase-specific conflicts of adulthood, and the antecedent phases with their contributory conflicts and fixations.

Adult Phase

The conflict involved in the task of the adult phase may be clarified by examining two contrasting cases. In one, the conflict was successfully resolved; in the other, a pathological outcome ensued. The two men I refer to are Freud and Schreber. The data on Freud's life situation, past influences, and conflictual processes are provided in Erikson's detailed analysis of the Irma dream (1954); while the basis for an understanding of the vicissitudes of object cathexes in the adult is found in Freud's study of the Schreber case (1911). The present discussion will be devoted to an examination of the processes involved in meeting the procreative task, particularly with respect to the regressive manifestations that mark the conflict.

As Erikson notes, the generative task which Freud successfully mastered involved self-exploration in the face of self-doubts stirred by isolation, criticism, competitiveness, and wishes for revenge. Object cathexes were challenged by regressive strains and role diffusion, as the developmental sequences underwent reversal through each antecedent phase, with the conflicts and resolutions contained therein. Identity challenges, oedipal conflict, defensive homosexual identification, and the whole range of pregenital drive derivatives (oral-tactual, anal-sadistic, voyeuristic, phallic-urethral), are all discerned in the dream. The successful ego mastery of the developmental tasks of each stage permitted an integrative outcome. Ultimately, the struggles of the past and present became fused through the equivalence of the oral cavity, the envied procreative inside of woman, and the mind of the investigator. Neutralization and reality gratifications provided the basis for the successful sublimation, enhanced then by cathexis of the products.

It may be noted that an essential feature of the masculine envy and emulation of the procreative function in this case was that the regressive aspects of the feminine identification did not threaten object cathexes prohibitively or irretrievably. ("Regression in the service of the ego" [Kris, 1936]; "cathectic displacement without regressive redifferentiation of ego" [Fliess, 1953]; "[t]emporary regressive mechanisms of identification induced in the service of the ego do not normally weaken the firm boundaries between self and object" [Jacobson, 1964]).

The conflict that for Schreber resulted in a pathological outcome rested precisely on the challenge to the ability to retain object cathexes in the course of regressive feminine identification. Whatever were the contributions coming respectively from challenges in the current life situation, unavailability of progeny, and conflict-enhancing influences of parents in earlier life, we can only surmise. However, the intrapsychic process is clear in respect to the main conflictual theme. The wish to enjoy copulation as a female, and the delusional system of world destruction which provided Schreber with the special mission of saving the world by becoming transformed into a female and procreating a new race, are interpreted by Freud (1911) as homosexual elements in a regressive process which was subjectively experienced as threatening because it involved decathexis of the world of love objects.[3] This became symbolized in the delusional belief that world destruction had resulted from removal of the rays of the sun, i.e., own cathexes of objects (which had been incorporated into the ego and which constituted the ego, and loss of which was tantamount to death). Freud's formulation considers paranoia to represent an attempted restitution of object cathexes, with negative valence. The regression then constitutes the "step back from sublimated homosexuality to narcissism" (1911, p. 72), and provokes violent conflicts on account of the threat to the subjective world when love is withdrawn. In other terms, conflict from regressive movement concerns the upsurge of aggression which cannot be neutralized as pregenital attitudes toward objects re-emerge.[4]

[3] The criticism of Freud's formulation by Macalpine and Hunter (1953) is based on a narrower interpretation of homosexual conflict than was evidently intended by Freud. They point out the disruptive effects of procreation fantasies insofar as these abrogate reality, despite the intrinsic ego-syntonic features and the potentialities for sublimation. However, they consider homosexual conflict only in terms of the implications for castration in the genital sense. It is clear that Freud was regarding homosexuality not merely from the viewpoint of this level of drive organization, but also as a symptom containing the return of the primarily repressed instincts involved in narcissistic fixation (pp. 67-68, 72). The tracing of the libidinal development from narcissism through homosexuality to heterosexual object love (pp. 60-61), and the description of the catastrophic feelings with reversal of this cathectic process (pp. 69-71), bear out the broader interpretation of homosexual conflict also as a dual process: regressive and reality-threatening or restitutive and object-preserving.

[4] In discussing a paper on phobias by Max Schur (1971), I suggested that the relationship between ego regression and "uncontrolled anxiety" involves experience that impairs successful operation of symbolic or equivalent gratifications, which it is the ego's task to provide. Equivalence in this sense is achieved through

In our everyday experience we deal constantly, in ourselves and in our patients, with the adult manifestations of
procreative strivings, with conflict, resolution, and symptom
formation, along one or another of the lines described in the
two foregoing cases. However, before proceeding with further
discussion, it would be well to mention some other contributions concerning the adult phase, and then to review the
role of feminine identification and striving in the male during
earlier developmental phases.

The concept of a masculine drive organization toward
fatherliness is discussed by Benedek (1959), who suggests that
it is based principally on biological dependency on the mother
and on continual developmental interactions between male
and female identifications. Parenthood for the father involves
revival of identifications with his own mother as well as father,
and integrates regressive maternal identifications, particularly
during his wife's pregnancies. The father's development in
maturity is influenced not only by the recapture of his own
childhood narcissism via the child, but further introjections
and identifications affect current and future potentialities.
Regressive influences and identifications naturally play an
important role in determining parental needs and strivings.

Jacobson (1950) also discusses the developmental forces in
parenthood, in terms of expressions of love, and advancement
of paternal identifications, as well as the omnipotent strivings
and regressive infantile conflict situations that may be revived.

Klein (1957) states that if a man's development has been
successful, he derives compensation for unfulfilled feminine

_____

identification, wherein object cathexis and narcissistic cathexis become comple-
mentary. Regression upsets the balance of such sublimation (the term applied to
this process by Freud [1923, p. 30]). The magnitude of object-renouncing regression determines the degree of danger, preponderance of primary process, refusion
of self and object representations (Jacobson, 1954), passive submission with devouring threats from the destructive character of pregenital attitude toward the
object (Freud, 1915). The conflict involved in identification has been indicated in
the description of rejection of identification because of the fear of being eaten
(Greenson, 1954); and in the fear of passivity which is the fear of helplessness or loss
of ego identity (Nunberg, 1953).

desires through a good relationship with the woman, by fathering her child, and by identification with the child, thus counteracting early envy of the mother's breast and other feminine attributes (especially the capacity to bear children).

Early Determinants

Pregenital

The equivalence of baby with that which has been eaten, and with the content of intestine and bowel, was recognized early in the theory of infantile sexuality (Freud, 1905; Abraham, 1913). Envy, covetousness, and possessive wishes were traced to experience of oral gratification, as was the identification with the bounteous mother (Abraham, 1924a). The mother identification takes place through the direct emotional tie (Freud, 1921, 1923), or regressively through introjection of the lost object into the ego (Freud, 1917a, 1921). The oral incorporation which forms the basis for the earliest identifications (Jacobson, 1964) would then serve as the model for later oral impregnation fantasies (Zilboorg, 1938). Such later fantasies as those of the woman swallowing and aggrandizing the male genitals (Fenichel, 1929), which may constitute one basis for envy of her power[5] (Boehm, 1930; Brunswick, 1940), indicate the continuing influence of early orality.[6] Envy of the female's breasts depends on cathexes of the oral phase, with later reinforcement from phallic displacements (Boehm, 1930). Fantasies of the smaller male penis entering a larger female penis originate in the feelings of superiority of the female breast, later displaced to genital organs (Abraham, 1925).

The oral cavity itself appears to serve as a prototype for all later ideas of body cavities (Lewin, 1953) and, according to

[5] See Lewin (1950) on the active-aggressive and passive-submissive attitudes which aim at making mother part of self or to become part of her.

[6] Ross (1965) refers to teaching as an expression of the wish to have children, rooted in oral feeding with later anal and phallic connections.

Spitz (1955), constitutes the precursor of perception, and the bridge between inner and outer perception. The cathexis of the "primal cavity," with subsequent shifts and displacements to other body cavities and to the contents thereof, is thus the crucial first source of internal fulfillment.

The anal phase of development is of primary importance in contributing to the passive-receptive incorporativeness that constitutes the principal pregenital determinant of the feminine tendency in men (Fenichel, 1945). The influence of anal-erotic experience on character, particularly on the sense of power to possess, preserve, and produce or create[7] has been thoroughly described in the literature.

The specific equivalence of feces and child, rectum and birth passage, is reinforced by the anatomical proximity (Andreas-Salomé, 1916), as well as by the other influences that determine cathectic displacements (similarity in structure and function, i.e., a mass stimulating a hollow organ [Freud, 1917b]; experiences of giving and receiving as object relation with the mother advances [Brunswick, 1940]; the contribution to later sexual development from the active and passive tendencies of the anal phase [Nunberg, 1947]). Transitional objects and the anal-baby concept indicate the sense of identification with the mother and with her functions (Kestenberg, 1956).

The role of aggression is clearly of fundamental importance in determining the character of one's identifications. The earliest attitude toward objects is one of hate, based on the invasion of narcissism by the flow of painful stimuli. Pleasure-providing objects are introjected, and object love as an antithesis to hate is achieved only when genital primacy is established (Freud, 1915). Regression to pregenital tendencies revives the annihilating impulses toward objects, as described earlier in this paper. The infant's oral and anal (and later

[7] Abraham (1920) shows the relationship between Creation myths and excretory process.

phallic) sadistic impulses and dismembering tendencies directed against the mother's body, which produce fears of
destruction and dismemberment (Klein, 1928; Schilder,
1941), call forth reparative impulses which provide the preliminary steps toward object love (Abraham, 1924b, p. 432).
The boy's identification with his mother based on the loss of
the love object has its earliest source in the pregenital experiences (Freud, 1923), on account of the envy of and rage
against the all-powerful and all-possessing mother (Klein,
1928, 1957; Socarides, 1953; Van der Leeuw, 1958).[8]

The pregenital wish for a child is based on the equation
breast = womb = intestine = feces = baby (Jacobson, 1950). As
development proceeds, the pregenital contributions to the
Oedipus complex may be noted in the equivalence of castration with loss of breast and of feces; of the wish for a child with
the wish for penis, feces, and breast; and of coitus with anal
and oral incorporation (Fenichel, 1945; Zilboorg, 1938).

Phallic and Oedipal

The displacement of pregenital to phallic cathexes determines
the further development of the breast = child and feces = child
to the penis = child equation (Freud, 1917b). Coexisting active
and passive tendencies are part of the phallic phase (Loewenstein, 1935), and are also carried over from the anal phase,

---

[8] Regarding primary identification, Greenacre (1953) states that the boy who
has been in close visual contact with the mother develops this, with bisexual splitting of the body image, even antecedent to the phallic phase. (The case I describe
herein confirms this). Fetishism has been studied by many, in the light of its implications regarding formation of ego and body image. I refer, e.g., to Freud (1927,
1940); Payne (1939), who points out the fetish is a defense against destruction
of the good parent; Gillespie (1940), who indicates the strong oral and anal trends
in the castration anxiety of the fetishist; Bak (1953), who suggests the triad of
fetishism, transvestitism, and homosexuality represent different phases of identification with the phallic and penisless mother, from pregenital identifications (cf.
also Fenichel on transvestitism [1945]); and Khan (1965), whose patient's foreskin
fetishism preserved the ego from disintegration by providing an identification with
the procreative and omnipotent mother.

and the boy identifies with the mother in wanting to get a baby from her or to give one to her (Jacobson, 1950; Kestenberg, 1956).

The importance of aggression in the phallic phase in determining the feminine attitude in men is described in detail by Jones (1933), who points out that the boy must pass through a satisfactory feminine stage before he can be masculine. Earlier oral or anal frustrations produce fixations which influence the phallic phase by means of the sadism common to them. The penetrating penis is used to reach oral aims and open the way to milk, feces, nipple, babies, and everything the child wants to swallow. The sadistic penis also has anal connections, to fetch the baby out of the bowel by means of the penis. The penis gets associated with acquiring, and any thwarting leads to fear of damage by the mother. The mother's withholding nipple equals the mother's hoarding nipple and penis. The mother's genital is phallic, having swallowed the father's penis (dragon of the cloaca). The boy wants to penetrate and crush or suck it. The father's penis is dealt with on apparent feminine lines, with oral- and anal-sadistic qualities. The annihilating attitude is the feminine one, with annihilation accomplished by mouth and anus, teeth, feces, and, on the phallic level, urine. This hostile tendency is behind the ambivalent attitude in all femininity in men. The ultimate aim is to rob the mother of her possession and destroy the dreaded object in order to insure safety. Penetration means destruction of own penis by projection of the oral and anal destruction to the cavity. The threat is that of castration of the boy or his father. The concept of the phallic woman provides a denial of the danger by offering reassurances regarding earlier oral need (Jones, 1933). (M. Klein of course has been foremost in advancing views of the importance of infantile sadism, based on envy, directed against the inside of the mother's body [1928, 1935, 1957].)

Predominance of passive tendencies in the anal phase predisposes to feminine identification and a negative oedipal development (Freud, 1923), which aims at replacing the mother but with accompanying castration fears (Freud, 1918). Further regression may result in paranoid tendencies, as described in the Schreber case. Normally, with the development of the Oedipus complex and the predominance of active wishes, the passive wish for a baby is relinquished and the identification with the father replaces that with the mother (Brunswick, 1940). Remnants of strong female identification may be recognized in the fantasies of penis as a hollow vagina, corresponding to those of vagina as an inverted penis (Ferenczi, 1925; Rangell, 1952, 1953).

Persistence of intense identification with the mother, and hence of envy of female procreation, has been noted in cases of: (i) identification with the phallic mother who will then love the boy-child; (ii) a turbulent anal phase which involves passivity, negative Oedipus complex, and fusion of anal and genital sensations rather than a shift to cathexis of penis (Kestenberg, 1956); and (iii) unmanageable hostility when a younger child is born at the peak of castration conflict (Jacobson, 1950).

Latency and Adolescence

Masculine identifications, which are normally strengthened during the phallic phase, achieve further consolidation with the ego advances and diminished strength of the instincts during latency (Anna Freud, 1936). Any identifications with the mother and newborn siblings that may have appeared during this phase tend to undergo reaction formation (Jacobson, 1950). As the equilibrium of latency wavers with the increased instinctual energies of the prepubertal period, aggressiveness intensifies, oral and anal tendencies reappear, and the conflicts of the earlier sexuality re-emerge (Anna Freud, 1936). As adolescence advances, renunciation of childhood objects and incestuous impulses leads to revival of narcissistic cathexes and restitutive object relations (Spiegel, 1951). However, the shift from the pregenital features of the prepubertal period to a more genital masculinity may only mask pregenital fixations in those cases where they prevail. Passive and feminine tendencies (as well as oral and anal fixations) may be overlaid by masculine activity with heightened genital cathexes, only to reappear in adult life when instinctual pressures again diminish (Anna Freud, 1936).

Conflicts between active and passive tendencies, occurring markedly in earlier phases and determined by environmental responses to the varying behavior of the child, contribute during the stages of sexual differentiation to the development of masculinity and femininity (Blos, 1962). The boy's preadolescent conflict is one of fear and envy of the female. The identification with the phallic woman alleviates castration anxiety in relation to the archaic mother (Blos, 1962; Jones, 1933).

The creativity of adolescence may be based on the narcissistic injury of the oedipal conflict, with consequent severe superego and marked mother identification, reviving earlier wishes to produce a child (Bernfeld, 1923, 1924).

In late adolescence, the strivings normally are active and phallic, with reaction against any desires to have children. This may represent a defense against the unconscious envy of woman's procreative ability (Jacobson, 1950).

The closing period of adolescence aims at providing stable ego interests and sexual differentiation and polarization, the core of the sense of identity. Blos refers to this as the "process of consolidation" (1962), Erikson speaks of the formation of "ego identity" (1956). Blos also describes "prolonged adolescence in the male" (a term proposed by Bernfeld [1923]), especially in boys whose mothers regarded them as great, when the world fails to confirm this. The basic identification with the mother creates a crisis regarding sexual identity in puberty. Perseveration of a bisexual position occurs, instead of the normal adolescent settlement of the conflict of bisexuality (1962).

Anthropological and Cultural Considerations

Studies of myths and rituals have provided a wealth of data relevant to the problems of sexual conflict and struggles over sexual identification. Interpretations have often differed, placing emphasis on one aspect or another of developmental processes with their multiple manifestations of regression and progression (Bettelheim, 1954). Influences that reflect the historical development of the race have also been discerned by many writers in various fields of the behavioral sciences.[9]

Bisexual strivings have been prominent in myths and rituals throughout man's history. The potentialities inherent in drives and organ modes become integrated, as development proceeds, under the influence of reciprocal parental patterns which are in turn determined by the particular cultural forces that prevail (Erikson, 1950). The drive components are thus molded by maturational sequences, societal processes, and regulating principles (Bernfeld, 1929; Erikson, 1950; Hartmann, 1939; Hartmann and Kris, 1945; Hartmann et al., 1946).[10]

Initiation rites have come under particular scrutiny, since ritual practices such as circumcision and subincision are so obviously related to bisexual conflict. These rites have been interpreted in various ways. First, as symbolic castration of the young by the old, to reinforce the incest taboo. Further, as representing a separation of child from mother, with ambisexual symbolism representing the attempt to master the trauma of castration and separation incident to growing up, by asserting that penis is vagina, male identical with female. There is thus a denial of the aggression and object loss provoked by the reality of growth (puberty, with progression of

[9] An interesting attempt to offer a synthesis is Campbell's *The Masks of God: Primitive Mythology* (1959).

[10] Hence, there is no point to arguing re constitutional sexual differences vs. personal experience involving pleasure or anxiety (Rado, 1940); or sex differences vs. social roles (Fromm, 1943).

libidinal development, reactively revives also the regressive infantile tendencies). The roles of being the wanderer and of being united with mother are simultaneously affirmed in this process (Róheim, 1945).[11]

Additionally, there is expressed in circumcision, an identification with the father and an affirmation of masculinity: the feminine aspect, foreskin (= vagina), is removed. At the same time, however, the castration threat inhibits masculinity, and reinforces the identification with the mother: (i) by the birth symbolism in the emergence of the glans from the foreskin like the infant from the womb; (ii) by equating glans and nipple, reviving identification with mother and gratification at the breast; (iii) by resymbolizing anal birth, enhancing the feelings of femininity based on anality. Anus and mouth, active and passive, masculine and feminine, are equally gratified in affirmation of bisexuality (Nunberg, 1947).

Initiation rites stand for more than an expression of feminine identification based on the mastery of castration and separation trauma (Róheim, 1945), and that based on the bisexuality calling for integration of feminine with masculine parts of the organism (Nunberg, 1947). According to Bettelheim (1954), they depict further the ambivalence regarding acceptance of, and attempts to integrate, the societally prescribed sex role. The ambivalence originates in pregenital fixations and is based on the envy of one sex regarding the sexual organs and functions of the other. "Vagina envy" of boys includes envy of and fascination with the female breasts, and lactation, pregnancy, and childbearing, according to evi-

---

[11] The ideas in the present paper came while preparing a discussion of the interesting paper by Leonard Shengold, entitled "The Royal Road" (1966). There he analyzed the conflicts and strivings that determined Freud's use of the metaphor of a journey in *The Interpretation of Dreams*. He recognized, among other things, the equivalence between mother's genitals and own mind, in the related passions for travel and self-exploration. I elaborated on the seemingly contradictory equations: journey = possession of mother; journey = death and going away from mother; and utilized the concept of crisis marking a developmental phase, with regression and threat to object cathexes.

dence from direct clinical observations, transvestitism in various forms, and from other phenomena. Circumcision, subincision, and stopping up of the rectum (as well as couvade)[12] represent attempts to assert that men, too, can bear children, that their sexual apparatus and functions are equal to women's, and that sexual maturity is possible. The initiation is a symbolic rebirth with male sponsors acting the part of those who gave birth to the initiates, and to pass from the phase of female dominance to one of male dominance (with an identification with the mother to compensate for her loss [Bettelheim, 1954]).

The masculine envy of women's childbearing power has been ascribed to another crucial historical determinant (attested to by the cults of Mother Goddesses), i.e., the feminine identification with the productivity of nature in agrarian cultures (Fromm, 1943), or in the period of racial development when there was utter dependence on chance multiplication of plant sources of food (Bettelheim, 1954). There is still another aspect of historical development that should be noted, namely, that in the hunting cultures, which antedated the planting cultures, the masculine psyche prevailed (Campbell, 1959, p. 351). The mythologies of the respective cultures have been interpreted in terms of the conflict between these two influences, just as in rituals the same conflict has been evident. Thus, in creation myths,[13] the "primordial androgynous giant" (Campbell, 1959) represents the construct of a bisexual

---

[12] Reik (1919) discusses couvade from the standpoint of the victory of man's tender impulses in the face of ambivalence toward the woman and toward the child who represents the totem animal and the reincarnation of the man's own father. Reik sees the assumption of the childbearing role as also reinforcing the incest taboo by displacing libido from mother to father. Zilboorg (1944) discusses couvade in the total context of the biological inferiority of the male, which calls forth a compulsive identification with the woman whom he hates, envies, and imitates. Wolff (1950) refers to couvade and other manifestations of man's envy of pregnancy in various cultures.

[13] In Babylonian and Hebrew myths of creation (Fromm, 1943); and in these plus Persian, Greek, Platonic, Hindu, Chinese, and primitive cultures (Campbell, 1959; Nunberg, 1947).

being who (as male) becomes separated from or gives origin to the female part, accounting for subsequent urges to reunite.

The mythologies and religions of various groups bear the imprint of the planting-matriarchal influences or of the hunting-patriarchal ones.[14] Mother Goddesses and priest cults of agriculturally based societies go along with the suppression of manifestations of the individual, with an outlook in which the individual is a cell, a part of the larger group; whereas in the shamanistic tradition of the hunters, individualism prevails (Campbell, 1959). The Promethean fire theft is a fitting model of the individual's challenging of the gods, of phallic competition, or striving against the homosexually tinged desire to extinguish fire (Freud, 1932). Freud's Promethean feat in challenging gods and hellfire to bring light to mankind (Shengold, 1966) required a regression to the homosexual conflicts and feminine identification (Erikson, 1954, 1955) for resolution and sublimation.[15]

Róheim conceptualizes sleep and the dream in similar terms.[16] Sleep is regression, the return to mother's womb and an introversion into own body, a death with relinquishing of the object world. Erotic tension counteracts anxiety re loss of object world, the dream represents genital libido, the object-directed trend (ego), set up against the regression to the womb. The shaman is the alter ego, awake while the person sleeps. The conflict is that of narcissism vs. object love, the regressive vs. the progressive trend of libido (1952).

[14] Nunberg (1947) describes the contrast between the patriarchal monotheism and the matriarchal polytheism; he sees the submission to the God Father of Judaism as a reaction formation against Mother-Son consort (incestuous) cults. Yahveh, he suggests, is a bisexual male, a derivative of the identification with the phallic mother.

[15] Erikson also refers to the puberty-rite character of the Irma dream, and the "repeated adolescence" of creative minds, the repeated reaffirmation of ego identity in the face of revived infantile pressures (1954).

[16] Róheim (1952) also refers to Jekels and Bergler (1940) on the life-death conflict in sleep and dream, as well as to Ferenczi (1924) on sleep as condensing regression to womb and pregenital and genital cathexis.

Campbell has advanced the interesting idea that we may currently be going through a period of transition, when "the binding of the shamans by ... the gods and their priests, which commenced with the victory of the neolithic over the paleolithic way of life, may perhaps be already terminating — today — in this period of the irreversible transition of society from an agricultural to industrial base, when not the piety of the planter, bowing humbly before the will of the calendar and the gods of rain and sun, but the magic of the laboratory, flying rocket ships where the gods once sat, holds the promise of the boons of the future" (1959, p. 281).

As noted previously (footnote 1), it has been suggested that man's rational and technological development itself originates as a compensation for his "womb envy," so that the return of the shamanistic influence and masculine ascendancy may result from such a self-fulfilling prophecy.

In summing up the cultural influence, the following may be stated: cultural needs that heighten the importance of feminine functions lead to certain enduring effects on the male, probably through maternally conveyed attitudes and activities directed toward the child. The result is that the child finds greater difficulty in abandoning early cathexes, and identifications become more conflict-laden. Denials and return of the repressed appear in symptoms and in the re-enactments of myths and rituals, as well as in other social expressions. In our present culture, it may be that a degradation of the role of motherhood has accompanied the transition from agrarian to technological predominance. The resulting conflict in women regarding masculine identification, and sublimations with an overemphasis on masculine strivings, may be contributing to an impairment of mutuality in the mother-child relationship, producing reciprocal conflicts in the child regarding his identification with the mother (reinforcing the other sources of castration anxiety already operating) — thus completing a vicious circle of envy as an expression of unavailability of conflict-free identifications.

Clinical Data and Implications

The material that follows illustrates a man's conflict over his sexual identification, with prominent interplay of regressive and restitutive processes. Procreative strivings represent a compromise, expressing envy of and competition with the incorporative female as well as the ego-directed object-preserving tendencies.

The patient, a writer in his early thirties, suffered from lifelong feelings of isolation which culminated in an acute panic reaction one day while he was engaged in some work which he regarded as unproductive. It was this experience that led to his undertaking psychoanalytic treatment, though there was a previous background of years of marital discord, with some attempt at counseling and psychotherapy for both partners. Many stresses had been piling up, and particularly difficult for the patient was his wife's growing assertions of independence, progressing to rejection, which included refusal of sexual relations. This had in effect brought to an end the basis for the mutual neurotic pattern that had characterized their relationship. Actually, the patient had felt forced into marriage. Although he had at first considered his wife to be warm, soft, tender, and beautiful, he had always been moved by a compulsive need to idealize relationships and to struggle against the sexual strivings that remained as a source of conflict from his earliest experiences. An oppressive sense of guilt had resulted from their premarital petting, which he felt his wife had exploited to trap him into the marriage. He reacted by withholding, premature ejaculation, and striking out physically. But when his wife became pregnant, he felt put into a box with no way out, and the marital relationship settled down to one in which he dominated and rejected, while she suffered passively and played on his feelings of guilt.

When finally her attitude had become more overtly rejecting, he experienced it as her having torn herself out of a mold he had tried to put her into. He felt that something inside him had died, that he could no longer dominate and possess her, that she in fact had gained control over him and no longer gave herself to him. Feeling empty, and desperate to get some token of love and to restore some feeling of warmth within himself, he threw himself into his work, but then began to feel that it was engulfing him. The episode of panic was described in terms of feeling a hot blackness enveloping and threatening to overwhelm and destroy him. He felt the urge to run, to emerge like a crab coming out of a shell.

The imagery relating to birth and emergence as against death and engulfment became meaningful as the history of his formative relationships with women followed upon his description of conflicts over sexual urges.

From earliest experiences, he had regarded sex as an all-encompassing force that sucked one in like a whirlpool; irresistible but dirty, destroying real relationship, a means of hurting and dominating, and a source of guilt. This he associated with what he recalled of his mother's attitude. In his view, she had regarded his father as inferior and had married solely for the purpose of obtaining a son, only to then discard the superfluous spouse. The parents were divorced shortly after the patient's birth. He grew up in a household of women and felt dominated by them. He recalled his mother as a feminist who wanted to exert control in a man's world. He described her as broad-shouldered, with tailored suits and a quick mind, boasting of being able to outdrive New York's cab drivers and outearn her husband. The patient remembered her as belittling men and their bodies, condemning sex as dirty, and regarding males as unacceptable, referring to male genitals as messy in contrast to the "neater" female genitals. To be acceptable to mother meant to renounce sexuality and masculinity.

The initial dreams were reported soon after the analysis had begun: "There was an older woman, wearing a hat and a khaki coat. We had some form of sexual contact, I hardly touched her, and awoke with a nocturnal emission." This was followed by another dream: "A fat man, a sheriff, arrested me. I couldn't learn what the charges were, nor make restitution. I was put into a cell, went to sleep, and awoke to find him in bed with me, masturbating all over me with his orgasm." The theme of soiling was thus prominent at the outset, and remained important throughout the analysis.

The relation to his sexual conflicts became evident through associations dealing with the strong arousal of erotic feelings toward his mother, who had displayed her nude body to him from early childhood on through adolescence. He recalled sitting on the toilet moving his bowels while watching his mother bathe and powder herself. She avoided kissing and hugging, withheld contact. His masturbation became compulsive after she had discovered it and expressed disgust, and in spite of his nurse's warnings that his penis would fall off. He sensed a need to punish and destroy himself. He thought of himself as a large penis, a rock overpowering and replacing the rest of his being, and he wished he could be cut off from it.

As analysis proceeded, the urges toward mother and the identification with her became clearer. He came to recognize that he related to women with an all-encompassing quality that he struggled against by trying to make such relationships asexual or antagonistic. Thus, the ambivalent feelings toward his mother were relived. He exuded an animal power which attracted women to him promptly. He longed for an ideal woman who would be tender, pure, warm, loving, untainted; yet he proceeded to stimulate, dominate, and overwhelm women. His urge was to cuddle and lose himself in the woman's warm body, or to crawl inside and attack and explode her; to suck her in, to mouth and caress the nipples, or to tear at the breasts and bite them off.

In reaction, his general demeanor was gentle, understanding, tolerant, forbearing, passive. But he could become bitter and vitriolic, loved to rub people's noses in the dirt, to create consternation by flaunting convention. Dirt, earth, darkness were associated with mother's dark room and its

familiar cosmetic odors. Curiosity (expressed during childhood in the dissection of frogs and snakes or putting them into
boxes) was mixed with a fear of touching the female genitals.

Being a very verbal person, his recollections and descriptions of childhood experiences came readily. The tendency to
intellectualize appeared as a residue of earlier life when repression, reaction formation, denial, and isolation of affect
had produced a constricted personality. But presently the
affects gained appropriate recognition and expression with the
revivals of older conflicts in the course of stressful current
experiences, in dreams, and in the transference neurosis. The
transference was positively toned, but with ambivalent under-
currents, mainly maternally centered, with repression and displacement of hostile feelings. Alternately, homosexual strivings expressed the need to incorporate a strong paternal model
to cope with the phallic and castrating mother.

Three types of acting out in the transference became
available for analysis, and proved valuable in providing insight and opportunities for resolution. These included derivatives of the oral, anal, and phallic drives (e.g., dependent
clinging, requests for medication; messiness, soiling; intrusive-
ness, bullishness).

Shortly after the beginning of treatment, with the outpouring of feelings toward the wife and mother, and with accompanying tension and sleeplessness, the patient began to
linger in clinging fashion at the end of the hours, and then one
day requested medication. Dealing with this by setting limits,
while accepting and interpreting his impulses, led to a recognition of the dependence on his mother and of her incorporative attitude toward him. The analytic material during the
next days turned to his rebellious activities in relation to
authorities, but then to his own tender, comforting ministrations toward his son during a critical illness in the latter's earlier
childhood. This led to further consideration of his relationship
to his two-year-old son, with whom he had identified strongly
and in whom he had rediscovered himself as capable of giving

and receiving love. He described the relationship in terms of contact on a deep meaningful level, one that formed the center of his life, the source of affirmation of something lovable within himself which made him feel whole. Through this relationship, he had "plugged into humanity." (The attitude toward his son as his womb-child-phallus is clear. The restitutive and liberating features are in marked contrast to the mother's aggrandizing and castrative attitude toward her child-phallus. The patient's attitude is based on his capacities for conflict resolution and sublimation.) Feeling, for once, free from the need to dominate, he could build things with and for the child. Contrasting this with the relationship with his wife, he stated that she too had made him the center of her world, but he felt this to be coercive so that he had been impelled to turn it against her, to destroy her.

The affirmation of wholeness and capacity for trust, which had been put to a test by the acting out of oral demands in the transference, were again challenged when the patient presented a situation that seemed to require that the analyst intervene by acting as his sponsor in a real life problem. Again setting limits, interpreting the domination via dependency and expressing confidence in the patient's ability to use his own resources, opened the way to further analysis of the drives that had called forth the oral regression.

The intense anger at not being given "support" was displaced to other people, but the analytic material then began to center on the father. The focus fell on his competitive attitudes toward his father, on the comfort of snuggling up to mother, and on an episode in which he had pressed himself upon his stepmother and had to be pushed off. A dream then appeared in which he found himself in a raging gun battle; and another in which he longed to go to bed with a beautiful woman who was enticing him but he refrained and felt victorious. Shortly after these dreams, he visited his father and felt surprised and nauseated to find himself physically attracted to his father's legs and fantasying father's penis in his mouth. He recognized in this his need to appease father. This realization was soon followed by a reassertion of masculinity when he participated in a community event with self-assurance and strength, which brought him praise and recognition as a leader. At this point he was then able to express the anger he had felt at father for the latter's failure to stand up to the castrative mother. His anger was expressed in a fantasy of rubbing father's nose in shit. The acting out of anal-aggressive tendencies in the transference took the form of messiness and smearing the analyst's furnishings with dirt which he tracked in. With interpretation, he recognized his defiance and provocativeness, his need to offend proper and dignified elders, like "shitting in the punch bowl at an elegant party." He recalled his tantrums as a child, and the punitive cold showers, the insistence on obedience, orderliness, and neatness. He had always longed to enjoy dirt in an earthy, acceptable way.

The intrusive impulses were expressed in many ways. He had a bullish approach which made it seem like he was always charging in. A significant confrontation occurred when he parked in the analyst's driveway, which led to the hour's being interrupted by a call requesting that he move out. He expected punishment, felt stripped naked with his genitals hanging out. But he was able to consider the possibility that he would not be rejected, and to proceed into the most sensitve area of his feelings of unacceptability. This involved his whole being and was based on the sexuality that he feared must contain the hatred he now recognized in his feelings toward his mother. He recalled with bitterness her having rejected his early needs for self-assertion, and described his "grabbed by the balls" feelings even at age three or four. He had learned to accept relationships based on hostile involvement and, whenever he moved toward relinquishing this, felt as though he were being pushed out of a womb. Clinging to an identification with the incorporative, intrusive, phallic mother meant preserving the only sense of security he had known. This was depicted in a dream of being in bed with a woman with big breasts, like mother's; sucking on her nipple which got longer and longer till it looked like a penis.

The task of re-establishing an identification with the intact male, of resolving the conflicts from identification with a castrative mother, proceeded slowly during the next year of analysis. With progression and retrogression, the working through gradually was accompanied by a lessening of aggressive attitudes, increasing satisfactions in relationships, reality gratifications in the form of achievements that led to acceptance by others and job stability. The sense of power inherent in collaboration culminated in an experience in which he teamed up with his wife in a certain enterprise; and this was followed by a sexual performance with potency and mutual orgasm for the first time in their marriage. His feeling at this point was that he was no longer afraid of his penis being cut off. He was now able to accept his body as a whole, and his penis with it.

After another particularly successful undertaking, the sense of wholeness of body-phallus was described in terms of feeling that he had created something, and that what he had produced was being accepted. He experienced this as a deliverance, and compared it with the euphoria he judged women must enjoy after childbirth.

In summary it is evident that the patient's conflict over sexual identification reflected his mother's penis envy, which promoted his castration anxiety and led to a pathological feminine identification. The central competition with and envy of the incorporative female (to rob mother of her possession: breast, phallus, womb, child) threatened his object cathexes. Procreative wishes, as compromise formations, expressed the aggressive drives as well as the censoring forces determining an attempted restitution. He identified with the castrated but revengefully castrating mother, sought to castrate himself by regressing to the womb, to be born anew with the child-phallus now his own. The wishes to aggrandize mother's contents and power were intrusive and incorporative, but with conflict and defense. Narcissistic injury imposed by oedipal frustration evoked regression to pregenital cathexes, recognizable in manifestations of soiling impulses, regressive narcissistic enjoyment of body products, with oral incorporation and passivity as reaction formation against phallic aggression (as described by Abraham [1917] in his paper on "Ejaculatio Praecox"). Passivity promoted feminine identification, negative Oedipus complex, homosexual regression, and castration fears. Thus, the vagina was dreaded and, regressively, love, envy, and hatred of the breasts were prominent.

The female was considered to be hoarding the nipple and penis which she had incorporated, and his striving to rob her by oral and phallic penetration led to the threat of destruction by the womb he sought to regress into. (Compare with Jones's description of the phallic phase [1933].)

Regression with reaggressivization and threat of object loss made the creative and procreative urges crucial. The dominant themes of death and rebirth, of engulfment and emergence, became the symbols of the repetition compulsion. That this must express a univeral conflict is evident from the myths and rituals of death and return from nurturing mother earth, a recurring theme from the earliest periods in man's history (Campbell, 1959). My previous discussion of the conflict between narcissistic regression and object love elaborates on this theme. Insofar as disruptive aspects of narcissism get equated with death, while integrative object love is equated with rebirth, the conflict between these fundamental principles is central to the conflicts of the procreative task.

The elements described in this patient can be recognized regularly in the most striking instances where early pathogenic influences are marked. Immaturity or instability in the parental objects who provide the models for identification predispose to regressive identifications based on part-object concepts (Sarlin, 1963), such as is illustrated in my patient's description of the penis replacing the whole self. Marked dependence on and ambivalence toward the mother prevent complete separation of maternal and self images (Jacobson, 1964). The broader question of man's femininity strivings per se is not separate from that of his envy of woman's procreative function. Heightened feminine identification stemming from pathogenic influence accentuates the conflict over procreative wishes, so that the former is a determinant of the latter. Further, the psychological significance of procreative function, from its cultural-historical roots, is integrally connected with femininity in all its aspects.

Instability or unreliability in the paternal model will impair the male's masculine identification by increasing the castration threats generated from pregenital phases onward in relation to the devouring mother imago. This is clearly an important factor in the case described above. In another patient whose case has been reported in an earlier paper dealing with a painful repetitive dream (Jaffe, 1957), the death of the father was the precipitating cause of an anxiety state. This event served to reawaken the threatening aspects of masculine identification, since an aggressive father had come to represent the patient's own repressed sadism (associated with early object loss: unavailability of body contact with a tuberculous mother, and then her death). On the other hand, he contrasted the nurturing care provided by a mother substitute and the association of the female with dependency, provisions, and invulnerability with the male as aggressive, endangered, and doomed to be stricken down. He openly expressed envy of the female for her organs, which he wished he had within himself, and dreamed of giving birth to a baby.

In the manifold everyday expressions of the struggle between regression and restitution, we see evidences of revival of the conflicts around every phase of development and fixation. Lewin (1954, 1955), especially, has pointed out the analogies between the analytic situation and regressive sleep, and the role of regression in affective, intuitive, and thinking processes has been well recognized. The restorative effect of

integrative capacities, which imply the availability of total relationship in contrast to part-object cathexes, undoubtedly is
involved in the sense of well-being in the procreating female,
and for the male when he succeeds in achieving it. The per-
vasiveness of the identifications of men with their pregnant
wives attests to the need for such restorative identification with
the secure and intact mother. Perhaps the custom in which the
father gives out cigars upon the birth of a child involves the
need for reassurance that penis-feces-nipple-child are possessions of the male too; and that his identification with the
fertile female reaffirms his wholeness, his object-relating
capacities in the face of disintegrative regressive pulls. Recently, an acquaintance was describing the restorative effects of a
weekend on her farm after the hectic week's activities in town.
Particularly impressive was her remark, "When I see how
plants grow despite all the adverse conditions, I feel I can do
the same." Regression in the face of hostile environment, leading to an identification with the soil and its procreative
powers, indeed represents the model for man's similar pattern
of regression and restitution, against the force of external and
internal onslaughts of aggression.

Needless to say, the analytic processs offers an opportunity for reintegration by facilitating regression, providing a new
model for acceptance of the reanimated conflict products, resolving ambivalence toward the disruptive internalized
feminine objects, and making conflict-free identifications
available.

Summary

The man's envy of woman's procreative function has several
sources:

1. *The sequence of experiences that are universal and
include:*

      (a) The experiences of the oral phase, which provide
the first identifications with the mother and the association

of her body and functions with the sense of internal fulfillment.

(b) The contributions of the anal phase to the passive-
receptive incorporativeness, which is the principal pregenital
determinant of the feminine tendency in men.

(c) Phallic cathexes that advance the equation of the
mother's organs with penis and child, and the desire to possess
all that the mother has inside of her as a defense against castration.

(d) The castration threats of the oedipal phase, which
may strengthen passive feminine identification as a defensive
tendency.

(e) Difficulties in settling adolescent bisexual conflicts, which may prolong an identification with the mother.

(f) Aggresive drives, which, when increased by any
factors at any genetic level, are of primary importance in producing conflict regarding tendencies and identifications.

2. *The conflict between regression toward narcissism
versus preservation of object cathexes,* which is a residue in
adult life of the conflicts of each antecedent developmental
phase. The regressive tendency revives feminine identification
(proceeds via homosexuality to the narcissism represented by
the womb), and even in daily normal functioning presents a
challenge to the phallic image of the self. The phallic self is re-
affirmed through restitutive tendencies from whatever early
experiences provided strength-giving identification with the
intact father and the procreative mother.

3. *The historical and cultural processes that emphasize
matriarchal elements* reinforce the masculine envy and the
masculine need to usurp feminine organ modes and functions
for reassurance of wholeness. *Competing patriarchal influences in a culture provoke in the mothers conflicts over their
identifications,* from which ensue tensions affecting mutuality
in mother-child relationships *and reciprocal envy and identification conflicts in the males.*

The patterns of development and regression, with evidences of conflict, may be recognized in analyses of men where resolutions are sought by sublimations based on identifications with the mother's good insides; or alternatively, symptom formation expresses the anxiety over such identifications on account of projected incorporative and castrative threats.

The therapeutic process is one that includes the acceptance of regression, with new reintegrative (including constructive feminine) models offered via the analyst's capacity to deal assimilatively with the patient's conflict products (interpretively, and with neither destructive incorporation nor castrative rejection). From this, the conflict-free component of maternal identification becomes more readily available.

REFERENCES*

Abraham, K. (1913), Restrictions and transformations of scoptophilia in psycho-neurotics; with remarks on analogous phenomena in folk-psychology. In: *Selected Papers on Psycho-Analysis*. New York: Basic Books, 1954, pp. 169-234.

_____ (1917), Ejaculatio praecox. In: *Selected Papers on Psycho-Analysis*. New York: Basic Books, 1954, pp. 280-298.

_____ (1920), The narcissistic evaluation of excretory processes in dreams and neurosis. In: *Selected Papers on Psycho-Analysis*. New York: Basic Books, 1954, pp. 318-322.

_____ (1924a), The influence of oral erotism on character-formation. In: *Selected Papers on Psycho-Analysis*. New York: Basic Books, 1954, pp. 393-406.

_____ (1924b), A short study of the development of the libido viewed in the light of mental disorders. In: *Selected Papers on Psycho-Analysis*. New York: Basic Books, 1954, pp. 418-501.

_____ (1925), An infantile sexual theory not hitherto noted. In: *Selected Papers on Psycho-Analysis*. New York: Basic Books, 1954, pp. 334-337.

Andreas-Salomé, L. (1916), "Anal" und "sexual." *Imago,* 4:249-273.

Bak, R. C. (1953), Fetishism. *This Journal,* 1:285-298.

Benedek, T. (1959), Parenthood as a developmental phase. *This Journal,* 7:389-417.

Bernfeld, S. (1923), Über eine typische Form der männlichen Pubertät. *Imago,* 9:169-188.

_____ (1924), *Vom dichterischen Schaffen der Jugend.* Vienna: Internationaler psychoanalytischer Verlag.

_____ (1929), Der soziale Ort und seine Bedeutung für Neurose, Verwahrlosung, und Pädogogik. *Imago,* 15:299-312.

Bettelheim, B. (1954), *Symbolic Wounds.* New York: Free Press of Glencoe.

* All references to *This Journal* are to the *Journal of the American Psychoanalytic Association.*

Blos, P. (1962), *On Adolescence*. New York: Free Press of Glencoe.

Boehm, F. (1930), The femininity-complex in men. *Internat. J. Psycho-Anal.*, 11: 444-469.

Brunswick, R. M. (1940), The preoedipal phase of the libido development. *Psychoanal. Quart.*, 9:293-319.

Campbell, J. (1959), *The Masks of God: Primitive Mythology*. New York: Viking Press.

Chadwick, M. (1925), Über die Wurzel der Wissbegierde. *Internat. Z. Psychoanal.*, 11:54-68.

Eisler, M. J. (1921), A man's unconscious phantasy of pregnancy in the guise of traumatic hysteria. *Internat. J. Psycho-Anal.*, 2:255-286.

Erikson, E. H. (1950), *Childhood and Society*. New York: Norton.

_____ (1954), The dream specimen of psychoanalysis. *This Journal*, 2:5-56.

_____ (1955), Freud's "The Origins of Psycho-Analysis." *Internat. J. Psycho-Anal.*, 36:1-15.

_____ (1956), The problem of ego identity. In: *Identity, Youth and Crisis:* New York: Norton, 1968, pp. 142-207; 208-231.

Faergeman, P. M. (1955), Fantasies of menstruation in men. *Psychoanal. Quart.*, 24:1-19.

Fenichel, O. (1929), The dread of being eaten. *Internat. J. Psycho-Anal.*, 10:448-450.

_____ (1945), *The Psychoanalytic Theory of Neurosis*. New York: Norton.

Ferenczi, S. (1924), *Thalassa: A Theory of Genitality*. New York: Psychoanalytic Quarterly.

_____ (1925), Contra-indications to the "active" psychoanalytical technique. In: *Further Contributions to the Theory and Technique of Psycho-Analysis*. London: Hogarth Press, 1950, pp. 217-229.

Fliess, R. (1953), Countertransference and counteridentification. *This Journal*, 1: 268-284.

Freud, A. (1936), *The Ego and the Mechanisms of Defense. The Writings of Anna Freud*, 2. New York: International Universities Press, 1966.

Freud, S. (1905), Three essays on the theory of sexuality. *Standard Edition*, 7:125-245. London: Hogarth Press, 1953.

_____ (1911), Psycho-analytic notes on an autobiographical account of a case of paranoia (dementia paranoides). *Standard Edition*, 12:3-82. London: Hogarth Press, 1958.

_____ (1915), Instincts and their vicissitudes. *Standard Edition*, 14:109-140. London: Hogarth Press, 1957.

_____ (1917a), Mourning and melancholia. *Standard Edition*, 14:237-260. London: Hogarth Press, 1957.

_____ (1917b), On transformations of instincts as exemplified in anal erotism. *Standard Edition*, 17:125-133. London: Hogarth Press, 1955.

_____ (1918), From the history of an infantile neurosis. *Standard Edition*, 17: 3-123. London: Hogarth Press, 1955.

_____ (1921), Group psychology and the analysis of the ego. *Standard Edition*, 18:67-143. London: Hogarth Press, 1955.

_____ (1923), The ego and the id. *Standard Edition*, 19:3-66. London: Hogarth Press, 1961.

_____ (1927), Fetishism. *Standard Edition*, 21:149-157. London: Hogarth Press, 1961.

_____ (1932), The acquisition and control of fire. *Standard Edition,* 22:185-193. London: Hogarth Press, 1964.

_____ (1937), Analysis terminable and interminable. *Standard Edition,* 23:209-253. London: Hogarth Press, 1964.

_____ (1940), Splitting of the ego in the process of defence. *Standard Edition,* 23: 271-278. London: Hogarth Press, 1964.

Fromm, E. (1943), Sex and character. *Psychiat.,* 6:21-31.

Gillespie, W. H. (1940), A contribution to the study of fetishism. *Internat. J. Psycho-Anal.,* 21:401-415.

Greenacre, P. (1953), Certain relationships between fetishism and the faulty development of the body image. In: *Emotional Growth.* New York: International Universities Press, 1971, pp. 9-30.

Greenson, R. R. (1954), The struggle against identification. *This Journal,* 2:200-217.

Groddeck, G. (1923), *The Book of the It.* New York: International Universities Press, 1976.

Hartmann, H. (1939), *Ego Psychology and the Problem of Adaptation.* New York: International Universities Press, 1958.

_____ & Kris, E. (1945), The genetic approach in psychoanalysis. *The Psychoanalytic Study of the Child,* 1:11-30. New York: International Universities Press.

_____ , Kris, E. & Loewenstein, R. M. (1946), Comments on the formation of psychic structure. *The Psychoanalytic Study of the Child,* 2:11-38. New York: International Universities Press.

Jacobson, E. (1950), Development of the wish for a child in boys. *The Psychoanalytic Study of the Child,* 5:139-152. New York: International Universities Press.

_____ (1964), *The Self and the Object World.* New York: International Universities Press.

Jaffe, D. S. (1957), Analysis of a repetitive dream with painful content. *Bull. Phila. Assn. Psychoanal.,* 7:50-55.

Jekels, L. & Bergler, E. (1940), Instinct dualism in dreams. *Psychoanal. Quart.,* 9:394-414.

Jones, E. (1933), The phallic phase. *Internat. J. Psycho-Anal.,* 14:1-33.

Kestenberg, J. (1956), On the development of maternal feelings in early childhood. *The Psychoanalytic Study of the Child,* 11:257-291. New York: International Universities Press.

Khan, M. M. R. (1965), Foreskin fetishism and its relation to ego pathology in a male homosexual. *Internat. J. Psycho-Anal.,* 46:64-80.

Klein, M. (1928), Early stages of the oedipus conflict and of superego formation. *The Psycho-Analysis of Children.* London: Hogarth Press, 1932.

_____ (1935), A contribution to the psychogenesis of manic-depressive states. *Contributions to Psycho-Analysis.* London: Hogarth Press, 1950, pp. 282-310.

_____ (1957), *Envy and Gratitude.* London: Tavistock Publications.

Kris, E. (1936), The psychology of caricature. In: *Psychoanalytic Explorations in Art.* New York: International Universities Press, 1952, pp. 173-188.

Landauer, K. (1931), Das Menstruationserlebnis des Knaben. *Z. Psychoanal. Päd.,* 5:175-184.

Lewin, B. D. (1950), *The Psychoanalysis of Elation.* New York: Norton.

_____ (1953), Reconsideration of the dream screen. *Psychoanal. Quart.,* 22:174-199.

_____ (1954), Sleep, narcissistic neurosis, and the analytic situation. In: *Selected Writings*, ed. J. A. Arlow. New York: Psychoanalytic Quarterly, 1973, pp. 227-247.

_____ (1955), Dream psychology and the analytic situation. In: *Selected Writings*, ed. J. A. Arlow. New York: Psychoanalytic Quarterly, 1973, pp. 264-290.

Loewenstein, R. M. (1935), Phallic passivity in men. *Internat. J. Psycho-Anal.*, 16:334-340.

Macalpine, I. & Hunter, R. A. (1953), The Schreber case. *Psychoanal. Quart.*, 22:328-371.

Nunberg, H. (1947), Circumcision and problems of bisexuality. *Internat. J. Psycho-Anal.*, 28:145-179.

_____ (1953), In: Problems of Identification, H. A. Wiggers, reporter. *This Journal*, 1:547.

Payne, S. (1939), Some observations on the ego development of the fetishist. *Internat. J. Psycho-Anal.*, 20:161-170.

Rado, S. (1940), A critical examination of the concept of bisexuality. *Psychosom. Med.*, 2:459-467.

Rangell, L. (1952), The analysis of a doll phobia. *Internat. J. Psycho-Anal.*, 33:43-53.

_____ (1953), The interchangeability of phallus and female genital. *This Journal*, 1:504-509.

Reik, T. (1919), *Ritual*. New York: International Universities Press, 1958.

Róheim, G. (1945), *The Eternal Ones of the Dream*. New York: International Universities Press.

_____ (1952), *The Gates of the Dream*. New York: International Universities Press.

Ross, H. (1965), The teacher game. *The Psychoanalytic Study of the Child*, 20:288-297. New York: International Universities Press.

Sarlin, C. N. (1963), Feminine Identity. *This Journal*, 11:790-816.

Schilder, P. (1941), Types of anxiety neurosis. *Internat. J. Psycho-Anal.*, 22:209-228.

Schur, M. (1971), Metapsychological aspects of phobias in adults. In: *The Unconscious Today*, ed., M. Kanzer. New York: International Universities Press, pp. 97-118.

Shengold, L. (1966), The royal road. *Amer. Imago*, 23:316-331.

Socarides, C. W. (1953), The development of a fetishistic perversion. *The Psychoanalytic Study of the Child*, 8:281-311. New York: International Universities Press.

Spiegel, L. A. (1951), A review of contributions to a psychoanalytic theory of adolescence. *The Psychoanalytic Study of the Child*, 6:375-393. New York: International Universities Press.

Spitz, R. A. (1955), The primal cavity. *The Psychoanalytic Study of the Child*, 10:215-240. New York: International Universities Press.

Van der Leeuw, P. J. (1958), The preoedipal phase of the male. *The Psychoanalytic Study of the Child*, 13:352-374. New York: International Universities Press.

van Leeuwen, K. (1966), Pregnancy envy in the male. *Internat. J. Psycho-Anal.*, 47:319-324.

Webster's New International Dictionary (1948), Springfield, Mass.: Merriam, 2nd ed.

Wolff, W. (1950), *The Threshold of the Abnormal.* New York: Hermitage House.
Zilboorg, G. (1938), Some observations on the transformation of instincts. *Psychoanal. Quart.*, 7:1-24.
———— (1944), Masculine and feminine. *Psychiatry,* 7:257-296.

3741 Huntington Street, N.W.
Washington, D.C. 20015

A NEW FEMALE
PSYCHOLOGY?

Peter Barglow, m.d. and
Margret Schaefer, ph.d.

MUCH OF THE IMPETUS for the recent proliferation of books devoted to the "nature of woman" stems from the women's liberation movement and probably from the antiwar and civil rights movements as well. The implications of these movements for psychoanalysis are difficult to identify precisely and are often contradictory. For instance, a male patient raged recently at one of us: "My wife wants to leave me! Her analyst turned her into a women's libber." On the other hand, women patients seen diagnostically are sometimes reluctant to see analysts or want to be referred only to female analysts in order to "avoid male chauvinist Freudian brainwashing."

Most of the recent books and articles on female psychology, reflecting current cultural trends, are critical of psychoanalysis. Many of them advocate the necessity for a

Peter Barglow is Associate Professor of the Department of Psychiatry at Northwestern University Medical School.

Margret Schaefer is Lecturer in the Department of Psychiatry at Northwestern University Medical School and an Assistant Professor of the Department of English at the University of Illinois at Chicago.

Books under review here:

Judith M. Bardwich: PSYCHOLOGY OF WOMEN: A STUDY OF BIO-CULTURE CONFLICTS. New York: Harper and Row, 1971.

J. Chasseguet-Smirgel, editor: FEMALE SEXUALITY. Ann Arbor: University of Michigan Press, 1970.

Elizabeth Janeway: MAN'S WORLD, WOMAN'S PLACE. New York: William Morrow, 1971.

Karen Horney: FEMININE PSYCHOLOGY, ed. H. Kelman. New York: Norton, 1967.

Jean Baker Miller, editor: PSYCHOANALYSIS AND WOMEN. New York: Brunner/Mazel, 1973.

"new female psychology" and imply that the time has come for massive revisions and a rethinking of previously accepted formulations. Unfortunately, many of the most popular recent works on the subject lack both scholarship and familiarity with psychoanalytic theory. Such books as Phyllis Chesler's *Women and Madness* (1972), Kate Millet's *Sexual Politics* (1970), Shulamith Firestone's *The Dialectic of Sex* (1970), a Marxist analysis, Germaine Greer's *The Female Eunuch* (1971), Eva Figes' *Patriarchal Attitudes* (1970), and Robert Seidenberg's *Marriage Between Equals* (1973), which take extreme anti-psychoanalytic positions, are either politically doctrinaire attacks on a Freud who is seen as "the strongest individual counterrevolutionary force in the ideology of sexual politics" (Millet, p. 178), or sensationalist popular psychology books which need not be considered here. Juliet Mitchell, a critic with impeccable feminist credentials, in her latest work, *Psychoanalysis and Feminism* (1974), points out that while many of these authors do pay a "formal obeisance to Freud" and his discoveries, they fail to understand the essence of the Freudian perspective in that they "implicitly deny the very notion of an aspect of mental life (expressed in its own 'language') that is different from conscious thought processes" (p. 8)—which is to say that they "deny the unconscious" itself. This is the major flaw of all these books: they are adultomorphic in the extreme. As she says, "the laws of the primary process . . . are replaced by these critics by those of the secondary process (conscious decisions and perceptions), and as a result the whole point is missed" (p. 8).

Her own book, however, also modifies Freud's notion of the unconscious considerably as she tries to make Freud acceptable to the feminist movement by reinterpreting his work in terms of Claude Lévi-Strauss, Jacques Lacan, and Friedrich Engels. The Oedipus complex for her turns out to be a kind of inborn racial memory of conflict over the economic barter of women, which, she claims, is the basis of all culture. The structures of the unconscious will be modified and the oppression of women will end when the economic system that engendered it, the nuclear family, will be destroyed. Whatever merits this idea has, it takes her just as far away from the psychoanalytic concept of the unconscious system as the books she criticizes.

In addition to implicitly denying unconscious mental processes and taking an adultomorphic view of Freud's theories, the arguments of most of the recently published criticisms of the psychoanalytic formulations of female psychology fail to make the crucial distinctions that need to be made between Freud's theory and contemporary psychoanalysis; between psychoanalysis and psychiatry, psychology, psychotherapy, counseling, and social work; between treating the patient's pathology and curing the "ills of society"; and between the idiosyncratic opinion or practice of some analysts and their social views and the mainstream of the thinking in psychoanalysis. The tendency is to lump all of these different points of view together, call the resulting mishmash "psychoanalysis," and soundly denounce it.

The books we have chosen for review here, however, while they are not necessarily psychoanalytic in perspective, do show some awareness of the processes of psychoanalysis as distinct from other psychological perspectives, and have some criticisms to make which merit our serious attention. The books are representative of the three major current theoretical approaches to female psychology: (1) that emphasizing social, cultural, and historical influences; (2) that emphasizing biological and ethological considerations; and (3) that emphasizing preoedipal infantile intrapsychic dimensions. The Miller volume, Elizabeth Janeway's work, and the writings of Karen Horney exemplify the first; the Bardwick volume the second; and the Chasseguet-Smirgel volume the third.

Our own orientation in this evaluation of critics of Freudian female psychology is that of developmental psychology, with an emphasis on the genetic point of view. Because we are concerned here with the problems of "normal" female development, we will not review material that emphasizes severe psychopathology, marked abnormality, or unusually severe childhood traumata. We will not attempt to defend or criticize the broad theoretical perspectives that characterize various schools of psychoanalysis, in the hope that what Greenson (1969, p. 513) described as "a real interchange of ideas among and within schools" will thereby be facilitated.

Social and Cultural Dimensions of Female Personality

The majority of the recent critiques are radically antibiological in perspective and criticize psychoanalysis for its neglect of social and cultural factors as major determinants of personality. They argue that analysts are too conservative and too heavily influenced by Freud and that they overemphasize or misuse biological determinants of female psychology while overlooking the influence of society. They tend to take a rather one-sided environmentalist point of view in the "nature versus nurture" controversy, and argue, in effect, that female psychological characteristics are the result of cultural conditioning rather than biological, developmental, or intrapsychic influences. They cite cross-cultural studies as proof of the enormous variability of so-called "male" or "female" personality traits, and they find evidence of an infinite and limitless modifiability of human beings through social conditioning. They argue that since most cultures in history, up to and including our own, have been patriarchal, that is, male dominated, the characteristics typically ascribed to women do not reflect woman's anatomy or biology or "nature," but reflect only their position of powerlessness, enforced servitude, and social inferiority in an androcentric society. Freud's formulations regarding the psychology of women, they charge, fail to take these social and political realities sufficiently into account and unwittingly betray the "male supremacist" bias of the middle-class Victorian culture to which he belonged.

The tone of the Miller volume, *Psychoanalysis and Women*, a collection of essays by various analysts critical of Freud's original theories, is well characterized by its book jacket blurb, which tells the reader that in this collection, "the still quite widely held *myths* [italic added] of penis envy, masochism, and innate passivity are challenged." For example, Clara Thompson, one of the earliest psychoanalysts to challenge Freud, writes that these and other personality characteristics Freud attributed to women derive from "Western woman's historic situation of underprivilege, restriction of development, insincere attitudes toward her sexual nature, and social and economic dependency" (Miller, p. 64), not from penis envy or from the difficulty of giving up the clitoris for the vagina. The greater narcissism and need for love that Freud described in women is not due to anatomical factors, as he thought, but represents simply "the excessive security needs typical of those in an actual position of economic helplessness" (p. 52). Alfred Adler, also anthologized in the Miller volume, rhetorically asks how, in a world where "masculine" signifies a "reserve of power and privilege" and the "glory of male domination," while "feminine" means "obedient, servile, subordinate," women could not be characterized by "submission, humility, and self-repression" (pp. 34-36).

The papers of Karen Horney (some of which are anthologized in this volume) also argue this position. Although Horney's early writings derive from traditional analytic material gathered in a clinical situation, her later works show a preoccupation with the purely social determinants of female personality. She too was one of the first psychoanalysts to differ sharply from Freud. In her 1926 paper, "The Flight From Womanhood," she points out that the formulations of Freud and his followers regarding female psychology which describe penis envy, feminine masochism, and inferiority show a striking resemblance to a male child's wishful fantasies and daydreams about women. She asks whether "masculine narcissism" could be responsible for the widespread conviction that penis envy alone accounts for so much of woman's psychology, including the female's castration complex and answers this dramatic question in the affirmative. However, she agrees that the girl's "narcissistic overestimation" of excretory processes during the phases of urethral eroticism, combined with the envy of the boy's exhibitionistic freedom in urination and masturbation give her a "realistic disadvantage."

Later on, however, she abandoned even this concession to Freud's anatomical and physiological emphasis. She felt that the mistaken male infantile beliefs about women codified as theory in Freud's formulations won acceptance because of the male-dominated nature of our culture and are believed as true to reality by adults because they compensate men for their envy of women's breasts, childbearing capacity, and motherhood. In her opinion, the "masculinity complex" in women is usually less important for the psychology of the woman than the comparable femininity complex (womb and breast envy) is for the psychology of man. (Bettleheim, 1962, documented and explicated this hypothesis later through his analysis of primitive puberty rites.) Eventually, Horney rejected entirely the idea of the castration complex and penis envy as part of "normal" (as opposed to abnormal) female development and saw in it, instead, the male narcissistic need to feel superior and to be envied for his genital equipment.

In "The Distrust Between the Sexes" (1931) and "The Dread of Women" (1932), she argued that many religious cults (e.g., that of the Virgin Mary), rituals and taboos (defloration, abstinence), and such myths as the story of Adam and Eve are the direct result of "misogynist" ideas resulting from man's fear and hatred of the sexually active woman, and reflect his envy of her childbearing capacity. The origin of this fear and hatred she finds directly in the male's infantile experience with the mother who evokes early rage by forbidding instinctual activity, thus stimulating oral-sadistic fantasies against her body. During the phallic phase, the little boy perceives his penis as much too small for the mother's genital and feels rejected, derided, and inadequate. He defensively denies the existence of the vagina and reinforces his self-esteem by debasing the female love object. This contributes to his "heightened phallic narcissism" and stimulates him to create and later to encourage the female self-concepts of inferiority typical of our culture. The myth of Adam and Eve, for example, devalues and denies the woman's capacity to give birth and denigrates her sexuality. Horney would agree with Ursula Brangwen in D. H. Lawrence's *The Rainbow* (1915, p. 171), who tells her husband, "It is impudence to say that Woman was made out of Man's body when every man is born of woman. What impudence men have, what arrogance!"

Still later in her career, in, for example, "The Problem of Feminine Masochism" (1933) Horney, however, rejected this notion of infantile experience as the decisive factor in the psychology of the individual, emphasizing instead the influence of postoedipal cultural experiences, namely, the "conditions of later life" and familial interpersonal variables. She rejected the traditional analytic position (later represented by Helene Deutsch, 1944-1945) in regard to masochism as a normal "outcome of the feminine constitution" and part of "women's anatomical destiny." She could find no persuasive evidence to substantiate the claim that adult women, because of biological realities and infantile fantasies, have desires for mutilation, a secret goal of rape, violence, and humiliation, or that they get masochistic satisfactions out of the pains of menstruation and childbirth (p. 215). Rather, she argued that such "satisfactions," along with the alleged passive narcissistic tendencies and penis envy that accompany them, were superimposed on women by patriarchal culture and society. She asked, could not the blockage of feminine outlets for growth and sexual expression in our patriarchal society, woman's economic dependence on men, and her becoming isolated in the spheres of family life, religion, and charity work account for the character traits usually attributed to women (p. 230)? To say that the woman is "naturally" masochistic merely absolves males of their guilt for exploiting her.

These ideas of Horney have become the common currency of most of the socially oriented critics of Freud, who do not go essentially beyond her criticisms. Elizabeth Janeway's book *Man's World, Woman's Place,* for example, which is representative of the sociologically oriented nonanalytic critiques of Freud that make up the largest part of the women's-movement literature, is in essential agreement with Horney and repeats many of her criticisms. Like Horney, Janeway believes that penis envy is a "fable originating on the male, not the female side" (p. 287), and that masochism is simply a choice forced on women by their social circumstance and serves "to absolve the man who inflicts . . . outrages on them of his guilt." Such feminine traits as flexibility, emotionality, and passivity she sees as socially adaptive responses which are required of women in their roles as wives, mothers, and homemakers, i.e., caretakers of men.

Janeway also holds that many of the personality traits attributed to women are male myths which express male infantile needs and wishes. Holding that myth "contain[s] psychic truth expressed symbolically" (p. 36), she, like Horney, spends much time analyzing myths for what she feels they can tell us regarding man's essential views of women. The primary myth man holds about woman, Janeway says, is the idea that her place is in the home. This idea, which imprisons woman with her children at home and seeks to keep her from the larger arena of public life, is a myth, she says, because it is not true to reality today, when at least 40 per cent (more as of this writing) of all married women are employed outside the home, and because it was not even true in the past. Following Phillipe Aries' theories (1962) in his *Centuries of Childhood* she argues that women then functioned in managerial capacities in medieval manors or in large communal villages. The myth simply serves the male childhood desire to recapture control and domination over the unfaithful, rejecting mother who destroyed the "Last Golden Age of early infancy" (p. 44). Men oppose women's working outside the home because their absence from the home recreates the threat of early mother loss in infancy.

The myth locating women forever in the home, Janeway believes, is itself the result of two related subsidiary myths—those of "female weakness" and "female power." She feels that the "myth of female weakness," which reveals itself in the image of women as inferior, childish, irrational, and passive, was buttressed by Freud's theories, and regards it, therefore, as another "Freudian" fable. However, this "myth of female weakness which preaches subordination of woman to man may merely mask its contrary, the myth of female power..." (p. 51). Thus woman may appear both as the "Mother Goddess who heals, renews, absolves, and offers life" (p. 48), culturally idealized as Mary, mother of Jesus, or worshipped as a fertility goddess; and as the "bitch-witch," the evil stepmother, or the castrating female, to whom Keats has given literary expresion in "La Belle Dame Sans Merci," and Wilde in *Salomé*.

The book's major insights into the myth of "man's world, woman's place" can be encapsulated by the well-known nursery rhyme:

> Peter, Peter, pumpkin eater
> Had a wife and couldn't keep her
> Put her in a pumpkin shell
> And there he kept her very well.

In analytic terms: Peter, the oral child, couldn't "keep" the preoedipal mother (in wife disguise) faithful to him. He masters the loss situation in adulthood by imprisoning her (in a weakened state, apparently) in a house symbolizing the shell remnant of his infantile oral longing. "And there he kept her very well"—at least until recently.

Psychoanalytically stated, Janeway's concept of myth is that it is a kind of socially shared transference formation. An amalgamation occurs between unconscious memories and experiences of the mother-child relation of primary narcissism and the conscious meanings and symbols of cultural myths, institutions, and fantasies that link the adult to his society. But it must be emphasized that the complex adult product, while incorporating transference and defensive remnants of its infantile origins, can undergo a change of function, become autonomous, and be further modified by culture. The relation between infantile experience, characterized by the primary process, and conscious adult fantasies, behavior, and societal structure is far too complex to be adequately explained by Janeway's (and other critics') assumption of a one-to-one relation between the two. The situation of male infantile loss of the mother could express itself in many other ways than in the "myth" of women in the home. There are an infinite variety of other defensive and reparative ego and superego formations and identifications that can be mobilized by the trauma of infantile narcissistic injury.

Granting that myth is a projection of infantile fantasies and wishes, the relation between myth and social reality, and between social reality and intrapsychic myth is more complicated than either Horney or Janeway admits. When we find that woman is given a powerful place in myth and literature (as Philip Slater points out is the case with Greek mythology and drama and Virginia Woolf says is true of English literature), while she has a minor public role and occupies a socially inferior position, what does this mean? Which reflects psychic reality more—the myths or the social behavior? We must be careful before we decide just what or whose kind of reality the myth reflects, or just what relation it bears to social behavior.

Gregory Zilboorg, an analyst anthologized in the Miller volume, has still another theory regarding man's attribution of weakness, passivity, envy, and inferiority to women. According to Zilboorg, man's insistence on the superiority of his penis, his hostility toward and envy of women (all of which he finds in Freud's formulations regarding female psychology) are defensive reactions against a recollection of his original weakness and inferiority regarding women. His ingenious argument is that patriarchy is not, as was once commonly thought, evidence of man's cultural or physical superiority over women, but of the very opposite, that is, of his original inferiority regarding her. Phylogenetically, the female, he argues, is "primary, more essential for the preservation of the race of living things, and therefore superior" (p. 94). The greater size and strength of the male higher mammal is not evidence of "male superiority," but of the opposite, it is the result of Darwinian natural selection by females who, in their choice of sexual partners, selected those males best suited to propagate the species. The human male through evolution developed muscular strength and physical stamina, just as the male bird developed colorful plumage, in order to attract the female. In prehistoric times, he postulates, "neither sex had any more idea of the connection between fertilization and reproduction than do animals. . ." (p. 96). Thus, women were able to exercise "supreme and final" choice in their selection of sexual partners and were the rulers of matriarchal societies which persisted into Mesopotamian and pre-Greek times and which can still be found today in some contemporary African tribes, such as the Awembas.

Eventually, however, Zilboorg postulates, one man became particularly powerful, healthy, and sexual by virtue of this very "enforced natural selection." Finding himself suddenly stronger than the woman, he gave expression to his hostility toward the primordial mother by performing the first "phallic sadistic act"—the "primal rape" (p. 99). This act, according to Zilboorg, became the origin of all later social organization, since it established male power, and led to the erotic and economic enslavement of women. And this *crime passionel* established a permanent male hegemony over women because its results were genetically inherited.

Zilboorg's argument is a version of the now popular "gynecocentric" point of view, which is adopted by some of the critics of Freud and which Zilboorg himself derives from the work of the late-nineteenth-century sociologist Lester Ward (1888). It has a kinship with those anthropological theories which posit an originally matriarchal organization of society in prehistoric times, such as put forward in the nineteenth century in the works of Johann Bachofen (1861), Friedrich Engels (1884), Robert Graves (1948), and more recently, in Erich Neumann (1964) and Joseph Campbell (1959).

A more elaborate but similar concept of female superiority and "gynecocentrism" has been revived by a more recent contributor to the Miller book, Mary Jane Sherfey. Although she says that claims "of innate female superiority based on a biological original-creation myth" are "totally unscientific and simply foolish" (p. 47), several of her theories belie this disclaimer. Like Ward and Zilboorg, she accepts as valid the existence of the matriarchal organization of prehistoric civilizations, on the basis of Masters' and Johnson's (1966) revelation of the female's "superior," indeed "infinite," orgasmic capacity. She believes the cornerstone of modern civilization to be not the "primal rape," but the "coercive suppression of women's inordinate sexuality" (p. 152), which was necessary before culture could evolve. She finds evidence of female primacy also in biology, though in embryology instead of phylogeny. "The early embryo is not undifferentiated, 'it' is a female" (p. 38). The penis and the scrotum are derived from an originally female *Anlage*; thus, "the penis is an exaggerated clitoris" (p. 34), and the scrotum is a further development of the labia majora. "If the fetal gonads are removed before differentiation occurs, the embryo will develop into a normal female, lacking only ovaries, regardless of the genetic sex" (p. 38).

Robert Stoller, reasoning about normative development from his studies of transsexual patients, at moments also comes close to a variation of gynecocentric speculation, while explicitly warning against formulations derived from man-kind's biological inheritance. He states, "in biology, animals and man, maleness is a quality differentiating out of a female *anlage.*" In normal male infant development there is a "proto-feminine phase." Masculinity is not a "naturally occurring state," but femininity is. "If boys, in the intimacy of the normal infant-mother symbiosis identify with their mothers . . . the boy who is to become masculine will have to repudiate that femininity" (in Miller, p. 248).

The belief in woman's primacy or superiority has found its way even into organically oriented articles about male and female sexuality, not in the Miller book. Gadpaille (1972), for instance, in a physiological review paper, offers the view that man's chauvinism and need to dominate women may be motivated by a denial of unconscious awareness of his greater biological and physical fragility.

It seems to us that arguments over whether the male or the female is biologically superior have no relevance to psychology. Verifiable data from biology and history do not confirm the primacy of either sex, nor can they be taken to suggest superiority or inferiority. While gynecocentric theories offer a balance to the previous androcentric ones and thus relieve male guilt, the former really have no more scientific basis than the latter. It is doubtful, furthermore, whether speculations regarding the structure of prehistoric social organizations and/or etiology of ancient social events can tell us much about the present-day psychology of women any more than considerations of embryological states can. The former requires us to accept a kind of Lamarckian reasoning with respect to the inheritance of acquired characteristics or a Jungian collective racial memory; the latter, questionable translations from the physical to the psychological.

Sherfey's conclusions regarding the primary "femaleness" of the human embryo are also a misinterpretation of the embryological evidence. The existence of embryonic bisex-uality in mammals has been clearly established. A "normal" female by definition cannot lack functioning ovaries, regardless of anatomical appearance. The chromosomally determined presence of androgen in the fetus is not an epiphenomenon, but is as integral to maleness as is external morphology. "Chromosomal sex is determined at the moment of fertilization" and therefore "it is not correct to speak of the 'innate femaleness' of the embryo" (Heiman, 1968, p. 410). As for woman's prehistoric ascendancy, Zilboorg's "primal rape" theory interestingly substitutes this event for Freud's analogous "primal murder" of the primal horde father (1913). The former cannot be substantiated any more than the latter. Lamarckian reasoning has been thoroughly invalidated by geneticists and anthropologists alike (Freeman, 1967).

It is interesting though not surprising that the emphasis on the effect a male-dominated society has on female personality has led many critics with this orientation toward an analysis of the history, prehistory, social institutions, myths, and traditions of culture and away from the consideration of individual female psychology and intra-psychic states. This change of focus is not hard to understand. If women's psychology is exclusively the product of an adaptation to male culture, if she is really a *tabula rasa* before culture imprints itself on her, then, in the strictest sense of the word, there really is nothing to "analyze." What must be "analyzed" instead is culture. But the psychoanalysis of cultural institutions, rites, and myths, as undertaken by these authors, is an extremely difficult endeavor, problematic in several ways. Robert LeVine (1973), for example, in his detailed theoretical explication of the methodology of psychoanalytic anthropology, feels that it is not possible to "psychoanalyze" cultural institutions at all. He argues that "Individuals, and only individuals, can be psychoanalyzed. Customs, institutions, and organizations cannot be..." (p. 209). They do not have an *analyzable* "superorganic" life of their own apart from the individuals who constitute them, and can only be analyzed in terms of the behavior and fantasies of the individuals who participate in them. In his studies of witchcraft accusations in sixteenth and seventeenth century England, he warns about the interpretation of religious symbols: "the first tenet [of a psychoanalytic approach to the meanings of religious symbolism] is that it is applicable only to individuals; it will establish the subjective meanings of a cultural symbol for the particular individual studied, not for other members of the group, who may or may not share those meanings" (p. 251).

In addition, it is important to realize that the mere fact of a correlation between certain social institutions and personality traits is not proof of a causal connection between the two. Mark Gehrie (1974) has commented on an attempt to demonstrate the causal connection between cultural conditions in the black ghetto with black suicide efforts: "In order to show that specific cultural conditions or sets of social institutions are responsible for certain individual behaviors, it is necessary to go beyond the assertion that particular behaviors may be shown to be consistent with the set of institutions; they may be consistent with many other sets of institutions as well. To go beyond such assertions, it is necessary to take a developmental perspective. . . ." Since none of the social critics we have discussed meet this requirement— few going beyond mere assertions of cause and effect—their ideas regarding the social origins of female psychology must be considered as yet unproven.

The assumption that cultural conditions of whatever sort can *by themselves* account for the behavior and the psychology of the individuals in a culture is questionable to begin with. Certainly, culture alone is sometimes responsible for the appearance and prevalence of personality traits alleged to characterize female behavior. But these traits may or may not reflect psychological reality. For example, Lifton (1965) has shown the passive-submissive quality supposedly so typical of the Japanese woman to be a superficial cultural trait unrelated to deeper psychodynamics; Lifton tells of the Japanese woman's way of treating her husband in public as "uncontested lord and master. . ." while in private exercising a pervasive authority over both husband and children (p. 44). In this ostensibly highly patriarchal culture, it is very often the paternal grandmother who is the supreme authority even when her son is middle aged or older, and who rules her clan with an iron hand. It is certainly possible that other global traits attributed to women, such as receptivity, emotionality, and even "normal feminine masochism," may be culturally created or rewarded manifestations, not representative of deeper intrapsychic constellations and without cross-cultural universality. But the idea that culture alone is responsible for intrapsychic as well as behaviorally manifest constellations is another matter. Based as it is, first of all, on the idea of the individual as an "empty organism," a *tabula rasa* without drives or wishes or fantasies of his own, it is an obviously unsound proposition. The evidence from biology, neurology (and yes, psychoanalysis) indicates that the individual, while enormously modifiable, is not infinitely so. He has inborn drives (and their psychic representations), an epigenetic developmental maturational timetable, and perhaps even inborn cognitive structures. Secondly, the cultural conditioning idea implicitly utilizes a behavioristic learning theory model for human behavior that is foreign to the psychoanalytic endeavor, which sees intrapsychic constellations as the final end-product of multiple complex actions between social institutions, rites, and beliefs, the individual's familial and social milieu, and his own drives, wishes, needs, and fantasies.

Let us grant that the patriarchial nature of the Victorian middle-class culture of which Freud was a member, and male psychological needs, probably did influence early theories of femininity and possibly were responsible for a number of persistent errors and distortions. Horney's suggestion that Freud did not sufficiently appreciate phallic narcissism and man's envy and "dread of woman," leading him and those influenced by him to mistaken ideas about women, is persuasive. Stereotypes such as those inspected by Janeway may have contributed to the perpetuation of some early errors even within the scientific community. However, the social analysts' attack on Freudian theory, particularly that of the most recent ones in the Miller book (Moulton, Symonds, Gelb, and Seidenberg) is characterized by a social-reformist zeal that, while most admirable in itself, confuses the role of the analyst with that of the political or spiritual leader. Although the title of the Miller book is *Psychoanalysis and Women* and its contributors are analysts, many of the papers reflect theoretical orientations that are not analytic in any sense of the word. The essays by Gelb and Seidenberg, in particular, are not based on analytic data and show a striking neglect of metapsychology, the technique and philosophy of psycho-analysis, and the development point of view. Gelb's is a moral argument charging analysts with being guilty "not only of being passive in the face of the continued denial to women of full participation in human life, but of embracing a decaying value system and of actually promoting deprivation" (p. 372). Seidenberg's presentation of psychoanalytic concepts in quotable phrases (i.e., the "trauma of eventlessness" [p. 353]), and his use of simplified social examples does not broaden either our analytic understanding or that of the lay audience to whom he speaks. It is striking, moreover, that he, together with Saltzman and Moulton and most of the nonanalytic critics continue to attack Freud's theories of women, stated well over half a century ago (though recently restated by Nagera, 1975), as if psychoanalysis had not changed dramatically since then. Their critique of Freud does not advance appreciably beyond that of Horney and her contemporary pioneer feminists, except in so far as they embrace the physiological data of Masters and Johnson and Mary Jane Sherfey to support their contentions that Freud erred. All are much more concerned with social advocacy than they are with broadening our analytic thinking. Judd

Marmor's worry is that today's analyst is faced with ideological problems such as what the proper therapeutic management of a "feminist" like Ibsen's Nora should be. Should he interpret "her 'penis envy' and her rejection of the normal feminine goals of wifehood and motherhood" (p. 204), or should he focus instead upon her "healthy" rebellion "and encourage her to move out of the home as a laudable effort at self-realization" (p. 204)?

But are these really psychoanalytic problems? Psychoanalysis, after all, is not an ideology (the critics to the contrary), but professes to be a science. An analyst who, motivated by even the sincerest desire to reform society encourages changes in patients consistent with his own personal ideology and must be said to run the danger of countertransference and transference interferences. An analyst's sympathy with the women's liberation movement (a sympathy we share, by the way) should not blind him to the fact that, for one patient, "women's liberation" might provide global rationalizations defending against recognition of intrapsychic responsibility for neurotic misery and thus reinforce avoidance of necessary psychoanalytic working through and constitute a resistance within the analytic situation. For another patient, it might represent evidence of an ability to act on her own values and wishes.

One might further add that while these critics magnify transference distortions of reality caused by male needs and wishes, they ignore the possible effect of transference distortions secondary to female rage at male domination and "oppression." An analytic understanding of female psychology requires that we be aware of both possibilities and that we consider the evidence from all sides. The contributors to the Miller volume, the late Horney, Janeway, and other social critics almost completely ignore the likelihood that female as well as male infantile needs might have shaped and still shape the structure of social and cultural institutions as well as female personality. To see culture and woman's character as so exclusively a product of *male* needs and fantasies is paradoxically to accept the patriarchal and androcentric position that culture is a specifically *male* function and woman merely man's creation—the very allegations that critics decry in Freud. It is highly unlikely that *male* desires and needs alone have shaped culture and women. It is certainly possible that the "myth" placing women into caretaking and childbearing roles in the home reflects female needs and desires as well as those of the male. To exclude all biological, developmental, and intrapsychic clinical data from consideration in such matters risks the danger of throwing out the baby with the bathwater.

The female infant's own response to the early loss of the mother might well push her, many years later, in the direction of seeking adult reparative compensation in the way her biology makes possible for her—in pregnancy and early motherhood. Childbirth offers a reparative possibility par excellence for early narcissistic injury. Freud's (1914) idea that "in the child which they bear, a part of women's own body confronts them like an extraneous object," giving them an opportunity for a "revival and reproduction of their own narcissism which they have long since abandoned" (pp. 89-91), might not be so far wrong. In her own child, the woman can once more recapture her own early narcissistic relation to her mother. Benedek (1970) noted that in pregnancy, "as metabolic and emotional processes replenish the libidinal reservoir of the pregnant woman" (p. 141), a supply of primary narcissism that becomes the "wellspring of motherliness" is again made available to her.

Female personalities, we believe, cannot simply be the product of a culture conceived of as exclusively male oriented. Intrapsychic constellations are the final end-product of multiple family interactions and attitudes, physical and environmental conditions, laws, customs, and religion; but they are also shaped by biology and anatomy, epigenetic and maturational considerations, and female as well as male infantile wishes. Psychological characteristics cannot be considered simply the result of social conditioning acting upon a *tabula rasa*. It is in fact the particular contribution of psychoanalysis to have focused on those aspects of reality that had been (and still are) too often ignored, not on the so-called objective reality of the external world, but on the subjective reality of intrapsychic and unconscious fantasies, wishes, needs, and drives. An anecdote that Betty Friedan (1963), the original modern feminist, reports about a psychoanalyst disillusioned with Freud's theory of femininity is instructive here.

One of the analyst's patients told of a dream in which she felt the self-fulfillment she would have if she obtained a job. His response was, "I can't analyze this dream away. You must do something about it" (p. 114). This interpretation, directed as it is toward conscious external reality instead of toward inner preconscious fantasy, highlights the contrast between the social analyst and the psychoanalyst.

Biological Dimensions of Female Personality

Bardwick's *Psychology of Women: A Study of Bio-Cultural Conflicts* (1971) is an attempt at a comprehensive description of female psychology based upon biological and psychometric studies as well as sociological and cultural data. The author is an experimental psychologist with prior publications of studies which identify physiological contributions to feminine personality development. This background explains the book's heavy emphasis on the biological contributions to female personality. Bardwick does, however, attempt to integrate the biological findings with data gained through psychological test evaluations, longitudinal observations of infant development, learning theory experiments, sociological studies of gender traits and attitudes, and brief clinical interviews.

Bardwick, who identifies herself as an anti-Freudian, devotes the first chapter of her book to attacking psychoanalytic theories of female personality, stating that "the fundamental assumptions of the psychoanalytic point of view seem ludicrous when they are divorced from the clinical situation" (p. 10). In light of her own heavy emphasis on biological factors, it is puzzling that she declares Freud's ideas about women a "perverted point of view" (p. 9). It is even more puzzling when it becomes apparent that her findings and conclusions actually closely parallel Freud's principal ideas about the feminine character. Her failure to recognize this contradiction, at best suggests intellectual scotomata in an otherwise sophisticated investigator. At worst, it reflects a blind antianalytic prejudice stimulated perhaps by the mass movements of contemporary social change for which psychoanalysis is a scapegoat on which to blame the status quo.

Bardwick examines a mass of evidence which leads her to the conclusion that the psychological distinction between males and females originates in prenatal and postnatal physiological, endocrine, and central nervous system differences. Much of the data she cites does lend itself to quantification and reliability across fields of investigation, and is skillfully compiled and integrated into the book. It can be only very briefly summarized here.

Bardwick's own studies corroborate prior investigations by Gottshalk et al. (1962), and Benedek and Rubenstein (1942) concerning the influence of different hormonal variables on personality. The data suggest that high self-esteem and outward, active, object-directed heterosexual tendencies in women can be positively correlated with high estrogen levels (Ivey and Bardwick, 1968; Benedek and Rubenstein, 1942), whereas depression, anxiety, and irritability correlate positively with low levels of estrogen and progesterone (Sutherland and Stewart, 1965; Benedek, 1959). High levels of progesterone during the secretory phase of the menstrual cycle or during pregnancy can be associated with an "increased integrative capacity of the ego," increased self-esteem, and an intensification of narcissistic receptive-retentive tendencies (Benedek, 1959). Oral contraceptive agents have been shown to produce similar results (Kane et al., 1966; Swanson et al., 1964).

Research also suggests that androgens are correlated positively with increase of genital sexual activity in both males and females. For example, androgen given to adult women may produce an increase in activity, aggressiveness, and frequency of sexual behavior (Kinsey et al., 1953; Kupperman, 1961). Intrauterine exposure of the female fetus to androgen has been positively correlated with later establishment of a more masculine than feminine psychosexual identity (Ehrhardt and Money, 1967). Bardwick, who draws freely on animal studies, also points to studies of rats and monkeys masculinized by testosterone who showed more "rough and tumble" play, threatening and mounting behavior than did normal females (Valenstein, 1968; Levine, 1966).

In regard to central nervous system differences, Bardwick presents evidence that "the influence of the sex hormones before birth involves the shaping of neutral circuits in the hypothalamus, which is the part of the brain that directly influences the endocrine system" (p. 83). "To the extent that there is central nervous system sex-typing, the predisposition to perceive and respond to stimuli will be influenced by the sex-type of the brain" (p. 88). Research indicates that androgens organize neural tissue in subhuman species—fish, amphibians, rats, guinea pigs, and monkeys (Gadpaille, 1972).

Much recent evidence, which she summarizes well, demonstrates the existence of constitutional psychomotor differences between boys and girls from birth on. At birth, girls demonstrate greater motoric passivity (Bell, 1960; Knop, 1946) and greater sensitivity to tactile and pain stimuli than do boys (Lipsitt and Levy, 1959). At six months of age, girls show greater "attention" to complex auditory stimuli (measured by cardiac deceleration) than do boys, and greater responsiveness to perceptions of human faces (Kagan and

Lewis, 1965). More aggressive play by male children than by female children has been documented at eight, thirteen, and 27 months of age (Kagan and Lewis, 1971). By thirteen months of age, girls display earlier language development, a preference for high complexity stimuli, and greater stimulus field dependency. Girls are also toilet trained at an earlier age. Many such distinctions can be traced into adolescence. For instance, the boy's superiority in tasks involving visual perception (Sherman, 1971 pp. 21-22) can also be noted in greater visual-spatial ability during adolescence (Macoby and Jacklin, 1975). Macoby and Jacklin consider aggressiveness (defined as destructive intent) and spatial talent to be genetically sex-linked. Biological gender contributions to behavior are also documented by Friedman and Richart (1975).

Clearly, a psychoanalytic theory of feminine personality cannot ignore the biological differences that these studies suggest. It seems probable that organic factors provide a solid foundation for sexual gender identity. However, Bardwick recognizes that, as repeatedly demonstrated by others (Stoller, 1968; Money et al., 1957), parental gender assignment and rearing outweighs biological factors by facilitating various kinds of learning through identification with both parents or through parental conditioning of behavior. Moreover, there is the problem of the translation of findings from human anatomy and physiology and primate behavior into psychology. This final step must surmount the formidable obstacles in mind-body conceptual integration and the barrier of human-animal distinctions. Keiser (1968), in a critique of Sherfey (also applicable to Bardwick), commented that there is "too great a freedom in equating physiological data with psychology, equating primates with humans . . ." (p. 455). Marmor (in Miller, 1973), points out, for instance, that male genital penetration of the female vagina cannot be conceptualized in terms of "active-passive" or "aggressive-submissive." The vagina can be conceptualized both as aggressive, grasping, holding, sucking organ and as a passive open receptacle. So far as the nonbiological determinants of female personality are concerned, Bardwick accepts the findings and conclusions of dozens of psychometric studies and psychological test observations that fit her generalizations without questioning the goals, methods, or quality of the research. Her interpretations of this material lack both a developmental perspective and metapsychological rigor. For instance, she cites several studies that prove that girls read and write much earlier than do boys (McCarthy, 1953; Terman and Tyler, 1954), and that girls tend to be more emotionally mature and less likely to require psychiatric treatment than do boys of comparable age. Instead of building upon her previous description of constitutional differences to explain these findings, she switches to a purely speculative mechanical psychological theory regarding the less turbulent resolution of the oedipal complex in girls, for which she offers not the least clinical evidence.

Bardwick's general psychological conclusion is that women are "more nurturant, dependent, receptive, maternal, intuitive, empathic, and emotionally labile" (p. 154), but are less aggressive and have lower self-esteem than men. The qualities of "nurturance" and motherliness originate in the physiological potential for pregnancy, and the "lability" is due to hormonal changes of the menstrual cycle. Biological and constitutional factors also account for the girl's lesser physical aggressiveness, motoric impulsiveness, and genital activity. Consequently, the girl has less fear of parental anger and less castration anxiety. She "is not forced to develop internal controls and an independent sense of self" (p. 16). Resulting female ego defenses and superego structures mature later and are less sharply defined. The girl is permitted to remain "affection seeking," "passive," and "infantile," longer than is the boy. Society sanctions or reinforces this prolonged state of dependency. It is lack of self-esteem that "most of all" distinguishes woman's personality from that of man. This is true particularly if she fails in the traditional feminine role: "if a woman has a feminine and normal core identity, failure in the feminine roles will preclude feelings of self-esteem" (p. 158). It is still true that "cultural and familial expectations and body needs converge to make marriage and children, love and nurturance, the most important of feminine psychological needs" (p. 162). Just as Freud and, more recently, Benedek thought, she also believes that pregnancy and lactation constitute the completion of psychosexual maturity in women.

But Bardwick does demonstrate with skill and conviction, in total agreement with Janeway, that for many women today, work, career, and intellectual creativity often become central life goals in spite of their conflict with the traditional female role of wife and mother. "In our masculine-oriented culture, a person is worth the market value of his skills and personality" (p. 166). She therefore argues that "in the reality of today, the pattern of compromise in which a woman works part-time, or works after the children are in school . . . is a more certain route to feelings of self-esteem" (p. 159). This proposition, which Janeway also argued, is quite reasonable and sound. The psychodynamics Bardwick delineates for the girl's ability to be independent in a career and to have a motivation to achieve is, however, clinically questionable.

She finds that the girl normally has less of an "independent sense of self" than the boy because her biologically lower levels of aggressiveness and genital impulsiveness allow her to remain more dependent on the parents. This tendency is reinforced by parents who permit (or even encourage) her to remain dependent, childish, and passive longer. The boy, by contrast, driven by a high level of impulses, becomes alienated from his parents, who react to his aggressiveness by pushing him away. "As the boy grows older [he] loses the external source of self-esteem [that his parents originally provide] and is pushed to develop internal independent sources" for self-esteem in himself. This formulation is contradicted by the comprehensive work, *Psychology of Sex Differences* in which Macoby and Jacklin (1975) found "a remarkable degree of uniformity in the socialization of the two sexes." They find, in fact, that "the studies that have identified any differential treatment ... have more often found great independence-granting to girls than boys." Bardwick's evidence is a primate study revealing that male baby Macaque monkeys were punished more and carried less by their mothers and quickly surpassed infant female Macaques in the rate of achieving independence from her (Jensen and Bobitt, 1968).

Bardwick's argument is that ambivalent mothers treat girls in the same way that boys are usually treated, and are thus more likely to produce achievement-oriented women. She cites a number of studies illustrating that a group of mothers who were ambivalent and withheld their love and support had girls who demonstrated higher scholastic achievement and motivation than was true of normal-control girls (Crandall et al., 1964). She concludes that "the development of achievement motives in girls requires a somewhat rejecting attitude by the mother when the girl is young ..." (Veroff, 1969); in fact, she says "it might take considerable maternal rejection, if not hostility, for girls to develop a high need to achieve" (p. 176).

Her reasoning in this matter, however, is inconsistent with the experience of therapists who penetrate even slightly beneath superficial defenses and who explore the early roots of personality traits. Only a theoretician far removed from clinical evidence would believe that an "independent sense of self" and high esteem could originate in early maternal rejection, parental pushes toward self-sufficiency, or societal expectations. There have been numerous studies documenting that maternal rejection is traumatic rather than beneficial for both sexes. Many such questions arise about the validity of her formulations and conclusions in these matters. One might simply ask, for example, if the young girl does not in fact develop "internal controls" as early and as solidly as the boy, why does she achieve earlier success in toilet training?

It is, perhaps, Bardwick's over-all method of inquiry into the clinical area of feminine psychology that presents the major problem, despite the validity of many of her conclusions. Can psychological tests, questionnaires, and a few interviews meaningfully identify broad motivations, character traits and conflicts? They are more likely to register simply conscious self-representations and rationalizations regarding real motivations.

Analysts disagree on the value for psychoanalytic theory of data derived from neighboring disciplines removed from the psychoanalytic clinical situation (Grinker, 1964; Gitelson, 1964; Stoller, 1968; Lustman, 1963). Nonanalytic research can provide critical evaluation or validation of some analytic hypotheses. There are, however, minimum standards for the quality of such work. It should utilize reproducible studies with careful use of scientific method, controls when possible, and have intrafield reliability. In this regard, Bardwick's book does not past the test.

Moreover, the researcher critical of psychoanalysis should have a basic understanding of metapsychology and some familiarity with the interrelation of theory formation and the analytic clinical situation. Bardwick's basic assumptions and her theoretical framework are left unstated but seem to be closer to those of experimental and behavioral than to depth psychology. Her deficient grasp of analytic concepts is exemplified by the following formulations: "The absence of an Oedipal crisis in girls is responsible for less mature defenses against sexual and aggressive impulses, the absence of an internalized ego ideal and greater dependence upon others (than in boys). . . . Therefore more energy is available for the conflict-free cognitive and perceptual spheres of the ego" (p. 17). These thoughts show, to say the least, an incomplete comprehension of both the Oedipus complex and the ideas of ego psychology. Her anti-Freudian stand itself reflects her misunderstanding of Freudian clinical method for, more than any other author discussed in this essay, she has offered massive evidence to corroborate Freud's theories of feminine passivity, masochism, and narcissism, without any awareness that she has done so.

Intrapsychic Dimensions of Female Psychology

Female Sexuality, edited by Chasseguet-Smirgel, amplifies theories formulated by Melanie Klein (1928, 1932), adopted by Ernest Jones (1932, 1935), and accepted in a modified form by the "English school" of psychoanalysis. The authors are preoccupied by the factors influencing feminine personality formations that originate in the first year of infantile life, and in fact consider the psychological experience of the infant-mother relation during this year to determine almost all future sexual development. Certainly, these writers are not the only ones (or the first ones) to turn their attention to this stage of life. Many analysts have noted Freud's failure to give sufficient attention to the obvious effect the archaic, powerful, controlling mother has on the child. Deutsch, as far back as 1925, Lampl-de Groot in 1928, and Brunswick in 1940, acknowledged the influence of the preoedipal mother.

Unlike the Kleinians, however, they did not modify or contradict Freud's theory, which assigns to the oedipal father the dominant influence in both normal and neurotic feminine personality structure. For most analysts, the oedipal constellation remains the crucial frame of reference for psychological development and sexual identity. Schafer (1973) recently noted that even the terms "*pre*oedipal" and "*pre*genital" anchor the roots of personality in the oedipal period and point to the relative neglect of the major early maternal factors the writers emphasize so dramatically in this book. Freud (1933) believed that prior to the phallic stage there was no difference in the sexuality of boys and girls, and often spoke of the little girl as though she were a little boy, going so far as to say "we are obliged to recognize that the little girl is a little man . . ." (p. 118). But the Kleinians are insistent on distinguishing the two from birth. Klein is very emphatic about the essential "femininity" of the little girl, positing an original "primary" vaginal awareness as well as an early *conscious* and *feminine* awareness of the father's penis—feminine in that she is said to recognize her mother from the beginning as an "inadequate sexual object" for her, in contrast to father.

The belief that the girl's sexuality is feminine from the beginning was already current in the 1930's (Müller, 1932; Horney, 1933), and was emphasized later by Brunswick (1940) who spoke of an "early vaginal sensitivity of anal origin." Today, the existence of an original feminine identity has been buttressed by contributions from biology and genetics (Stoller, 1968, 1976; Sherfey, 1973) and by Benedek's (1970) pregnancy studies. It has been tentatively validated by child observation studies (Galenson and Roiphe, 1976) and theoretically explicated by Barnett (1966). Thus, most analysts can agree with Jones's (1935) observation that "there is more femininity in the young girl than analysts generally admit ..." Unfortunately, however, the Kleinian analysts make the girl's "femininity" dependent on an inexplicable ability to recognize the father as an "authentic" and the mother as an "inadequate" sexual object in the first year of life, which is hardly commensurate with what we know of infantile perceptual-cognitive capacity in this period. It would require the use of a Jungian archetype theory to account for a cognitive capacity to distinguish the genitalia of mother and father and recognize either parent as an "adequate" or "inadequate" sexual object at this early stage.

For the Kleinians, psychosexual development begins when the little girl, frustrated by the maternal breast, turns directly to an oral incorporation wish for the paternal penis, which is perceived as a separate part of the mother's (not the father's) body. This so-called "pregenital penis envy" forms a significant part of Kleinian theory. Important fantasies of the girl during this time include those of the "usurpation of genitals and other properties of the parents' bodies," and of removing the "breast-penis" from mother—fantasies associated with primitive envy and rage, producing fears of cruel retaliation in the form of fantasied bloody damage to the infant's own internal organs. As the oral penis wish directed toward mother merges into an oral incorporative penis wish toward father (the "fellatio fantasy"), the organ site, which the child associates in fantasy with the reception of the penis, changes progressively from the mouth to the anus to the vagina—all in the first year of life.

The resulting final vaginal desire for the father's penis is quickly frustrated by paternal rejection of the little girl's love. The rejection is said to have two consequences: (1) It produces phallic penis envy leading to idealization of the desired male organ. This constitutes the phallic phase, which is considered a defense against the recognition of paternal rejection, and which contains a regressive tendency towards a revival of oral paternal or even maternal penis envy. (2) It initiates the nuclear Oedipus situation. Thus, Jones (1927), can speak of the "direct transition between oral and oedipus states" (p. 450).

At this point, the girl's mother becomes a rival for the father's love and a competitor for the possession of the penis or its symbolic, magical, idealized qualities. The penis can be coveted now as an instrument to express hatred for the mother. Also, because the girl's love for father was transferred from the intense maternal relationship, it includes remnants of primitive pregenital (oral and anal) aggression. This accounts for an unconscious hatred for the father and is said to produce a universal feminine guilt toward males. This guilt, consciously experienced by the girl in the father relationship, can spread to inhibit her realistic achievement and creativity. Repression of the hatred, they theorize, could account for the often described spiritualized, sublimated character of female sexuality. The positive ("libidinous") portion of the oedipal wish for the penis is transformed into a desire for a penis-child, or is sublimated into such feminine emotions as spirituality and gratitude.

These formulations clearly conflict with Freud's views of the Oedipus complex (Freud, 1924, 1925, 1931; Calogeras and Schupper, 1972), not only because of their emphasis on the preoedipal period itself, but also because they hypothesize what amount to precisely delineated *oedipal*, not preoedipal, experiences in the first one and a half years of life. Freud himself considered the oral period "dim and shadowy," subject to "inexorable repression" and felt that the decisive events in the girl's sexual development took place much later, in the phallic phase. The girl, then recognizing her "castrated" state, turns away from the mother in disappointed anger for having provided her only with a clitoris, an "inferior penis," and turns to her father's love and his penis. That is to say, Freud felt that the castration complex initiated the girl's Oedipus complex. For him, the assumption of female identification also involved a shift from activity to passivity, from a self concept including an inferior penis (the clitoris) to a castrated self concept corresponding to a shift from clitoral cathexis to vaginal cathexis. And unlike Klein and Jones, Freud (1937) felt that penis envy constituted the "bedrock" of unconscious frustration throughout life.

Kleinian metapsychology places much greater emphasis on the vicissitudes of oral and early phallic aggression than on the vicissitudes of the Oedipus complex proper. Kleinians view these as determining decisively all later development of personality. In fact, they ascribe the differences between the normal male and the normal female personality to the differences in the original intensity of the hostile wishes toward the breast-penis image. The contributors to *Female Sexuality* feel that the early life experience of girls is much more characterized by primitive rage, aggression, and sadism than that of boys. They believe that "the sadistic-oral and sadistic-anal phases . . . are extremely violent in girls" (p. 44) because the mother is only a poor substitute for what would constitute a "truly adequate sexual object," i.e., the father (p. 72). The girl therefore perceives the mother as more frustrating and rejecting than does the boy. Moreover, she fears a retaliatory "revenge against the inside of her body," since she lacks an external body organ (penis) of her own onto which she can displace her fears. Furthermore, unlike the male child, the girl cannot transfer her sadism from mother to father (who is needed as a "mature" love object). The result is that the introjected breast-penis-mother produces a punitive superego precursor that is only slightly modified by later identification with the devoted, indulgent, feeding "good mother."

The massive negative (aggressive) components of the phallic penis wish and its associated affects may motivate a variety of defenses. Destructive (penis) wishes and corresponding retaliatory fears can necessitate a splitting of parental and part objects (breast, phallus) into "all-good" or "all-evil" imagos. Denial, repression, idealization, reaction formation, or masochistic turning of hatred toward internalized objects may be other consequences. In marked contrast to Freud, the Kleinians thus argue that the girl's later superego is "more powerful and therefore stronger and more severe than that of the boy" (p. 34). Later oedipal paternal deprivation revives oral breast penis envy and its destructive components. Intense sadistic strivings may be projected onto the penis, making it dangerous and threatening. And it is "the introjection of this penis which forms the nucleus of the paternal superego" (p. 34).

Historically, the Kleinian view of the feminine superego as stricter than the masculine provides a counterbalance to Freud's (1924) depiction of the feminine superego as weak and defective. But both views remain unsubstantiated. Yorke (1971) and Muslin (1973) have explored in detail the incompleteness of the Klein-Jones concept of the superego.

It is interesting that the Kleinian paradigm of the conflict-ridden, turbulent mother-daughter relation, as opposed to that of the more conflict-free mother-son relationship, echoes in some measure Freud's (1933) own idyllic picture of the early mother-son situation as "altogether the most perfect, the most free from ambivalence of all human relationships" (p. 133). However, Freud emphasized the real attitudes of the mother "object" toward the male child, not the infantile perceptions of her created by various introjections and projections emphasized by the Kleinians.

Female Sexuality contains many vivid clinical examples of adult psychoanalyses. The material is full of illustrations of the revival of the infantile states and affects described above. Most genetic reconstructions include good and bad objects and breasts, but the omnipresent penis reigns supreme. Jones's adjective "phallocentric," intended for Freud, applies much more aptly to these writers. Interpretations are directed almost exclusively toward the unconscious, recalling the flavor of the old Id Master Groddeck (1928) himself in his *Book of the It*. The concepts of ego resistance, character formations, the adaptive point of view, and the principle of multiple functioning are missing.

The book's major contribution is found in several imaginative re-creations of infantile narcissistic fantasies and images. For example, one author notes that when the pregenital mother withholds narcissistic confirmation, the girl infant "attempts to give it to herself, thereby becoming essentially narcissistic ..." (p. 73). But since this attempt lacks the foundation of "solid maternal love," it is bound to fail in some measure, and, as a result, the girl is forever "more dependent on her love objects than is the boy" (p. 73). (This formulation, however, again assumes that the girl infant can, before the age of one, recognize the fact that the father is her "authentic" sexual love object.)

Later, women are said to seek narcissistic gratification above all else. "Women offer themselves sexually in order to be loved, while men love in order to be satisfied" (p. 70), says Maria Torok (pp. 35-70), who also notes that the possession of the envied penis can represent "satisfactory narcissistic confirmation for a woman." Penis envy can camouflage "a painful feeling of deficiency," a wish for pleasure, a desire for power, strength, or autonomy, a "revolt against the omnipotent mother," or even a "desire for maturation and development." Narcissistic needs can be satisfied later in life by physical beauty, by having a baby, by reality accomplishments, or, vicariously, through marriage.

Narcissistic Dimensions of Female Personality

The Kleinian writers are not the only analysts who emphasize the need for self-esteem-maintenance, or a "painful feeling of deficiency" as the central issues in feminine psychology. Janeway, for instance, noted that the woman's "feeling of superiority" and "guiltless power" (pp. 54-55) in the mothering experience were compensatory for the humiliation of having to function in "man's world." Most of the works under review here directly or indirectly argued that both male and female narcissism influenced or dominated analytic theories of female sexuality. Many of the social critics, for example, felt that most of the major formulations about the personality of women originated in "male narcissism," and expressed efforts to hide feelings of male vulnerability by depreciating and degrading women.

On the other side, many critics agree essentially with Bardwick's formulation that "most of all, lack of self-esteem" was the variable that "repeatedly differentiated women from men" (p. 2), and that women do have a pervasive sense of inferiority. Unlike Freud, however, who had the same views, they felt the reason for this to lie in woman's actual position in patriarchal culture, society, and history. Horney summarized this view when she suggested that the masculine orientation of our society produced in women "a regarding of [themselves] as weak, helpless, or inferior ..." (p. 229).

Freud (1914), too, felt that narcissistic pathology particularly distinguished the woman's personality from the man's, but ignored cultural influences when he wrote: "different lines of development correspond to the differentiation of functions in a highly complicated biological whole" (p. 89). He concluded that the girl's perception of her castrated state constituted a special narcissistic injury which caused her to develop, "like a scar, a sense of inferiority" (1925, p. 253) and a "narcissistic sense of humiliation" (p. 256). In puberty, he believed, the "maturing of the female sexual organs ... seems to bring about an intensification of the original narcissism" (1914, p. 88).

It is, however, extremely difficult to demonstrate that there is a gender-linked difference in the self-esteem of men and women, or that women have more narcissistic pathology than men. Macoby and Jacklin (1975), surveying research in this area, found no distinction in self-esteem between boys and girls. Freud's emphasis on the presence or absence of the penis as the major determinant of self-esteem ignores the complexities of its roots, its maintenance, and its regulation. Moreover, his emphasis on the all-determining character of the narcissistic injury of not having a penis places the pathology of self-esteem very late in the phallic phase. Kohut (1972) has pointed out that the penis is only transitorily, not originally, or exclusively, or permanently, the leading zone of bodily narcissism, commenting, "The significance of the genitals during the phallic phase is determined by the fact that at this period, they temporarily constitute the *leading zone of the child's* (bodily) *narcissism*..." (p. 374). The narcissistic cathexis of the penis at this time is analogous to "the narcissistic cathexis of feces during the anal phase of development and the narcissistic cathexis of certain autonomous ego functions during latency..." (p. 374). Freud's association of female narcissism almost exclusively with the lack of a penis is probably incorrect. If the sight of the anatomical distinction between the sexes has such a major impact on the psychology of the female as Freud suggested, a narcissistic fragility must already have pre-existed (Schafer, 1974).

The development and establishment of a healthy narcissism begins much earlier than Freud thought and depends primarily on the primitive parent-child state and separation-individuation processes. It is therefore not possible to attribute lack of self-esteem or narcissistic pathology to women on the basis of their feelings about not having a penis. It is interesting to note that most critics of Freud implicitly seem to accept his idea that women have lowered self-esteem and are more "narcissistic" (i.e., have more narcissistic pathology), since this seems almost impossible to prove in any case. The degree of narcissistic pathology in an individual depends neither on the presence or absence of the penis nor on women's position in a male chauvinistic culture, but grows out of the primitive and specific child-mother interaction.

The only reasonable conjecture possible at this time about the relation between narcissism and gender is that the sexes seem to have differing timetables for the development of narcissistic disequilibrium. We hypothesize that the girl may have an initial narcissistic advantage, which she gradually loses during the anal, phallic, and oedipal phases, which present her with more gender-specific narcissistic traumata; and the boy may have an initial disadvantage, which he overcomes because the later developmental phases present less difficulty for him than for the girl.

The boy's initial narcissistic disadvantage in comparison to the girl springs from certain developmental, maturational, and biological factors that cause him to put a greater strain on the mother's empathic capacity in the second half of the first year of life than does the girl. His greater physical aggressiveness, his tendency toward more movement in space (Bell, 1960), and his greater size (Garn, 1958), all of which may be related to prenatal androgen production, make him more difficult to soothe and probably serve to push him away from the favorable mother-child symbiosis earlier than the girl. Tolpin (1971) has pointed out that "it is simply impossible for the mother to hold and calm the larger, more active, and alert infant of the second half of the first year in exactly the way that she held and cradled the physically more immature infant with whom an almost complete sense of physical merger is possible" (p. 324). This condition would be exacerbated for the boy because he is larger, more active, more aggressive, and probably less soothable than the girl during the earliest six to eight months of life. Thus, the boy's emergence from the protection of the mother-infant symbiosis is probably more traumatic than the girl's, who is able to retain it longer and benefits from the lesser strain she puts on the mother's empathic capacity. We hypothesize that this specific narcissistic trauma might retard the boy's development for a time and thus account for the incontestable evidence of the infant boy's slower mental achievements in the areas of conation, cognition, verbal development, emotional maturity, and toilet-training success we described earlier. Further, in the second and third year of life, the boy faces the difficulties of what Greenson (1968) calls "dis-identification." In order to attain a healthy sense of maleness, the boy, unlike the girl, must replace the primary object of his identification, the mother, and must identify instead with the father. This constitutes still another narcissistic trauma of the preoedipal period which threatens the boy in other developmental areas. The girl, on the other hand, we posit, has an initial narcissistic advantage over the boy because, being smaller, less aggressive, less active, less inclined to move away from the mother in the second half of the first year, she does not put as much early strain on the mother's capacity for empathy and optimal frustration, and therefore is for most mothers easier to pacify. Thus, she is probably usually able to remain in the protection of the mother-infant symbiotic relation of maximal empathy longer than the boy, and therefore enters the separation-individuation phase less traumatically and with a stronger self than does the boy. This, along with the fact that she does not have to face the strains of the "dis-identification" process, we posit, can account for the girl's often-noted early developmental superiority.

The late preoedipal period just prior to the opening of

the oedipal situation, however, is probably somewhat more narcissistically difficult for the girl than for the boy. (This constitutes a contrast to the relatively greater ease with which the girl can achieve primary identification.) The male child has the opportunity to overcome initial narcissistic traumata because during the anal and phallic phases the penis can be used advantageously for exhibitionistic narcissistic purposes during urination and erection. Unlike the girl, he need not suffer the narcissistic injury implied by the need for a change of object (the mother) when he moves from preoedipal to oedipal sexuality. The boy's oral-anal relation with the mother merges almost imperceptibly with the phallic and oedipal phases of his development. The boy moves into the oedipal phase from preoedipal sexuality without a change of object, and, optimally, he receives admiration and narcissistic sustenance for his phallic exhibitionism from father and mother. His idealization of the latter is frustrated gradually by her failures to respond to his exhibitionistic seductive efforts. The relation with his father remains unchanged until the advent of competitiveness and castration anxiety during the oedipal period.

By contrast, the girl's situation with her mother must change radically. The mother must be relinquished at least temporarily as the primary love-object. This essential process is inevitably accompanied by massive disappointment. Cognitive and affective comprehension of the mother's primary genital sexual loyalty to the father constitutes a painful rejection for the little girl and is another source of narcissistic injury. Turning away from mother produces "separation anxiety attendant upon traumatic disillusionment" (Gedo and Goldberg, 1973, p. 118). Furthermore, the mother failed to provide her with the (then highly prized) penis and is perceived as incapable of filling up the girl's inner space with penis or child (Barnett, 1966).

There may be another gender distinction between boys and girls in the establishment of "perceptual object constancy" (setting up of "physical boundaries of both self and object" [Burgner and Edgcumbe, 1972, p. 326]). One factor assisting the boy to establish such boundaries is the accessibility of the penis to manipulation and visual exploration that makes it possible for the one-year-old boy to connect what he feels with what he can see. He can compare "early scrotal and deep testicular sensations with the more acute and localizable sensations of his penis" (Kestenberg, 1968, p. 507). The sensory experience provided by contact between the penis (part object) belonging to the external world and the boy's hands or clothing is not available to the girl (Barnett, 1966). Such considerations may have implications for the reported superiority of boys in the performance of analytical cognitive tasks involving spatial perception and their greater field-independence ability shown by performance on "Rod and Frame" tests (Sherman, 1971, pp. 21-22).

The presence of the father becomes a major factor during the second year of life. He can represent outside reality by supporting the tendencies of both male and female for autonomy, helping prevent reunion with or engulfment by the mother. Typically, he encourages the boy competitor to separate from, not cling to, the mother more actively than he does the girl. He is obviously another available object for identification and may reinforce or inhibit the acquisition of various functions. Coming in at intervals from the world outside in contrast to the intense mother-child relationship, he is a figure idealized early and may avoid the ambivalence caused by daily familiarity. The child, particularly the boy, relates to him more around movements in space, and he is associated with running, throwing, dexterity, and brightness. The mother is more important at times of distress, need, and fatigue (Abelin, 1971). These qualities resonate again with the autonomous givens of infants of both sexes. How does the girl build up a representation of herself as feminine? It is highly unlikely that, as Freud (1933) put it, "the little girl is a little man" until she discovers her lack of a penis and acknowledges herself as castrated. Penis envy is probably not the only or the usual core stimulus for the girl's basic gender identification. It too often has become an overcondensed, overused, and simplistic explanation of complex psychic phenomena. The time-honored stature of the concept may have obscured at times the fine details of the girl's positive feminine narcissism, hiding rather than revealing its early fragility, its emergence from separation-individuation, its foundation in primitive parental mirroring, and its connections with biological factors in early psychosexual development.

The girl's gender self-image, we believe, is built upon a biologically based femininity that is facilitated or inhibited by parental mirroring responses leading to a variety of identifications with gender traits of her mother and secondarily her father. Admiring maternal or parental response to "feminine" qualities, including the childbearing and mothering functions, fosters the creation of a nuclear gender-self constellation that coincides with or even precedes castration anxiety and penis envy. At what age could the girl mentate a pregnancy-baby concept and relate it to her own body? Cognitively, this could be accomplished between eighteen and 24 months. During Piaget's stage six of the sensorimotor period, "the infant is able to use mental symbols and words to refer to absent objects." The child is capable of "deferred imitation" and can evoke "an absent model in some internal symbolic form, for example, by means of visual image" (Ginsburg and Opper, 1969, p. 39). The positive pregnancy and beautiful motherhood image-concept, in Blum's (1976) words, emerges as "more than an id wish ... or consolation for fantasied castration, [but as] a most coveted aspiration of the maternal ego ideal" (p. 176). Blum emphasizes the importance of maternal ego and superego identification in feminine development and in the regulation of feminine interests and attitudes.

What about the penis envy and castration anxiety Galenson and Roiphe (1976) describe as being typical of the normal girl during the second half of the second year of life? At this time and during the third year of life, penis envy does become a major motivational force which we do not seek to minimize. But its course always depends upon what has gone before. The idea of a baby may now compensate the girl for her lack of a penis and be in a sense a substitute for it. However, behind the wish for a baby can be found significant earlier narcissistic configurations.

These formulations are consistent with the positions of Klecman (1976) and Stoller (1976) who doubt that penis envy is usually "the initiator of feminine gender identity," but differ from those of Kestenberg (1956a, 1956b) who emphasized the crucial significance of early vaginal sensations for the psychology of the girl. Kestenberg thought that early undischarged inner sensations and vaginal excitations and tensions were the basic source of the girl's need for a child and "the girl's creation of her very own fetish, her doll baby" (1956a, p. 277). Evidence for the existence of early vaginal excitations is, however, ambiguous. Equating such metapsychological concepts as "excitations," "tension," "biological urge," and "vaginal desires" requires vast theoretical leaps which are made unnecessary by the use of the narcissistic frame of reference. Our emphasis on the prephallic origin of the girl's wish for a baby is, of course, also contrary to the major thrust of Freud's (1917) description of the origin of the woman's wish for a child: "At first they had wanted a penis like a man; then at a later, though still childish, stage there appeared instead the wish for a baby" (p. 129), a position adopted by H. Deutsch (1944-1945), and recently restated by Nagera (1975). Our position is nevertheless in harmony with several unpursued avenues of Freud's (1917) thinking about the origin of a girl's wish for a child. The theory of anal erotism is a narcissistic bridge between the meaning of feces (*Lumpf* in *Little Hans* [Freud, 1909]) and the first-baby concept. Earlier, Freud (1914) offered narcissistic women a road that leads to complete object-love: "In the child which

they bear, a part of their own body confronts them like an extraneous object, to which, starting out from their narcissism,
they can then give complete object love" (pp. 89-90). (Note
the absence of any reference to the penis.) If reproductive
potential and mothering capacity are treasured and mirrored
by the parents, representations of pregnancy and childbearing, or breast symbolism will become highly cathected core
attributes of the primitive mind-body self. If parents respond
positively and nontraumatically to the female qualities of tne
girl, femininity will be reinforced and built into the cohesive
self. Blum (1976) noted, "both parents foster and orient the
feminine individuation of their daughter, and the love and
approval of both mother and father confirm a positive
feminine identity, body image, and ego ideal." These views
also agree with Easser (Panel, 1976) in considering feminine
sexual identity "inseparable from an evaluation of the whole
self-system...requiring that [the woman] experience pleasure
and enjoyment in her body image, including all its sensations."

Achievement of pregnancy and motherhood constitutes a
subsequent pillar of feminine self-esteem, particularly when
culturally reinforced. Mankind has certainly changed its
values massively since those primitive times when visual por-
trayals in sculpture and painting identified a woman by
breasts and protuberant abdomen and a man by an erect
penis. But the central importance of the pregnancy potential
is not diminished by these changing values. Almost every child
has the opportunity to identify with parenting models, and
most societies still provide ample admiration for the realization of maternal potential.

REFERENCES*

Abelin, E. L. (1971), The role of the father in the separation-individuation pro-
    cess. In: *Separation-Individuation*, ed. J. B. McDevitt & C. F. Settlage. New
    York: International Universities Press, pp. 229-252.
Aries, P. (1962), *Centuries of Childhood*. New York: Knopf.

* All references to *This Journal* are to the *Journal of the American Psychoanalytic
Association*.

Bachofen, J. J. (1861), *Das Mütterrecht: Eine Untersuchung Ueber die Gynaiko-kratie der Alten Welt.* Stuttgart: Krais & Hoffman.

Barnett, M. C. (1966), Vaginal awareness in the infancy and childhood of girls. *This Journal,* 15:129-141.

Bell, R. Q. (1960), Relations between behavior manifestations in the human neonate. *Child Develop.,* 31:463-477.

Benedek, T. F. & Rubenstein, B. (1942), *The Sexual Cycle in Women.* Washington, D. C.: National Research Council.

———— (1959), Sexual functions in women and their disturbance. In: *American Handbook of Psychiatry,* ed. S. Arieti. New York: Basic Books, pp. 727-748.

———— (1970), The psychobiology of pregnancy. In: *Parenthood,* ed. J. Anthony & T. Benedek. Boston: Little, Brown, pp. 137-151.

Bettelheim, B. (1962), *Symbolic Wounds.* New York: Collier Books.

Blum, H. (1976), Female psychology, masochism, and the ego ideal. *This Journal,* 24(5):305-351.

Brunswick, R. M. (1940), The preoedipal phase of the libido development. In: *The Psychoanalytic Reader,* ed. R. Fliess. New York: International Universities Press, 1948, pp. 261-284.

Burgner, M. & Edgcumbe, R. (1972), Some problems in the conceptualization of early object relations: Part II. The Concept of Object Constancy. *The Psychoanalytic Study of the Child,* 27:315-333. New York: Quadrangle Books.

Calogeras, R. C. & Schupper, F. X. (1972), Origins and early formulations of the Oedipus complex. *This Journal,* 20:751-775.

Campbell, J. (1959), *The Masks of God.* New York: Viking Press.

Chesler, P. (1972), *Women and Madness.* New York: Avon.

Clower, V. (1976), Theoretical implications in current views of masturbation in latency girls. *This Journal,* 24(5):109-125.

Crandall, V., Dewey, R., Katowsky, W., & Preston, A. (1964), Parents' attitudes and behaviors and grade school children's academic achievements. *J. Genetic Psychol.,* 104:53-66.

Deutsch, H. (1925), The psychology of women in relation to the functions of reproduction. *Internat. J. Psycho-Anal.,* 6:405-418.

———— (1944-1945), *The Psychology of Women.* New York: Grune & Stratton.

Ehrhardt, A. A. & Money, J. (1967), Progestin induced hermaphroditism. *J. Sex Research,* 3:83-100.

Engels, F. (1884), *The Origin of the Family, Private Property, and State.* Chicago: C. H. Kerr, 1902.

Figes, E. (1970), *Patriarchal Attitudes.* London: Faber & Faber.

Firestone, S. (1970), *The Dialectic of Sex.* New York: William Morrow.

Friedman, R. C. & Richart, R. M. (1975), *Sex Differences in Behavior.* New York: Wiley.

Freeman, D. (1967), Totem and Taboo: A reappraisal. *The Psychoanalytic Study of Society,* Vol. 4, ed. W. Muensterberger & S. Axelrad. New York: International Universities Press, pp. 9-33.

Freud, S. (1909), Analysis of a phobia in a five-year-old boy. *Standard Edition,* 10:5-149. London: Hogarth Press, 1955.

———— (1913), Totem and taboo. *Standard Edition,* 13:1-161. London: Hogarth Press, 1955.

———— (1914), On narcissism: An introduction. *Standard Edition,* 14:73-102. London: Hogarth Press, 1957.

_____ (1917), On transformations of instinct as exemplified in anal erotism. *Standard Edition,* 17:125-133. London: Hogarth Press, 1955.

_____ (1924), The dissolution of the Oedipus complex. *Standard Edition,* 19:173-179. London: Hogarth Press, 1961.

_____ (1925), Some psychical consequences of the anatomical distinction between the sexes. *Standard Edition,* 19:243-258. London: Hogarth Press, 1961.

_____ (1931), Female sexuality. *Standard Edition,* 21:233-243. London: Hogarth Press, 1961.

_____ (1933), Femininity. *Standard Edition,* 22:112-135. London: Hogarth Press, 1964.

_____ (1937), Analysis: terminable and interminable. *Standard Edition,* 23:216-253. London: Hogarth Press, 1964.

Friedan, B. (1963), *The Feminine Mystique.* New York: Dell.

Galenson, E. & Roiphe, H. (1976), Some suggested revisions concerning early female development. *This Journal,* 24(5):29-57.

Gadpaille, W. J. (1972), Research into the physiology of maleness and femaleness. *Arch. Gen. Psychiat.,* 26:193-206.

Garn, S. M. (1958), Fat, body size, and growth in the newborn. *Human Biology,* 30:265-280.

Gedo, J. E. & Goldberg, A. (1973), *Models of the Mind.* Chicago: University of Chicago Press.

Gehrie, M. (1974), Presentation. Anthropology and Psychoanalysis Workshop, Chicago Institute for Psychoanalysis. Unpublished.

Ginsburg, H. & Opper, S. (1969), *Piaget's Theory of Intellectual Development: An Introduction.* Englewood Cliffs, N. J.: Prentice Hall.

Gitelson, M. (1964), On the identity crisis in American psychoanalysis. *This Journal,* 12:451-476.

Gottschalk, L. A., Kaplan, A. S., Gleser, G. D., & Winget, C. M. (1962), Variations in magnitude of emotion. *Psychosom. Med.,* 24:300-311.

Graves, R. (1948), *The White Goddess.* New York: Creative Age Press.

Greenson, R. R. (1968), Dis-identifying from mother: its special importance for the boy. *Internat. J. Psycho-Anal.,* 49:370-374.

_____ (1969), Origin and fate of new ideas in psychoanalysis. *Internat. J. Psycho-Anal.,* 50:503-515.

Greer, G. (1971), *The Female Eunuch.* New York: McGraw-Hill.

Grinker, R. R. Sr. (1964), Psychiatry rides madly in all directions. *Arch. Gen. Psychiat.,* 10:228-237.

Groddeck, G. (1928), *The Book of It.* New York: International Universities Press, 1976.

Heiman, M. (1968), Discussion of Sherfey's paper on female sexuality. *This Journal,* 16:406-416.

Ivey, M. E. & Bardwick, J. M. (1968), Patterns of affective fluctuation in the menstrual cycle. *Psychosom. Med.,* 30:336-345.

Jensen, G. D. & Bobitt, R. A. (1968), Monkeying with the mother image. *Psychology Today,* 1:41.

Jones, E. (1927), The early development of female sexuality. *Internat. J. Psycho-Anal.,* 8:459-472.

_____ (1932), The phallic phase. *Internat. J. Psycho-Anal.,* 14:1-33.

_____ (1935), Early female sexuality. *Internat. J. Psycho-Anal.,* 16:263-273.

Kagan, J. & Lewis, M. (1965), Studies of attention in the human infant. *Merrill-Palmer Quart.,* 11:95-127.

_____ (1971), *Change and Continuity in Infancy.* New York: Wiley.

Kane, J. F., Daly, R. J., Wallach, M. H., & Keeler, M. H. (1966), Amelioration of premenstrual mood disturbance with a progestational agent (Enovid). *Dis. Nerv. Syst.,* 27:339-342.

Keiser, S. (1968), Discussion of Sherfey's paper on female sexuality. *This Journal,* 16:449-456.

Kestenberg, J. S. (1956a), On the development of maternal feelings in early childhood. *The Psychoanalytic Study of the Child,* 11:257-291. New York: International Universities Press.

_____ (1956b), Vicissitudes of female sexuality. *This Journal,* 4:453-476.

_____ (1968), Outside and inside, male and female. *This Journal,* 16:457-520.

Kinsey, A. C., Pomeroy, W. B., Martin, C. E., & Gebhard, P. H. (1953), *Sexual Behavior in the Human Female.* Philadelphia: Saunders.

Kleeman, J. (1976), Freud's views on early female sexuality in the light of child observation. *This Journal,* 24(5):3-27.

Klein, M. (1928), Early stages of the Oedipus conflict. *Internat. J. Psycho-Anal.,* 9:167-180.

_____ (1932), *The Psychoanalysis of Children.* London: Hogarth Press and Institute of Psychoanalysis.

Knop, C. (1946), The dynamics of newly born babies. *J. Pediatrics,* 29:721-728.

Kohut, H. (1959), Introspection, empathy, and psychoanalysis. *This Journal,* 7:459-483.

_____ (1971), *The Analysis of the Self.* New York: International Universities Press.

_____ (1972), Thoughts on narcissism and narcissistic rage. *The Psychoanalytic Study of the Child,* 27:360-400. New York: Quadrangle Books.

Kupperman, H. S. (1961), Sex hormones. In: *The Encyclopedia of Sexual Behavior,* ed. S, Ellis & A. Abarbanel. New York: Hawthorn.

Lampl-de Groot, J. (1928), The evolution of the Oedipus complex in women. *Internat. J. Psycho-Anal.,* 9:332-345.

Lawrence, D. H. (1915), *The Rainbow.* New York: Viking Press, 1967

LeVine, R. A. (1973), *Culture, Behavior and Personality.* Chicago: Aldine.

Levine, S. N. (1966), Sex differences in the brain. *Scient. Amer.,* April:84-90.

Lifton, R. J. (1965), *The Women in America.* Boston: Houghton Mifflin.

Lipsitt, T. P, & Levy, N. C. (1959), Electrotactual threshold in the human neonate. *Child Develop.,* 30:547-554.

Lustman, S. L. (1963), Some issues in contemporary psychoanalytic research. *The Psychoanalytic Study of the Child,* 18:51-74. New York: International Universities Press.

Mahler, M. S. (1965), On the significance of the normal separation-individuation phase. In: *Drives, Affects, Behavior,* ed. M. Shur. New York: International Universities Press, pp. 161-169.

Macoby, E. E. & Jacklin, C. N. (1975), *Psychology of Sex Differences.* Stanford, California: Stanford University Press.

Masters, W. H. & Johnson, V. E. (1960), The sexual response cycle of the human female: gross anatomic considerations. *Western J. Surg. Obstet. Gynecol.,* 68:57-72.

_____ (1966), *Human Sexual Response.* Boston: Little, Brown.

McCarthy, D. (1953), Some possible explanations of sex differences in language, development and disorders. *J. Psychol.,* 35:155-160.

Millet, K. (1970), *Sexual Politics.* Garden City, N. Y. : Doubleday.

Mitchell, J. (1974), *Psychoanalysis and Feminism.* New York: Pantheon.

Money, J., Hampson, J. G., & Hampson, J. L. (1957), Imprinting and the establishment of gender role. *Arch. Neur. & Psychiat.,* 77:333-336.

Müller, J. (1932), A contribution to the problem of the libidinal development of the genital phase of girls. *Internat. J. Psycho-Anal.,* 13:361-368.

Muslin, H. L. (1973), The superego in women. In: *Moral Values and the Superego Concept in Psychoanalysis,* ed. S. C. Post. New York: International Universities Press, pp. 101-125.

Nagera, H. (1975), *Female Sexuality and the Oedipus Complex.* New York: Jason Aronson.

Neumann, E. (1964), *The Great Mother: An Analysis of the Archetype.* Princeton: Princeton University Press.

Panel (1961), Frigidity in women. B. E. Moore, reporter. *This Journal,* 9:571-584.

Panel (1976), The psychology of women: Late adolescence and early adulthood. E. Galenson, reporter. *This Journal,* 24:631-645.

Schafer, R. (1973), The idea of resistance. *Internat. J. Psycho-Anal.,* 54:259-285.

—————— (1974), Problems in Freud's psychology of women. *This Journal,* 22:459-485.

Seidenberg, R. (1973), *Marriage Between Equals.* New York: Anchor/Doubleday.

Sherfey, M. J. (1973), *The Nature and Evolution of Female Sexuality.* New York: Random/Vintage.

Sherman, J. A. (1971), *On the Psychology of Women.* Springfield, Ill.: Thomas.

Slater, P. (1971), *The Glory of Hera: Greek Mythology and the Greek Family.* New York: Beacon.

Stoller, R. J. (1968), *Sex and Gender.* New York: Science House.

—————— (1973), Presentation to Chicago Psychoanalytic Associaton. Unpublished.

—————— (1976), Primary femininity. *This Journal,* 24(5):59-78.

Sutherland, H. & Stewart, I. (1965), A critical analysis of the pre-menstrual syndrome. *Lancet,* 1:1180-1183.

Swanson, D. W., Barron, A., Floren, A , & Smith, J. A. (1964), The use of norethynodrel in psychotic females. *Amer. J. Psychiat.,* 120:1101-1103.

Terman, L. M. & Tyler, L. E. (1954), Psychological sex differences. In: *A Manual of Child Psychology,* ed. L. Carmichael. 2nd ed. New York: Wiley.

Tolpin, M. (1971), On the beginnings of a cohesive self. *The Psychoanalytic Study of the Child,* 26:316-352. New York: Quadrangle Books.

Valenstein, E. S. (1968), Steroid hormones and the neuropsychology of development, In: *The Neuropsychology of Development: a Symposium,* ed. R. L. Isaacson. New York: Wiley, pp. 1-39.

Verhoff, J. (1969), Social comparison and the development of achievement motivation. In: *Achievement Related Motives in Children,* ed. G. Smith. New York: Russell Sage Foundation, pp. 46-101.

Ward, L. (1888), *Pure Sociology.* New York: Macmillan, 1914.

Woolf, V. (1929), *A Room of One's Own.* New York: Harcourt, Brace, 1959.

Yorke, C. (1971), Some suggestions for a critique of Kleinian psychology. *The Psychoanalytic Study of the Child,* 26:129-155. New York: Quadrangle Books.

Northwestern University Medical School
303 East Chicago Avenue
Chicago, Illinois 60611

NAME INDEX

439

SUBJECT INDEX

445